OUT OF GALILEE

Out of Galilee

Christian Thought as a Great Conversation

M. Darrol Bryant

WIPF & STOCK · Eugene, Oregon

OUT OF GALILEE
Christian Thought as a Great Conversation

Copyright © 2018 M. Darrol Bryant. All rights reserved. Except for brief quotations in critical publications or reviews, no part of this book may be reproduced in any manner without prior written permission from the publisher. Write: Permissions, Wipf and Stock Publishers, 199 W. 8th Ave., Suite 3, Eugene, OR 97401.

Wipf & Stock
An Imprint of Wipf and Stock Publishers
199 W. 8th Ave., Suite 3
Eugene, OR 97401

www.wipfandstock.com

PAPERBACK ISBN: 978-1-5326-3848-0
HARDCOVER ISBN: 978-1-5326-3849-7
EBOOK ISBN: 978-1-5326-3850-3

Manufactured in the U.S.A.

Centre for Dialogue & Spirituality in the World Religions
Renison University College/University of Waterloo

Contents

Preface | vii
An Historical Timeline | ix

Part I: Approach and Context | 1
    Chapter 1. An Introduction to Christian Thought as a Great Conversation | 3
    Chapter 2. The Jewish/Greek/Roman Matrix | 12

Part II: Beginnings and the First Centuries: 30-325 | 23
    Chapter 3. The Coming Kingdom & the Formation of the Canon | 25
    Chapter 4. Christian Practice & the Exemplary Christian | 38
    Chapter 5. Articulating the Faith: Two Christian Apologists Justin Martyr & Tertullian | 46
    Chapter 6. Irenaeus: The Three-Articled Faith | 56
    Chapter 7. Speculative Thought: The Search for the Language of the Relationship of the Christ to God | 66

Part III: Ecumenical Symbols & Classical Christianity: 325-1000 | 83
    Chapter 8. Seven Ecumenical Councils 325-787: Creeds, Councils, & Empire | 85
    Chapter 9. Augustine: Architect of Western Christian Thought | 100
    Chapter 10. Eastern Voices: Wisdom in the East | 119
    Chapter 11. Benedict and the Rise of Monasticism, Boethius and the Via Positiva, Dionysius and the Via Negativa | 133

Part IV: Medieval Christian Thought: 1100-1500 | 151
　Chapter 12. On the Way to the Medieval Synthesis: Anselm's Faith Seeking Understanding and Abelard's New Dialectical Method | 153
　Chapter 13. Grammars of the Spirit: Bernard, Hildegard of Bingen, Francis of Assisi, Bonaventure, and Julian of Norwich | 166
　Chapter 14. The Quest for Synthesis and the Emergence of Theology as the Science of God in Medieval Christian Thought | 178

Part V: Reforming Christian Thought: 1500-1780 | 191
　Chapter 15. Protestant Reformers: Luther, Calvin and Zwingli | 193
　Chapter 16. Anabaptist and Anglican Reformers | 216
　Chapter 17. Reform in the Catholic World: Erasmus, Ignatius and Teresa | 225
　Chapter 18. Reforming the Reformers: Three Protestant Movements: Pietists, Puritans and Methodists | 237
　Chapter 19. Christian Thought in the Americas | 253

Part VI: The Enlightenment and Beyond: 1780-1950 | 267
　Chapter 20. The Rise of Modern Science, the European Enlightenment, and the Beginnings of Modern Christian Thought | 269
　Chapter 21. Three Movements of the Nineteenth Century: Existential Christian Thought, the Oxford Movement and the Social Gospel | 282

Part VII: Contemporary Christian Thought: 1920-2017 | 293
　Chapter 22. The War to End all Wars and the Beginnings of Contemporary Christian Thought | 295
　Chapter 23. The War to End all Wars and Contemporary Catholic Thought | 308
　Chapter 24. The Great Conversation Revisited: Beginning the Third Millennium | 321
　A New Postscript | 325

Appendix | 329
　Words from the Great Conversation of Christian Thought
Bibliography | 365

Preface

THIS GUIDE TO THE story of Christian thought grows out of my teaching over the past forty years. For three-quarters of that time, I have taught courses in the history of Christian thought to undergraduates at Renison University College, University of Waterloo. I have long felt the need for a readable and reasonably sized introduction to that great conversation of Christian thinkers through the ages. There are many multivolume histories of Christian doctrine and teaching. But where was the shorter volume that could introduce the student to that great conversation? I hope this volume fills that need. I see it as a guide to the story of Christian thinkers across the ages wrestling with the meaning of the faith that arose in response to Jesus of Nazareth.

Of course I am dependent upon the work of others who have toiled long and hard and with greater depth and insight into that history than I have here. They have investigated that history and particular figures within it in ways that have taught me much, and I have borrowed shamelessly from their works. I have read and used their translations of the works of the Christian thinkers included in this volume, my own knowledge of the original languages in which Christian thinkers through the ages wrote being so rudimentary as to be virtually nonexistent. I also learned from scholarly interpretations of these same works. However, I offer here my own interpretive readings of these figures. These readings are necessarily selective. Many of these Christian thinkers wrote much more than I could read, and I have focused on the works that I considered most fitting for my purposes here. No one-volume account of that great conversation among Christian thinkers could be exhaustive. Rather, I regard the figures discussed here not just as particular voices but also as representative of types of Christian thinking. In my selection I have stayed, on the whole, with figures who have been important to more than one generation and, in the post-Reformation era, to more than one denomination. In many of these cases I have then offered my own analysis of their contribution to Christian thought. But I have also included, wherever possible, the actual words of a particular figure. Again, it was necessary to severely limit the amount of direct quotation I could include, but the notes direct the reader to the sources in English. I do feel that it is important for the student of Christian thought to hear the words of the particular figures I have included here so I have included some of those words in the appendix.

I have divided this text into twenty-four chapters, which means two chapters per week in a twelve-week term with time left for a mid-term exam. Each chapter includes a summary, questions that address what is presented in the chapter, and footnotes that point to possibilities for further reading. I have used this format in my classes over some years with good success. I feel that I have succeeded when students discover figures in this great conversation who move them and lead them to further study. I'll always be grateful to the student who wrote in her course evaluation: "I really loved learning about Augustine. Augustine rocks!"

This guide to Christian thought has been unfolding over a long period of time. In the mid-1980s I was asked to prepare my on-campus course on the history of Christian thought for distance education. I asked Gail, one of my students who had taken another class of mine, if she would mind keeping a good set of notes that I might have at the end of the course. I felt her notes would be better than mine and it would help me in preparing the course for the distance education format. I was amazed when a week later, after a couple of classes, she turned up with twenty typewritten pages of notes. It was a verbatim transcript. "How did you do this?" I exclaimed. "Before I came back to school I was a court reporter," she said. By the end of the course I had two hundred pages.

For the next decade I was only able to work on this project in bits and pieces. Then finally, in the fall of 2010, I had a non-teaching term that allowed me to work on this volume, and in the fall of 2012 I was on sabbatical. Along the way, many people have read parts of this volume and given me the benefit of their critical responses: my colleagues A. James Reimer and James Gollnick and my former students Ron Dueck and Victor Froese. I am also grateful to Val Lariviere for her assistance over several years and for the editorial work of Susan Hodges Bryant. Then in 2015-16, I engaged Bob Chodos, a seasoned editor, to go through the whole volume. He turned these earlier efforts into the book you now hold in your hands.

Finally, it is to my students in the history of Christian thought over the past twenty-five years that I am most grateful. They were the ones who challenged me to render the figures we were studying together accessible. If I have been successful in these efforts, then it is my students whom I must thank.

M. Darrol Bryant
Easter Week, 2017

An Historical Timeline

c. 2000 BCE the Call of Abraham

c. 1200 the Exodus

750 ff. the Prophets

570 the Babylonian Captivity

4 BCE the Birth of Jesus

26-30 CE the ministry, crucifixion & resurrection of Jesus

40s & 50s the writings of Paul

50s to 90s the writing of the Gospels

70 the Destruction of the 2nd Temple in Jerusalem

150-220 the writings of the early Christian apologists: Justin Martyr, Tertullian, & Irenaeus

185-254 Origen writes *On First Principles*

200s the early Christian writings composing the New Testament are largely in place

313 Christianity is legalized in the Roman Empire

325 Constantine becomes the sole Emperor of the Roman Empire and favours Christianity

325 the first Ecumenical Council at Nicea: Christ as "very God of very God..."

381 the second Ecumenical Council is held in Constantinople, the Cappadocian Fathers, especially Gregory of Nyssa are influential, get the full Nicene Creed

352-430 Augustine writes the *Confessions*, the *City of God*, & *On the Trinity*

415 The Fall of Rome

431 the Council of Ephesus

451 the Council of Chalcedon proclaims Christ is "truly human, truly divine"

AN HISTORICAL TIMELINE

480-525 Boethius writes the *Consolation of Philosophy*

c. 520 Dionysius the Areopagite, a Syrian monk, champions the *via negativa* in mystic writings like *Divine Names & Celestial Hierarchy*

480-543 Benedict of Nursia established the Benedictines, a monastic rule that builds on the Desert Fathers & Mothers of 3rd century ascetics. Spreads across Christianity

800-877 John Scotus Eriugena writes *The Voice of the Eagle*

1056 the East-West Schism divides Christianity between the Roman Catholic and Eastern Orthodox

1095 Pope Urban II initiates the Crusades

1109 St. Anselm of Canterbury, author of the ontological argument dies.

1151 Hildegard of Bingen writes the *Scrivias* (Know the Way) & the *Book of Divine Works*

1226 St Francis of Assisi dies having founded the Franciscans and, together with Clare of Assisi, the Order of St. Clare

1274 St. Thomas, the greatest of the Scholastics and author of the *Summa Theologica* dies, as does St. Bonaventure who wrote the *Soul's Journey to God*.

1350 the Black Plague devastates Europe

c.1400 Julian of Norwich writes her *Showings* and of "God, our Mother."

1492 Columbus discovers the "New World" and Jews are expelled from Spain

1517 Martin Luther posts his "95 Theses" and the Reformation begins

1525 the Peasant War rages in Germany

1527 Felix Manz was executed in Zurich, the 1st martyr for the Anabaptist cause.

1536 Jean Calvin publishes the 1st edition of his *Institutes of the Christian Religion* and assumes leadership of the Reformation in Geneva. Menno Simons renounces his priestly vows and joins the Anabaptists.

1537 Bartolome de las Casas writes *The Only Way* defending the indigenous peoples of the New World and criticizing the Spanish ways of conversion

1540 St. Ignatius of Loyola establishes the Society of Jesus (the Jesuits)

1545-63 the Council of Trent reformulates Catholic teaching and renews Catholic practice

1577 Teresa of Avila publishes *The Interior Castle* on the interior life.

1594 Richard Hooker publishes the *Laws of Ecclesiastical Polity* important for the Anglican tradition

1611 the King James Bible was published in England

1618-48 the Thirty Years War began as a conflict between Catholics & Protestants. It ended with the Peace of Westphalia that recognized the principle that the religion of the Sovereign would be the religion of the realm. The options were Catholic, Lutheran or Calvinist.

c. 1650 George Fox founds the Society of Friends, known as the Quakers

1687 Isaac Newton published his *Philosophiae Naturalis Principia Mathematica* that laid the foundation for a new science of the natural world.

1740s the Great Awakening in the American Colonies, Jonathan Edwards published his *Religious Affections*

1750 ff. The emergence of the European Enlightenment that pitted the religion of reason against the religion of revelation and the publication of the *Encyclopedia* in France

1781, 1793 Immanuel Kant publishes his *Critique of Pure Reason* and *Religion within the Limits of Reason Alone*

1790s the French Revolution and the beginning of the Industrial revolution in Great Britain

1830 Friedrich Schleiermacher, regarded as the Father of Modern Theology, publishes his *Christian Faith*

1844 George Williams founds the Young Men's Christian Association (YMCA)

1848 Karl Marx and Friedrich Engels publish the *Communist Manifesto*

1855 Lady Mary Jane Kinnaird & C. Emma Roberts found the Young Women's Christian Association (YWCA)

1869-70 1st Vatican Council. It proclaimed the teaching on papal infallibility

1880s The Scramble for Africa, the Modern Missionary Movement, the Social Gospel Movement

1893 the World's Parliament of Religions in Chicago

1906 the Azusa Street Revival in Los Angles led by William J. Seymour marked the beginning of the Pentecostal movement in the USA

1910 the World Missionary Conference in Edinburgh, Scotland

1932 Karl Barth begins the publication of his 16 volume *Church Dogmatics*

1934 the Barman Declaration opposes the Nazi supported "German Christians"

1939-45 the Holocaust or *Shoah* and the murder of 6 million Jews

1941 Reinhold Niebuhr publishes the *Nature & Destiny of Man*

1945 the Lutheran Pastor and opponent of the Nazi regime Dietrich Bonhoeffer is hung. His *Letters & Papers from Prison* were published in English in 1953.

1948 Founding of the World Council of Churches in Amsterdam

1961 Karl Rahner publishes Vol 1 of his 21 volumes of *Theological Investigations*

1962-1965 2nd Vatican Council especially *Nostre Aetate* or *Declaration on the Church's Relations with non-Christian Religions*

1963 Dr. Martin Luther King Jr., the head of the Southern Christian Leadership Conference gives his "I Have a Dream" speech, a landmark in the American Civil Rights movement

1965 Nullification of the mutual anathemas of the 11th century between the Roman Catholic and Orthodox Traditions.

1976 the Episcopal Church in the USA approves the ordination of women.

1999 the Lutheran World Federation and the Vatican sign the Joint Declaration on Justification

2000 Pope John Paul apologizes for the sins of "Roman Catholics in the name of the Church" in the last millennium, naming, specifically, the Crusades, inquisitions, forced conversions in the Americas, religious intolerance, and injustices towards women and the poor.

2000 the remarkable growth of Pentecostal Christianity across the globe in the past century

2006 the Methodist Council adopts the Lutheran/Catholic Declaration on Justification

2013 Pope Francis, an Argentinian, became the first non-European Pope in modern times. He is also the first Jesuit Pope.

2015 *Laudato Si: On Care for our Common Home,* an encyclical by Pope Francis addresses global warming and environmental issues facing our planet. It is widely endorsed by other religious authorities including HH the Dalai Lama and leading scientists.

PART I

Approach and Context

THE FOLLOWING TWO CHAPTERS provide an introduction to the Great Conversation. They outline the approach that this book takes to the story of Christian thought and sets Christian thought in context.

Chapter 1 presents the idea of Christian thought as a conversation that seeks to unfold the meaning of the revelatory events that lie at the beginning of the Christian era. Those events are witnessed to in the Christian writings that come to be known as the "New Testament," they become the apostolic witness. For Christian thinkers the life, teachings, death and resurrection of Jesus of Nazareth are central. And our approach seeks to unfold that great conversation that began in response to Jesus the Christ and continues down to today. Moreover, in approaching that conversation we want to proceed in an historical and descriptive way—seeking to describe that thought in the context of its time. At the same time we proceed in a way that is existential and ecumenical—seeking to understand the meaning of that conversation for people's lives and in a way that is not biased to one or another branch of Christianity.

In Chapter 2, we set the great conversation in its initial context, the matrix of its emergence. Jesus and his initial followers were all members of the Jewish community, and theirs was a Jewish world. This is the primary matrix out of which Christian thought emerged. But the time of Christian beginnings in Israel were also ones in which Romans were in political control and in which Greek culture was pervasive. For example, early Christian writings were composed in *koine* Greek, rather than Hebrew. And it was the Roman authorities who crucified Jesus. This multifaceted context is the matrix of Christian thought.

Chapter 1

An Introduction to Christian Thought as a Great Conversation

A Prologue

It was the summer of 2002, when I walked the brown hills of Israel looking down on the blue Sea of Galilee. It had been a long journey from the small wooden church on the Dakota plains, where I sat in the front pew mimicking the gestures of the pastor. More than forty years of studying the history of Christian thought and the great traditions of the religious life of humankind had also intervened. Here I was, finally, walking where Jesus walked. The sun was hot, the air dry, the sky blue. In Jerusalem, three weeks before, bombs had gone off as the intractable conflict continued. Earlier, I had been in Jerusalem and made my pilgrimage to the Church of the Holy Sepulchre (or the Church of the Resurrection as the Orthodox call it). I had also been to Gethsemane, and at the back wall of the Tantur Centre on the edge of Jerusalem viewed Bethlehem across the blockade. But it was here on these sun-browned hills that I felt most moved, most connected to the one my childhood church had called "Our Saviour." In the front of that church there had been an image of Jesus walking on the Sea of Galilee — the same sea that now sparkled in the sun below me — with a hand reaching down to Peter. Here again, I imagined, an open hand reached out, a gesture of compassion tinged with dismay from the Prince of Peace.

When I returned to Canada, I decided to retitle my account of the story of Christian thought. I would now call it *Out of Galilee: Christian Thought as a Great Conversation*. For it was there, in Galilee, that the story began. It began with the response of some fellow Galileans to the teaching and life of Jesus of Nazareth; it began with a response to the one who invited them to follow him as he marked out the way to God. It is a Way found in the Gospels written years, perhaps decades, after the events that blazed through the Galilean countryside and ended in the city of Jerusalem. They would speak with marvel of what they had witnessed. Matthew, one of those early disciples, would see Jesus as the Christ, the anointed one, "the son of David, the son of Abraham," while Mark would write of "the beginning of the Gospel of Jesus Christ, the Son of God." Luke would write of the divine-human Saviour who, following his death and resurrection, would walk unrecognized with his disciples to Emmaus until "their eyes were opened" in the breaking of bread. And. John would write, "In the beginning was the Word, and the Word was with God . . . and the Word became flesh and dwelt among us, full of grace and truth."

Yet the events that marked Jesus' life—his teaching of the Kingdom of God, his parables, his healings, his conflicts, his death in Jerusalem and his astonishing resurrection—went virtually unnoticed by the wider world of his time. No one paid much attention to what happened in an obscure but troublesome corner of the Roman Empire in the early part of what we now call the first century. However, for the followers of Jesus, these were revelatory events. They disclosed a new era in God's dealing with humanity. Peter, Andrew, Mary Magdalene, John, Matthew and the others who had responded to his outstretched hand and followed him had come to believe that he was "the anointed one," the long awaited Messiah, "the Word made flesh."

These deeply held convictions fueled the Jesus movement, first within Jesus' own Jewish community, and then, especially in response to Paul more than a decade later, among the Gentiles. Paul had not known Jesus "after the flesh" but had encountered the Risen Lord while on his way to Damascus and been given the vocation to spread the message that came "through a revelation of Jesus Christ." (Gal 1:11) Paul, known as "the Apostle to the Gentiles," was instrumental in spreading the Christian message beyond the boundaries of the Jewish world.

However, both the revelatory events and these efforts on behalf of the new faith also raised questions that were to demand responses from the very beginning of the Christian era. What was the relation of this new movement to its parent tradition? If Jesus was the Messiah, then when will the Davidic Kingship be reestablished? What did it mean when Paul told his followers: "God had raised him from the dead?" How was it that this Jesus revealed God? What were the teachings that this new community should follow? What should be its practice, its rituals? Did it have a scripture? The questions were myriad and troubling even among those who had turned to this new movement and it was not always clear where one turned to find an answer. Of course, there were the first followers of Jesus, the disciples now regarded as Apostles, but how available were they, and to whom, and when?[1]

As the early followers began to realize that Jesus' crucifixion was not the end, but that he was living in their midst, the convictions that inspired them concealed a question. What was the relationship of Christ, now risen, to God, the one Jesus called *Abba*? This issue was troubling not only for the Jewish followers of Jesus but for the Greek/Gentile followers too. In the *shema* from Deuteronomy 6.4: *Hear! O Israel the Lord our God is one* . . . Jews proclaimed the oneness of God. While some Greek/Gentiles believed in many gods, others, more philosophical, believed in an unchanging God. Could such views be squared with Christian affirmations of Jesus as Lord? Moreover, what exactly did Christians mean when they called Jesus "Lord" or the "Christ"? Though these were titles and names given to Jesus, it was not until four centuries later that Christians, gathered for a great council in Chalcedon outside Constantinople, would say of Jesus that he was "fully human and fully divine."

In seeking to answer these and other questions, Christians held firm to their conviction that Jesus' life, death, and resurrection was central to the truth they sought. The answers to these questions were articulated generation after generation, in diverse cultural settings, in different ages, and thus the great conversation unfolded.

Christian Thought as a Great Conversation

The focus of this book is not so much on the history of dogma or doctrine narrowly considered as on the way that Christians articulated the faith given to them and that fashioned their very being. In addition to doctrine, there are grammars of the spirit, ethical discourse, practical concerns, directions for ritual and many other things that are part of Christian thought. These aspects of the great conversation are included here. It was not until the eleventh century that Anselm, a monk and later a bishop, defined Christian thinking as "faith seeking understanding." This phrase best captures the way

---

1. Disciples in this context are the 12 followers directly linked to Jesus. Apostles are messengers with the task of spreading the teachings to others. Here this means the disciples minus Judas plus Paul.

we see this unfolding conversation over the ages of the Christian era, these two millennia.

Of course, as Huston Smith reminds his readers in *The Soul of Christianity*, that thinking unfolded within a worldview that saw the finite enfolded in the infinite.[2] This worldview was the great unanimity prior to the emergence of the modern secular West. In more mythological terms, it was a two-tiered universe, a world above and below. For the Abrahamic traditions, it was God, under various names, who created the universe, as Smith notes, while other traditions used other terms to speak of this world above and below.

We in the modern west tend to assume a one-dimensional world known through empirical instruments, whereas ancient thinkers assumed that reality was multidimensional and everywhere suffused with Spirit. Jesus lived in a constant awareness of his *Abba* (Father), and Paul would say of God, "In him we live and move and have our being." (Acts 17:18) Others in the other great religious traditions would speak of this multidimensional reality in their own terms—Confucians of "heaven and earth," and South Asians of *samsara* and *nirvana*—but all would agree there is a More that enfolds the Here and Now. While the modern dissent from this traditional worldview has rendered it more difficult for those of us raised in the modern era to hear aright thinkers of an earlier age, it is essential that we acknowledge their worldview so that we can hear them in their own terms.

What is it that we should hear. We should hear the ways that Christian thinkers in different eras, in different cultural milieus, in different social settings give expression to their faith seeking understanding—their ways of articulating the meanings of this faith. For while faith may be given, once for all, the way it is heard and articulated by Irenaeus and Origen in the second and third centuries is not identical to the voices of Augustine and Gregory of Nyssa in the fourth century. Nor with those of Hildegard of Bingen in the twelfth century, Bonaventure in the thirteenth, Jean Calvin in the sixteenth or Paul Tillich or Karl Rahner in the twentieth century. It is my conviction that our understanding of the Christian faith grows and expands by listening to these many, many voices as they contribute to the great conversation that is the history of Christian thought. They contribute even when they disagree with one another, as when Athanasius thundered against Arius in the fourth century or as Abelard did when he wrote against Anselm's view of the atonement in the twelfth. For these are challenges within the circle of believers vying with one another for the truth given in faith. Often, the different voices are responding to different circumstances

---

2. See Smith, *The Soul of Christianity*, 1-35.

and different social settings and drawing on different resources within the longer tradition. Moreover, they are aware that the truth they seek always exceeds their words.

This means that we see Christian thought as unfolding as a great conversation seeking to articulate:

1. The inner dynamics of the Christian faith to witness to the life, death, and resurrection of Jesus of Nazareth, the Christ;
2. The demands of the wider culture for an account of the faith of this new religious movement; and
3. The variety of issues that arose as Christianity sought to relate to the demands of the diverse social settings in which it found itself and the ineffable mystery of the sacred.

Along with the diversity of Christian thought, it is equally important that we acknowledge its multiformity. Eugen Rosenstock-Huessy notes that human beings find themselves on what he calls the "cross of reality," simultaneously facing inward and outward, backwards and forwards. There is the interior world as well as the outer world of society and creation, the pull of the past as well as the future. As we attend to the interior world, our thinking moves more in a spiritual and mystical way, whereas when our attention moves to the social world and creation then our thinking moves in a more social way. When we are attending to the past, our thinking is historical. Moreover, the future beckons and demands a response. All these dimensions are present in Christian thought in a given generation and era, and its story is not complete without each of them.[3]

Approached in this way, we will discover that Christian thinking has been plural in nature from the very beginning. Far from being a defect, the plurality that one discovers in Christian thought arises from the very quest for universality that marks revelatory events. This plurality, reflected in the four Gospels—Matthew, Mark, Luke, and John—comes to be foundational for the Christian Scriptures. As Rosenstock-Huessy has remarked, the four gospels establish "the rule that one truth must be expressed in different ways for different times of life." Then, he continues, the Gospels are like "movements of a symphony" in which "the whole truth is only conveyed . . . together."[4] In this view, which I share, plurality (along with diversity and multiformity) is the way to the truth of the whole. Rarely does the story of Christian thought achieve this sublime state, but it does point

---

3. See Rosenstock-Huessy, *The Christian Future*, 92–112, and 165. See also Rosenstock-Huessy, *Speech & Reality*.

4. Rosenstock-Huessy, *The Christian Future*, 99.

in this direction: in the diverse voices in different settings and times, we see the unfolding quest for the truth of God. Christian thought becomes a multi-voiced, multi-faceted and continuing conversation concerning the fundamental claims of the Christian faith, a rich narrative of faith seeking understanding across the ages of the Christian era. It becomes the great conversation.

Our Approach to the Great Conversation

Already in the book of Acts, the men and women of the early Christian community were those "belonging to the Way." (Acts 9: 2) The Way initially charted by Jesus of Nazareth and now followed by those who came after. Indeed, that Way was being lived in the lives of those inspired by those early followers who were preaching this new Gospel, the Good News. In the midst of this movement, questions arose about this Way and its meaning for its followers. Historians now tell us that the first followers of Jesus were all Jews, and for much of the century beyond the time of Jesus the Christian movement is a Jewish movement. Paul had taken the Christian Gospel to the Gentiles, and in writing to the Romans had said of the Gospel: "it is the power of God for salvation to everyone who has faith, to the Jew first and also to the Greek." (Rom. 2:16) Behind this bold declaration lay the challenge at the very outset of the Christian movement to extend the Gospel beyond the boundaries of the Jewish world. Later we will look more closely at this issue, but here it is important to see that this is but the first moment in the perennial challenge of Christianity to relate its message to changing circumstances, to new challenges.

In using the image of "a great conversation," I do not want to suggest that Christian thought is mere chitchat. It is a living process of listening and speaking, speaking and listening in the crucible of life itself. It is, as mentioned earlier, a process and event within life enfolded in the Beyond about the way things are, or as Calvin said 1,500 years after Jesus, "about God and the soul." Rather than searching for the "one right voice" or overly burdening the inquiry by seeking to distinguish those elements in a particular figures thought that were judged orthodox from those that were judged heretical (a judgment always made from a later vantage point), we want to see what Christians over the centuries thought about the Way. We want to see something of the impact on their lives. We want, for example, to see what Origen (185–254) thought about the Christian faith in his own time and in his own terms rather than asking about how "orthodox or heterodox" he was. We want to meet Julian of Norwich (1342–1423) and hear her speak of "God our Mother," exploring what she means by such a statement. We want to hear Pope John XXIII in his own terms as he calls on the Church "to let the winds blow through." In short, our approach to Christian thought is historical and descriptive rather than normative; it is existential and ecumenical, rather than deductive and confined to a particular denominational slant.

A Brief Overview & Timeline for the Great Conversation of Christian Thought

Finally, it might be useful to provide a brief overview and timeline for the journey that lies ahead. Here, we have divided the great conversation into six periods. The first is from 25 to 325, the period of beginnings to the first ecumenical Council at Nicea. This period includes the time from Jesus' life, death and resurrection in Jerusalem through the beginnings of the spread of Christianity and its experience of persecution as an outlaw religion down to the time of Constantine and the fateful decision to make Christianity the religion of the Roman Empire. During this period, we see the early shaping of the Christian *koinonia* (community) and the emergence of Christian writings, beginning with Paul's letters in the 40s and then the Gospels later in the first century, which added to the Hebrew Bible to form the Christian sscripture. We also see an understanding of the Christian faith as, in Irenaeus' words, a "three-articled faith," affirming "faith in one God . . . maker of heaven and earth, the seas and that in them is" as well as in "Christ Jesus, the Son of God, who became incarnate for our salvation" and "in the Holy Spirit." It is, says Irenaeus boldly, "this kerygma and this faith the Church, although scattered all over the whole world, diligently observes."[5]

We then turn to the second period, 325–1000, the period of the ecumenical councils and classical Christianity. When, under the Emperor Constantine, Christianity was acknowledged as a legitimate faith and then later became the official religion of the Roman Empire, its status in the world was forever altered. The major councils of the Christian church, began in 325 and continued over the next 450 years. After the major shift from an outlaw religion to the official religion of the Empire, another significant change occurred in the fifth century with the fall of Rome. After Rome fell, monasticism flowered within Christianity and it increasingly assumed all kinds of social functions over the next few centuries. At the end of this period, and the end of the first millennium of the Christian era, Christianity divided

---

5. See Kerr, *Readings in Christian Thought*, 27 is a section on Irenaeus. This quote is from page 29.

into Orthodox or Eastern and Western Christianity. Earlier there had been schisms, or divisions, within Christianity, notably in the Donatist churches of the fourth century and the Nestorian churches of the fifth century that made it all the way to China. But the largest split occurred in 1000 when the tensions that had long been evident between Orthodox and Catholic Christianity resulted in the Bishop of Constantinople and the Bishop of Rome declaring their separation from each other.

The third period in our account of Christian thinking is from 1000 to 1500, the medieval period. With the rise of the universities in the West, we see the emergence of a new kind of thinking in Christian circles. Thomas Aquinas called it a "sacred science" or "theology, a science of God." At the same time, we see great efforts to chart the spiritual life in the life of Francis of Assisi and the writings of figures such as Bonaventure and Hildegard of Bingen. In the West, medieval civilizations blossomed and declined, and as the period ended Western Christianity became fragmented with the Protestant Reformation.

The fourth period in our account is from 1500 to 1750. During this period, Western Christianity was fractured into many Protestant churches—Lutheran, Reformed, Anglican, Anabaptist and others—along with Catholic and Orthodox Christianity. Martin Luther, an Augustinian monk in Germany who broke with the Catholic Church, was the first of the great reformers. But reform took place within the Catholic tradition as well. Over these centuries, many new Protestant movements emerged and flourished, some of them in the new worlds of the Americas that Europeans had recently discovered. The period was marked by intense conflict among Christian groups in Europe, including years of warfare.

The fifth period of our story stretches from the publication of the first volume of the *Encyclopedia* in France in 1751 to the world wars of the twentieth century. Beginning in the mid-eighteenth century, we see the emergence of the movement that would come to be known in the West as the European Enlightenment. (In the East the term is related to Siddhartha Gautama and his experience of Enlightenment c. 500 BCE.) The European Enlightenment dramatically altered the cultural landscape within which Christianity found itself. The Enlightenment gave rise to the modern era with the new political philosophies of Locke and Rousseau, the thought of Voltaire and Kant, the French Revolution of 1789 and the flourishing of the modern sciences. In the Enlightenment, with its desire to be free of the Church, the Western world was dramatically altered—-and so was Christian thinking.

The modern period continued to unfold in the industrial revolution of the nineteenth century and the emergence of a technological culture, especially after the world wars of the twentieth century.

The sixth period in the continuing conversation for the truth of what was given in the revelatory events at the beginning of the Christian era stretches from the beginning of the "war to end all wars" in 1914 down to our own time of transition. Beginning after World War I and continuing after World War II, we saw Christian thought return to the perennial questions basic to the Christian faith. We also saw the emergence of an ecumenical movement that began to heal the divisions that had beset Western Christianity since the Reformation, and even made dents in the thousand-year-old split between the Christian East and West. We now find ourselves in this contemporary or postmodern era. The great conversation continues as Christians explore the revelation given in the life, death and resurrection of Jesus of Nazareth. It is to the context for the unfolding of that great conversation that we now turn.

Review

1. Why can Christian thought be seen as a "Great Conversation?"
2. What are the four elements of the approach taken here to Christian thought?
3. What was the worldview in which Christianity began—and in which Christian thought was largely articulated until modern times?

Chapter 2

The Jewish/Greek/Roman Matrix

In this chapter, we want to focus on three topics:

- the Jewish heritage and matrix out of which Christianity comes
- the Greek cultural world which has an impact on Christianity
- the Roman Empire in which Christianity emerges

The Jewish Matrix

CHRISTIANITY EMERGED WITHIN THE context of the Jewish world. Not only were Jesus and his followers Jews, but also their sense of the world, their culture, and their habits had been forged in a Jewish matrix. As a consequence, Christian thinking was initially identical with Jewish thinking even though it came to diverge as Christianity unfolded. Early Christian and Jewish thinkers shared a belief in God as the creator of the heavens and the earth, and as transcendent of every created thing. In terms of that fundamental starting point, there is continuity between Christian and Jewish thought. But as Christianity developed and sought to understand the relationship of Jesus the Christ to God, there emerged an understanding of God as trinity, as "one in three, three in one." This understanding separated Christian thought from the strict monotheistic traditions of Judaism, even though Christians continued to affirm that God is One and that they were not polytheists. The Christian doctrine of the trinity arose over a period of time as Christian thinkers reflected upon how Jesus is related to God. We will discuss this below.

In addition to the belief in a transcendent creator God, Christianity is one with its Jewish forbears in that it affirms that the central dynamic in reality is the encounter between God and humankind. God is the creator of heaven and earth and all that is. God is the one who creates man and woman in God's own image, the one who called Abraham, the one who led the people of Israel out of bondage in Egypt, the one who creates a Covenant with his people, Israel, the one who, as says the prophet Amos, demands justice. Christians believe that the divine-human encounter continues to unfold in the events that surround Jesus' life. Indeed, the early Christians believed that Jesus is the Messiah, the anointed one of God.

The belief in Jesus as Messiah came to be foundational for Christian thinking even though early Christian understandings of the Messiah diverged from the longer Jewish messianic tradition. In the longer Jewish tradition, that messianic dimension is understood primarily in terms of a covenant relationship between God and a particular people, Israel. However, within the Jewish world there were divergent understandings of "the Messiah." Some looked for a more collective Messiah, some for a restored Davidic King, some for an eschatological figure, and so on. In Christianity, as it unfolds, that divine-human encounter is increasingly understood in terms of the relationship that people have with Christ as the incarnate word of God.

A third element of continuity between Jewish and Christian thinkers is the belief and affirmation that history is purposive. There is a kind of inner direction to the historical process that stretches from creation, as that process is finally articulated in Christian thought, through the fall and redemption, all the way to the end of history or the consummation of the historical process. History is not simply repetition or the endless recurrence of cycles. There is an inner linear dynamic that unfolds over time, so that history itself becomes very important within Christian thinking. This unfolding history is related to God's purposes and intentions.

Thus, early Christianity is a new religious movement that emerges in the Jewish world that has important points of continuity with the longer Jewish tradition and yet moves beyond some of its central affirmations. Aside from these points of continuity, three other aspects of the ancient Jewish world also provide background for early Christianity.

Early Christianity stands initially within the prophetic tradition of Judaism. The Jewish tradition is complex, but it is particularly the prophetic tradition that is crucial for Christian thought. The prophetic dimension of Jewish thought affirms that the divine intention, expressed in the symbol of the Kingdom of God, is one that will be realized in space and time. Thus Christianity, by placing itself in this dimension of Judaism, takes on a worldly focus in its beginnings. When Jesus announces his ministry in the Gospel of Luke, he reads from the prophet Isaiah: "*The Spirit of the Lord is upon me, because he has anointed me to preach good news to the poor. He has sent me to proclaim release to the captives and recovering of sight to the blind, to set at liberty those who are oppressed and to proclaim the acceptable year of the Lord."* Then he says, *"Today, this scripture has been fulfilled in your hearing."* (LK4:18-21) Jesus takes up his own position and his own understanding of his work and ministry squarely within the context of the prophetic tradition of Judaism. So from the beginning, there has been a large element in Christian thinking which centres on the theme of the coming reign of God. And, of course, it is over the interpretation of this prophetic tradition that there is major conflict between the Jewish and Christian traditions. Christians identify Jesus as the Messiah while the Jewish tradition still awaits the fulfillment of its messianic beliefs.

For Christianity, the prophetic tradition of the Hebrew Scriptures is realized in the life and ministry of Jesus of Nazareth. In the prophetic tradition, one of the central questions concerned the coming of the Messiah, and for Christianity the Messiah is the one who has come in the person of Jesus. Thus one of the challenges for early Christianity is to try to show how, in the events of Jesus' life, this prophetic tradition has been fulfilled. In the first decades of the Christian era, this was a much contested issue. Later generations of Christians assume that Jesus as Messiah was a self-evident matter, but this was not so for early followers of Jesus.

For the larger Jewish community, the prophecies concerning the Messiah remain to be fulfilled. It is important to understand that, while Christianity emerged within the matrix of the Jewish tradition, it also offers an interpretation of that tradition which is very different from that maintained within Judaism itself.

In the Christian scriptures we can see that it is not a simple matter to affirm that Jesus is the Messiah. Some contemporary scholars of the Christian scriptures say that the earliest Christian belief was that when the Messiah comes, the Messiah will be Jesus. There is a gradual movement backward in time in these Christian writings from the belief that Jesus will be the Messiah when the Messiah comes, to the belief that the Messiah has already come in the present and was Jesus, to the belief that Jesus was the Messiah from the very foundations of creation—that he existed with God at the beginning and has come into the world at this moment in time. This is related to the Christian doctrine of Incarnation, which has its roots in the early Christian writings but was developed more fully in later centuries.

A second strand of Judaism that is important for the development of early Christianity is what scholars call intertestamental Judaism: Jewish life and thought between 400 BCE and the beginning of the Christian era. From this period, early Christianity gets the belief that God mediates himself to the world through supernatural beings such as angels, a belief that is a rather late development within Judaism. After 587 BCE, when a large portion of the Jewish population was marched off to Babylon—it was the period of the Babylonian Captivity—Jewish thought was influenced by other traditions of the Near East. This influence meant that more "otherworldly" or "supernatural" elements were incorporated into the Jewish worldview than had been there before. It is important to know that there is tension within Judaism between the earlier prophetic traditions and later traditions—evident, for example, in the book of Daniel. In Daniel, we see more emphasis than in other biblical writings on the "supernatural" elements of God's relationship to the world.

A third element of the Jewish tradition important for Christianity is Alexandrian Judaism—the Judaism that emerged in the city of Alexandria in Egypt. The works of Philo of Alexandria (30 BCE—45 CE) exemplify this strand of Judaism. Philo reflected on what was happening in Judaism as it encountered the larger Greek world, and his Jewish thinking was influenced by Greek philosophical ideas. He is important to later Christian thought in that we see in his work an attempt to reconcile the Jewish scriptures with Greek philosophical traditions. He did that through what is called an "allegorical method of Biblical interpretation." In the Alexandrian tradition, there was a movement away from the literal interpretation of scripture towards a more differentiated reading. This shift was partly due to a desire to relate the Jewish scripture to the philosophical tradition. Philo maintained that the God we find in Scripture is a transcendent God. But drawing on the Greek philosophers, he asked this question: if God is utterly transcendent, how does God make himself known to human beings?

For Philo, the way in which God makes himself known to human beings is through his own self-revelation, which is present in Scripture. But, he argued, we must maintain the distinction between God and Scripture. To maintain this distinction, Philo used an analogy drawn from the Platonic tradition's concept of the difference between the world of reality and the world of appearances. For Philo, Scripture is to be understood as a shadow of the truth, a manifestation within which truth is to be found. The truth which is found in Scripture is a spiritual truth. Thus Philo saw the need to develop a method for the interpretation of Scripture which allows us to penetrate through the shadow to the light which stands behind it. For Philo, that meant an allegorical method. We must exert ourselves to see what the true meaning of Scripture is. We must, as it were, see through Scripture to the transcendent reality that stands behind it, because that is where the truth of Scripture lies.

In attempting to interpret the Hebrew Scripture in this way, Philo was trying to reconcile the truth that is given in scripture with the truth that is given in philosophy. For Philo, that philosophy was particularly the philosophy of Plato. Philo believed that truth was one and sought a method that could preserve his own commitments to scripture but also incorporate what he was discovering in the writings of the philosophers. He believed that the truth that was revealed in scripture—as it were, in its shadows or appearances—had to be penetrated, and that when we discovered that truth, it would be consistent with the truth disclosed by the philosophers.

One term that Philo used to speak about what mediates between the world of truth and world of appearances was the "*logos*"—the Word. The *logos* is, in Philo's thought, that reality through which an utterly transcendent God mediates himself to the world of space and time. Philo's notion of the *logos* is a complex one. For Philo *Logos* means that principle by which God creates and orders the world, and it also refers to the means/reason by which the mind apprehends truth or reality. Philo was seeking a way of interpreting both Scripture and philosophy.

We have discussed Philo as an example of the kind of creative ferment that was going on in the religious world of Judaism as it attempted to relate its understanding of the God of Israel to the philosophical traditions of the Greek world. In this process, it began to incorporate certain Greek ideas—such as the *logos* or *word* or *reason*, through which God enlightens the minds of human beings—in an attempt to bring about reconciliation between the kinds of truth that are found in Greek philosophical culture and those found in the Hebrew Scriptures.

Later, we will see similar processes going on within Christian thinking. Christianity would struggle with the problem of reinterpreting the Hebrew Scripture in the light of its beliefs that the Messiah had come in Jesus of Nazareth and that Jesus is the one through whom God had been disclosed. Christian thinkers would also try to understand this Jesus in relation to the Greek world and its notions of truth and reason. Like Alexandrian Judaism, early Christianity would generate allegorical interpretations of Scripture and develop the concept of *logos*—the mediating reality between the world of appearances and the truth.

Greek Culture and Philosophy

The second contextual factor for the unfolding of Christian thought was Greek philosophical culture. Ever since the time of Alexander the Great (356BCE - 323BCE), Greek philosophical ideas had permeated the ancient world, and that philosophical culture also had a formative impact on Christianity. The early Christian community had its origins in and around Jerusalem, but with the missionary activity of the Apostle Paul, the early Christian community moved beyond the confines of Jerusalem into Asia Minor and around the Mediterranean basin. In these diverse settings, the Christian community was called upon to understand itself in relation not only to its original Jewish context but also to the Greek philosophical culture. Thus, Greek thinking about the world had an impact on Christian thought.

When we talk about philosophy in the ancient world, we are not talking about philosophy as we experience it in the contemporary world, as a department in the university. In the ancient world, philosophy was understood as the quest for wisdom, and we might say that it was more or less the religion of the intellectual classes. It was a way of understanding the world and human life within it.

One key strand of Greek thought is derived from the Greek philosopher Plato. The Platonic view makes a distinction between a world above our world, described as the world of real or ideal forms, and the realm of appearances, which is this world, described as a shadow or reflection of the realm above. For example, Platonists would say that in terms of justice and goodness in the world of space and time, we encounter in this world only reflections of the realm of justice and goodness which lies above and beyond this realm of appearances. A view of reality which divides reality into different levels was very common in the ancient world: there is a realm above and a realm below.

This two-fold reality is also related to the philosophical issue of trying to relate the one and the many. In the realm of appearances, we have many; but all those many gain their essential identity from their participation in the one which lies behind the many. In the Platonic scheme of things, the realm of the many, the realm of appearances, has its reality by virtue of its participation in the deeper realm of forms. The true identity of anything in our perception of things is not its material identity but its spiritual identity, its participation in the realm of forms.

Here's an illustration to help clarify this view. What is it that makes us all human beings despite all our differences—some bigger and some smaller, some younger and some older, some with dark skin and some with light skin, and so on? Normally, we do not have any trouble recognizing human beings as human beings in spite of their various shapes and sizes. How is it that we know them? Is it because they all participate in a common essence or a common form: our humanness? Platonists would say yes to that question.

What is our humanness? For the Platonists, it is that we are all rational creatures and we all have a desire for the good (both qualities that we easily attribute to ourselves, but often question in others!). The Platonist would say that we understand reality through participation and recollection. The Platonic traditions claim that the human mind has access to the world which lies behind the world of appearances. For example, the Platonist would say that we have knowledge of justice in its ideal form, and it is that knowledge which allows us to recognize instances of justice or injustice in the world of appearances in which we live.

The Platonic viewpoint is quite foreign to modern approaches to the world. Rather than claiming prior knowledge of ideal forms—of justice, for example—the modern view says that we see particular instances of justice or injustice and we then generalize from those many instances. In other words, we notice similarities and abstract from the particulars to come up with a general idea. The Platonic tradition, on the other hand, places primacy on the mind having direct access to the spiritual world or the world of forms which lies behind things. Based on that knowledge, we identify qualities and things in the everyday world of appearances.

When Christianity moves into the larger Greek world, it begins to articulate its own self-understanding in relation to Greek philosophical categories and an essentially Platonic conception of the world. We will see how this works out in Christian thinking about God and the world.

Another element of the Greek philosophical tradition, different from the Platonic view, is the Stoic philosophy that grew out of the work of a man named Zeno around 300 BCE. Zeno argued that the purpose of life was to overcome all passions, to place virtue at the heart of one's life and to live a life in accordance with nature. Stoicism also emphasized the brotherhood of all men, but this brotherhood was meant in a fairly exclusive sense. For the ancient Stoics, there was an order to the universe; that order was called "fate." Fate was impersonal, ruling all things, and the task of human life was to come to understand that impersonal fate and to live in harmony with it. This tradition was very influential in the Roman world of the first and second centuries, and there are similarities between some early Christian ideas and some Stoic ones. The similarities suggest not only that some early Christian thinkers borrowed ideas from the Stoic world, but also that they found these ideas to be congenial to what they already believed. Moreover, in seeking to make themselves understood to audiences steeped in Greek thinking, Christians sometimes articulated their own views in terms drawn from Stoic or Platonic philosophy.

Thus as Christianity moved outside of the matrix of its Jewish origins, it increasingly drew upon Greek philosophical concepts to articulate its own view of God, of reality, and of the life that humans should live in this world. And while Christianity adopted some of the language and ideas of the Greek philosophical traditions, it also transformed these ideas. For example, there are parallels between early Christian notions of providence and Stoic notions of fate, but the ideas are philosophically and psychologically different from each other. Christians, like Stoics, affirm that there is an order to creation; but unlike the Stoic idea of an impersonal fate governing all, the Christian idea of order is grounded in a beneficent God giving meaning to all of life's events. This difference substantially alters the whole idea.

The Roman World & Empire

As we begin our exploration of Christian thought, it is important to remember that the larger social world within which Christianity unfolded was shaped by Roman civilization. During its earliest period, Christianity was an outlaw religion often subject to persecution by the Roman authorities because of its refusal to acknowledge the Roman gods. It was for this reason that one of the charges levelled against Christianity was that it was "atheistic"—that is, Christians did not worship the Roman gods. There was a conflictual relationship between early Christianity and the Roman world—after all, the Romans had put to death the Christian Messiah. But the attitude of the Christian community shifted and became more differentiated. Paul, the Apostle to the Gentiles, often traded upon his Roman citizenship even though he too was put to death by the Romans. Nero, the Roman emperor, accused Christians of instigating the fire in Rome in the 70s.

But in the fourth century, the situation changed, and it changed dramatically. Changes began when Constantine legalized Christianity in the Edict of Milan in 313. Christianity became the official religion of the Roman world in 380 during the reign of Emperor Theodosius (379-395). It very much affected the shape that Christianity took and the thought of Christian thinkers. Christianity increasingly incorporated into itself the Roman passion for order and social stability, which certainly affected the way the Christian church came to see its social function.

Emerging within Roman civilization was a network of roads and commerce between peoples that was relatively new in the ancient world. This possibility of wide-ranging connection was important to early Christianity. It facilitated the spread of Christian ideas and its development in widely separate contexts. There were little outposts of Christian believers in Egypt, in cities in Asia Minor such as Ephesus (in today's Turkey), in Rome and in North Africa, as well as in Israel and the ancient Near East. These places were all part of the Roman Empire—and communication between these different centres was sporadic and limited. One couldn't keep in touch by phone or solve problems by sending a fax or an e-mail.

Paul was a Roman citizen, and at times he used his citizenship to get himself out of difficulties. It facilitated his movements around Asia Minor to cities like Ephesus and Corinth, where he established communities of Christians, and to Rome.

One of the things that Roman civilization bequeathed to Christianity is a concrete example of the possibility for human beings to live within one large social network with diverse cultural traditions and multiform social practices, and that peoples can be woven into a common social order. While Christianity was critical of aspects of this imperial society, it also absorbed aspects of the Roman world into itself. For example, the idea of a universal society is one that Christianity tried to promote and develop. And while critical of specific religious dimensions of Roman society, Christianity was also dependent upon the social network of Roman society to promote its own message and vision of how things stand between God and the human race. Even today, the largest grouping of Christians is the Roman Catholic Church.

Summary

It is important to understand some of these background features of Christianity because the world in which Christianity emerged was a world that had shape to it. It was not an empty landscape waiting to be written on. Not only were Jesus and his early followers Jews, but a Jewish world was the matrix of Christianity. However, that Jewish world had already been permeated by elements of Greek culture and philosophy, and the earliest Christian writings were in *koine* Greek and not Hebrew.

The larger society was Roman, encircling the whole of the Mediterranean basin. It was not a neutral world but a world already shaped by centuries of human culture: Hittite, Egyptian, Greek, and Roman, to name just a few. Christianity unfolded in relation to these older and larger cultural realities, which posed limitations as well as opportunities for the development of Christian thought.

Review

1. What ideas did early Christian thought share with the longer Jewish tradition?
2. How important was Greek thought and culture to early Christian thinking?
3. Did the Roman world have an impact on Christian thinking?
4. Who was Philo of Alexandria?

PART II

Beginnings and the First Centuries: 30–325

IN PART II OF the Great Conversation, we look at the emergence of Christian thought in the first three centuries of the Christian era. Chapter 3 outlines the emergence of the early Christian community as a "spirit-filled community," living in the hope of the Coming Kingdom. We see how that community moved out into the Gentile world and the issues that arose in that process. The Hebrew Bible was the Christians' first scripture, but as early Christians began to write of their experiences, the process of forming their own scriptural canon began.

In Chapter 4, our investigation extends to early Christian practice as we examine the *Didache*, an early Christian writing known as the *Teaching of the Twelve Apostles*. Here we see how early Christians dealt with the problem of persecution. In this phase, the "martyr" emerged as the exemplary Christian. In Chapter 5, we move into the second century of the Christian era and examine early Christian thinkers such as Justin Martyr and Tertullian. They were known as "apologists" who sought to articulate the Christian faith to the Roman world (Justin Martyr) and within the Christian community (Tertullian).

Chapter 6 focuses on Irenaeus, an exceptionally important Christian thinker at the end of the second century. Irenaeus understood the Christian faith as a "three-articled faith," and he articulated the basic Christian story as one that moves from creation to the fall and redemption and on to consummation. Chapter 7 looks at Origen, a great Alexandrian who turned Christian thought in a more speculative/philosophical and doctrinal direction.

Chapter 3

The Coming Kingdom and the Formation of the Canon

THIS CHAPTER LOOKS AT Christian thought in the first hundred years, from 50 to 150. Try to imagine a community scattered around Jerusalem, out to Damascus, up into Asia Minor and down into Egypt—and perhaps as far away as the coast of India. Imagine a Christian community that has no churches dotting the street corners of towns and cities across the world. Think of a community that has no structured clergy and no clear system of authority. Think of an early community that has no nuanced creedal statement or a Bible as we know it— the Hebrew Bible being their only scripture. Imagine an early community that knows nothing of the theological developments that characterized the third and fourth centuries, a period in which many of the basic teachings of Christianity become articulated.

A Spirit-filled Community

The character of this early community is reflected to us in the *Acts of the Apostles*, which tells us about the founding of the early Christian community in terms of the events of Pentecost. We need to think of a spirit-filled community, one that believes that something decisive has occurred through the resurrection of Jesus, an event which still has early Christians bewildered and astonished. This community is in the very beginnings of the process of self-definition and beset by a whole number of practical problems as well as profound theological issues.

The *Acts of the Apostles* begins in the following way:

> *In the former book, O Theophilus, I spoke of all that Jesus did and taught from the beginning until the day on which he was taken up, after he had given commandments through the Holy Spirit to the apostles whom he had chosen. To them he presented himself alive . . . appearing to them . . . and speaking of the kingdom of God. (Acts 1:1–3)*

The "former book" that is spoken of here is the Gospel of Luke: Luke/Acts is a two-volume work. During this period of early Christianity, the very texts that became part of the Christian Bible were still in the process of formation. Even those few that had been written were likely not widely known to the whole community, except in oral fragments. Thus we are speaking about a period before we have the full Christian Scripture. This Christian community is still in the process of sorting out who this Jesus was and what his life and ministry, and especially his death and resurrection, mean. It is a community that is still dependent upon the living proclamation of the disciples who knew Jesus, such as Peter and John, and early Christians such as Paul who did not know Jesus "in the flesh."

The Delay of the Parousia

In the early Christian writing called the *Acts of the Apostles*, the Christian community is concerned with a number of matters. Two provocative questions arise. When is the kingdom going to come? And how are we to live as we wait?

The question of when the kingdom is going to come is the first question addressed in the *Acts of the Apostles*. This writing reveals that one of the first things the early Christian community believed about Jesus was that he was the Messiah. The community also believed that with the Messiah comes the kingdom. The Jewish community expected that the coming of the kingdom meant the restoration of Israel, and the early Christian community, particularly the community in and around Jerusalem, shared this expectation. According to the *Acts of the Apostles*, one of the first questions the apostles asked Jesus after his resurrection was, *Lord, will you at this time restore the Kingdom of Israel?* Jesus answered, *It is not for you to know times and seasons which the Father has fixed by his own authority* (Acts 1.6–7).

In the interim, there is a gift promised to the Christian community, the gift of the Holy Spirit. Early in the *Acts of the Apostles*, the story is told of the bestowing of this gift in the experience of Pentecost. Luke paints the picture of a group of rather dispirited Christians gathered in Jerusalem suddenly filled with the spirit. Onlookers wondered if they had been drinking. And though they spoke many languages, they understood one another (Acts 2). Pentecost is interpreted as the founding of the *ecclesia*, the community, the church. However, it is perhaps more helpful to see this event as the founding of the early Christian community, because the word *church* has a whole set of associations for us that are not quite accurate in relation to this earliest community.

Thus in the *Acts of the Apostles*, the early community received, first, a question mark as to when the kingdom that Jesus inaugurates is going to be fully realized. Second, it received the gift of the spirit when there is speaking in many tongues and yet everyone understands. The third element crucial to the self-understanding of early Christianity is the command that *you shall be my witnesses in Jerusalem . . . to the end of the earth* (Acts 1:8). Thus early Christians received a vocation as a community to be witnesses to what has occurred in and to Jesus, in whom and through whom salvation has come:

> *And when he had said this, he was lifted up before their eyes, and a cloud took him out of their sight. And while they were gazing up to heaven as he went, behold, two men stood by them in white garments, and said to them, "Men of Galilee, why do you stand looking up to heaven? This Jesus who has been taken up from you into heaven, shall come in the same way as you have seen him going up to heaven"* (Acts 1:8–11).

These elements constituted the foundations of the early Christian community: the belief that in Jesus, the Kingdom has begun to dawn and is beginning to take shape among them; that the community is to be guided by the power of the spirit; and that the early Christian community, especially the disciples/apostles, has a vocation to be witnesses throughout the whole world. When we think about those who received this testimony and witness, we must remember that we are initially talking about very small numbers of people in and around Jerusalem. Furthermore, they don't yet have a set of definitive Christian writings regarded as authoritative within the Christian community, aside from the Hebrew Bible.

What is the authority in terms of which the early Christian community lives? It is the testimony of the disciples and later of Paul, the first great missionary and Apostle, who have gone out from Jerusalem to bear witness to what they have seen and heard. The groups of people who heard their preaching and teaching may have heard the disciples or the apostle Paul for a few hours, a few days, or perhaps weeks, but then they wouldn't see them again for a long time. The apostles didn't take up residence in these communities, taking time to fully impress upon the people they came into contact with their understanding of what had occurred in the life, death and resurrection of Jesus. Nor could they leave behind them a book in which the Christian story could be found, although they could point to the Hebrew Scripture and explain how they believed its promises pointed to Jesus. Consequently, the early Christian groups were left in large part to their own devices. They had received the gift of the Holy Spirit, which would instruct them and lead them.

At the same time as they were teaching, the apostles were themselves going through a process of trying to understand what had occurred in the events of Jesus' life, death and resurrection. On some issues, the disciples and apostles found themselves in conflict with one another. There was a meeting spoken about in Acts as the "Council of Jerusalem," sometimes called the first ecumenical council. This Council reflected the practical problems that beset the early church—practical problems with deep theoretical import. To solve these problems, the early Christians turned to the disciples and leaders for their adjudication and consideration.

The Council of Jerusalem

Chapter 15 of the *Acts of the Apostles* says that some men came down from Judea and were teaching the brethren that u*nless you are circumcised after the manner of Moses, you cannot be saved.* (Acts 15:1) The early Christians saw themselves in the context of their Jewish forbears, viewing the law that had been given to Moses as binding upon the Christian community. And Jesus' own life and ministry was directed to the people of Israel. They were the people of God from whom he came and by whom he was partly received and partly rejected. However, when Paul came along, he understood the life, ministry, death and resurrection of Jesus differently from other Jews. He saw it as a message for the whole world — that is, for non-Jews (the Gentiles), as well as Jews. And so a major question for the early church was the extent to which following the laws of Moses is required for membership in the new community. Must the new converts be circumcised in order to be saved? Must they follow the dietary laws of the Jews?

Some taught "yes" and others said "no." Paul, having preached to the Gentiles, is particularly important here. Thus at the council in Jerusalem, Barnabas and Paul recounted *what signs and wonders God had done through them among the Gentiles.* (Acts15:12) Peter supported the work among the Gentiles and said that everyone *shall be saved through the grace of the Lord Jesus.* Then James uttered his judgment to the council: *We should not trouble those of the Gentiles who turn to God.* (Acts15:19) Thus he argued that the full law of Moses is not obligatory. In their opinion, this was what God called for in relation to the Gentiles. A new set of conditions applied for membership in the people of God.

Thus while many believed that the Jewish traditions had to be maintained, Paul, Barnabas and some of the others offered another view. They believed that people would be saved through the grace made available through Jesus, but that the Jews were still to follow the law of Moses. Paul seemed to hold the view that the law given to Moses remained valid for the Jewish community but was not obligatory for non-Jews entering this new dispensation. So in answer to the question "What shall we say to the Gentiles when we preach among them?", the conference responded as follows: *As for the Gentile believers, we ourselves have written our decision that they abstain from idol offerings and from blood and from what is strangled and from immorality.* (Acts 15:20)

The council of the apostles, the early disciples and the early teachers was the first structure of authority in the Christian community. Questions were referred to the disciples, this time meeting as a group, and their responses were decisive within the community. We have only this one instance of such a meeting recorded in the *Acts of the Apostles*. But we can imagine that there may well have been other such meetings to address all sorts of practical problems and questions that arose in the day-to-day life of these widely scattered early communities.

Paul and the Delayed Parousia

It is clear from the *Acts of the Apostles* that there was a widespread belief within early Christian communities that the kingdom would come soon . Many scholars, especially recent ones, have made a great point of this belief in speaking of the delay of the *parousia* (the coming kingdom). The much-anticipated kingdom was not immediately realized in a visible way. Some modern scholars even define the coming of the kingdom as the birth of the spirit-filled community that grew out of the Pentecost experience.

When is the kingdom coming and what shape will it take? There is no simple answer, but we need to be aware of the power of this expectation for early Christians. The coming of the kingdom is the horizon within which the early community unfolded, with the expectation among some that it would occur soon. Thus the delay of the *parousia* was a crucial factor in early Christian experience. Martin Werner, a contemporary German scholar believes that it was so decisive that it alone prompted the development of

Christian thought.[1] Werner's view is overstated, but it does underscore the significance of the question of the coming kingdom. We also see this as a central issue in the letters of Paul to the communities he founded.

Paul addressed issues that arose within these communities in letters of encouragement and criticism that he wrote to them. In the first of his two letters to the Thessalonians, Paul had said something about the coming of the Lord that had created confusion, and so he wrote them a second letter. In the first letter, in Chapter 4, he wrote,

> *But we would not have you ignorant, brethren, concerning those who are asleep, that you may not grieve as others do who have no hope. For since we believe that Jesus died and rose again, even so, through Jesus, God will bring with him those who have fallen asleep. For this we declare to you by the word of the Lord, that we who are alive, who are left until the coming of the Lord, shall not precede those who have fallen asleep. For the Lord himself will descend from heaven with a cry of command, with the archangel's call, and with the sound of the trumpet of God. And the dead in Christ will rise first; then we who are alive, who are left, shall be caught up together with them.* (I Thessalonians 4:13-17)

Apparently, some in the community believed that Paul was telling them that the coming of Christ was imminent and the kingdom was going to be established very soon. They thought he meant that the kingdom would come within the lifetime of living members of the community.

However, this wasn't the point that he wanted to make. Paul wrote a second letter in which he repeated what we saw earlier in the *Acts of the Apostles*: that day is still far off, we don't know the time, and we simply have to wait upon God to bring about his kingdom. He urged the Thessalonians "concerning the coming of our Lord Jesus Christ . . . not to be quickly shaken in mind" (II Thess. 2.1). However, there is evidence in the letters of Paul that he shared the belief that the kingdom was coming soon. For example, on the question of marriage, he advised the Corinthians that it is best not to marry because the kingdom is near at hand, and when it comes, everything will change. Paul writes, "*Are you free from a wife? Do not seek marriage . . . the appointed time has grown very short . . . the form of this world is passing away*" (I Cor. 7: 25ff.).

Nevertheless, that first generation of believers did marry, and now they had children and the challenge of instructing their own children in the faith. As the expectation of the imminent kingdom began to wane in intensity, questions such as how to instruct new believers and how to instruct a

---

1. See Werner, *The Formation of Christian Dogma*.

second generation came to the forefront. What should they be taught about the events that occurred before they were born?

Remember that in 50, 60, 70 or 80 teachers and parents could not hand children and new believers the New Testament because this collection of twenty-seven books did not yet exist. They might have had the Pauline writings—some may have been written in the 50s—but these letters are very specific, written to particular communities about particular issues. We do not know how widely they were known. The gospels—Matthew, Mark, Luke and John—came later. The early believers lived by the stories that were transmitted orally by the apostles and other early missionaries. These stories were passed on from person to person and from generation to generation.

As it began to dawn on members of the early Christian community that the kingdom might still be a ways off, they increasingly turned their attention to practical issues. Three of the crucial issues were the Scripture they shared, the persecution they endured and the unity of the Christian community they hoped for. Here we will look at the emergence of the Christian scripture; we will take up the other issues—persecution and unity—in the following chapter.

Towards the Christian Canon

For the Christian community, the first scripture was the Hebrew Scripture. As my former colleague John Miller insists, Christians have always been a people of the Bible, but their first Bible was the Hebrew Scripture. Later, Christians were to call this first Bible the "Old Testament." But that Scripture was now being interpreted in a new light, in the light of the life and death of Jesus. Christians believed that a central teaching of the Hebrew Scripture was the prophecy of the coming of the Messiah. The Christian community believes that the Messiah, the anointed one, was Jesus of Nazareth. Thus the early followers of Jesus, Jews like Jesus, came to understand their first Bible in a distinctive way, a way that was different from the way it was understood by other Jews. For example, in the early Christian writings we see efforts to prove these prophecies and to draw from the Hebrew Bible the texts that they now saw confirmed in the light of what happened in and around Jesus.

According to contemporary scholarship, the oldest writings incorporated into the Christian canon—the accepted group of early Christian writings—are the letters of Paul (40s–50s), followed by the Gospels (60s–100), and the other writings (70–100).

It is important to know that there were other writings, including gospels that were not accepted into the canon of early Christian writings. By excluding these other gospels, the early community set some limits upon what was considered a faithful witness to Jesus Christ. One example we have of a gospel that didn't make it into the New Testament is the *Gospel of Thomas*, the so-called *Secret Sayings of Jesus*. This is a text we have only recently recovered, from an ancient Christian library found in Egypt in the 1940s. This particular book—a collection of sayings—was attributed to the Apostle Thomas and was said to contain the words of the living Jesus. There is some ambiguity about the meaning of "the living Jesus." It seems at some points to mean sayings that Jesus communicated secretly to his disciples before his death and, at other points, to mean words from the resurrected Jesus, not spoken during his life and ministry but spoken to Thomas after his resurrection.

Many of the parables and stories found in the *Gospel of Thomas* are similar to stories that we have within the synoptic gospels and the Gospel of John. They vary somewhat in their emphasis. For example, we read in the *Gospel of Thomas*:

> *These are the secret words which Jesus the Living spoke and which Didymus Judas Thomas wrote. And he said, "He who will find the interpretation of these words will not see death . . . " And later, "Jesus said, If those who draw you say to you, Lo, the kingdom is in heaven, then the birds of heaven will precede you, if they say to you, it is in the sea, then the fish will precede you. But the kingdom is within you and outside you . . . When you know yourselves, then you will be known; and you will know that you are the sons of the living Father."*[2]

This text echoes words and ideas from the synoptic gospels, but there are also things that we don't find in those gospels. Why is this text not included in the Christian canon?

We can only speculate. Contemporary scholars believe that part of the reason is that this gospel was only known to a very small part of the Christian world, the Gnostic Christian communities in Egypt, and was not widely circulated. It also contains certain theological tendencies, certain interpretations of Jesus that are at odds with the beliefs of the wider Christian community. This gospel is seen as coming out of a milieu that was strongly influenced by what we call "Gnostic" beliefs—from the Greek word "*gnosis*," to know. The Gnostic communities tended to downplay the historicity of Jesus and to see Jesus as a kind of spirit who temporarily donned, but very quickly shed, human flesh. So, in Thomas's Gospel, the story of Jesus' crucifixion plays a very minor role. To the Gnostics, Jesus was someone

---

2. See Grant and Freedman, *The Secret Sayings of Jesus*, 112–15.

who could not be really touched by such an event because the real Jesus hid behind his fleshly form. This issue was a very contentious one in the early community. There are not a lot of writings that address themselves to this issue, but we can better understand it by comparing the *Gospel of Thomas* with the gospels in the New Testament.

The synoptic gospels (those of Matthew, Mark and Luke) emphasize Jesus in his historical setting. He is a teacher from Galilee. His life includes teaching, healing, gathering disciples and his mission to Jerusalem. The accounts of Jesus in the gospels included in the Christian scripture focus on the stories of his passion, the entry into Jerusalem and his crucifixion—events that the New Testament writers saw as being at the heart of the Jesus story. The events themselves as well as the way the story is told emphasize the mysterious humanity of Jesus. On the other hand, the *Gospel of Thomas* downplays Jesus' humanity by focusing on his living spiritual reality.

The *Gospel of Thomas* and other early writings were excluded because they were not considered faithful witnesses to Jesus Christ. Thus, the very process of forming the canon also came to define the boundaries of the early Christian community. Certain texts were designated as authoritative, and communities which accepted these texts were within those boundaries. Those that did not agree—or that accepted additional texts—were thus in an uneasy relationship with the wider Christian community.

The first Christian writings that we have are Paul's letters from the 40s and 50s. They are followed by the synoptic gospels from the 60s and 70s, with John's gospel probably much later. Then there were other writings from the second half of the first century some of which were eventually included in the Christian canon but took a long time to be universally accepted. Among those is the book of *Revelations*, which some Christian communities were doubtful of into the third and fourth centuries. They were not sure whether it should be included or excluded. Another book that was under some suspicion was the book of *Hebrews*. Should it be in or not? Similar questions were raised about the books of *James, Second Peter, Second and Third John*, and *Jude*. We don't know why these books were regarded with suspicion in some quarters. We only know that in certain communities, these books were not included in the canon early on.

A few other books were very close to being included but did not make it. Those include the *Didache* (discussed below), a book called the *Shepherd of Hermas*, and another called the *Apocalypse of Peter*. These books were widely accepted, but were not finally included. Though they were generally attributed to the apostles, their authorship was always in doubt. Authorship was crucial in determining which writings would be in and which would not. If it was believed that the apostles authored them or the authority of the apostles stood behind them, then they usually became part of the Christian canon.

According to modern historical critical judgments, even the gospels included in the canon were not written by the people that tradition says wrote them. However, the view of the early Christian world was that they were written by the authors to whom they are ascribed (or in the case of the Gospel of Mark, by someone very closely associated with the apostle), and thus carried the mantle of the apostles. In the case of these three books mentioned above that were not included, there was just too much doubt about whether they came from the apostles or one of the close followers.

The process of defining the canon was a gradual one, taking place over a considerable period of time. It would seem that the criteria for entry into the Christian canon included the following: apostolicity (written by an apostle or close follower), universal usage and faithful witness to the events. Some contemporary scholars see universality as an important factor in deciding which books were considered authentic witnesses to these early events. If the book was known to all parts of the early community, it was considered authentic. If it was known only to some, it didn't usually make it into the canon.

The last criterion, faithful witness, is difficult to specify, but we can get some idea of it by reading, for example, the *Gospel of Thomas*. The story of Jesus there has a distinctly different feel and a different view of Jesus from the story told in the canonical gospels. In some sense, there are also differences among the four gospels that are included in the Christian canon. But the Thomas gospel apparently goes beyond the acceptable range of faithful witness.

However, what actually determined the canon is finally a matter of speculation, since there was no recorded meeting of people to decide these questions. It was probably a more informal process, one largely hidden from us. In reconstructing the process, we must use our imaginations, for there is little documentary evidence that tells us how it happened.

Marcion: A Defining Moment in the Process

A central issue for Christian thinking, and one that was in the background in the process of forming the canon, came to a head in relation to a second-century Christian thinker named Marcion. He came from the area around the Black Sea, became a Christian, and moved to Rome where he established a school for the study of the Christian message. Marcion did much to push the community to resolve the question of what belonged in the canon.

Marcion refused to employ the "allegorical" methods of exegesis then current in much of the Christian world for interpreting Scripture, and he found himself unable to reconcile the Hebrew Scriptures (what Christians would later call the Old Testament) with the teachings and message of Jesus, particularly as that message was articulated in the writings of Paul. Marcion argued that there was a great discontinuity between the Christian message and the message of the Hebrew Scriptures. Indeed, he claimed that the Christian god was not the same god as the Jewish god. In his view, the only authentic Christian writings were ten of the letters of Paul and an abbreviated version of the Gospel of Luke.

The problem for Marcion was what he saw as the discontinuity between the Yahweh of the Hebrew Bible and the Abba (Father) that Jesus addressed. His particular interpretations of Paul and Luke portray God as a god of grace and redeeming love, and it is this God—not the Yahweh of the Hebrew Bible—who is revealed in Jesus Christ. Marcion's view would have limited the canon to the letters of Paul and the Gospel of Luke. Christianity for Marcion was wholly a gospel of love, which stood in opposition to what Marcion saw as the legalism of the Hebrew Bible.

Marcion built a whole theological system around his interpretation of the differences between the Jewish God and the Christian God. The larger number of Christian communities rejected his views, but those views and the communities upholding them survived into the third and fourth centuries. Their growth and persistence posed a threat, representing a rival interpretation of Christianity and the Christian canon. Subsequent Christian thinkers have wrestled continuously with the issues that he raised—and in popular Christianity down to the present day, there are those who assert a fundamental difference between the God of the Christian Old Testament and the God of the Christian New Testament. But the Christian leadership in Marcion's time rejected his view, insisting that the God of the Jewish Scriptures is the same God revealed in the Christian writings. The wider community thus rejected Marcion's limitation of the canon to the letters of Paul and the Gospel of Luke.

As the content of the canon was determined, groups that followed dissidents such as Marcion were eventually excluded from the wider Christian community. Having a canon partly means that those who do not agree with it are excluded, since the Christian canon is one element that defines the boundaries of Christian thinking. Defining these limits is part of the struggle that begins in the second century over the question of the canon. Many of the people whom we will look at shortly addressed this issue of what should be normative in the early Christian community.

The Christian Canon at the End of the Second Century

By the end of the second century, there was widespread agreement on which books were a part of the canon and which were just on the fringes. The first official document that we currently know that includes the twenty-seven books found in the current canon comes from the year 367. In that year, Athanasius, the Bishop in Alexandria, wrote a letter in which he included all the twenty-seven books that we now include in the canon. There are earlier documents which included most of these books, but not all of them.

Through the first three centuries, the Christian canon of Scripture—that is, the writings to be added to the Jewish Bible or what later came to be called the Christian Old Testament—was still being formed. Thus Christian thought began before there was a complete and acknowledged canon of Scripture. Moreover, the process of determining the canon was a long and difficult one that is largely hidden from view. We simply don't know how the decisions were made that resulted in these new writings being added to the Christians' first Bible, the Hebrew Scriptures.

Summary

In the first generations after Jesus' life, death and resurrection, the early Christian community struggled to find its way. This process was complicated by the seeming delay in the expected coming of the kingdom. We see this in the early writings of Paul, the Apostle to the Gentiles. As the good news of the Christian story made its way beyond its original Jewish context, new ways of understanding Jesus begin to emerge as well as new ways of understanding what it meant to be part of the community of faith. While the early Christian community was a "people of the book," Christians now understood that book as witnessing to Jesus, the Messiah. Gradually, the early stories and memories of Jesus were incorporated into writings: the letters of Paul, the gospels and other writings. Through a process that we can only imaginatively reconstruct, certain of these writings were incorporated into the Christian canon. While Marcion attempted to restrict the Christian writings to the letters of Paul and the Gospel of Luke, excluding the Hebrew Bible, the larger community reaffirmed the Hebrew Bible as its own along with the newer Christian writings.

Review

1. Some have described the early Christian community as "spirit-filled." Why?
2. What was the first Christian scripture?
3. Who was the "Apostle to the Gentiles"?
4. Why was the Council of Jerusalem important?
5. What were the earliest Christian writings?
6. Why were some writings included in the Christian canon and others excluded?
7. Who was Marcion? Why is he important in the process that led to the formation of the Christian canon?

Chapter 4

Christian Practice and the Exemplary Christian

WHILE THE CHRISTIAN COMMUNITY remained scattered through its first century, it increasingly spread across the Roman world and even beyond. It was thus troubled by the question of how it could create unity of practice, rite and belief. The establishment of a Christian canon was a step in that direction, but to prevent the spirit-filled community from exploding into a number of unrelated fragments, more was required. With this in mind, we continue our exploration of early Christian thought in relation to the issues that faced Christians as they sought to give shape to their community and their practice. We look at the *Didache*, a writing that was on the edge of the canonical process, for the light it sheds on early Christian thought, as well as other writings that addressed the unity of the Christian community and the martyr as the exemplary Christian.

Didache: A Manual for Christian Living, A Glimpse of Early Christianity

The full title of the *Didache* is *The Teachings of the Twelve Apostles*. It is a small book which runs to about eight pages in modern translation. It summarizes some of the views and practices of the early Christian community and is ascribed to the apostles in a general way, but not attributed to any one of them in particular. This book, widely circulated in the early church, was then lost and wasn't rediscovered until the nineteenth century. We don't know exactly where it comes from, but it is generally regarded as giving us a glimpse into early Christian practice and beliefs. In particular, it sheds light on the practical issues dealt with late in the first and into the second century. It offers some advice on how to deal with matters like the rituals of baptism and the Eucharist, as well as with pesky "apostles and prophets" who turn up in one's community from time to time.

The Didache begins as follows: *"The Lord's teaching to the heathen by the 12 apostles . . . There are two ways, one of life and one of death, and between the two ways there is a great difference."* Early Christianity is presented as a *Way*, and it presents the ways open to humanity as two. One is *the way of life* and other is *the way of death*. They are dealt with very briefly. The way of life, says the Didache, is this: *"You must love God who made you and second, your neighbour as yourself, and whatever you want people to refrain from doing to you, you must not do to them."* This summary draws upon the great commandment that Jesus repeated and is a variation on the Golden Rule. Then follows a whole set of maxims, including *"bless those who curse you, pray for your enemies, fast for those who persecute you"* and so on. Following are many very specific teachings and moral guidelines as to the kind of life that will characterize those who follow the Way, the way of life. The way of death, by contrast, is *"wicked and thoroughly blasphemous,"* and many sins are listed.

The text is moralistic, straightforward and free of abstraction. It reflects the extent to which the concerns of the first century were practical preoccupations rather than large speculative questions. The message of the apostles has been heard. Jesus the Messiah has come and now there are the practical issues of how one should live. The focus of the text is on distinguishing those who are on the Christian side from those who are not. The *Way of Life* is clearly the Christian way.

The Didache also offers descriptions of early Christian rituals such as baptism and the Lord's Supper—and of how to deal with prophets who come into the community. The Didache says this about baptism:

> *Give public instruction on all these points and then baptize in running water in the name of the Father, and the Son and the Holy Spirit. If you don't have running water, baptize in some other. If you can't in cold, then in warm. If you have neither, then pour water on the head three times in the name of the Father, and the Son and the Holy Spirit. Fast first for one or two days.* [1]

---

1. See Richardson, *Early Christian Fathers*, 171–79.

The instruction is simple, straightforward, and very practical. For example, regarding baptism, there is a preferred form, but if it is inconvenient or impossible, there are alternatives.

In regard to the Eucharist, the text says that only those who are baptized should be allowed to participate in the Eucharist, and it gives instructions about how the Eucharistic rite should be performed: *"This is how to give this. First in connection with the cup: We thank you Father for . . . Then in connection with the piece of bread broken off the loaf: We thank you our Father . . ."*

The Lord's Prayer is mentioned in the text, with the suggestion that the prayer be recited three times a day. There are also instructions for how to treat wandering apostles and prophets. The *Didache* says that you should welcome anyone who comes your way, but if the teacher proves a renegade, then pay no attention to him. It notes that one of the marks of a true apostle and prophet is that he doesn't stay too long: *"You should welcome everyone on arriving as if he was the Lord, but he mustn't stay beyond one day. If he stays three days, he is a false prophet!"* Perhaps if we had heeded this view, the history of Christianity would have been very different! The text goes on to say that on departing, the itinerant figure should not accept anything except enough food to carry him to his next lodging, and he must not ask for money. If he does, warns the *Didache*, this marks him as *a false prophet*. Again, here is some stunning advice that points to an apparent problem for the early Christian community: how to determine which of the many prophetic voices is authentic and should be heeded.[2]

The *Didache* conveys the sense that the early community lives under the threat of persecution when it speaks to its readers about being courageous in the face of persecution and difficulties. It concludes, as the Book of Revelation concludes, with a reminder that the Lord is coming and so the difficulties now being endured are temporary. This injunction points to an issue that is very important to the early community: persecution and martyrdom.

Persecution and Martyrdom: Defining Exemplary Christianity

Throughout the first three centuries of Christianity, the community experienced persecution and opposition. This persecution was sporadic and didn't touch every part of the community in the same way. It probably began with Nero blaming Christians for the fire in Rome in the early 70s. After the

---

2. See especially ibid., 176.

70s, there were periods of intense persecution followed by periods when Christians would be left alone. During periods of persecution, Christians were often put to death. They became, for early Christians, exemplary figures, as martyrs for the faith. They offered a model of the ideal for the early Christian community. Polycarp (70–c.155), a bishop and himself a martyr, spoke of martyrs as "models of true Love." [3]

Among the writings that were important to the early community were the letters of Ignatius of Antioch. It is thought that Ignatius lived from 35 to 107 though these dates can't be firmly fixed. Ignatius reflects a certain development within the early community in that he was always referred to as a bishop, one of those people who had responsibility for the oversight of the Christian community in a particular city. He is known as the Bishop of Antioch and may have been the second or third bishop of that community. So we see that early on in the Christian community, figures emerged who exercised some authority in relation to the gathered group in a particular town or area. One can view the emergence of bishops and other leaders as a response to very practical problems that arose among Christians who understood they were living by the present inspiration of the Spirit and through the presence of the risen Jesus.

We have already seen that the early community took the Hebrew Scripture as its Bible. But this scripture is understood in the light of the recent events around which the early community had come into being. Moreover, there were people who, almost daily or weekly, felt they were visited by Jesus in dreams or visions, as well as being addressed by the Holy Spirit. With a multiplicity of voices, all claiming the warrant either of scripture or of direct inspiration, what would happen when these views differed from one another or were contradictory? One person would take a lesson form a vision of Jesus, another would understand Scripture to teach something different on the matter, and a third would feel that his or her view was inspired by the Holy Spirit. How could the matter be settled when a number of people claimed Jesus spoke directly to them? The rise of bishops—shepherds responsible for several congregations—unfolded against this kind of background.

Although Ignatius is known as the Bishop of Antioch, we know very little about him except for what we learn from the letters he wrote on his journey from Antioch to Rome. He was being taken by a guard of ten soldiers to be put to death. On his trip, he passed through many towns where there were Christian groups, and he stayed with the people in these towns. Then he wrote letters of encouragement to the various churches that he

---

3. Richardson, *Early Christian Fathers*, 131–58, this quote, 131.

had visited. One letter he wrote ahead to the Christian church in Rome is striking. He begged those in Rome not to interfere at all in his case, nor do anything that would deprive him of martyrdom. Nothing should be done to prevent him from following that path which had been opened before him. When Ignatius wrote about martyrdom he, first of all, saw it as an opportunity to *"imitate the passion of my God,"* and he noted that he was *"voluntarily dying for God."* As a martyr, he would be following Jesus' way.[4]

Martyrdom was, for Ignatius, the way of discipleship. He considered it part of being a genuine Christian. In the letter, he clearly expressed his impatience to quickly get to God, and there was no more certain way than through the experience of being put to death for the faith. Because he held martyrdom in such high regard, there is a great deal of discussion in his letter about the *"blood of Christ."* Through martyrdom, Ignatius' blood is mixed with the blood of his God. In some ways, this emphasis is a bit distasteful to us, but we have to recognize the extent to which the early Christian community began to understand itself as a suffering community. As Ignatius said in his letter, *"The source of our unity and election in relation to God is our genuine suffering which we all undergo in a variety of ways."*[5]

Martyrdom was just an extreme example of the general situation of the Christian community—*genuine suffering which we all undergo*. Ignatius was not counselling people to go out of their way to seek martyrdom; indeed, he expressly forbade it. His point is that when this experience befalls a Christian, then that person should not resist but simply let events unfold, responding with courage and faithfulness and trusting that all unfolds in the providence of God. Faithfulness is the core issue. Christians were charged with the crime of refusing to worship the Roman gods. For the Christian this is not a crime, but simply part of being a Christian.

Another example of such a model is Perpetua, who takes her place in a long line of Christian martyrs going back to the first century. She lived in Carthage in North Africa and died in 203 before a public audience when she was thrown to wild animals in the local arena. She wrote that *"while I was still with the police authorities . . . my father out of love for me tried to dissuade me from my resolution.* But she rejected his arguments, declaring that she could not be *"anything else than what I am, a Christian."* During the period when she and her infant son were imprisoned with other Christians, she wrote, *"I nursed my child, who was already weak from hunger. In my anxiety for the infant I spoke to my mother about him, tried to console my brother, and asked that they care for my son."* These were difficult days for her, but she said

---

4. Ibid., 104–5.
5. Ibid., 87.

that once "*I was granted the privilege of having my son remain with me . . . I immediately regained my strength. Suddenly the prison became my palace, and I loved being there.*"

During her imprisonment, Perpetua had dreams and visions that comforted her. One had her ascending a summit and encountering "*an immense garden*" where she was welcomed by "*a tall grey-haired man dressed like a shepherd*" who said "*Welcome, my child*" and offered her a "*morsel of the cheese he was making.*"

Perpetua continued to resist her father's entreaties. When she was brought before the governor, Hilarion, and asked to "*offer sacrifice for the emperor's welfare,*" she replied, "*I will not . . . I am a Christian.*" The sentence was passed on Perpetua and those with her: "Condemned *to the beasts.*" And their response? "*We were overjoyed as we went back to the prison cell.* Shortly after, she died in the arena.[6]

It is important for us to see how the early Christian community defined its sense of discipleship in these events, as well as identifying the exemplary Christian. In this process, Christians take the suffering and death of their Lord, Jesus Christ, as the clue to living their own lives in the world, as their Way. In later eras, we see other models of the exemplary Christian emerge: the holy monks of the desert, the saints of the MIddle Ages, the visible lay saints of Calvinism, the born-again Christians of the evangelical movements, the existential and socially engaged Christians of the modern world. All of these models of the exemplary Christian draw upon the scriptural witness, but appeal to different elements of that witness.

To the martyr of early Christianity goes the honour of precedence.

In a situation where one expects to suffer persecution from following Jesus as the way to God, the issue is how one deals with that persecution. It is remarkable how members of the early Christian community took their experience of suffering and turned it on its head. They transformed it into the occasion for faithful witness to their suffering and redemptive Lord. The letters of Perpetua and Ignatius are just two examples of the way these remarkable early Christians dealt with a hostile world. They helped establish the martyr as the exemplary Christian of early Christianity.

The Unity of the Church

Martyrdom for the faith is not the only subject of Ignatius's letters. The second theme of the letters is the unity of the church. One growing problem towards the end of the first century was schism and division within the early

---

6. See Perpetua at www.eyewitnesstohistory.com/martyr.htm.

community. What constitutes the unity of the church? For Ignatius the unity of the church lies in the obedience that the members of the community give to church authorities. In the *Didache*, which may reflect a period before Ignatius, the emphasis was on apostles and the prophets as the ones who bear witness to the primary events at the fountainhead of Christianity. By the time of Ignatius, at the end of the first century, the issue had shifted. The apostles were now dead, and increasingly, all those who were among the original witnesses to the events were also dying. The focus of authority now shifted to those people who exercised certain offices in the early community: figures such as presbyters and especially bishops.

As people cleave to their bishops, like Ignatius, they gain unity among themselves, which reflects the true nature of the church. The church as a community of love is characterized by unity. Ignatius contended that the bishop stands in the community as the representative of God, and to defer to the bishop is equivalent to deferring to God. It is interesting that, in Ignatius's view, there was no sense of some intermediary authority—such as Scripture—between God and the bishop. Later, once a body of writings had been established as authoritative texts, this situation became more complicated. The bishops then were not to act contrary to Scripture. But in Ignatius's time, the Christian Scripture was still fluid.

In Ignatius's argument the bishop is equivalent to God. What is striking for historians of Christianity is the fact that the notion of apostolic succession that emerges elsewhere is absent in Ignatius. Ignatius did not rest his argument on the fact that he, as a Bishop of Antioch, was a successor to one of the original apostles. Others, such as Clement (c. 100), did make this argument from lineage or succession, and this notion became very important in Christian thought. There is direct transmission of a tradition from master to disciple, teacher to student, founder to follower. But Ignatius put forward an archetypal argument: there is a heavenly order of things, a divine pattern, and that heavenly or divine pattern is reflected in the order of life within the church in which the bishop plays the dominant role. In the heavenly realm, God presides over all things. In the church, to the extent that it reflects this heavenly realm, the bishop plays this fundamental role. Moreover, a bishop, as Ignatius saw him, was also an administrator, a liturgical officer and a prophet. Obedience to the bishop, Ignatius believed, was the primary way that the church could avoid internal division.

Summary

The challenges for the first generations of Christians were many and varied. The community of the followers of Jesus—from those who confessed that he was the Messiah to those who saw him as their "Lord and God"—was in the process of formation. They were developing the ritual practices that would become central to the community gathered in worship and remembrance: baptism, Eucharist, prayer and the reading of Scripture. In response to the persecution they suffered, the early Christian martyrs gave shape to the exemplary faith of those who followed their Lord. Initially a spirit-filled community, Christians also found their way to a more structured community headed by figures with authority—presbyters and bishops responsible for mediating the witness of the early apostles. And as the first generation died out, the new generations began to clarify their own canon to include new Christian writings. These elements would all contribute to the unity of a community continually beset by division while striving to be faithful to the one who was central to its faith.

Review

1. Why is the *Didache* important to the great conversation?
2. What do you think of Polycarp's view of the martyrs as "models of true love"?
3. Who was Perpetua?
4. How is Christian unity maintained, in Ignatius' view?

Chapter 5

Articulating the Faith

Two Christian Apologists: Justin Martyr and Tertullian

WE BEGAN THIS ACCOUNT of the history of Christian thought at the very beginning: with the way the early followers spoke of Jesus and what they believed had been disclosed to them in Jesus' life, death and resurrection. We have seen something of that early Christian thought in the previous chapters. Now we turn our attention to some figures of the second century who were known as early Christian apologists—figures who represent the starting point for many accounts of the history of Christian thought. They are called "apologists" not because they said they were sorry for being Christians. They were apologists in the old sense of the word—figures who articulated a reasoned defence of the Christian faith to those outside their community, as well as against those within the community whom they considered wrong or mistaken. The first example we will discuss is Justin Martyr, who died a martyr under Marcus Aurelius in 165.

Justin Martyr (100–165)

Justin was a Greek-born citizen of the Roman Empire. He was trained as a teacher of Platonic philosophy and came to embrace the Christian faith. He opened the first Christian school in Rome and offered an important defense of Christianity to both Roman and Jewish opponents. It is important when we look at Justin Martyr to recognize a fundamental assumption he made about reasonable discourse—an assumption not shared by all those who are remembered as early apologists. Justin's *First Apology* was directed

> to the Emperor Titus Aelius . . . Pius Augustus Caesar, and to Verissimus his son, the Philosopher, and to Lucius the Philosopher, son of Caesar by nature and of Augustus by adoption, a lover of culture, and to the Sacred Senate and the whole Roman people—on behalf of men of every nation who are unjustly hated and reviled.[1]

Note especially what follows:

> *Reason requires that those who are truly pious and philosophers should honour and cherish the truth alone . . . The lover of truth ought to choose in every way, even at the cost of his own life, to speak and do what is right . . . Since you are called pious and philosophers and guardians of justice and lovers of culture, at least give us a hearing—and it will appear if you are really such.*

Thus Justin reached out to his readers on the basis of reason, urging them to exercise their own reasonableness and commitment to truth. Paul Tillich, a twentieth-century Christian thinker, saw in Justin Martyr an attempt to find common ground with his readers. We Christians, Justin Martyr was saying, are committed, as you are, to truth, and I will show you the connections between the truth of Christianity and your truth. He thus acknowledged that there was truth around prior to the Christian revelation. He spoke of "*seeds of truth,*" that were there before the time of the Christian revelation and were found in the work of some of the early philosophers and the prophets.

Starting with these seeds, he offered a reasoned account or a reasoned defence of Christianity, an apology for the faith. That defense has two aspects: one in relation to practical matters, and one in relation to philosophical matters. Justin Martyr was aware, living in Rome, that there was much misinformation about Christianity. Because of persecution, the Christians did much in secret, sometimes meeting in the catacombs beneath the city. They did not have synagogues as the Jews did where people could see what their practices looked like, and this situation led to misunderstanding, suspicion and rumours. For instance, early Christians were accused of being atheists and cannibals, among other there things. They were accused of atheism because they didn't believe in the Roman gods, and as atheists because the God they worshipped were invisible. This was very disturbing for the Romans. The notion of cannibalism came about as a result of people

---

1. See Richardson, *Early Christian Fathers*, 242.

hearing about the Eucharist. In simple language, Justin Martyr explained the Christian beliefs and practices to non-Christians. For example, Justin wrote,

> On the day called Sunday there is a meeting... [during which] the memoirs of the apostles or the writings of the prophets are read... [and] the president then urges us to the imitation of these noble things... Then we all stand together and offer prayers... Then bread and wine and water is brought and distributed to all... and a collection taken... to take care of the orphans and widows...[2]

His description of the Eucharist distinguished the Christian practice from the practices of other mystery religions that abounded at this time, specifically the mysteries of Mithra, an ancient mystery religion that did many things in secret. One of the characteristics of these rites was that only the initiated could participate. Justin Martyr wanted to make the point that Christianity was not committed to secret rites. It was only because of the hostility towards Christianity that its public rites were often practiced in secret. Justin wanted these practices to be known and went to great pains to explain them.

But Justin's principal concern was a philosophical one. According to Justin Martyr, Christians honour Christ "in accordance with reason."[3] Indeed, for Justin Martyr, Christ is "the Word (logos/reason) of God."[4] He acknowledged that there were those outside the Christian community who lived by reason and that they had to be respected. A love of truth linked all: Christians and non-Christians. Justin Martyr made this philosophical point in his writings to show that Christianity was the fulfillment of all the inclinations, desires and movements towards truth that are part of the human race.

Justin's view of the human race was limited to the Jewish and Greek worlds. He attempted to show that just as the Jewish prophets foretold the coming of Christ, so the Greek philosophers, especially Plato, had shadowy intimations of Christ. Now that Christ has come, he argued, we see the reason of things with clarity. In an important passage from *The First Apology of Justin, the Martyr*, he said that "*we have been taught that Christ is the First-begotten of God, and have previously testified that he is the Reason of which*

---

2. See Kerr, *Readings in Christian Thought*, 24.
3. See Martyr in Kerr, 22.
4. See Martyr in Richardson, 258.

every race of man partakes." And since Christ is "*Eternal Reason or the Logos Incarnate,*" he now fulfills what others knew only dimly.[5]

What was Justin doing in this text? For one thing, we see that as Christianity moved into the larger cultural world of the ancient period, it developed an understanding of Jesus as "Logos." Jesus is the "Eternal Reason/Logos" or the "Eternal Word." This idea emerged in early Christian thinking partly to satisfy the drive within Christianity towards universality. We have discussed the debate in the New Testament about whether or not the ministry of Jesus was for the Jews alone or also included the Gentiles. We noted that Paul was the champion of the belief that Jesus is of significance not only for the Jews but also for the Gentiles and for everyone. Jesus' significance is not confined to the small group of people who knew the Hebrew Scriptures, but is of importance to all human beings, and the salvation mediated through Jesus is of universal significance.

Christians argue this point by first expanding the terms in which they speak about Jesus. Initially, Jesus is the Messiah, the fulfillment of the Jewish prophecies. But he is also the "Logos," the "Word made flesh," the one "who exists from the foundation of the world" and "the one through whom the creation was made." In Justin Martyr, Jesus the Christ is this universal "Logos," "Eternal Word," or "Reason." And Jesus Christ as the Logos or Eternal Reason precedes the historical Jesus:

> *We have been taught that Christ is the First-begotten of God, and have previously testified that he is the Reason of which every race of man partakes. Those who lived in accordance with Reason are Christians, even though they were called godless, such as, among the Greeks, Socrates and Heraclitus and others like them; among the barbarians, Abraham . . . Elijah, and many others . . . those who lived by Reason and those who so live now are Christians, fearless and unperturbed . . .* [6]

Thus for Justin, Jesus Christ is that Wisdom and Word, that Truth and Reason that humanity has been searching for and has sometimes glimpsed and sometimes partially grasped. But now that Logos/Reason has been made known:

> *Jesus Christ alone was really begotten as Son of God, being his Word and First Begotten and Power, and becoming man by his*

---

5. See Kerr, 24.
6. Ibid., 24.

will, he taught us these things for the reconciliation and restoration of the human race.[7]

In Justin's perspective, in the Christian story, what Greeks have always dimly known and always dimly sought has been made known to us. It has been disclosed, revealed or uncovered in the figure of Jesus of Nazareth. Now we do not have to search blindly, but can look directly at this man and see what we—and you—have always sought in striving for wisdom and understanding.

Thus, apologists such as Justin attempted to engage the larger cultural and philosophical world in dialogue, not on the basis of absolute discontinuity between Christian faith and other ways of life but of some common ground on which dialogue can be initiated. For Justin, that common ground was the Logos, the Word or Reason. In his plea to the Emperor, we see an appeal to that commonality with his audience: we are all rational human beings who are in favour of truth and want to know the truth. Then he tried to show that Christians are lovers of truth and doers of justice.

Justin Martyr defined Christianity in the person of Jesus as the bringer of wisdom, and it is in that wisdom that salvation lies. Humanity before the appearance of the Logos, the Divine Word, moved in darkness or in twilight in its efforts to make its way towards the truth. But now with the coming of Jesus, the Son of God, or as Justin Martyr said, "the first begotten of the Uncreated," we have disclosed wisdom and truth in which the fullness of life is to be found.[8] There were anticipations of this full revelation of God in both the philosophies of the Greek world and the prophecies of the Jewish world, but it is in the Logos that the fullness of God's wisdom is made known.

Justin Martyr, the first of the apologists of the second century, attempted to reach out to the wider society and culture, urging people to be faithful to their own desire for truth. He then offered an account of the Christian faith that centres on Jesus, the Christ, as the embodiment of wisdom, reason, truth. There is no record of any response from the Emperor or the Senate or any of the people to whom he addressed his *Apology*. Indeed, he would die a martyr's death at the hands of those he sought to engage.

Tertullian (150-225)

We are now going to move across the Mediterranean Sea to North Africa and the figure of Tertullian, one of the earliest and greatest of the African

---

7. Ibid., 24.
8. Ibid., 25.

fathers of the Christian Church. He came from the area around Carthage, near where Tunis, the capital of Tunisia, now stands. His father was a military man, and Tertullian was educated in rhetoric and law, living for a period in Rome. He was converted to Christianity as an adult. He became a very passionate and partisan advocate of the Christian faith, employing what he knew (which was a great deal) in the service of the faith. He was the first of the early fathers who wrote in Latin. His use of Latin signalled the growth of Christianity among the Latin-speaking Roman population. A gradual shift was taking place: Christians remained a prescribed minority within the Roman Empire, but their numbers were growing. At the same time, ironically, we see in Tertullian that in some respects, Christian thinking was accommodating itself to that cultural world.

Unlike Origen later on, Tertullian was a practical thinker not a speculative one. He wrote very extensively, producing more than thirty volumes, and there was virtually no topic current in the community of his day that he did not touch or express some opinion on. Like Irenaeus, he directed much of his writing against the Gnostics, and he was particularly hostile to what he called their speculative theology. Tertullian is sometimes spoken of as an early Christian apologist, but he worked on the basis of assumptions that were very different if not in complete opposition to those of an apologist like Justin Martyr.

Justin Martyr wanted to see the continuity between the Christian revelation and other forms of reason, and for him, the philosophers were ultimately to be reconciled with Christianity. Tertullian held another view. For him, there was no connection whatsoever between Athens and Jerusalem. Athens symbolized the Greek philosophical world and mind, and Jerusalem the transformative Christian revelation. Those two worlds, for Tertullian, stood in absolute opposition to one another. In one of his books, called *Prescription to Heretics,* he said,

> *"I have no use for a Stoic or a Platonic or a dialectical Christianity. After Jesus Christ we have no need of speculation, after the Gospel no need of research. When we come to believe, we have no desire to believe anything else."*[9]

He thus argued that Christianity is a complete answer to life's questions, and for any question that might arise we need only understand what is already present within Christian revelation. We have no need of any other sources of knowledge to help us. Tertullian was thus an important figure in the formation of what we call the *"Regula Fidei or Rule of Faith."* He defined

---

9. See Tertullian in Kerr, 39.

what the apostolic faith was according to the apostles and early fathers, and he felt that what had been handed down from earlier generations was completely adequate. There was no need for anything more, no questions that remained to be solved.

Tertullian's distaste for any kind of speculation was related to his conviction that Christianity was primarily a moral teaching. Justin Martyr understood Christianity primarily as wisdom, and Irenaeus understood it as a way of salvation. For Tertullian, Christianity was primarily a moral teaching, centred on living the moral life. One of the major questions he addressed was how one lives as a Christian in the world and the relationship between the Christian faith and culture.

It is because of his views on these issues that he has been held in high regard by Christians through the ages. For example, Tertullian argued that Christians could not serve in the army, and he is always cited as the first Christian thinker who dealt explicitly with this question in his writings. His view is quite interesting because his father had been a military man, but Tertullian rejected military service as incompatible with Christianity. He cited two reasons why Christians should not serve in the army. The first is that the oath to serve God and the oath to serve man are incompatible. A person who joined the military was obliged to swear allegiance to the Emperor. For Tertullian, this allegiance was incompatible with a person's ultimate loyalty, which was to God. His second argument stemmed from his interpretation of the events in Gethsemane described in the gospels. When they came for Jesus at Gethsemane, Peter grabbed someone's sword and cut off a soldier's ear, but Jesus took the sword away from him. In Tertullian's view, when Jesus disarmed Peter at Gethsemane, he unbelted every soldier.

This example illustrates how Tertullian read the New Testament as containing very concrete teaching on virtually any question that might arise. We must look at what Jesus said and did in order to know how we should live. Using this approach, Tertullian contributed to one of the major tasks of the second century: the effort to generate a summary statement of what Christians believe. Tertullian contributed to that effort In his *Prescriptions Against the Heretics,* he wrote,

> *My first principle is this. Christ laid down one definite system of truth which the world must believe without qualification, and which we must seek precisely in order to believe it when we find it . . . You must seek until you find, and when you find, you must believe. Then you have simply to keep what you have come to*

believe, since you also believe there is nothing else to believe, and therefore nothing else to seek.[10]

There was nothing irenic in Tertullian's approach; unlike Justin Martyr, he made no effort to find any common ground with those outside the Christian community. Nor was there any effort to understand the grounds of what one believes, as there would be later in Origen. For Tertullian, there was "*one definite system of truth*," which he summarized in his *Regula Fidei*, or *Rule of Faith*:

> *We believe that there is but one God, who is none other than the Creator of the world, who produced everything from nothing through his Word, sent forth before all things; that this Word is called his Son . . . brought down by the Spirit and Power of God the Father into the Virgin Mary, was made flesh in her womb, was born of her and lived as Jesus Christ; who thereafter proclaimed a new law and a new promise of the kingdom of heaven, worked miracles, was crucified, on the third day rose again, was caught up into heaven and sat down at the right hand of God; that he sent in his place the power of the Holy Spirit to guide believers; that he will come with glory to take the saints up into the fruition of the life eternal . . . and to judge the wicked . . . after the resurrection of both good and evil with the restoration of their flesh.*[11]

What Tertullian did not say, and what we must say looking back on this period, is that this single definite system of truth is one of several created through a process of reflection that went on in the Christian community throughout the first two centuries. Jesus does not offer a summary of what it is that one is obliged to believe. The summary of the law that he offers is that one should love God and the neighbour as oneself. That is all. Jesus speaks in parables, and the gospels offer the story of his life. The effort of summarizing Christian belief went on in the centuries following his life.

Tertullian saw his summary as definitive and clear enough that we should be able to present it as the totality of what Christians are obliged to believe. In his view, it provided a basis for judging other interpretations or other developments within the early Christian community. Tertullian was very much against speculation and felt that all the attempts to offer a more philosophical account of the Christian faith were simply wrong. Far from being subtle, Tertullian was very direct and forceful in his presentation of what we ought to believe.

---

10. Ibid.
11. Ibid. 40.

Tertullian's summary, the *Regula Fidei,* is similar in its three-part structure to Irenaeus's summary, which is probably earlier, and the later one of Origen. All these summaries begin with an affirmation of one God, the Creator. They then offer a summary account of Jesus as the Word of God, and close with a third part dealing with the Holy Spirit. But there are also significant differences in the summaries. At this point in the history of Christian thought, there was no agreed-upon, authoritative account of the Christian faith that was universally held in the Christian community. However, Christian thought was moving in that direction. In the subsequent centuries, Christian belief was codified in the ecumenical councils of early Christianity.

One of the distinctive features of Tertullian's thought is his attempt to understand the conflict between Christianity and the wider culture. He was one of the first Christian thinkers to pit Christ against culture, and one of the most important. While Justin Martyr tried to show how Christianity was the fulfillment of tendencies present in the wider culture, Tertullian moved in a different direction, presenting Christianity's relationship to the culture as one of conflict and opposition.

Fundamental to that conflict between Christ and culture is the issue of where one's loyalty lies. For Tertullian, the Christian's primary loyalty is to God. That loyalty stands in tension with and, in some respects, in contradiction to civil or Roman society, especially in its demand that Christians acknowledge the cult of the Emperor. As we have seen, Christians had from the very beginning said no to this demand of Roman society. For Tertullian, loyalty to the Emperor must give way to loyalty to God, and it is on that basis that he posited a fundamental conflict between the Christian faith and the life of the wider culture.

Curiously, however, in his defense of Christianity Tertullian argued that the ruling authorities should not persecute Christians because, of all people, they are the most reliable. They keep to themselves and live orderly and moral lives. In this important respect, they are good members of civil society even though their primary loyalty is to something beyond the civil order—the transcendent God. Tertullian understood the relationship between Christianity and culture in the context of Christianity being a minority religion. This issue would return and become much more complex when Christianity became dominant and loyalty to God could result in criticism of various forms of established Christian society. We will come back to that later on.

We have emphasized the extent to which Tertullian identified the heart of the Christian faith with the moral life. Although Tertullian's writings contributed significantly to the establishment of the Apostolic Rule in "mainstream" Christianity, his emphasis on the moral ideal as the centre of Christianity took him to the fringes of the Christian community. Late in Tertullian's life, he became associated with the Montanist sect, which he saw as reflecting the ascetic and strict moral ideal of the Christian faith.

Summary

The apologists of the second century reveal two faces: one looking outside, the other looking inside the Christian community. A figure such as Justin Martyr sought to dissuade those outside the circle of the faith community from their hostility to the Christian faith. Indeed, he argued that to acknowledge the Christian faith is to acknowledge truth itself in Jesus Christ, the Reason/Logos of God. Tertullian, on the other hand, looked within the Christian community and sought to create a uniformity of belief and behaviour. The differences between these figures can be characterized in a number of ways, turning on such issues as the relationship of faith and reason, Jerusalem and Athens, faith and philosophy. While Justin Martyr saw Athens fulfilled in Jerusalem, Tertullian saw antipathy between the two and regarded philosophy as "the source of all errors." Tertullian sees Christ as being in opposition to the dominant culture and urged the Christian community to centre its life wholly on its Lord, against the culture of the Empire: no kneeling to the Roman gods, no participation in the Roman armies. Justin Martyr saw Christ as above the dominant culture and as calling the culture towards its fulfillment in God. The differences in the thought of these two figures reflect conflicting currents in Christian thinking through the ages. Yet each contributed to that great conversation which is Christian thought.

Review

1. What was Justin Martyr's view of the "Logos"?
2. How did Tertullian view the relationship of "Athens and Jerusalem"?
3. What is the "*Regula Fidei*"?

Chapter 6

Irenaeus: The Three-Articled Faith

IN THIS CHAPTER WE look at a third Apologist. Irenaeus (130–202) came from a different background. Born in the east, probably in the city of Smyrna, he was a student of Polycarp, Bishop of Smyrna and an early Christian martyr. Irenaeus then moved west, was educated in Rome and ended up on the far western frontier of the Roman Empire, in Gaul—what is now France. It was in Gaul that he did his major work. This gives us a sense of the growing universality of Christianity. Irenaeus grew up in one part of the world, was educated in another and lived out his life in a third. His writings affirm the universality of the church. He made an important contribution to the definition of the Christian canon, arguing against Marcion's truncated version of the Bible and in favour of the inclusion of the Hebrew Scripture and the four gospels. Irenaeus tried to do what he could to foster a sense of unanimity within the Christian world and contribute to a summary of the Christian faith.

The Regula Fidei or Apostolic Faith

As we have already seen in Tertullian, these summaries of the faith were known as the *regula fidei* or the Rule of Faith. They were an attempt to offer a summary of Christian teaching, a summary which, it was said, comes from the Apostles and is to be found everywhere within the Christian community. The effort to articulate and establish a rule of faith reveals the twofold problem that Christianity was facing: on one hand, a desire for an internal clarification of the faith of the Christian community in the face of the divergent opinions found within the community itself, and, on the other, the challenge of defining the faith over against alternative accounts of reality. Irenaeus articulated his understanding of the Christian faith against those tendencies and positions within the Christian community that he considered heretical. Central to this challenge was the form of religious and philosophical life known as Gnosticism, a movement that was partly external to the Christian community and, in the form of Christian Gnosticism, partly within it. Irenaeus's most famous writing, known by its short title, *Against Heresies*, says it all.

Irenaeus was neither a speculative theologian like Origen nor a philosopher like Justin Martyr. He was a bishop, a man of the church concerned with the spiritual well-being of his community. He sought to give some guidance to the faithful, some understanding of the rule of faith that should be at the heart of the community. The full title of *Against Heresies*—the *Refutation and Overthrow of the Knowledge Falsely So Called*— reflects the way Irenaeus saw his own situation in the context of early Christianity. He was worried about Gnosticism, especially Christian Gnosticism, which for Irenaeus was the "knowledge falsely so-called" that he sought to combat, to distinguish from what he regarded as central to the Christian faith. He undertook this task on the basis of his understanding of what Tertullian had called the *Regula Fidei* and what Irenaeus called "The Apostolic Faith." This "apostolic faith" is what Irenaeus saw as having emerged from Christian experience over the first century and a half of its existence. He summarized it as follows:

> *The Church, although scattered over the whole world even to its extremities, received from the Apostles and their disciples the faith in one God, the Father, Almighty, Maker of Heaven and earth, the seas and all that in them is, and in one Christ Jesus, the Son of God, who became incarnate for our salvation, and in the Holy Ghost, who by the prophets proclaimed the dispensations, the advents, the virgin birth, the passion and resurrection from the dead, the bodily ascension of the well-beloved Christ Jesus our Lord into heaven, and his Parousia from the heavens in the glory of the Father to gather all things in Himself...* [1]

Although the early Christian creed known as the Apostles' Creed is a later document—the earliest documented version we have comes from the fifth century—its language is very similar to that of Irenaeus. Such statements represent a tendency to give an "apostolic" account of the Christian faith.

---

1. Irenaeus in Kerr, 29. See Richardson, *Early Christian Fathers*, 343–97 for a fuller account of Irenaeus.

A Three-Articled Faith

One of the things that began to emerge in Irenaeus and other figures from this time is an understanding of Christianity as *"a three-articled faith."* These three articles constitute the fundamental structure in terms of which Irenaeus understood the Christian faith: an understanding of God as creator, an understanding of God as redeemer, and an understanding of God as sanctifier. Or, to speak in Trinitarian terms—which were not yet fully developed—we see in Irenaeus an understanding of the Christian faith as faith in God the Father, God the Son and God the Holy Spirit.

The three fundamental moments are among the things that distinguish the Christian faith from all other faiths and from those faiths within or on the edges of the Christian community that claim to be a part of the Christian tradition. Christians, as we see in Irenaeus and others, are those who speak about God as Creator, Redeemer and Sanctifier. Irenaeus was the first great creedal theologian in the Christian tradition, the first Christian thinker who tried to understand the systematic implications of these three central affirmations. He wanted to understand the relationships between these three moments of Christian faith. To gain a full statement of the Christian faith, we have to address ourselves to all three of these issues.

Note the difference between Irenaeus' formulations and what we saw in Justin Martyr. Irenaeus has a structural clarity about the Christian faith—the three-part faith—that we do not find in Justin Martyr. Justin Martyr understood the Christian faith primarily in terms of wisdom: true philosophy, knowledge of a way of life that centres in right thinking and right living.

Irenaeus was certainly in favour of these things, but his way of understanding the path of salvation, that way of life that Christianity brings, is in terms of these three elements of the Christian faith. These are embedded in the Christian story, the context of the apostolic faith. We will follow the structure of this three-articled faith in our discussion of Irenaeus's considerable contribution to the great conversation.

By the time we get to Irenaeus, the Christian story had begun to take normative shape. The story begins with Creation, the first moment, and continues through the Fall to Redemption, and on to Consummation. This Christian story is the context for Irenaeus's account of the Christian faith, the three-articled faith.

The Christian Story: Creation the First Moment

We begin, then, with the first article: the affirmation concerning God the Creator. For Irenaeus this was the first fundamental Christian affirmation. He affirmed his belief in *"One God, Father, Almighty, Maker of Heaven and earth, the seas and all that in them is."* It was on this basis that he attacked the Gnostic Christian view that God is not the creator of the heavens and the earth—a view that Irenaeus considered a heresy. The difference between Irenaeus's affirmation of the belief in God as the Creator of all and the Gnostic view of the "demiurge" as the creator of the universe was a primary issue in the disagreement between the two.

In looking at Irenaeus's writings, we often pass over the material about God as "creator and father" rather quickly because it is all so familiar to us. It is a commonplace of the Christian faith, isn't it? But we miss something essential when we do that: the extent to which early Christians had to fight hard for the belief that God was the creator. With whom did they fight? They were countering certain Gnostic accounts of reality along with more philosophical accounts that made creation some mysterious event of some creative principle, not linked with the personal God as it is in Christianity. What Irenaeus understood the Gnostics to be teaching was the doctrine that the creation of the world—and certainly there was more than one view of creation among the Gnostics—was basically a trick, accomplished not by the true God but by a lower god that was sometimes referred to as the "demiurge." This lower god created the material world to entrap the spirit, which was in us but caught in flesh within the material realm. This created realm was not our proper home, nor was it the proper setting for the unfolding of our deepest nature. Rather than this lower, trickster creation, our proper home, as spiritual beings, is some wholly spiritual world which lies behind creation and in relation to which the true God exists.

It is in this framework, Irenaeus thought, that Gnostic Christians interpret the life of Jesus. The function of Jesus for the Gnostics was to be our spiritual guide who could lead us out of this lower, material world back to our true and proper spiritual home. He was an emissary from the true God, the high God, who stole down into this dark realm that the demiurge had created to try to rescue these spirits which had been trapped in this lower world and lead them back to their proper home. Irenaeus tried to establish a very different doctrine of creation, and of God, from what we find in the Gnostic writers, the "heretics" that Irenaeus was writing against. Irenaeus argued that *"the rule of truth we hold is that there is one God Almighty, who made all things by His Word, and fashioned and formed that which has existence out of that which had none."* Later, in another writing, Irenaeus said,

> It is well that we should begin from the first and principal heading: the creator God, who made the heaven and earth and all that is therein; whom they blasphemously describe as the "fruit of a defect," and show that there is nothing above Him nor after Him, and that it was not by compulsion but of His own free will that He made all things, since He alone is God, alone is Lord, alone is Creator, alone is Father, alone is the container of all things and the cause of the existence of all things."[2]

These words of Irenaeus contain some very crucial Christian thinking as well as some important affirmations, ones that not all Christians subscribed to in Irenaeus's day.

What does it matter who the creator is or what the status of this creator is? For Irenaeus, this was the fundamental point that needed to be made: the God that the Christians worshipped is the God who made this creation as the proper home and setting for his creatures, and the bodies that God gives the creatures are not foreign to God, inhibiting the life of the spirit, but the proper setting for the human spirit. We are a unity of body and spirit, and Irenaeus makes this point about human nature by affirming that God—the only One and True God—is the author of creation. Irenaeus was trying to find a way to say to his congregations: this world around you, this creation, is the world that God has made for us and in which we are to live out our lives. In this way, he gave content to the texts in Genesis that speak of God as creating the world and then seeing that it was "good." Irenaeus said that those who are trying to tell you that this world is absurd, meaningless, and senseless are wrong. This is God's creation and it is in this context that we were meant to be, not somewhere else.

Irenaeus spent a great deal of time in his writings trying to establish his Christian doctrine of creation. This was part of his contribution to the effort to grasp and summarize the apostolic tradition. Moreover, Irenaeus sought to unfold those convictions in contrast to other philosophical and theological views, views sometimes found within the Christian community and sometime beyond it. Other issues arose in relation to the second and third elements of the three-point faith.

The Fall and Redemption: The Second Moment

For Irenaeus, Christians affirm that God is the creator of the world, and they also affirm that the world is fallen. Something happened in the beginning that skewed creation, making it not quite what God had intended. That

---

2. Ibid., 32.

is the Christian doctrine of the fall. Sin and death enter the world at that point. This doctrine of the fall then sets the context for the second element of the Christian faith: the affirmation of God as Redeemer, the bearer of salvation. The word *salvation* is derived from "salvus" meaning 'sound' or 'whole' or 'well' in relation to health. Salvation comes in Christian contexts to mean, "to be made whole." Irenaeus liked the phrase "man fully alive." Irenaeus clearly saw that some healing of our humanity was required. His writings were very important in relation to this second element of Christian faith—the belief in God as Redeemer. Irenaeus was one of the first Christian thinkers to offer a systematic account of what it is that the coming of God the Redeemer effects. What does the Incarnate Christ do or effect?

Before answering that question, you have to answer a prior question: what is the problem to which the Christian doctrine of redemption is the answer? Jesus, the Son, the Redeemer, comes into the world to redeem fallen humanity. Irenaeus is known as the father of a doctrine of redemption which understands redemption as restoration. He wrote,

> *The Word who was in the beginning with God, through whom all things were made and who was always present with the human race . . . was united with His creation, and became man subject to suffering . . . the Word became flesh . . . God recapitulating the ancient creation of man in Himself, in order to slay sin, to remove death's sting, and restore man to life.*"[3]

What the Redeemer does is restore to humanity what was lost in the fall. In the fall our humanity was damaged or injured so that now the humanity we have is something less than what God as creator originally gave to humankind. So what the Incarnation means, in Irenaeus's thinking, is that God takes into Himself our fallen humanity and raises it back up to its full power. According to Irenaeus, "the glory of God is man fully alive." This phrase was used in the title of a long-running Canadian television program, *Man Alive*.

Humanity is restored in Christ, according to Irenaeus. Irenaeus saw that what was damaged in the Fall was the *imago dei*, the image of God in which humankind is created. The *imago dei* is the dignity of the human being. What is restored through Christ is that original image, the *imago dei* in which men and women were created.

This also led Irenaeus to argue against "docetic Christologies," those teachings that denied Christ the fullness of humanity. The "docetists," some of whom were also Gnostics, maintained that in the Crucifixion, Christ appeared to suffer but did not really suffer. Irenaeus argued against these views

3. Ibid., 37.

as diminishing Christ's humanity. Rather, Irenaeus insisted that Christ suffered fully, that he truly died on the cross and that God raised him up. And in that rising, humanity is restored.

This was Irenaeus's account of the second element of Christian faith: God as Redeemer comes into this world, which is good but fallen, reverses this process that was initiated by the fall, and restores humankind to its original status.

But of course, one could say that that is very nice, but look around us. The world still seems to be very chaotic and confused: evil is still in the world. Isn't this evidence that this is not the world that God created? It looks as if these other forces that came into human life through the fall are very much in evidence. They are around us everywhere, and we still see them.

Consummation: The Third Moment of the Christian Story

Irenaeus answered the question of why evil persists in the world by invoking the third element of the Christian faith: the belief in God as Sanctifier or Consummator. The redemption which is accomplished in and through the Incarnation is in a process of being completed. That is, we are in an interim position in terms of God's eternal plan and purpose. We are between times: between the moments of creation, a moment of completeness and wholeness, and the end time, when the whole creation will be restored to God. History is the time in between creation and consummation. As creatures living in this in-between-time, we have begun to experience the restoration which is accomplished in Christ, but it is not yet completed. What the Spirit is doing now is sanctifying our lives and transforming the creation. Eventually, what God has begun in Jesus Christ will be completed and realized throughout the whole creation. It is a process of being divinized—lifted up into the life of God.

Irenaeus's understanding of the work of the Spirit as a sanctifying and consummating work is articulated against another group that he perceived as a threat to Christian faith: the Montanists, a small group that had grown up around a prophet by the name of Montanus (mid-2nd century). In their beginnings within early Christianity, the Montanists believed that the spirit that Jesus promised that he would send, the Comforter, had come in the Prophet Montanus. In the Gospel of John, Jesus says that it is a very good thing that he go away because, if he does not go away, then we will not receive "the Comforter." The question for the Montanists was, "When is the Comforter coming?" The Christian community had already answered that question by saying that the Comforter came at Pentecost. Montanists expected something more. They believed that the Holy Spirit had come and was joined to this figure Montanus (c. 170 CE), who would now usher in the last days and last stages of God's redemption of the world.

Montanists were filled with the Spirit. Montanus and some women prophets claimed to receive special visions from God as to how we should live and what we should do in this particular moment of time. Irenaeus felt that Montanism was a premature anticipation of the Christian hope for the consummation of creation. They had leaped over God's timetable. God's work of reclaiming creation for Himself is something that goes on over a long period of time, and this was a wrong anticipation of this Christian hope for the consummation of all things.

Some have argued that we should see Montanism as an early protest movement within Christianity against the institutionalization of the Christian faith and an attempt to recapture some of the vitality that they saw as more characteristic of the early Church, and there is some truth to this view. But the Montanists' understanding of the Christian belief in the Spirit as involving some kind of sudden transformation of things clashed with Irenaeus's understanding of the way in which the Spirit worked. Rather, for Irenaeus, the Spirit worked to bring God's creation to its proper end over a long, long period-of-time. There will be a time when the millennium will come, when the Kingdom of God will be visible in the order of time and space, but that time is still ahead of us.

One of the impressive things about Irenaeus is the way he sought to link these three beliefs—creation, redemption and consummation—to one another. He was perhaps the first to see how these teachings/doctrines were interrelated, how each of them affects the other two. If you understand creation in a certain way, that will have implications for your doctrine of redemption. And your view of sanctification will be affected by your understanding of creation and redemption, and so on. We have to grasp the fullness of the Christian faith and understand each dimension of that "three articled faith" in relation to each other. Irenaeus was probably the first figure in the history of Christianity who grasped fully the systematic implications of each of the elements of the Christian faith.

The Bible, the Spirit and the Body

By Irenaeus's time, the Christian community largely accepted the Jewish Scripture as its own. The early Christian community believed that in Jesus the Messiah had come, and that was how they then read the Jewish

Scripture. In the newer Christian writings, Christianity made the case for their reading of Scripture in the light of their belief that Jesus Christ is the incarnate Word. In Irenaeus's time, the issue of the Bible—what was it? what did it contain?—was still alive and controversial. What writings were to be included in the Christian Bible? Which of the early Christian writings were to be excluded? Later Christians, having lost any awareness that the Christian Scripture unfolded over time, assumed that we always had the Bible whole and complete. But that is not the case. We have to realize that the Bible was first of all the Scripture of the Jews, and that the Christian Bible is the Jewish writings plus the early Christian writings that were accepted into the Christian Scripture or canon. Irenaeus played an important role in defining the early Christian Scripture.

Irenaeus introduced into Christian thought the idea of a "New Testament" and an "Old Testament," a new covenant and an old covenant. For Irenaeus, there is a unity to Scripture, but there is also diversity. Irenaeus was very aware of Marcion and wrote against him, largely in terms of his teaching about creation—Irenaeus saw Marcion as a Gnostic—and implicitly against his view of Scripture. For example, Irenaeus wrote that there are four gospels—and only four—because there are four directions and four points to the Cross.

Irenaeus' doctrine of creation also led him to have a more positive view of the relationship between the spirit and the body. He saw them as belonging together, in contrast to writers like Tertullian, Origen and later Augustine for whom the spirit and the body were in opposition. This opposition between the spirit and the body had several sources. One was the early Christian writings themselves, which sometimes—in some Pauline writings for example—present the spirit in opposition to the flesh. Other elements of the New Testament are ambiguous on this question. Another source was Christianity's relationship to Neo-Platonism where there is a strong body/soul dualism. Here the body is the source of those unruly passions that the spirit must subdue. And yet another source was the ascetic emphasis within Christianity itself, especially in the early Desert Fathers. Many of the early monastic pioneers understood Christianity as a discipline of the body which was looked upon as the source of passions—especially sexual ones—that have to be tamed if not overcome.

In a central way these currents came to be part of Augustine's thinking, and he was perhaps the most influential thinker in the history of Western Christian thought. This would become an issue that bedevilled Christian thought through the ages. Christianity would have done well to have heeded Irenaeus on this issue for Irenaeus taught the goodness of creation: body, soul and spirit.

Summary

We have given considerable attention to Irenaeus because he represents a new development within Christian thought: He articulated an understanding of Christianity as a three-articled faith and saw the Christian story as stretching from creation to consummation. Irenaeus was among the first to see the interdependence of the Christian affirmations: that how one conceives the Fall, for example, affects how one sees redemption. The Christian story was increasingly understood as a story of creation, fall, redemption, and consummation that was increasingly moving into the centre of Christian thought. And Irenaeus saw more clearly than others that each affirmation in the story has implications for the other elements, and that we need to see those implications. This Irenaeus did largely in relation to Gnostic Christians who, in his judgment, had gotten it wrong. The creation that comes from God is good, though the divine image in humanity is in need of healing. Christ as the Redeemer of our humanity restores our broken humanity to God. Thus through the Incarnation, God becoming human in Jesus Christ, our humanity is lifted up into the life of God. Irenaeus wrote that "He became man that we might become God." This was the good news that Christians had seen and now proclaimed.

Review

1. What is Irenaeus's "three-articled faith"?
2. Why is it said of Irenaeus that he understood "redemption as restoration?"
3. Why was the doctrine of creation such an important issue for Irenaeus?

Chapter 7

Speculative Christian Thought
The Search for the Language of the Relationship of the Christ to God

DURING THE FIRST, TWO centuries of the Christian era, the energies of Christian thinkers sought to establish the foundations of the Christian community. What were the boundaries of belief in that community? What were its normative sources? What should be the patterns of organization within church life? How would the community settle doctrinal disputes? Were there limits to the diversity of teaching about the Christian faith? How would the community identify what was central to Christianity?

By the third century, the Christian community had come to believe that God was the Creator, the Redeemer and the Sanctifier or Consummator of all things. Increasingly, the Christian faith was regarded as, in Irenaeus's words, "a three-articled faith." However, how is the Christian community to understand the God who was above us, with us, and in us? The issues that came to dominate Christian thought were understandings of these matters with more depth and addressing the implications of each article of the faith for other Christian affirmations. How, for example, could the God who is creator of all things be present in Jesus as the Christ who is the bringer of redemption? If we say that God is in Jesus Christ, does that mean that God died on Good Friday? Who is this God with us in Jesus Christ and how is that God related to the God above us, the Creator of heaven and earth? Moreover, how is God with us in Jesus Christ related to God the Holy Spirit? How could God be simultaneously with us and in us? Were these mysteries too great for us to penetrate? Here we explore these questions looking at

Origen, one of the greatest philosophical and speculative thinkers of early Christianity.

Origen: Biblical and Speculative Christian Thought

Origen (c. 185–254) grows up in Alexandria, arguably the most cosmopolitan city of the ancient world. Because of its position in Roman civilization and its fine port, Alexandria was not only a centre of trade but also a melting pot of various races, cultures, philosophies and religions. It had once housed the finest library of the ancient world, the library of Alexandria. Origen went to the famous Christian school founded by Pantaenus in Alexandria in the mid-second century. Clement of Alexandria (c.150–220) was Origen's predecessor at the school and a remarkable Christian thinker who compared Christian ideas with those coming from the East, including Buddhist and Hindu notions.

Origen was a very precocious young man, extremely bright and able. When he was sixteen, Christians were being persecuted in Alexandria. Origen was saved from martyrdom when his mother hid his clothes so he could not go out into the street. His father, however, was arrested and imprisoned. In an exchange of letters, Origen encouraged his father to maintain his fidelity to the faith. His father certainly did and was eventually put to death as a Christian martyr. Shortly after this time, when he was eighteen, Origen became the head of the school in Alexandria. This was a remarkable thing for a young man his age and well reflected his intellectual abilities as well as his own deep commitment to the Christian faith.

I mention this context for Origen because one of the things that characterizes him and makes him so important in Christian thought is that he was the first great philosophical Christian thinker. This was partly encouraged in him by the context of his life. In the school at Alexandria, he was constantly in touch with and responding to the kinds of criticisms that were levelled against Christianity by people of other persuasions—philosophers, gnostic thinkers, people of other cultures. For centuries there had been an important Jewish community within Alexandria, and earlier we noted that Philo (c. 20 BCE) had come from this community. And in a sense, all of these people provided the context for Origen's Catechetical School. It was in relation to this rich intellectual milieu that he articulated and defended the Christian faith. For Origen there were no questions that were out of bounds—that could not be raised and should not be addressed. In this he was very different from Tertullian, who felt that everything that was necessary had been given in the tradition. Consequently, according to Tertullian, what we needed to do was simply to believe what had been given to us. Origen's view was more nuanced.

Like Tertullian, Origen felt that there was a core tradition that had been handed down and must be accepted. What was that "core"? Origen wrote,

> The holy apostles, when preaching the faith of Christ, took certain doctrines, those namely which they believed to be necessary ones, and delivered them in the plainest terms to all believers, even to such as appeared to be somewhat dull in the investigation of divine knowledge.[1]

But he also felt that there were all kinds of other questions that Christians should address. Such questions were not only permitted but necessary if one were to grow in wisdom and understanding. So, Origen continued,

> ... the grounds of their statements they left to be investigated by such as should merit the higher gifts of the Spirit and in particular by such as should afterwards receive through the Holy Spirit the graces of language, wisdom and knowledge.

There were other doctrines, said Origen that the Apostles gave but did not explain. In both cases—the foundations of some doctrines and these other doctrines—the "how" or "why" was left to those who came after who "should prove to be lovers of wisdom." Origen clearly believed himself to be one of those "lovers of wisdom."[2]

In his *On First Principles*, we find Origen's summary of the core of apostolic teaching:

> That God is one, who created and set in order all things, and who when nothing existed, caused the universe to be ... Then again: Christ Jesus, he who came to earth, was begotten of the Father before every created thing ... he emptied himself and was made man, was made flesh, although he was God ... and this Jesus Christ was born and suffered in truth and not merely in appearance ... he truly rose from the dead ... and was taken up into heaven ... Then ... that the Holy Spirit is united in honour and dignity with the Father and Son."[3]

His summary of the apostolic teaching is similar to what we saw in the other figures we have looked at, Tertullian and Irenaeus. However,

---

1. See Kerr, *Readings in Christian Thought*, 43.
2. Ibid. 44.
3. Ibid. 43-44.

Origen's account contains important phrases like "not merely in appearance," which is a rejection of more Docetic and Gnostic versions of Christology, versions that diminished the humanity of Christ. Moreover, Origen wanted to say more about what it is that Christians believe and to take seriously the questions that were being raised within the Christian faith as well as by those outside.

Interpreting the Bible

Origen was also a very fine biblical scholar. Many of his writings were philosophical and speculative, but he wrote even more extensively on the Christian Scriptures. He spent a great deal of effort in trying to establish an authoritative version of the Septuagint, the Greek translation of the Hebrew Bible. He put together a volume called the "Hexapla" which placed side by side all the versions of what Christians called the Old Testament in order to compare the different translations. From these scholarly efforts Origen wanted to extract the best translation of the Bible.

Origen is also reported to have written commentaries on virtually every book in the Bible and on many books more than once. It is said that he wrote eight commentaries on the Book of Genesis, and five on Lamentations. He wrote many commentaries on the Book of John and the Book of Revelation. His commentaries were extensive and learned. It is said that he devoted an entire volume to the opening line of the Gospel of John: "In the beginning was the Word . . . " We know this more by legend than by direct evidence because in the century after his death he came under attack and many of his writings were lost to us. He was remarkably prolific and offered some very important insights on the question of how we were to interpret scripture.

The interpretation of scripture was an issue and problem for Origen. Indeed, it had been a problem from the beginning when the Christian Bible was the Hebrew Bible, now read through the eyes of a community that believed the Messiah had come in Jesus the Christ. Earlier, the controversy surrounding Marcion's views of Christian scripture had led to a reaffirmation of the Hebrew scripture as part of the Christian scripture. And Irenaeus had given us the language of Old and New Testaments. However, it was Origen who gave us the first theoretical account of how we should interpret scripture.

Origen argued that we find in the sacred writings three levels of meaning. He wrote that we must

> ... *portray the meaning of the sacred writings in a threefold way upon one's own soul so that the simple man may be edified by what we may call the flesh of the scripture... the obvious interpretation; while the man who has made some progress may be edified by its soul, as it were... and the man who is perfect... may be edified by the spiritual law... For just as man consists of body, soul, and spirit, so in the same way does the scripture, which has been prepared by God... for man's salvation.*"[4]

The first level of interpretation is what Origen called "the flesh of the Scripture." This is the obvious or surface interpretation. The second level is for one who has made some progress in the faith, those whose Christian faith has been deepened by study and the life of discipleship. This is the "wisdom of Scripture," the soul of Scripture. This level addresses us more deeply than the first. The third level is the "spiritual law" of Scripture. This level is for those who have achieved the highest degree of perfection in the Christian life. Thus we see in Origen a complex hermeneutical or interpretive scheme. It is made even more complex by Origen's attempt to correlate each level of meaning within Scripture with one's level of advancement in the Christian faith. It was, Origen believed, only as we grew in our faith that we could come to see and understand these deeper levels of meaning within Scripture.

We can all gain some glimpse of Origen's view when we recall how differently Scripture has struck us as we have read and reread it at different times and ages. When we read it as a seven-year-old we grasp it differently than when we read it as a forty-year-old. I think Origen recognized this and tried to incorporate this into his view of what modern scholars call hermeneutics, the art of interpreting a text.

Origen understood the Christian faith in general and Scripture in particular as providing us with "saving knowledge/wisdom." This is what the Christian message brings to us. There are levels and degrees in terms of our understanding of this "saving knowledge." The first time we read Scripture, we tend to read it at the "bodily" or obvious, literal level. But as we continue to read and study Scripture, a second level of meaning begins to emerge. This is what Origen saw as its moral meaning.

However, there is a third and deeper level, what Origen called its spiritual meaning. As an example of the issue that he was trying to deal with in the interpretation of Scripture, Origen discussed some of the terms and words that we find in the creation story in the Book of Genesis. "There are,"

---

4. Ibid. 45-46. For further study see *Origen, On First Principles*.

wrote Origen, "certain verses or short passages of Scripture which . . . have no bodily [literal] sense at all." Then, he continued,

> *Now what man of intelligence will believe that the first and the second and the third day, and the evening and the morning existed without the sun and the moon and the stars? . . . Who is so silly as to believe that God, after the manner of a farmer, "planted a paradise eastward of Eden," and set in it a visible and palpable "tree of life" . . . and when God is said to "walk in the paradise in the cool of the day . . . "*

If such statements were not meant to be taken literally, what did they mean? "I do not think anyone will doubt," wrote Origen, "that these are figurative expressions which indicate certain mysteries through a semblance of history and not through actual events." In words that are almost contemporary in their ring, Origen explained that he was not denying the historical elements of Scripture, but seeking to rescue the reader of scripture from silly conclusions. "Our contention," he wrote, "with regard to the whole of divine Scripture is that it all has a spiritual meaning, but not all a bodily meaning . . . Consequently, the man who reads the divine writings must exercise great care."[5]

It is important to see, as we do in Origen, that the question of the interpretation of scripture and how it is to be rightly understood is a problem that emerged early in the history of Christianity. It is not a late problem that arose only in the modern world in the light of the historical critical examination of scripture. Early Christian thinkers were also aware of the interpretive issue and sought to address it. There was a need to distinguish among those things that had literal meaning, those that had figurative meaning, and those that had spiritual meaning. God gives us the spiritual meaning through the Scripture so that we might come to saving knowledge of God. This for Origen was the primary purpose of Scripture and so he argued that we must take great care in the interpretation of Scripture and not misunderstand what God—for Origen believed that Scripture is inspired—is trying to communicate to us in and through these writings.

This brief discussion of Origen's view of Scripture should not be taken to mean that Origen played fast and loose with Scripture or that he did not take it extremely seriously at its literal level. For example, Origen himself took in an absolutely literal way the statement in Scripture about becoming eunuchs for the kingdom of heaven (MT. 19:12), as he had himself castrated when he was a young man.

---

5. See Kerr, *Readings in Christian Thought*, 45-47.

Apophatic Thinking

The other side of Origen, one as important as his biblical scholarship, is his philosophical theology and his attempts to answer the objections to the Christian faith that had been made by the opponents of Christianity. Origen sought to offer a comprehensive statement of what Christians hold and believe. This is found in his book called *On First Principles*. This book was written when Origen was in his forties and is an attempt to offer a comprehensive statement on a whole range of issues that have arisen in the encounter of Christianity with other philosophical and religious traditions and in its own internal reflection. Here we will look briefly at Origen's view of creation, redemption, and consummation.

First, however, we need to understand that Origen was an apophatic thinker. That is, he recognized that God was ineffable or beyond the full grasp of our words and concepts. Thus all efforts to articulate the truth or meaning of God are inadequate to the reality of God. Here the language of faith is understood as a pointing to the Ultimate, rather than a definitive fix on the truth of God.

Origen's Teaching on Creation, Redemption and Consummation

Keeping this in mind, let us look at Origen's teaching concerning creation. This is a very cursory and simplified version of Origen's teaching, a view that takes seriously the biblical teaching on creation and other philosophical views. He affirmed the biblical view that God created the world and that there was nothing but God before creation. But he went beyond the biblical teaching when he argued that God calls creation into being through a process of emanation, a flowing forth from God. Like some of the early Greek philosophers, Origen emphasized that God creates out of God's own divine nature or reality. This is a spiritual process that creates spiritual intelligences or souls. It is God's own reality that becomes the reality by which and through which God creates.

Later on, there is an issue of creation out of nothing and doctrines of emanation became a very controversial issue among Christian thinkers. For Origen, when God creates, God creates spiritual beings or spiritual intelligences whose defining characteristic is that they are creatures of freedom, endowed with free will. As creatures of freedom, these created beings can turn either towards God or away from God—they have the freedom to move closer to God or further and further away from God. As some of them do move further and further away from God—the image here is of God as light—they become darker and darker, and in a sense more and more material. In that way they experience a fall.

By and through the exercise of their own will, these spiritual beings of intelligence and freedom move away from God and so the fall, for Origen, is grounded in the misuse of the freedom that these spiritual beings have. This then sets up the problem to which Christianity is the answer. As these spiritual beings move further and further away from God, and in a sense fall out of union with God, there has to be a way to bring them back into union with God. That was Origen's understanding of the function of Christ. Christ is the bringer of "true knowledge" or "saving knowledge." As he brings this saving knowledge to these fallen spiritual beings, people like you and me, and then as we accept it and grow in that saving knowledge, we are brought back into union with that original source of our being, the Creator of Heaven and Earth.

Central to this process is the figure of Jesus the Christ. Christ for Origen is the incarnate Word of God (Logos). He is the second image of God, true wisdom, the "*mediator between all creatures and God, whom the apostle Paul announces as the firstborn of the whole created order.*" This divine or cosmic Word becomes incarnate and takes on flesh. "*We are numbed*," said Origen, "*with wonder at the fact that this nature, higher than all, emptied itself of its condition of majesty and became a human being living among human beings.*"[6] It is this Mediator who leads fallen creatures out of their bondage and returns them to the true source of their life and being.

Here Origen skirted Gnostic thinking that sees Christ as the bearer of a secret knowledge or wisdom. But Origen differed from Gnostic Christians in his insistence that this is a public knowledge or wisdom that is available to all and not just to the initiated. It is the saving knowledge or wisdom given to humanity in Christ and in Scripture.

The third element of Origen's teaching in his book *On First Principles* is that the end or the consummation of all things involves the return to the beginning. This was Origen's view of what the Greek Christians call *apokatastasis* or cosmic consummation. Again, we will say this in a simplified form. What Origen was arguing here is his "eschatology," what God is doing or achieving through the divine or incarnate Word. Origen's answer to that question was that eventually all creatures will return to their origin in God. Nothing that God created will be lost to God because everything was created out of God. For God to lose something of that divine reality out of which God created creatures would mean that in the end God would be

---

6 See Norris, *The Christological Controversy*, 73-74.

less than what God was in the beginning. Hence all things have to return to God. He appealed to Paul who said, that "God will be all in all" at the end.

The implications that Origen drew from this Pauline view became problematic for some other Christian thinkers in the West. One of these implications was his belief in universal salvation—all creatures will be saved eventually. For Origen the emphasis was on eventually restored to God. What this means, said Origen, is that we should not think of "hell" as something eternal. Rather, he contended, hell becomes for those who do not turn to God in this world another stage that fallen spirits must go through on their pilgrimage to their eternal home. So hell becomes an extended reform school for the spirits that do not make it during their lifetime.

To tie together universal salvation with his idea of freedom, Origen said that God's love is so compelling that eventually all beings will freely choose to return to God. The consummation of all things gets extended. In temporal terms, it might take eons for a freely chosen return to the origin to occur.

Origen was recognized by his contemporaries as an extremely fruitful and important Christian thinker. A century later, some in Latin Christianity blamed Origen for many "wrong" teachings that came into the Christian church, one of these being this doctrine of universal salvation. But in his own time he was highly respected—as he continues to be in Orthodox Christianity with its teaching on *apokatastasis*. In later centuries, many Western Christian thinkers would also hold the view of a universal restoration of all to God. It is important to understand figures in the history of Christian thought in relation to the different settings in which they lived and worked.

The last of Origen's great contributions was his writing called *Contra Celsus*. Celsus was a Greek philosopher who wrote a very sharp critique of Christianity, arguing that it was silly from beginning to end. The ruin of Celsus's library still stands in Ephesus (modern Turkey). Origen wrote a very fine response to Celsus showing how he constantly misrepresented what Christianity taught and believed. Origen's defense of Christian teaching was so impressive that it effectively ended ill-informed rejections of Christianity of this kind in the ancient world—something like the views we see in Richard Dawkins and Christopher Hitchens in our own time.

The Search for a Language of Christ and God

In Origen we see some of the philosophical and speculative questions that get addressed by Christian thinkers. It is not self-evident how we can speak about God simultaneously as Creator, Redeemer and Consummator. What does this say about the divine nature? How is it possible for God to be all of these things and how is God in each of these things? The efforts of Christian thinkers in the third and fourth centuries were directed at trying to give answers to these questions. We need to understand more precisely not only the philosophical issues that underlie Christian teaching but also how the different elements of the Christian faith relate to one another. Origen, for example, taught that God alone is *autotheos*—literally "from himself." God is from God and in God from all eternity. And the early Christian community understood that Jesus Christ is the bringer of salvation. While the early community—except for Marcion and some others—clearly affirmed that God is the Creator, how do we understand the relationship between the Creator and the Bringer of Salvation? How does this fit with that early of Christian affirmations that Jesus is the Messiah, the Anointed One, the one whom God anoints in order to accomplish a certain task?

In the first couple of centuries there was not much reflection on how Jesus the Christ is God. Certainly it was believed that Jesus is Lord and that Jesus is the Messiah and the Son of God. But Christians used such affirmations without seeing that there is any difficulty in affirming with Ignatius that "Jesus Christ is our Lord and God" and affirming that God alone is *autotheos*, from God.

When Origen tried to define more closely who the Eternal Logos—the Word made flesh—was, he often described the Logos as the First Begotten. Some heard this as implying a time when the First Begotten was not. And yet, the Gospel of John says that the Word was in the beginning and the Word was God. Does this text suggest that there was a moment when the Word was not with God because the Word had not been created? Origen did not want to say that. He said that the Logos is eternally generated from the Father, but at the same time he wanted to say that the Logos is not the Father. On one hand, he wanted to distinguish between God the Creator and God as the Logos or the Word. On the other hand, he wanted to establish some fundamental continuity or even sameness between God and the Word.

Origen tried to do that by saying that the difference between God himself and the Word is that the Father is alone (*autotheos* or from himself) and the Son or the Logos is the eternally generated, the First Begotten from the Father. But he said at the same time that the Son is eternally begotten so as to get away from the suggestion that there was a time when he was not. To say that he was eternally begotten is to make a logical distinction and not a temporal distinction. There is a distinction between God the Father and God the Word, but it is purely a logical distinction and not a temporal distinction. You could not say that there was a time when the Logos was not. In temporal terms, the Logos always was, but the Word became flesh, became

Jesus Christ, at a particular moment in time, lived for thirty years, and was crucified, buried and resurrected.

Another question is: how is that Eternal Word related to Jesus since there was clearly a time when Jesus of Nazareth was not? Whatever else we want to say about the birth narratives in the Gospels, Jesus is presented as being born at a particular moment in time. Matthew begins by listing the genealogy that precedes Jesus. So clearly Scripture speaks about Jesus as having a beginning. Jesus of Nazareth was born of Mary. So what is the relationship between the Word/Logos, who was with the Father from eternity, and Jesus, born of Mary at a particular moment in time? How are they united with each other? Origen argued that the Eternal Logos united itself with the soul of Jesus such that the soul of Jesus receives the Eternal Logos completely. The soul of Jesus thus merges into the power and the light of the Eternal Logos. But, of course, to say that is to raise some other problems. Early Christians also wanted to say that Jesus is a truly human figure, and they resisted Docetic and Gnostic views of Jesus that qualified his humanity. They wanted to affirm his humanity on the one hand, but then it seemed it was being taken away with the other because they also wanted to affirm that Jesus is the Christ, the eternal Logos.

In this way, the issues that arose in the third and fourth centuries of Christianity concern the understanding of the Christ Christians confess as the bringer of salvation. All these Christian thinkers were united on the conviction that Christ is the bearer of salvation, the one who mediates between the Divine and the human. But how precisely to understand this mediator, this Logos made flesh, was an immensely perplexing issue. It exceeded the human mind. Origen once remarked that of the many issues that Christians ponder,

> *There is one that exceeds the capacity of the human mind for admiration . . . I mean the fact that that great power of majesty divine, the very Logos of the Father as well as the very Wisdom of God, in whom all things visible and invisible were created, must be believed to have been circumscribed with the human being who appeared in Judaea; and what is more, that the Wisdom of God must be believed . . . to have been born as a small child, and to have squalled in the manner of crying children.*" [7]

This is the puzzle, problem, and mystery that these different Christian thinkers were trying to understand. How can we understand or hold together these two affirmations that seem to be central to Christian faith: the belief in the eternal Word of God and the human Jesus? When Origen concluded

---

7. Ibid., 74-75.

his effort to understand "these very difficult questions about the incarnation and the deity of Christ," he remarked that should "someone come up with better ideas and can confirm what he says with plainer assertions from the Holy Scriptures, let them be accepted instead of what we have written."[8]

In more formal terms we could say that the issue is the incarnation. From the biblical traditions, the regula fidei (rule of faith), at baptism and when new people came into the Christian faith, they repeated the formula that God was made man or that God was incarnate in Jesus. But the thinkers within the Christian community wanted to understand this belief and its implications. This shows how understanding follows what is already confessed or believed. Christians believed in the incarnation; now Christian thinkers were trying to understand it.

In part, the incarnation was a troubling and perplexing issue because the development of Christian thinking at this point reflected the impact of Greek philosophical categories on the articulation of the Christian faith. With the Greeks and from the Greeks, the Christian thinkers had increasingly come to understand that a fundamental characteristic of the Divine, or of God, was that God was impassable or unchanging. And yet, one of the things that we certainly notice when we read the Gospel stories or hear accounts of Jesus' life is change. He is born and grows up; he moves here and there; he dies and is resurrected. This presents the problem of trying to link together the assumed unchanging nature of deity or divinity with the changing life of the bringer and bearer of salvation. But need we think of the divine as unchanging?

To further complicate the issue, there was the question of how Jesus mediates the divine life to us. As Christian thinkers sought to understand the One who is their origin, their redemption and their end, they found themselves moving towards Trinitarian doctrine. As they entered the third century, most Christians believed that God is Creator, Redeemer and Sanctifier. But how precisely did they understand these three dimensions, or masks, or personae of God? From its Jewish forebears, Christianity had inherited the belief that God is one. Now some people both within and outside the Christian community began to feel that Christians were talking in a way that sounded as if there is more than one God. There is God the Creator and Father; God the Logos, the Word, the Christ; and God the Spirit. Did Christians really believe that God is one? Or did they believe that God is two, or three, or more? All of these issues became intertwined with one another, and that is why it took so long for these matters to be sorted out.

---

8. Ibid., 81.

At the beginning of the third century, probably more than anyone else, Origen tried to hold together in a coherent way all these different elements of Christian affirmation and articulate a whole understanding of all of these matters. When Origen did this, he said very explicitly that his understanding was very imperfect. It was just an attempt to understand how all this fit together.

In the period after Origen, the kind of synthesis that he had achieved began to break down. Different people focused on different aspects of Origen's teaching, and many of these people came to hold views which, in the history of Christian thought, are referred to as "monarchian" views, a way of understanding the relationship of Jesus to God while preserving the unity or the monarchy of the Christian belief in God.

Dynamic Monarchian Views

Monarchian views get divided into two different camps, sometimes called "dynamic Trinitarianism" and "modal Trinitarianism." Dynamic monarchians like Theodotus, who was a Christian layman in Rome in the early third century, argued that Jesus was a man on whom the divine Spirit descended in his baptism, giving him at this point in time a messianic vocation. What distinguishes Jesus from other human beings, and what especially relates him to God, is not some characteristic of his nature. He is not like God in some way. Rather, Jesus has a special task to fulfil, a messianic vocation. And the divine Spirit, after Jesus' baptism, is enabling him to fulfill that task.

Within these views emerged an "adoptionist Christology"—the view that Jesus is a man adopted by God to fulfil a certain mission or vocation, a certain task. Theodotus preserved the unity of God by not identifying Jesus with God but arguing that Jesus fulfils a task for God. Jesus is a man who is adopted through the Spirit and given this special vocation. And Jesus comes ever closer to God by increasingly identifying his life with God's purposes and will.

A similar dynamic monarchian view was that held by Paul of Samosota (200–275), a bishop who said that when Christians speak about the Logos and the Spirit in relation to God they are speaking about certain qualities and not about persons. The Logos and the Spirit, then, are eternal powers or potentialities of God, and these potentialities of God are present in Jesus. Like Theodotus, Paul of Samosota argued that there emerged a unity of Jesus' will and love with the will and love of God. So, as Jesus developed and grew and increasingly understood the will and love of God, he received more and more of God's Spirit and God's Logos, so that he finally came to be united with God in terms of his will and love. For Paul of Samosota, Jesus then became one with God. This came about in terms of the unity of his will and love with that of the Father. In the views of both Theodotus and Paul of Samosota, there was a time when Jesus was not one with God. For Theodotus, Jesus in a sense never becomes one with God. This is more ambiguous in Paul of Samosota, who seems to say that Jesus— over a period of time, as he unites himself with God's will and love—receives from God more of his Spirit and Logos until he achieves a kind of unity with God. Again, the point of this way of understanding Jesus is to preserve the unity of the one God.

Neither Paul nor Theodotus came to see the question of the relationship of Jesus to God in terms of an identity of nature. It is rather a question of a unity of will and purpose.

Modal Monarchian Views

The modal monarchians went in a very different direction. One of those directions is represented by Praxeus (c. 190), who argued the Virgin had given birth to God Himself, and that God suffered and died. Hence one could say that the heavens were emptied when the incarnation took place. There was no longer some God beyond, but God came wholly into time in the figure of Jesus. The universal Creator was wholly in the figure of Christ, so when Jesus Christ suffered and died on the cross and was resurrected, it was God Himself who had suffered, died and been resurrected. Praxeus felt this had to be maintained to prevent Christianity from becoming polytheism. God was one, not two or three. If God was one, it had to be argued that that one God was wholly present in Jesus—not some part or some aspect, but God Himself. God's mode of existence shifted—it changed from the God above to the God who was wholly with us in Jesus Christ to the God who was the Holy Spirit.

Another modal monarchian view was that of Sabellius (c. 215), who asserted, it is said, that "the same is the Father, the same is the Son, and the same is the Holy Spirit." Sabellius wanted to argue that there is but one God and that God is essentially the same in the Father, the Son and the Spirit. The differences, in his view, are the differences of different faces, appearances, or modes of manifestation of that one same God. Sabellius was moving more towards the Trinitarian formula that became familiar, indeed the standard, after the ecumenical councils of the fourth and fifth centuries. But it was not yet that kind of Trinitarianism because Sabellius' view did not adequately maintain the distinctness of the Father, the Son, and the Holy

Spirit. For Sabellius, the same God is present under these different faces or appearances of deity.[9]

Athanasius: A New Voice on the Incarnation

At the beginning of the fourth century a new figure appeared in Egypt. His name was Athanasius (296–373) and, like Origen, he was an Alexandrian. Around 315 he published a remarkably powerful treatise entitled *On the Incarnation of the Word*. It was addressed to Macarius, a young Egyptian who was considering Christianity. Athanasius centred his presentation of the Christian faith on "the divinity of the Word of the Father ... his universal providence and power ... that the good Father through him orders all things ... all things are moved by him and in him are quickened." It is this cosmic Word: that has "been manifested to us in a human body for our salvation."

Some of the other Christology's of this time began with the human figure of Jesus and tried to figure out his relationship with God. In contrast, Athanasius began with the Eternal Word of God who is incarnate in Jesus the Christ. In more contemporary terms, we would call this a Christology from above, rather than a Christology from below. In beginning with the Word of God and then speaking of the Incarnation, Athanasius articulated a crucial principle of his thought: the identity of the Creating and the Redeeming Word of God. As Athanasius asserted, "the renewal of creation has been the work of the selfsame Word that made it at the beginning." Thus Athanasius first spoke of the Creation: "Out of nothing, and without its having any previous existence, God made the universe to exist through his Word." This entire creation is from God and humanity is made "after his own image." Furthermore, humanity is made "for incorruption," but having "rejected the contemplation of God ... no longer remained as they were made." Herein lay the reason, Athanasius continued, for the incarnation of the Word:

> *His coming down was because of us ... our transgression called forth the loving-kindness of the Word" who "for our salvation he dealt so lovingly as to appear and be born even in a human body.*"[10]

Or, again,

> *He took pity on our race and had mercy on our infirmity ... and, unable to bear that death should have the mastery—lest the*

---

9. See Tillich, *A History of Christian Thought*, 65-80 for a fuller discussion of these figures.

10. See Hardy, *Christology of the Later Fathers*, 55-59.

> *creature should perish, and his Father's handiwork ... be spent for naught—he takes unto himself a body, and that of no different sort from ours ... for it belonged to none other to bring man back from the corruption which had begun than the Word of God, who had made them from the beginning.*[11]

Thus, Athanasius argued that the reason for the incarnation was the redemption of humanity which, created in God's image but corrupted by the Fall, could be restored only through the Word which had created us. Only the Word, Athanasius argued, had the "power ... to turn the corruptible to incorruption." He affirmed that the Word "was made man that we might be made God."[12] Athanasius thus challenged all with his powerful treatise On the Incarnation. Jesus as the Christ was none other than the Incarnate Word of God who had rescued the creation and restored it to communion with God.

Athanasius was for forty-five years a controversial Bishop in Alexandria. Throughout his long career he was deposed and then restored to his office of bishop several times. But his views would become the standard by which all other accounts of Christ would be measured. Later they would become enshrined in the first ecumenical council at Nicea (325 C.E.).

But in his very own backyard there was a rival view, held by Arius who asserted that there was a time when the Word was not and thus challenged Athanasius's view of the identity of God and the Word. Arius (c.280–336) was a popular Alexandrian priest in a section of the Christian community that had always been closely related to Greek thought. He was a highly revered person, and one who understood himself to be following the lead of Origen in his teachings. The position that he came to articulate was one that would preserve the oneness of God and the view that God alone was from God.

We don't have actual writings that are directly from Arius. Thus we must reconstruct Arius' view through his critics and opponents. It seems Arius argued that Christ as the Logos is a special creation of God and thus, said his critics, subordinate to the Father. His arguments were presented not so much in learned treatises as in popular teaching and song. For Arius, the nature of God was beyond comprehension, a view shared by other Greek-thinking Christians. And this God was so far beyond humanity that God could not become God in human form. Therefore, what God did in order to mediate between God and the world was create a second reality, the Divine Logos, which is certainly much higher than human, but somewhat lower—at least this is what Athanasius thought—than the ineffable God. Thus the Logos is, Arius' critics argued, a semi-divine creature. And,

---

11. Ibid., 62 and 64.
12. Ibid.73 and 107.

apparently following Origen, Arius argued that only God was unoriginated. God is only Himself from eternity and the Logos is a created being—a very high being in terms of a hierarchy of beings, but not God Himself. Thus the battle was joined.

Summary

Throughout the third century, then, there were many different figures contributing to the large and complicated discussion going on within the Christian community as Christians tried to understand the nature and character of Jesus in relation to God. We see in Origen a remarkable philosophical openness to questions that underlie and surround the apostolic teaching. We see him wrestling with the issue of the interpretation of Scripture. We also see a kind of speculative inquiry that was new in Christian thought. While many of Origen's views became controversial, his efforts marked a significant contribution to the great conversation. He saw the necessity of addressing the difficult issues and he contributed significantly to the efforts to find a language adequate to the relationship of Christ to God.

It was a given among Christian thinkers that God was One. This had been part of Christianity's inheritance from the Jews, the people of Jesus. And yet, Christians had come to believe that the Risen Christ was their Lord and had, as Irenaeus had earlier affirmed, "become man in order that man might become God." This was also a view held by Athanasius early in the fourth century. Was that possible if Jesus Christ was not, in some sense, God? Athanasius said no as he argued for his understanding of the Incarnation. But Arius said that Athanasius's view compromised the unity of God. And so the debate continued. The conflict between Arius and Athanasius would come to a crisis in the fourth century, when. these matters came to the first ecumenical council at Nicea for resolution.

Review

1. What was Origen's view of biblical interpretation?
2. Did Origen believe that speculation is appropriate for the Christian thinker?
3. What are "monarchian views"?
4. Why is Athanasius's view of Christ sometimes called a "Christology from above?"

PART III

Ecumenical Symbols and Classical Christianity: 325–1000

IN PART III WE move into the early ecumenical councils of the Christian tradition, beginning in 325 at Nicea. This Council occurred in the context of a sea-change that had begun under the Emperor Constantine. Christianity went from being an "outlaw religion" to becoming a legitimate religion of the Roman Empire and in the 380s the official religion of Rome.

The councils were called to address controversial issues within the Christian world. They resulted in symbols or creedal statements that sought to state the faith of the Church. In Chapter 8 we outline the contentions at issue at each council and the symbols that emerged.

In the midst of these councils, there emerged a figure, St. Augustine, who would be fundamental for the Western, or "Roman Tradition" within Christianity, as we see in Chapter 9. There were also some important Eastern voices. as we see in Chapter 10, especially those known as the Cappadocian Fathers: Basil the Great, Gregory of Nazianzus and Gregory of Nyssa. Their voices continue to be exceedingly important for what later came to be known as the "Orthodox tradition" of Christian thought. In Chapter 11, we look at the emergence of monasticism and the figure of Benedict of Nursia, as well as Boethius and Dionysius, who speak for the "via positiva" and the "via negativa" respectively. Taken together, all of these contributions to the Great Conversation served the emergence of what might be called "Classical Christianity."

Chapter 8

The Seven Ecumenical Councils 325–787
Creeds, Councils, and Empire

WITHIN THE ROMAN EMPIRE the early fourth century was a troubled time. Divisions and rivalries challenged the stability of the empire. In the battle of Milvian Bridge in 311, Constantine, one of the rivals for the crown of emperor, was successful in defeating his opponents. It is said that he fought under the banner of the cross. The irony seems to have escaped the notice of his contemporaries. The cross, a Roman instrument of punishment and death on which Jesus died, had now become the emblem of a Roman army.

The next year, Christianity was legitimated, and in 325 it was favoured by Constantine and became the preferred religion of the emperors. Christianity became the official religion in 381 under the Emperor Theodosius and pagan rites were forbidden in 391.

These developments shifted the whole character of early Christian discussion and debate. Christianity had been a minority—indeed an outlaw—religion, often persecuted and attacked. In 325 Christianity became the religion Constantine supported. This change in its social status had consequences for the whole of the Christian community and a profound impact upon Christian thinking, debate and discussion. Christianity now became linked to the political order in fateful ways.

In addition to whatever religious and theological motives he may have had, Constantine had certain political purposes in mind when he made Christianity the preferred religion of the Empire. What Constantine very much wanted to happen, and believed would happen, was that making Christianity the official religion would bring order and stability to his Empire. However, as he came to know something more about Christians, he discovered that there were deep divisions within the Christian community on profoundly important doctrinal questions, as well as on the question of the relationship of the Church to political life. How could an internally disagreeing religious community serve the imperial political purposes of unity and order?

Earlier debates within Christianity had gone on for a long time and had a variety of outcomes. Either a position had come to commend itself throughout the whole Church, or different views had just persisted in various parts of the growing community, or various views had just faded away. But now there was a political element introduced into the whole discussion. Shortly after Constantine announced his preference for Christianity, the first ecumenical council of the Christian community was called. *Oikumene*, the Greek term from which "ecumenical" is derived, means "the whole inhabited world."

Council of Nicea, 325

In 325 Constantine ordered the calling of the first ecumenical council at Nicea, his summer residence southeast of Constantinople, now Istanbul in Turkey. The bishops assented and gathered for this first council in that same year, 325. This council is often referred to as the Council of the 318—roughly the number of bishops that were involved in the deliberations.

In the beginning, these ecumenical councils had two purposes. One was the political purpose of establishing uniformity of doctrine within the Christian Church so that the religion would better serve the purposes of unity and discipline within the Christian community, and by extension within Roman society. The other was the religious and theological purpose of clarifying disputed points in relation to the faith of the Church. While both were important, the presence of the political factor very much changed the nature of the discussion within the Christian community. Indeed, some Protestant and Anabaptist thinkers in the sixteenth century saw the recognition of the Church under Constantine as "the fall of Christianity." I feel that goes too far, but it does point to the dramatic new situation of Christian thinking.

Constantine's own religious views are very much in dispute. Some thought that he privately tended towards an Arian position. We don't know how true that is, but we do know that the Council of Nicea became the forum within which the debate between Arius and Athanasius came to a head. And in terms of the central streams of Christianity, it was settled.

So a debate that might have gone on over a much longer period of time, through an exchange of writings and creative conflict within the boundaries of the Christian community, was now taken into a politically charged and legally binding context. Here the Church gathered in an ecumenical council would declare itself one way or another on the issues that divided Athanasius and Arius. The council decided against Arius and in favour of Athanasius. It agreed with Athanasius's claim that Christians believed that the incarnate Word of God, Jesus the Christ, was fully God. Sometimes the debate between Athanasius and Arius is characterized as a debate over an iota—over an i—since the debate came down to whether or not Christ was *homo-ousios* or *homoi-ousios*: that is, of the same substance as God or of like substance. Athanasius pushed for the view that Christ was "very God of very God," while the Arians said that Christ was "the created Logos/Word of God." The Arian forces were willing to say that Christ or the Logos was like the Father—the created Logos of God. But the Athanasian group argued that the nature of Christ and the Father were identical. So, it is a question of whether it is homoousios or homoiousios: of the same substance or like substance.

The Stakes at Nicea

The issues that dominated the Christian community over the next 150 years centred on defining the language that is appropriate to the expression of the Christian faith. Do we understand that Christ is of the same substance or essence or like substance or essence? The "like" idea was rejected because it was said that it introduced an element of subordination into the relationship of the Logos to God. Opponents of Arius argued that it presented Christ as lower than the Father.

This may seem like a very fine distinction. What is at stake here? This is a much debated issue, but it seems to me that it is ultimately the understanding of the salvation that is mediated by Christ to humanity. In Athanasius's writing on the incarnation, he used a formula that is very important in understanding what was at issue for him. That formula was that "Christ became man in order that man might become God." He was made human so that our humanity might be lifted up into the life of God; the Logos was incarnated so that humanity might be divinized. And Athanasius also argued that if the Incarnation were not "done by means of the body, humanity would not have been divinized."[1]

---

1. See Norris, *The Christological Controversy*, 91.

What was at stake for Athanasius in the conflict with Arius is not a mere technical point but understanding the nature of the salvation that comes to human beings in and through the Word. For Athanasius, when we talk about salvation, we are talking about the transformation or divinization of human nature. For the purpose of Christ is to heal humanity, to restore humanity to union with God. For Athanasius, this involved the recovery of the image of God (imago dei) which was humanity at creation, but was wounded by sin and is now healed in Christ so that the life of humanity might be lifted up again into the life of God.

Thus, for Athanasius and those thinkers that followed him, salvation is ontological/spiritual and not just moral. That is to say, salvation involves a transformation of the very being of humanity, not just a transformation of human actions. If Christ as the bringer of that salvation is not of the same substance as the Father, then his capacity to bring this ontological or spiritual change about is, in Athanasius's view, thrown into question. If he is not truly of God, how can we be confident that through him we are restored to union with God? If this Word is a lower deity, then whatever he does must be something other than bringing us back to union with God because he is himself not God. What may appear to be merely technical disagreements—should we say homoousios or homoiousios (with or without the i), of the same substance or like substance with the Father—are actually something more. Athanasius argued that it is the same substance in order to be sure that the salvation that the Word/Logos mediates to humanity is capable of doing what he understood salvation is supposed to do: bring about a transformation in the very being of human beings. Athanasius said that Christ was "humanized in order that humanity might be divinized."

For Athanasius the concern was to see in Christ the restoration of humanity. Christ restores humanity by becoming human. In taking up our humanity Christ divinizes humanity by lifting it up into the life of God.

While implicit in the Scriptures—when Paul, for example, asserts that "in Christ God was reconciling the world to himself" (II Cor. 5.19)—this whole argument reflects a change in Christianity from much of earlier Christian thought. The earliest Christian documents that we have can be read as arguing that Jesus as the Christ brings about a moral transformation. He is the one who reflects the will of the Father perfectly, and Christianity is primarily engaged in the transformation of the human will to bring that will more into conformity with Christ, whose will is one with the Father. And thus the transformation that takes place is more in the moral life: "Be perfect just as your heavenly Father is perfect." But at Nicea it was Athanasius that prevailed.

Nicea was the first of seven councils of the early Church. These councils came to loom very large in defining the Christian faith, or better in expressing the faith of the Church. Here we pay special attention to the first four councils as they focused on the Christological issues. There was also an element of discipline attached to the councils. Disciplinary action was taken against those who held contrary views, with bishops sometimes being removed when the views they held were anathematized at a council. At this time no one was put to death for holding views that a council declared heretical, but that did happen later, in the Middle Ages, at some councils within the Western Catholic tradition.

Council of Constantinople, 381

Arius died about eleven years after the Council of Nicea. The controversy went on after Arius's time, and even Athanasius recognized that there were some ambiguities in the council decision. Athanasius was even removed as a bishop at Alexandria, then restored, then removed, then restored again according to whether the sitting emperor favoured the Arian or the Athanasian view. After Constantine's death, he was succeeded by his son who was very pro-Arian, and it looked for a time as if everything was going to shift and go in the Arian direction. But those Arian views ultimately lost and the Athanasian side again prevailed at the second council, at Constantinople in 381.

While Nicea proclaimed that Christ was fully God or homoousios, this did not wholly solve all the questions being considered. There were many important developments between the Council of Nicea in 325 and the Council of Constantinople in 381. Chief among those developments was the work of the Cappadocian Fathers: Basil the Great, Gregory of Nazianzus and especially Gregory of Nyssa, who clarified the language of *ousia* or "substance/essence" and *hypostasis* or "mode of being/persona." In these terms Basil the Great was able to identify both what was identical –the divine substance or reality—and what was particular –the particular mode of God as Creator or Father and as Son or Redeemer. One of the analogies he used was speaking about humanity as of identical essence or substance and about Peter, Paul and Mary as particular human beings. So now there was an understanding that the Father, Son & Holy Spirit were one in *ousia*/essence/sub-stance and three in *hypostatsis*/mode of being/persona.

Many of the same issues that had arisen before resurfaced at Constantinople because of a lack of full clarity in the Church's teaching on Christ. But the central specific issue at Constantinople was one raised by Apollinaris, who was a supporter of Athanasius. Apollinaris argued that Christ was fully God, but in asserting the unity between the Logos and the humanity of Christ spoke about the human person as composed of a soul, flesh and the spirit. Apollinaris then argued that when the Logos was incarnate in Jesus the Christ, the Logos replaced the spirit in Christ and wholly dominated the humanity of Christ. In a sense, the creed that emerged from Nicea defining the Christian faith led to the problem that the Council of Constantinople addressed: if we affirm that Christ is "very God of very God," how should we understand the humanity of Christ? Apollinaris, in his efforts to try to speak out of the faith of Nicea. ended up speaking in ways that called into question whether or not there is a full human nature within Christ. So Constantinople opposed Apollinarianism, and while it wanted to reaffirm that Christ is fully human, it didn't quite do that. Rather, it reaffirmed Nicea and its teaching that Christ is homoousios without attempting to address the issue of what is involved in the full humanity of Christ. It is from Constantinople that we get the "Nicene Creed."

Council of Ephesus, 431

The third of the seven ecumenical councils, the Council of Ephesus in 431, addressed the issue of what was called Nestorianism. Nestorius was a bishop in Constantinople. In trying to be faithful to the understandings that had emerged at Nicea and Constantinople, Nestorius argued that in Christ we have two separate persons—one divine and one human. He saw these two merged in each other. Nestorius was in part reacting against an understanding that had emerged after Constantinople, which—in his view inadequately—stated that there were these two natures present within the figure of Jesus Christ. His opponents reacted against his understanding of two persons in Christ and their merging in each other.

Another aspect of Nestorius's position was his argument against the teaching that Mary was *theotokos* or the mother of God. Instead, Nestorius asserted that we should understand Mary as theodochos or the recipient of God. Again this was perceived by some as qualifying or obscuring the extent to which Jesus was fully human, and by others the extent to which he was fully God. The issues arising after Constantinople concerned how to understand the relationship between the human and the divine within the person of Christ.

These are very complicated disputes, requiring a more detailed analysis than we can offer here, and the metaphysics of it all was often clunky and obscure. The best that we can do is to try to point to the meanings at stake in these controversies. Such an approach helps us to see why the councils ended up affirming what they affirmed in the creeds. The Council of Ephesus found against Nestorius for his lack of definition of how these two separate persons were related to each other in the figure of Jesus Christ and affirmed that really in Christ we have but one person. But the Church was moving towards a clearer definition, which would emerge at the next council, at Chalcedon, with the statement that there are two natures within Christ but only one person.

Some bishops did not accept Ephesus, their churches became known as the Nestorian Churches of the East.[2] They were regarded as heretical for teaching that Christ has only one nature (monophysite) or, later, that Christ had only one will (monothelitist). They could not accept some affirmations of Ephesus but they did not disappear. Rather, they continued as churches separated from those who accepted the creeds of the Councils. This was one of the sad consequences of the councils. The Nestorian Churches of the East continued—some down to the present day—and made significant contributions to the great conversation of Christian thought.

Council of Chalcedon, 451

The Council of Chalcedon addressed the issue of Eutychianism. Eutychias, an opponent of Nestorius, was attempting to be faithful to what he understood to have been said at Ephesus. But he was accused of confusing the two natures of Christ when he denied that the personhood of Christ was one with ours throughout Christ's entire life. Eutychias ended up saying that after the union of the human and the divine in the incarnation, there was really only one nature in Christ.

The Council of Chalcedon provided the famous but controversial formula that came to define the orthodox view of Christ within Christianity: Jesus the Christ is fully human and fully divine. In the person of Jesus Christ we have two natures that are related to one another in what is called "hypostatic union."

---

2. The phrase "Churches of the East" can be confusing. It is a phrase that is now sometimes used to refer to all the churches of the East, both Orthodox (the Orthodox Churches in communion with the Patriarch of Constantinople) and the Nestorian Churches, the Coptic Church of Egypt, the Ethiopian Church, and others. Sometimes it is used just in relation to the Orthodox Church in communion with the Patriarch of Constantinople. One has to look at the context. It should be noted that the first use of the phrase Roman Catholic Church for the Catholic Church is 1208. For the period being discussed here they were all just Churches or Christian.

Through these first four councils, we can see the emergence of two tendencies. One tendency was to affirm that Christ was fully of God. It was felt that only in this way could the salvation of humankind be assured, a salvation that saw humanity divinized in Christ. And at the same time, there was a tendency to affirm the full humanity of Christ, which asserted itself in reaction to every statement about the divine Christ that made him less or other than human. Only if Christ were fully human could he identify with humanity, and we with him. Obviously, these tendencies were in conflict with each other. Throughout these first four councils, we can see how affirmations that Christ was one with God would lead to further affirmations that would compromise Christ's full humanity. And then the opposite problem was how to affirm the fullness of Christ's humanity without compromising the way in which Christ was fully God. So what did Chalcedon do? Astonishingly, it said Jesus Christ was both fully human and fully divine. It defied logic and accepted paradox, affirming that the Lord Christians worship and adore is, at once, fully divine and fully human.

Understanding Chalcedon

How are we to understand this? At one level we can't, even if we can see why Christians came to affirm the creed that arose from these councils. But there is something we can understand. At Chalcedon, the Church arrived at a set of affirmations that should govern Christian thinking about Christ. What the majority of the Church here realized is that it wanted to affirm that Christ is fully God and fully human. These then become the guidelines, the outer boundaries that should govern Christian thinking about Christ. These affirmations never fully explicate how exactly these terms are to be understood and how they clarify the person of Christ. They are symbols and not conceptions. They state the faith or convictions of the Church, even if we are uneasy about their metaphysics. They resolved the century and a half of debate by saying we want to affirm both things: Christ is fully divine and fully human. While this paradoxical affirmation is, in itself, difficult to understand, I think that we can see some of the logic that led to it.

Let's look again at what happened over the first four councils. They began with Athanasius insisting that the Incarnate Word is fully God, nothing else and nothing less. Then Apollinaris, who supported the Council of Nicea and affirmed that Christ is fully God, got into trouble when he started talking about the humanity of Christ. That is what the next council saw, and so it said, "No, that is not the way to say it: human nature is body, soul and spirit and so we have to maintain the presence of all of these elements within the figure of Christ. Then just when that seemed to get settled, Nestorius came along and said, "If we have this fully human nature in Christ, how is that related to the divine nature, and don't we really have here in effect two persons somehow in this one figure, a divine person and a human person?" Then the Church responded and said, "No, that is not what we want to say either. Let's leave it at a general level since we don't know precisely how to say it, but we do know that we want to say that Christ is both fully human—and thus related to us—and fully divine—and thus able to relate us to God."

Mystery and Meaning

These are the affirmations or rules that should govern thinking about Christ, and this leads to the proper definition of a mystery: we know more than one thing to be true, but we can't fully grasp, and don't know how to articulate, the relationship between these two things. We want to say that Christ is fully God in order to be sure that what the figure of Jesus Christ mediates to us is of God and can relate us to God. We have to say that. On the other hand, for us to be related to this figure, we have to affirm that he fully shares our humanity. Otherwise he gets too distant and we don't have any understanding of how we can share in his life. So it's as if the Christian community says, "We know we want to say these two things, but how to understand the relationship between them is a mystery." This is not meant to be evasive or to shut people up. Nor does it mean that we shouldn't think about that relationship or try to understand it. However, it is an incredibly difficult thing to understand and probably beyond our capacity to fully figure out. You can think about it for your whole life if you want to, and in a sense that is what the Church does as Christian thinker after Christian thinker tries to understand this mystery. But every thinker comes up against the limitations of the human mind to fully grasp the ineffable truth of God.

The language of these debates—ousia, hypostases, natura, persona, divine, human—is often obscure to modern students. The metaphysics is often clunky and wooden. To understand these debates, we need to recognize that they were bounded by assumptions that made their resolution exceedingly difficult. The first of those assumptions was the belief that God was one: the monotheism that Christianity assumed from Judaism, and with it the rejection of polytheism. This was a given. It was also a given for these Christian thinkers that God was unchanging. This was a view inherited from the Greeks. And the third assumption was that Christ became human so that the human might be lifted up into the life of God. This view had become so obvious by the end of the second century that it was just assumed in these debates. Given these assumptions, Christian thinkers attempted to answer the question of how God was present in Jesus Christ and what Christ meant for humanity. The symbols of faith, the creeds that emerged in these councils, were their answer, their consensus affirmation of the faith. They didn't so much answer the questions as mark out the boundaries of affirmation for the normative or orthodox faith of Christianity.

Where in the life of the Christian community did these affirmations or symbols belong? Not long after Nicea, that council's affirmation or Creed began to be recited in the churches as part of their liturgy. When this happened, the affirmations found their proper home: they were symbols of what Christians affirmed. This was the proper context of the councils: to clarify the faith of Christians. The imperial aim was often at cross-purposes with this spiritual aim and compromised what unfolded in these councils. However, the symbol of Nicea/Constantinople, the Nicene Creed, found its way to its proper setting in the worship life of the community. It was here that the assembled congregation recited the faith that marked Christianity. It is this creed that has been central to the faith of most Christians since the fourth century.

After Chalcedon: The Last Three Councils

There were three further councils after Chalcedon: Constantinople II in 553, Constantinople III in 680 and Nicea II in 787. Constantinople II and III returned to issues that had been raised by Nestorius. Constantinople II reaffirmed earlier decisions and rejected the Monophysite views of Theodore, Theodet and Ibas for their suspected Nestorianism, the view that Christ has only one nature. In its decree, the council affirms that "there are the two generations of God the Word, one before ages of the Father, non-temporal and bodiless, the other at the last days when the same came down from heaven and was incarnate of . . . Mary, and born of her."[3] And at Constantinople III, the bishops gathered to reject the views of the monothelites who believed that in Christ we have only one will. Constantinople III affirmed that in Christ there are two wills in accordance with Christ's two natures, one fully human and one fully divine.

---

3. See Hardy, *Christology of the Later Fathers*, 379.

Defining the Human

What is interesting here is how these councils were also developing an understanding of what is involved in being human. Understanding the nature of the human/man was not an issue at the council of Nicea that affirmed the divine nature of Jesus. But this was confusing to someone like Apollinaris (d. 390). It seemed to undermine the humanity of Christ. So Apollinaris taught that Jesus had a human body, a rational soul, and a divine mind—a monophysite view. But others rejected this view seeing it as compromising Christ's divinity. It wasn't until Chalcedon that we get the paradoxical affirmation that in Christ we have two natures, one divine, one human in one person. And then the centrality of the will to being human became an issue later on, as we see in the fourth century, especially in a figure like Augustine. During these early centuries of the Christian era, a shift was taking place in terms of the understanding of humanity. If we understand the will as essential to humanity, then how do we understand Christ? The debates about the humanity and divinity of Christ contributed to thinking about some larger issues related to understanding what is involved in being human and what is involved in being God. In a sense, what was affirmed at Chalcedon is the mystery of the person, because the statement that Christ is a person who has within himself two natures makes the notion of what constitutes a person considerably more complex. After that time, Christian thinkers began to develop an understanding of what it means to be a human person that reflected and drew upon the understandings that developed at the level of the Creeds on the humanity and divinity of Christ.

At the last ecumenical council, Nicea II in 787, the issue was iconoclasm or the destruction of religious icons/symbols. Although there were no painted or sculpted images of Christ for more than one hundred and fifty years after Jesus' death, such images began to be widely used when Christianity was made the religion of the Roman Empire. Some felt that images violated the commandment against graven images and were idolatrous. Others believed that images were necessary to instruct believers in the truth of Christianity since not everyone could read the Bible. The council of Nicea II decided that icons were allowed and could be venerated, but could not be worshipped. Worshipping icons would be idolatrous. However, if icons were seen as pointing to a truth beyond themselves, they could be honoured or venerated without being worshipped. In large measure, this was a controversy between the Eastern (Greek, Syrian, later Russian) churches and the Western (Latin) churches. The views of John of Damascus, one of the great Eastern Christian thinkers of the mid-eighth century, prevailed.

Nicea II was the last council that brought together the whole Church. Many councils were called after this time, but the split between the Eastern and Western churches— between Rome and Constantinople—meant that large sections of the Church did not participate in these councils. Only the seven councils discussed here were received by the whole Church—meaning the Western Church and the Eastern Church except those that were excluded after Nicea, Constantinople, Ephesus and Chalcedon, groups like the Nestorian, Coptic, Syrian, and other Christian groupings—as occasions on which there was a meeting of minds about important issues.

Councils and Christian Thought

How do we understand these early ecumenical councils in relation to Christian thought? I think that we should see them, to use their own word, as "symbols" of the Christian faith, symbols that serve to establish the boundaries of Christian affirmation. They were a continuation of earlier efforts to identify a "regula fidei" or rule of faith. And while they offered a confession of, or witness to, where Christians put their trust, they did not specify in detail the positive content of the Christian faith. For example, when the Council of Nicea, together with the Council of Constantinople, affirmed that Christ is fully God, they told us what the Church affirms about Christ, but they did not offer a full account of what it means to say he is fully God.

Indeed, immediately after Nicea, we see various people understanding "fully God" in different ways. They still wanted to know what it means to say that Christ is fully God, especially since Jesus Christ is so obviously human. It is almost as if the Christian community lurched from one council to the next saying, "This is what we hold dear, but no, that is not quite what it is that we want to say" about the divinity and humanity of Christ. Finally, at Chalcedon, we get to a place where both things were affirmed—Christ is fully human and fully divine and there are two natures in one person. In doing this, the Church offered a symbol or confession that should regulate and guide Christian thinking about the person of Christ. But this is not a full account of what it means to say that Christ is fully human and/or fully divine—or that he has two natures in one person, or that he has two wills, or any other of the specific affirmations of the councils. It only provides the Christian thinker with boundary affirmations: when you think about Christ, remember that there are two things you must affirm, that Christ is fully God and fully human.

The people who were declared heretics at a given council had been in good standing up to that point—often holding the office of bishop, the highest ecclesial position available. When the Church gathered as an ecumenical council ruled against them, they were often removed from their positions since their efforts were determined to be unhelpful in the process of trying to clarify what the Church should hold. When we look at what comes out of a council, we always find a statement of what the faith of the Church is: a creedal statement called a "symbol." The conclusion of the Council of Chalcedon, for example, states where it is that Christians put their trust, it is a symbol of their collective affirmation.

In most Christian churches, it is the Nicene Creed—so called even though it was actually formulated at Constantinople—that is recited during worship as the statement of what the Church believes.[4] This is repeated Sunday after Sunday: this is what we affirm/believe. It was not the primary concern of the Councils to give us detailed theological treatises. Rather, a council would conclude by saying what, in its judgment, Christians should affirm and confess. This would always come in the form of a symbol of faith. The beginning of the Nicene Creed is typical: "We believe in one God, Father . . . ." A council would also specify certain ways of stating the faith and say, "These are not acceptable." At the end of the Council of Constantinople, we have these words: "This wise and saving symbol of the divine grace . . ."[5] The council was trying to find the most appropriate way to give expression to what is held in the hearts and minds within the Christian community, even when it is paradoxical and beyond conceptual grasp. Huston Smith once remarked about the "clanky metaphysics of the early creeds."

We also see in these councils the extent to which the creedal Christian faith came to be stated and articulated in the light of Greek philosophical categories. One of the major problems that lies behind these various councils is the relationship between the Greek heritage and understanding of God as impassable or unchangeable and the Jewish view of God as One and wholly transcendent. Because of the interface of these views, Christians found it very problematic to say how this unchanging deity could be present in a human form, in a human person without falling into polytheism. Would the creeds have looked the way they do if early Christian thinkers had had access to other philosophical traditions? That is a speculative but interesting question. The question that arises later is how binding these formulations of the Christian faith are on people, especially those who were never influenced by the philosophical traditions that shaped these early creeds.

---

4. I am aware that after the Reformation many Churches recite the Apostles Creed and that there are Christian churches in the modern and contemporary world that do not incorporate a creed into their worship.

5. See Norris, *The Christological Controversy*.

I think that we should see the creeds of the councils as a quite magnificent achievement within early Christianity. Bringing together the Christian faith and Greek philosophical categories was an impressive accomplishment. But one of the issues that arises is whether or not there could be another articulation of the Christian faith that does not use and depend upon these Greek categories. This became an issue for Christianity in later centuries when it moved into the Indian, Chinese and sub-Saharan African worlds. Then Christians discovered something they hadn't realized for centuries: that cultural factors—which at the time were not regarded as specific to a given culture but were seen as universal categories—influenced the formation of the Christian creed. But this is a question that came much later, and it generated a great deal of difficulty within the Christian world. Some of the early missionaries felt that it was really important to immerse themselves in the culture of China, as early as the 7th century or India in the 19th and 20th centuries, and learn its cultural outlook so as to gain some understanding of how the world they had entered was put together. Furthermore, they believed that one should try then to articulate the Christian faith in those terms.[6]

This caused considerable difficulty for some missionaries. For the moment, however, it is important to see that Greek philosophical categories had an impact—for good and for ill—on the formation of the creeds of the early Christian Church.

Finally, the term ecumenical comes from the Greek word oikumene which means "the whole inhabited world." These councils generated "symbols" of the faith, and statements on issues of doctrine, worship and discipline that were regarded as binding on all Christians. It was in the ecumenical councils that normative symbols of the faith emerged. The symbols of the councils did not end discussion about the Christian faith, but they gave a symbol or creed that reflected the consensus of the Christian community. These councils are highly regarded in both the East and the West, as they are said to reflect an undivided Christianity.

Summary

The early ecumenical councils loom large in the history of Christian thought. The creed or "symbol of faith" that emerged at Nicea-Constantinople becomes the creed most often recited by Christians in worship down through the ages. These councils also provided some boundaries to govern Christian

---

6. See for example Palmer, *The Jesus Sutras*, and the writings of Abhishiktanada, especially *Hindu–Christian Meeting Point*.

thinking about controversial issues. For example, Nicea said that Christ was "very God of very God," Chalcedon that Christ was "fully human, fully divine," and Nicea II that icons should be "venerated but not worshipped."

Review

1. What were the ecumenical councils?
2. Why are Nicea and Chalcedon important?
3. What issue did each address?

Chapter 9

Augustine

Architect of Western Christian Thought

Augustine of Hippo, 354–430

ALTHOUGH AUGUSTINE LIVED DURING the times of the early ecumenical councils and the great Christological debates, he did not play a significant role in them. It was as if they were going on around him without his even being aware of them. He was born in North Africa into a religiously mixed family. His mother, Monica, was a Christian and his father was a pagan. Following a common practice of the time, Augustine was not baptized as an infant. Baptism was understood as a cleansing of sin, so if you delayed it until later in a person's life then there would not be much time to be sinful after baptism. Hence baptism was often deferred, sometimes until a person's deathbed. Augustine's mother did not want to leave it that long, but she thought it might be preferable to leave it until he was a teenager.

Augustine actually became a Christian much later in his life and only after a very long and difficult struggle. That struggle is recounted in one of his great writings, called the *Confessions*. This book is the story of Augustine's life from his birth through his childhood, his education and his eventually becoming a teacher of rhetoric and making it within the imperial centres of the Roman Empire to his conversion.

The imperial heartland was across the Mediterranean in what we now call Italy. First at Rome and later at Milan, Augustine held positions under the imperial government as a teacher of rhetoric. Earlier he had been seriously involved with the Manicheans, an important religious movement with roots in the ancient Near East that understood the cosmos as a great struggle between the forces of good and the forces of evil. Augustine was also heavily influenced by Neoplatonism, a very important philosophical and religious movement within his lifetime.

In his twenties Augustine learned from the Neoplatonist's something that was very important to him: to think of God in immaterial terms. God was spirit. Thinking of God in material terms had been a problem for Augustine. Coming to view God as spirit was an important moment in his intellectual conversion.

He was in his thirties when he is finally converted to Christianity. His wish after that was to return with a small group of friends to North Africa and live in a small Christian monastic/philosophical community, where he and his friends could engage in contemplation and the deepening of their spiritual life. He did go back to North Africa, and he did found his community. But on one occasion he decided to go into the nearby town of Hippo. His reputation as a good and pious man preceded him. Thus, according to the legend, when he came into the church in Hippo, people grabbed him, brought him to the front of the church and told the bishop to make him a priest. The bishop did, and later made Augustine his assistant. When the bishop died, Augustine became the Bishop of Hippo. Then, for the remaining forty years of his life, Augustine was a very influential thinker within the Christian world. He redefined the Christian faith in ways that dominated Western Christian thought for centuries, in some ways down to the present day. He is arguably the most influential thinker in Western Christianity.

A large part of that influence is due to his *Confessions*. The other text that did much to establish his influence was his *City of God*, written after the "barbarians" (the Germanic tribes) from the north overran Rome in 410. No one had any memory of there ever having been a time when Rome wasn't the ruling power of the world. It's fall was an extremely distressing event. It was as if the end of the world had arrived. Civilization was collapsing. Many people believed that the reason that Rome fell in 410 was that the Romans had abandoned their ancient religion and had adopted Christianity. So, Augustine's *City of God* was partly written in response to that contention. He began writing this book in 410 and wrote it over the remainder of his life, completing it by the time the barbarians overran his own city of Hippo in 430.

In the *Confessions* and the *City of God* Augustine articulates his influential understanding and vision of the Christian faith. Augustine dealt with very fundamental issues but in novel ways. His *Confessions* and his *City of God* both represented innovative forms of Christian thinking. The *City of God* was published in pieces because people wanted to hear what Augustine said in answer to the charge that Rome fell because of its conversion to Christianity. So every time Augustine finished one of the chapters (they were called "books"), it was copied and circulated. Then people waited for the next installment. The whole work contains twenty-two books and runs to over a thousand pages. Our review of Augustine will be much shorter.

These two books—along with many other things that Augustine wrote, including his *De Trinitate*—made him the thinker who had to be dealt with in relation to virtually every issue that came up in subsequent Western Christian thought. Here I outline some of the elements of Augustine's understanding of the Christian faith and focus on his Christian vision—his understanding of the human journey to God, individual and collective.

In a sense Augustine's great contribution is that he took the great doctrinal battles as resolved and shifted the focus to trying to understand what the Christian faith is in relation to the life of human beings, both individual or personal and social or collective. In both these respects he made many important contributions. But the Eastern churches do not hold Augustine in such high regard and refuse to see him as one of the "fathers of the church." Their criticism of Augustine, one now shared by many in the Western church too, is that his thought is skewed because of its overemphasis on sin. We will come back to this issue.

Augustine's *Confessions*

In large measure, Augustine's importance lies in his articulation of a compelling understanding of human life in the light of Christian faith—what we might call a "Christian anthropology." The *Confessions* is a book that, in large part, grows out of Augustine's own experience. It tells the story of his life up and through the time of his conversion to Christianity. It is not, however, an autobiography, nor is it a modern "true confession." The point of the story is not simply to elucidate the moment of his conversion but to show how God's grace—despite Augustine's turning away from God—was the decisive factor in his life from the very beginning.

The *Confessions* opens with these words:

> *Great art thou, O Lord, and greatly to be praised; great is thy power and infinite is thy wisdom' (Ps. 145:3). And man desires to praise thee, for he is part of thy creation; he bears his mortality about with him and carries the evidence of his sin and the proof that thou dost resist the proud. Still he desires to praise thee, this man who is only a small part of thy creation. Thou hast prompted*

him that he should delight to praise thee, for thou hast made us for thyself and restless is our heart until it comes to rest in thee.[1]

What is crucial here is, first, Augustine's conviction that we are made for God and made to praise God. And, second, that we are restless until we come to rest in God. These twin affirmations are fundamental to Augustine's understanding of what we are as human beings and what is going on in our lives. When Augustine tells us his story in the *Confessions*, it is, of course, a retrospective account—an account told from the standpoint of his conversion. So it is informed by crucial religious assumptions. It is not a straightforward chronological account of the story of his life in terms of the assumptions that dominated him at different moments in his life. It is a retelling of his story in the light of the things that he has come to affirm: that we are made for God, that we are continually seeking God, and that we are restless until we rest in God. So when he looks back on his life, he sees these principles at work. It is the perspective in which he reinterprets his own life in order to show how all that restlessness is really a kind of blind searching for God in the midst of all the other events that befall him.

Restless and Seeking God

Augustine was born into a family where his mother was a Christian and his father was not. Augustine tells us that as an infant he was jealous of his mother's attention to others, as a child he was troublesome to his teachers, and as a teenager he did terrible things like stealing some pears from an orchard with his friends: "All these things . . . can be occasions of sin because . . . if we are too much tempted by them we abandon those higher and better things, your truth . . . and you yourself."[2] Then when he went to Carthage, "where I found myself in the midst of a hissing cauldron of lust,"[3] he was caught up in the passions of sexual longing. Later, when he became a teacher of rhetoric his life was caught up in vain pursuits of ambition and position. Augustine remarks that "I was led astray . . . and led others astray . . . we were alike deceivers and deceived in all our different aims and ambitions."[4]

---

1. See Augustine in Kerr, *Readings in Christian Thought*, 51. See also St. Augustine, *Confessions*, 21.
2. See St. Augustine, Confessions, 49-53.
3. Ibid., 55.
4. Ibid., 71.

What's going on here? Is Augustine retelling his life in order to confess his own sinfulness? No, he is pointing to something deeper. Augustine realizes that in the middle of this twisting and turning of his life, there is something else at work, something more powerful and more significant than his understanding and his will. It is loving grace. It was providing for him through his mother's love, his teacher's instruction and his own desire for the good. It was calling him to his true happiness—to rest in God. It was there in the midst of all of his twisting and turning and attempts to turn away. It was that reality that was attempting to restore him to himself by restoring him to the Creator who made him, as he made all creatures.

For Augustine, this restlessness and turmoil that characterized his life were in a hidden way a search for God. That search was, as it were, in, with and under all of the other events of his life. We are creatures who are made for God and we are restless until we come to rest in God.

Sin as the Tendency of the Self to Turn In On Itself

Another element in Augustine's understanding of what we are as creatures is that we are fallen, or sinful. While we are made for God and restless until we rest in him, there is a contradiction that runs through our lives. That is the evidence for Augustine of the presence of the fall—Adam's fall—not only as an event at the beginning of time but as it affects every one of us. The story of every man or woman recapitulates the story of the human race in that we are made by God, for God, but there is something that intervenes to turn us away from God. This is Augustine's definition of sin: "the tendency of the self to turn in upon itself." It is the placing of one's self—rather than God—at the centre of things. And it is this tendency, which we all know in our own experience, that becomes, for Augustine, evidence of our fallenness, our sinfulness. Or, we might call this an inner tension or contradiction—is this the right term—that permeates human life: while we are made for God, we tend always to turn in upon ourselves rather than allowing our lives to open out to their divine source and divine goal. We came from God, and for Augustine we go to God as the telos or goal of human life. Augustine shows us this other presence in our lives—the tendency for us to turn away from God and for the self to turn in upon itself. This is how Augustine understands the presence of sin in human life.

This contradiction within the human heart also expresses itself in a number of other tensions that are to be found within the human soul. They are seen in the struggle between the passions and the intellect, which is a major issue for Augustine. In the experience of growing up, Augustine felt that the passions run ahead of our understanding, often leading us in directions of their own making before we can fully grasp what is going on in our passionate nature. For Augustine, one of the tasks of the Christian life is to bring the passions and the understanding into increasing harmony with each other. Augustine experienced St. Paul's statement in Romans 7:19-20: "For I do not do the good I want, but the evil I do not want is what I do. Now if I do what I do not want, it is no longer I that do it, but sin which dwells within me." This is, for Augustine, evidence of the contradiction that runs through human nature; it is the disordering of our nature that comes from the fall. Technically, it is Augustine's doctrine of concupiscence, that is, a 'wound of our original nature, a tendency to turn away from the good.'

It is also reflected in the contradiction between lust and love. For Augustine, underlying every lust is a more genuine desire, which is to love and to be loved. But oftentimes that gets confused with lust, which is basically evidence of our turning in upon ourselves so we don't regard the other as a genuine other, who is to be respected in and of their own right. When caught in lust we see the other as mainly something that will satisfy this lust and desire within ourselves, rather than as a person to be loved for who they are.

For Augustine this is evidence for the presence of sin within the human heart. There is similarly a kind of contradiction that pervades the intellectual life of human beings. The dynamic of the intellect is to go to God. The tendency of fallen intellects is to place themselves at the centre of the universe and to make their own understanding decisive in terms of a way or a point from which one can judge everything else. And so Augustine came to believe that it is important for the intellect to submit itself to an authority beyond itself. Theoretically that authority is God, but practically it turns out to be the Church, which we have to heed in our lives for the understanding and the intellect to unfold as they should.

The Goal that is God

What is Augustine saying? Augustine understands the human being as a creature of will, intellect and passions or feelings, a creature made for God. But since we are fallen creatures, these powers of the human soul are disordered. To give one example, when Augustine was eighteen or nineteen years old he encountered a work of Cicero's called *Hortensius*.[5] This book played a very important role in Augustine's life because it awakened in him a love for wisdom.

5. See St. Augustine, *Confessions*, 58.

It awakened this intellectual passion. But a love for wisdom doesn't necessarily mean that the current content of one's mind is true wisdom. In Augustine's case, his journey led him through a number of religious and philosophical views. From them he learned things but also found them wanting in certain respects. For example, when he became a Manichean, he saw the world as a conflict between good and evil. These eternal ontological principles are at war with each other, and the war that is taking place throughout the cosmos is also reflected in the inner war in the heart between the powers of good and evil. But finally, after a long and difficult struggle, he came to see the limitations of the Manichean view and moved beyond it in his journey towards becoming a Christian.

Finally, after fourteen or fifteen years, he discovered what the proper object of this love for wisdom was: truth. The intellect, above all, desires truth. And that desire for truth is, for Augustine, synonymous with God, because God is truth. "True happiness," said Augustine, "is to rejoice in the truth, for to rejoice in the truth is to rejoice in you, O God, who are the Truth."[6] It was only when his desire for truth came to rest in the reality of God that he found the object of his longing. The point here is Augustine's analysis of this power of the human soul—the power of the intellect and the desire to know truth. He asked, "What is the proper goal of that power of the soul?" His realization was that the proper goal of the intellect or the mind is truth. And, for Augustine, truth is God.

Likewise, if we look at the will and ask, "What is the proper object of the will? What do we aim for in making decisions? Augustine's answer is that what we aim for is the good. When we are confronted by options and then decide, "Well, I am going to do this rather than that," it is because we think that by doing this we move towards the good. We desire to do the good. And it is the proper function of the will to lead us to the good. Thus, as we understand ourselves more deeply, we come to understand the good we see more deeply. And as Augustine's story shows, we also come to understand that the good is also rooted and grounded in God. So, just as the intellect seeks truth so the will seeks the good and both come to rest in God.

Likewise the passions or the feelings. What is their object? For Augustine, the object of the passions and the feelings is harmony, and that becomes the beautiful. And of course the beautiful is not, finally, anything apart from God. That too is God. When we analyze the term more fully, God is the true, the good and the beautiful. And this is why Augustine says, "We are made for God." What are we as human creatures? We are the powers of the human soul: the intellect, the passions and the will. And all of these

---

6. Ibid., 229.

dimensions of the human personality drive us towards God, in which they achieve their fulfilment and completion. But the problem is that these powers of the human soul, in the condition that we are in and under which we experience them, are disordered or fallen. These powers of the human soul are disordered as a consequence of sin, which Augustine characterizes in the most general way as "the tendency of the self to turn in upon itself." We are not what we were meant to be.

The powers of the human soul, rather than going towards God as they should, are caught in other knots. Rather than the will going towards the good, which is God, we find that people say instead, "I do what I want to do. Don't tell me what I should do or what is right to do. It is my will and I will do what I want to do." And rather than the intellect going to the truth, which is God, we find the intellect turning away from the truth or confusing its own desires with the truth of things. The evidence of the disordered intellect is that we simply assert the truth of whatever happens to be the content of our own mind. We stubbornly insist on the truth of our own self-centred views. We don't want to hear anything else. And rather than the passions going to beauty or harmony, which is God, they become distorted by our tendency to be self-centred and desire only what we want.

Augustine saw this disorder, manifest throughout the human personality, as the source of our unhappiness. It generates more restlessness, more unhappiness, because even though we make these strong affirmations of our conviction that we are the centre of the universe, these powers of our soul aren't happy there because they know that it isn't true, it isn't good, it isn't beautiful. They want something more. And that more that they want is something beyond where we are at a given moment. And only when they reach their proper end will the person enter a kind of repose, a peace. They only achieve peace when they finally come to rest in God. But Augustine is aware of how powerful these contradictions are in a human life, how powerful this disorder is. Indeed, for Augustine, it is the source of evil in the world: that is where evil arises.

The Origin of Evil

Following the Biblical tradition, Augustine affirmed with Genesis that creation is good. Then where does evil come from? This was something that puzzled Augustine a great deal. His questioning is there in the *Confessions* when he tells his own story of stealing some pears. Some modern psychological critics of Augustine have shaken their disapproving heads over this story, thinking that Augustine makes too much of such a trivial and ordinary event: as young boys stealing pears. They miss the point. What Augustine was trying to explore and understand in a totally trivial event was a deeper mystery which he saw at work within his own heart. Within his own being and life, he saw a tendency—he named it in various ways—to do something less than the good he should do. Why did he steal the pears? Was he hungry? No. Did he steal the pears in order to make himself one of the fellows? That was part of the motivation. There were a few guys together and someone said, "Let's steal the pears." You don't want to be a jerk and not participate in this event.

But that wasn't an adequate explanation for Augustine. He pondered this problem and it became an issue that he returned to in his life again and again. This was an issue that he had struggled with as a Manichean. The Manicheans gave an account of evil that says there are two eternal principles that are in opposition to one another—the power of good and the power of evil. But as a Christian he knew there was one thing he couldn't say: that evil comes from God. Augustine didn't want to say that God is responsible. Rather, Augustine located evil in the human person, the tendency of the self to turn in upon itself and to make itself the centre of things.

Another way Augustine spoke about evil is that evil arises when we choose nothing. Or, to say it another way, when we choose a lesser good. A contemporary figure like Paul Tillich would say: when we choose nonbeing. Evil is a certain kind of absence. We turn away from the good, and rather than choosing good we choose something less than that. It is a negative reality that arises in the human soul and in human life as a turning away from the good. To take Augustine's example, he didn't have to steal the pears from the pear tree. After the boys stole them they just threw them away, highlighting for Augustine what a pointless event this was. This action involved choosing nothing, choosing some lesser good, turning away from the good. This notion of the origin of evil became a very controversial view within the history of Christianity. But it is one major understanding of evil in the Christian tradition, and Augustine makes some very important contributions here.

Augustine's Conversion and Transforming Grace

But now we need to return to Augustine's story and its conclusion: his conversion. It is here that we can see a very controversial aspect of Augustine's view of human nature and the human journey. Given Augustine's view that the human heart is disordered, then we have to ask: what can lead human beings back to our proper life, the life for which we are made? In looking at his own life, Augustine couldn't discover in himself a power, ability, strength or virtue which could account for the fact that he finally turned towards God. When he looked at himself and examined himself, what he found was that rather than turning towards God, he was always turning away from God. As an infant he was jealous when another infant was fed before him. As a little boy he failed to heed his mother, father and teachers. As a young man in Carthage he was caught in a "cauldron of lust." As a young professional he was beset by ambition and deceiving himself and others. He looked at all these things and could not find something within himself that would account for his conversion.

One can see him struggling in the events leading up to his conversion. It is as if he were saying to himself, "I know, I know, I know that I need to rightly order these different desires in me, all of these loves that are so strong within my being, and I can't find in myself that power to do it."[7] It was this sort of experience that led Augustine to the view that the renovating power in human life is not a human power but a divine power.

Humanity is a ruined house, and we need someone to come in and do some renovations. When Augustine looked for this restorative power, he could not find it in the human heart, in the human soul, but he found it as something that is active on the human soul, transforming it, renovating it, restoring it. The name he gave to the renovating power is grace. Grace is the loving power of God to create, preserve, recall, restore, renovate and lead humanity back to union with God. This is the end for which we were created, to come to rest in God, and this power is the only power that can lead us to this genuine capacity to rest in God. It is the light and love of God, a power from above, a divine power: the power of grace. And grace is what God gives to human life; it is present to all lives before we ever ask for it.

Augustine saw the power of grace present in how God orders creation long before we ever come on the scene. Augustine pointed out as he went through the various stages of his life evidences of that grace all along the way. When the child is born, milk comes. God makes creation in a way that generates these things that are necessary for the sustaining of human life. We don't make them; they are just "given" to us, as it were. Commenting on his infancy, Augustine noted how these gifts of parental care, feeding and love and his mother's milk are finally to be understood as from God. They are all from God. God is the cause and source of things, though they are through things that God made. God is the formal cause, human beings the efficient cause. The mother, the nurse, the one who cares for the child co-operate, as it were, with God's grace in nourishing human life. But we have to understand where they come from: Augustine's answer is that they are from God. We have no

---

7. See especially Augustine's *Confessions*, 78-82 and 161-65.

power within ourselves that is wholly our own. Grace was working in Augustine and around him as it is in every human life.

Finally, as he recounted in the *Confessions*, he is in the garden and he hears children say "Take up and read." He wonders what game are they playing but then decides that it must be a divine voice. So he picks up the Scripture and reads the page to which he opens. He is finally converted and his soul is flooded with peace. Augustine wrote of this moment,

> *I was ... weeping in the most bitter contrition ... when I heard the voice of a boy or girl ... chanting ... "Pick it up, read it; pick it up, read it" ... Damming the torrent of my tears I got to my feet, for I could not but think this was a divine command to open the Bible and read the first passage I should light upon. I had heard how Anthony, accidentally coming into church while the Gospel was being read, received the admonition as if what was read had been addressed to him ... So I quickly returned to the bench where Alypius [his friend from Milan] was sitting ... I snatched it [the Bible] up, opened it and in silence read the paragraph on which my eyes first fell: "Not in rioting and drunkenness, not in strife and envying, but put on the Lord Jesus Christ and make not provision for the flesh to fulfill the lusts thereof" (Rom.13.13). I wanted to read no further, nor did I need to. For instantly, as the sentence ended, there was infused in my heart something like the light of full certainty and all the gloom of doubt vanished away.*[8]

This was the culmination of a process that had been going on throughout his whole life and it finally clicked at this moment. Out of that experience he came to hold a very high doctrine of grace. It is God's grace—the Lord Jesus Christ—that redeems, renews and renovates the human being. It is grace that can overcome the disorder in the human heart. It is grace that can restore us to ourselves. It is grace that leads us to rest in God.

Pelagius and Augustine

The centrality of grace to Augustine becomes evident in his later controversy. with Pelagius. Pelagius was a monk from the British Isles who had made his way to Rome where he was an important teacher. In talking about the powers of the human soul, he argued that human beings have the capacity in themselves to turn towards God. Augustine argued that, after the fall,

---

8. See Kerr, *Readings in Christian Thought*, 56-57. For an interesting interpretation of Augustine's "conversion" see Garry Wills, *Augustine's Confessions*. I read it many years after I had written my account of Augustine's conversion.

human beings in and of themselves don't have the power to turn towards God, but God's grace gives them that capacity. Augustine's own experience was fundamentally on the side of wonderment at his own conversion: "I couldn't do it. God really did something here. God pursued me for years and years, from the time of my birth, through all of my life." This was Augustine's sense of things.

In the controversy with Pelagius, he insisted that we should not ascribe the power of turning to God to the human being. Why not? Because if we do, we are ascribing to ourselves a strength and honour that isn't ours. We really have to see how everything comes to us from God. It became a bitter debate, one of those moments in Christian history when two rival understandings of the human situation get generated. The division continues down to the present day.

There are people who are basically Pelagian in their outlook and others who are basically Augustinian in their outlook. What divides them is the relative role that each gives to the human factor in the process of salvation. Pelagius argued that we have the capacity to turn towards the good and all human beings are obliged to exercise that capacity. Augustine didn't agree. He saw grace as given in life, but it was a special infusion of grace that allowed human beings to turn towards God. It is not just a matter of exercising a capacity that we all have; it is a matter of God enabling our wounded self to turn to God. These are dimensions of life that remained puzzling for Augustine. But in later years he basically said that this is the kind of thing that is in the providence of God. We don't fully understand this, but some people do turn towards God. It is part of the way that God orders things. This leads to a doctrine of divine foreknowledge or predestination. However, as Augustine remarked,

> *The conclusion is that we are by no means under compulsion to abandon free choice in favour of divine foreknowledge, nor need we deny—God forbid!—that God knows the future ... We accept both. As Christians and philosophers we profess both—foreknowledge, as part of our faith; free choice, as a condition of responsible living.*[9]

It has always seemed to me that there was something wrong with this debate. Augustine just couldn't see what Pelagius was trying to say and vice versa. For, as Augustine admitted here, he did not want to deny human agency in the affairs of the heart. Nor did Pelagius deny the presence of grace in the human journey.

---

9. Kerr, *Readings in Christian Thought*, 61.

Another controversy that was important in Augustine's life was with the Donatists, a group within the church in North Africa that argued that the larger Church had developed too mechanical and magical a view of the sacraments. The larger Church failed to realize, said the Donatists, that the moral quality of the priests affects the sacraments. Indeed, rituals performed by immoral priests do not work. Moreover, the Donatists also said that the recipients should be leading blameless lives when they participate in the sacraments. Against the Donatists, Augustine defended the view that the sacraments are in and of themselves effective. They work because they are rituals instituted by God to heal and redeem the human race. You can't make the effectiveness of the sacraments depend upon the moral quality or the lack thereof of a given priest—and certainly not on the recipient. They work just by being properly performed. This came to be the view that the sacraments work because they are done: ex opera operato.

Augustine's larger theological views grew out of his own experience. He came to understand his life as the story of how human beings are constantly being pursued by God and turning away from God, and how no matter how much we turn away from God, God still pursues us. He universalized this story as the human story: humanity is in flight from God, but God never abandons his creatures. He goes after them. Why? Because what God wills for us is our good. God is our maker, redeemer and consummator. We see this most perfectly in the mediator between God and man, Jesus Christ, in whom we see perfected humanity: humanity turned towards God, humanity that has found itself in God. For Augustine, Jesus as the Christ is the mediator, the one who mediates to humanity this homecoming to a gracious God.

Augustine's *City of God*

In addition to his understanding of the human journey to God, Augustine is very important in terms of the social journey to God—the contribution he made to the great conversation in his *City of God*. As Augustine wrote,

> *My dear, Marcellinus: This work which I have begun makes good my promise to you. In it I am undertaking nothing less than the task of defending the glorious City of God against those who prefer their own gods to its Founder. I shall consider it both in its temporal stage here below (where it journeys as a pilgrim among sinners and lives by faith) and as solidly established in its eternal abode.*[10]

---

10. Augustine, *City of God*, 5. Later, Augustine notes that "In truth those two cities are interwoven and intermixed in this era and await separation at the last judgment." 46.

Augustine dealt with the question that occasioned the writing of this book: the view of some that the reason Rome fell in 410 was that it had become Christian. More importantly, he went on to articulate a more comprehensive Christian vision of society, including an understanding of how society relates to the Kingdom of God, Augustine's *City of God*. Here I offer a very schematic and condensed view of Augustine's social vision.

Augustine, of course, rejected the idea that Rome fell because it had become Christian. Rather, it fell because of its own inherent flaws and because all human cities are subject to change. They are not eternal cities. Augustine disagreed with those who thought that the fall of Rome presaged the end of the world. "Wake up!" he said. "Let's think about this!" We have to understand that the proper and final end of humanity is the heavenly city: the saints in communion with God. That is our final and proper home. Our other, and more temporary, home comprises the human communities that we build in this world. But these communities are only temporary and passing; they are subject to time and to the flawed and fallen nature of our humanity. Thus a principal task of Augustine's writing was to clarify these two ends or goals of humanity: the eternal city or the "city of God" and the temporal city or the "city of man."

What is the origin and nature of these "two cities," and the relationship and difference between them? There are, Augustine argued, basically two kinds of human association. There are those human cities that come together out of self-interest and self-love. These are the cities like Rome. They aim at their own glory and seek domination over all. This is the human city. But there is also another kind of human association: the Church. It is made up of people who come together out of a love for God. They aim at the glory of God and they seek perfect peace and union with God. This is the heavenly city.

Augustine does not see the cities of man made up of people bound together by self-love in wholly negative terms. They can lead to some relative goods. They have the positive function of generating a kind of unity among people. They do keep in place our conflictual nature. But these cities are also flawed and subject to change. They come and they go. The city of God, on the other hand, is made up of those people whose lives are centred on God. They have rightly ordered their loves and love God above all. They realize that here they are pilgrims moving towards the eternal City that is always beckoning.

The point that Augustine made—what confused so many people in relation to the fall of Rome—is that we have failed to understand that the ends of human beings are twofold. We have both a natural end and a supernatural end. Humanity's supernatural end is to enjoy eternal felicity in the communion of the saints in heaven with God. That is our highest end. The other end that we have is a natural end within this world, this temporal order, and that is a life of relative justice, relative peace, relative harmony and the like. But all of these goods, while they are goods, are not our highest goods. They are all relative goods. The total fulfilment of these goods, Augustine argued, is something that we can't fully realize in time. We can only get these things beyond time in eternity because the character of our living in time is that everything changes. Rome had fallen, and even Augustine's contemporary St. Jerome thought that meant the end of the world. Had we been abandoned by God?

Augustine asked another question: What did you ever expect from your life in time? We confuse our supernatural ends with our natural ends. We expect from human life, from social institutions, things which they can never produce. They can only produce relative peace, harmony and justice. They come and go and you shouldn't invest an expectation for perfect harmony, justice and peace in the temporal order. You only get these things in the communion of the saints in heaven with God.

Augustine was trying to suggest that the reason there is some confusion—even among Christians—about the reason for the fall of Rome is that they didn't adequately distinguish the city of man from the city of God. Consequently they confused the two ends of humanity, the natural end and the supernatural end. For Augustine, the longing for peace and perfect justice and perfect harmony are all appropriate human longings, but they only achieve their proper end and goal beyond time in the order of eternity. This world is a place of pilgrimage towards our proper home, which is not in the order of time but beyond time in the communion of the saints in heaven with God. And the other end we have is the natural end within time, wherein we can only achieve relative harmony, justice and peace.

Augustine turned to the Christian sources and argued that history, the story of man's life in time, is exemplified in the story of Cain and Abel. Here Cain kills his brother instead of loving him. This dynamic of fratricide is the consequence of the fall. It is the permanent condition of our life in time, only qualified by God's grace. It is the divine presence which seeks to lift our vision beyond the temporal order and to return creatures to their true and proper end—their higher end—which is the love of God. In effect, Augustine argued that we shouldn't invest too much expectation in what we can obtain in terms of the social and temporal order, but realize that what we long for most deeply will only be obtained beyond time.

In time these two cities are mixed up with each other. They are intertwined so that in terms of any particular human life it is difficult to know with any certainty whether or not that person is, finally, a citizen of the heavenly city or of the human city. I think that Augustine had his own life in view when he said this. A person at a given moment may appear to be wholly caught within the net of her own self-love, but at a later point in time, it may become clear that she actually undergoes a conversion and comes to place the love of God in the centre of her life. It works in the other direction too. Someone who appears to have his life characterized by the love of God may fall out of grace and really come to be caught in the net of self-love. This means that, for Augustine, the order of time is characterized by ambiguity. We all must wait for the last judgement for complete clarity as to who is and who is not a part of the City of God. In speaking about the last judgement, Augustine used the parable of the wheat and the tares that grow up in time and only at the harvest are finally separated from each other.

This was also Augustine's way of speaking against chiliastic movements, movements that believed, like the Donatists, that God's kingdom comes in the order of time. It was a way of restraining enthusiasm within the Christian community. It was Augustine's understanding of the Christian faith that while Christians live in the order of time, they have to live with a certain amount of ambiguity. We have to keep our eyes focused on those things which are above because in the order to time we will never be able to fully satisfy the longings for perfect peace, harmony and justice. What God is doing in the historical process, we might say, is trying to reclaim for God citizens of the heavenly kingdom, a kingdom that is always ahead of us and beckoning us.

Augustine's work here was very important and influential. It set the tone of Christian thinking in the West over the next centuries. There was sufficient ambiguity within Augustine's own views that some came to understand him as arguing that the community that in time most reflects and embodies the aspiration for the City of God is the Church and the institution in time which embodies self-love is the state. This issue of the relationship between the Church and the state would become a very important one in coming centuries. And when the Church is identified as the community in time which points towards the City of God, then in any conflict between the Church and the state, the Church should play a larger role and the state should play a subordinate role. Whether or not one understands Augustine in this way, it is clear that he didn't believe that the temporal order could bear the coming of God's kingdom because it is subject to change. The coming of God's kingdom means something beyond time.

Augustine on the Interpretation of Scripture

While Augustine is not especially known for his scriptural writings, he did have a nuanced view on the interpretation of the Bible. Jerome (347–420), Augustine's contemporary, had translated the Bible into Latin. Jerome's translation was known as the Vulgate and it was the version of the Bible known in the Catholic world down into the twentieth century when newer translations began to replace it.

Augustine saw that there were four different aspects to be distinguished when reading Scripture. First, there was the literal/historical element that dealt with historical events. Then there were the allegorical and moral elements that address the questions of what we should believe (the allegorical) and what we should do (the moral). And beyond these, there was the mystical dimension of Scripture that answered the question of what we should hope for.

Augustine did not write many exegetical works: he wrote works dealing with Genesis, Romans, Galatians and the Sermon on the Mount, but these were not commentaries in the modern sense. They were, rather, more general explorations of the major themes of the text. The final chapters of the *Confessions*, for example, are indicative of Augustine's writings on Scripture. Here he engaged Genesis to discern its general view of creation—and to criticize contemporary views that he rejected, such as those of the Manicheans. But his schema for the interpretation of Scripture is worthy of consideration.

Augustine on the Trinity: A "Psychological" Reading

I conclude this discussion of Augustine with a reference to his *De Trinitate* (On the Trinity), which shows the shift that has taken place in Christianity. By the time of Augustine, many of the doctrines that we consider central to Christianity were fairly well established. In other words, it was increasingly obvious throughout the Christian world by Augustine's time that when Christians speak about God they are speaking about God as Trinity, as "three in one and one in three." That formula was widely held and shared within the Christian community and was the distinctive element in the Christian view of God. Increasingly, the doctrine of the Trinity was a "given" in the Christian tradition—in Augustine's time it was not as contentious an issue as it had been. His efforts were not devoted to establishing the doctrine, but rather to unfolding and understanding what it is that Christians believe. This became increasingly characteristic of Christian thinking from this time on, as reflected in Augustine's aphorism, "I believe in order to understand."

Christian thinking takes place within the circle of faith and not from the vantage point of some disinterested observer. We begin by reflecting upon what the community of faith holds to be true about God, Christ, the Holy Spirit and all the other topics that come up for reflection. We seek to understand more fully what it is that is believed. To use an example, we can say that for Augustine we find ourselves in love and then we try to understand that love in which we find ourselves. Reasoning doesn't make us love. Thinking can only help us to understand being in love. What our reflection does is deepen our understanding of the love in which we find ourselves. Our understanding can go deeper, but it is never able to get behind that love and establish it on some other foundation. As we reflect upon things, we hopefully gain greater inward illumination about what we are seeking to understand.

This is especially clear in relation to Augustine's reflection on the Trinity. There is no argument for the Trinity in *De Trinitate*. Rather he is just seeking to understand more deeply how God is one in three and three in one. His explorations of the Trinity are often referred to as a kind of psychological Trinitarianism because in trying to understand the internal relations of the persons of the Trinity, he drew his analogy from the powers of the human mind. When we examine the mind, what we discover are memory, intelligence and understanding. These are powers of the same mind, yet it is possible to distinguish them from one another. Often in *De Trinitate*, he employed analogies from the life of the mind to help us understand how things can be three in one and one in three. There is, said Augustine, this same kind of mystery of three in one within our own psyche.

The other analogy he used is the nature of love, the connection between the lover, the beloved and the love between them. When Augustine analyzes love, he shows it to have a Trinitarian structure. There is the lover and the loved and the love that binds those two things together. This is another way that he tried to talk about the Father and Son and Spirit. The Father is the source of love, the Son is the object of the Father's love and what binds the Father and Son together is love, the Holy Spirit.

These analogies help to show that "three in one" is not a wholly strange notion. We can't know the inner relations between the Father and the Son and the Holy Spirit directly, but we can approach them by analogy. What that does is move our minds towards the reality of the Trinity which we are trying to understand. So while the Trinity always exceeds our grasp in terms of being able to fully explain it, it is very present to our lives and to our experience. There is a kind of distance and closeness for Augustine to the truth about God. We can know by analogy either through the life of the mind or as creatures who love.

Augustine knew that the tradition of Christianity contained this belief in God the Father, Son and Holy Spirit. You meditate upon that belief seeking to find analogies in life that help you see this relationship of the three in one, and in that way the mind is lifted up to contemplation. For Augustine and for the later theological tradition that came after him, the primary purpose of theological reflection is contemplation, and that is the link to understanding. It isn't really an explanation; the best that we can attain is contemplation.

Summary

It is difficult to summarize the significance of Augustine for the great conversation of Christian thought. Part of the reason for this difficulty is the magnitude of his contribution. At the same time, it must be noted that his influence was on Western Christianity and not Eastern Christianity. Indeed, Eastern Christians do not consider Augustine one of the "fathers of the church." They take this more critical view of Augustine because they see in him an emphasis on "original sin" and human sinfulness that skewed his Christian thinking. For Eastern Christianity, the first thing that must always be said of humanity is that we were created in the image of God, the imago dei. This, in the view of his critics, was not characteristic of Augustine. As a result, Augustine did not have a significant impact on Eastern Christianity.

But in the West, he was the premier Christian thinker down through the Middle Ages and even among the Protestant Reformers. Augustine not only influenced figures like Anselm, Thomas Aquinas, Bonaventure and Hildegard of Bingen but was also the Christian thinker most often cited by Martin Luther—who was an Augustinian monk—and Jean Calvin during the Reformation. His *City of God* and *Confessions* are the most widely read texts of Western Christianity. These writings provided a view of humanity in relation to God in both individual and social terms that was determinative for Western Christianity.

Review

1. What are the principal writings of Augustine?
2. What did Augustine mean when he spoke of the "disordered soul"?
3. Why is the heart "restless until it comes to rest in God"?
4. What is the "Eastern critique" of Augustine?

Chapter 10

Eastern Voices

Wisdom in the East

EARLIER, IN OUR DISCUSSION of the ecumenical councils, we encountered the Cappadocian fathers—Basil the Great (330-379), Gregory of Nazianzus (329-389) and Gregory of Nyssa (334-395)—and their contribution of the language of ousia/hypostasis to the Christological and Trinitarian debates between the Council of Nicea (325) and the Council of Constantinople (381). In this chapter, we look further at their contributions to the great conversation, as the Cappadocians remain foundational figures in Christian thought in the East. We then look at the later figures of John of Damascus and Gregory of Palamas, figures also important in the great conversation as voices from the East.

The Cappadocian Fathers and Eastern Voices

The Cappadocian fathers—the name comes from a region called Cappadocia in the Byzantine world, now in modern Turkey—had a tremendous impact on Christian thinking, especially in the East and to a lesser extent in the West. Although the official date of division between East and West is 1054, the seeds of that division were sown much earlier. Despite the terminology of East and West, the difference between the Orthodox and the Catholic is not a geographical question but rather a difference in temper of mind and ways of thinking. The Eastern fathers were Greek and wrote in that language, while the formative figures in Western Christianity typically wrote in Latin. It is sometimes said that the Greek-speaking Christian thinkers emphasized the mystical and spiritual dimensions of the faith, and the Latin-speaking Christian thinkers emphasized the moral and rational dimensions. There is some truth in this characterization, but it should not be overstated. Nor should the later categories of Eastern and Western thought obscure the many convergences between Christian thinkers writing in Greek and those writing in Latin. More important than their differences are their actual contributions to that great conversation within the family of Christian traditions.

Basil the Great

Basil came from an aristocratic family and was known for his great organizational abilities. Like Augustine, Basil had been a student of rhetoric, and he had studied in Caesarea, Constantinople and Athens. When he was thirty-four, he reluctantly entered the priesthood and in 370 he became the Bishop of Caesarea, the capital of Cappadocia. He was very influential in the development of monastic rules in Eastern Christianity, while it was Benedict's Rule that came to dominate monasticism in Western Christianity.

At the Council of Nicea in 325, the conflict between Athanasius and Arius had been decided, and the Arian affirmation that "there was a time when the Logos was not" was declared heretical. More affirmatively, Nicea had determined that the Incarnate Word of God, Jesus the Christ, was "one in being with the Father." Basil, along with the two Gregory's—of Nyssa and of Nazianzus—championed this affirmation. Following Athanasius, the Cappadocians believed that unless Christ was fully God, our humanity could not be lifted up into the life of God or made one with God. It was this faith that the Cappadocians defended.

It is said that these Eastern thinkers were very concerned with an ontological anthropology—that is, an understanding of humanity in relation to God. To understand humanity's relationship to God is the way to the real essence of human beings. Basil is thought of as a second Athanasius because he too was concerned about the human condition and the exaltation of the nature of man. As Bishop of Caesarea, he was a social worker, building hospitals and hospices and orphanages. He was also a reformer of the liturgy of the East. He died two years before the second ecumenical council, the Council of Constantinople.

Basil the Great contributed significantly to Christological and Trinitarian thinking with the two words *ousia* and *hypostasis*. Ousia is the Greek term for the essence or substance of God, which is unique and found only in God. Hypostasis, also Greek, means "existence in a particular mode," or the manner of being of each of the persons in the Holy Trinity. It is sometimes said that ousia is the aspect common to the three persons of the Godhead, and hypostasis is the particular mode of the Father, Son or Holy Spirit.

For Basil, the Trinity is one Reality (ousia) or Godhead manifest in three distinct hypostases or faces. In his view, the Holy Spirit is a distinct manifestation of God, rather than—as taught by later Western Christianity—being generated by God the Father and the Son.

Gregory of Nazianzus

Gregory was a close friend of Basil's. They had been students together, and Gregory, like Basil, came from an aristocratic family. Also like Basil, Gregory was a humanistic Christian thinker and a great orator. Gregory was fascinated with monasticism, which was flourishing in his time. This monasticism had little to do with withdrawal from the world and more to do with the rigorous pursuit of spiritual depth. He would later write a collection of the wisdom of the "Desert Fathers."

Against his will, his father ordained Gregory a priest. He subsequently disappeared for a number of years. He later regretted his action and returned to serve as a priest and then bishop in a small town. He was persuaded to serve as the Bishop of Constantinople, where he remained for two years before returning to his small town and later retiring to his family estates. Gregory was a reflective person who preferred to live a quiet life and write poetry. However, while in Constantinople he wrote and delivered five important speeches/sermons on the divinity of the Word. It is for these sermons, often called the *Theological Orations*, that Gregory is known.

In his Orations, Gregory of Nazianzus expressed a characteristic conviction of the Cappadocians in relation to God:

> *It is difficult to conceive God, but to define him in words is an impossibility . . . In my opinion it is impossible to express him, and yet more impossible to conceive him . . . even to those who are highly exalted, and who love God.*[1]

Here Gregory is writing against the Eunomians, who held to an extreme Arianism that claimed that Christological questions could be settled by "simple reason," since it was clear to them that "the Father is greater than the Son and that the Son is subordinate to the Father." Gregory ridiculed their views. Yet, he insisted, I must not be misunderstood . . . For we ought to think of God even more often than we draw our breath . . . It is not the

---

1. See Hardy, *Christology of the Later Fathers*, 138.

continual remembrance of God that I would hinder, but only the talking about God . . . when unreasonable . . . without reverence.[2]

However, reverential thinking about God does not make for easy conceptualization of God. "It is one thing to be persuaded of the existence of a thing," said Gregory, "and quite another to know what it is."[3] At the same time, Gregory believed that it is our nature as human beings to "long for God . . . but [be] unable to grasp him."[4] God so surpasses us as to be wondrously beyond us. This is the point he made in the first two Orations. It is only in the third Oration that Gregory actually said what it is possible to say, modestly and reverentially, concerning the Word.

He said that the God we "hold in honour" is a monarchy that is not limited to one person, for it is possible for unity . . . to come into a condition of plurality; but one that is made of an equality of nature, and a union of mind . . . – a thing which is impossible to the created nature—so that though numerically distinct there is no severance of essence. Therefore unity . . . found its rest in trinity. This is what we mean by Father and Son and Holy Ghost."[5]

And, contrary to the Eunomians, Gregory maintained that "there was never a time when" this Trinity "was not."[6] Of course, said Gregory, this concept of the Trinity is difficult to grasp, for these matters related to God "belong to God alone" and do not have analogs "common to other beings."[7] That the Trinity is not temporal is crucial to rightly grasping, albeit in a very limited way, the truth of God. This ineffable reality—the reality of Godhead as Trinity—always exceeds us. Gregory then proceeded to argue that this eternal Word assumed our humanity for "our salvation" and "in order that I too might be made God so far as he is made man."[8] In quoting Athanasius, Gregory aligned himself with that view of sanctification as deification that is characteristic of Eastern Christian thought.

Gregory of Nyssa

Gregory of Nyssa was a younger brother of Basil and their elder sister Macrina. From this well-to-do Christian family with ten children came

2. Ibid., 130-31.
3. Ibid., 139.
4. Ibid., 145.
5. Ibid., 161.
6. Ibid., 163.
7. Ibid., 167.
8. Ibid., 173.

three bishops and the remarkable Macrina, whose intellect and devotion had a great impact on her younger brothers. Educated at home and in local schools, Gregory was initially not inclined to the religious life. He became, like Augustine and his brother Basil, a professor of rhetoric and was married for a time. But under the influence of Gregory of Nazianzus, who was a friend, as well as his brother Basil and sister Macrina, he gave up secular life and followed his brother and sister into the monastery.

He devoted himself to prayer and study and was especially influenced by the writings of Origen. In 372, he was made a bishop and dragged into the doctrinal and political squabbles of his time. He followed Basil in his commitment to Nicea, and defended the fullness of Christ's divinity against Arian views and the fullness of Christ's humanity against Apollinarian views. He was deposed from his seat as bishop but then restored to his see at Nyssa, where the people of his diocese met him with great joy. He was in Constantinople for the ecumenical council of 381.

Gregory was primarily an intellectual given to a life of prayer, study and writing. But his position as bishop led him to spend most of his energies writing against "the enemies of truth." This was the phrase he used in his major work *On Not Three Gods*, in which he joined the Cappadocians in defense of the Nicean faith. Here, Gregory acknowledged that the question of the Trinity is "very difficult to deal with." But even "if our rather feeble powers of reason prove unequal to the problem, we must guard the tradition we have received from the Fathers as ever sure and immovable, and seek from the Lord a means of defending our faith." It would seem, Gregory acknowledged, that "we must say there are three gods," but he rejected this as "blasphemy." Further, he says, "we must confess one God, as Scripture bears witness, "Hear, O Israel, the Lord thy God is one Lord" and also "avoid similarity with Greek polytheism." Thus, on the one hand, there is the weight of tradition clearly committed to the belief that God is one. The oneness of God is, for Gregory, a given. But he also did not agree with those who say that if you affirm that God is one, then you "must deny divinity to the Son and the Holy Spirit." Gregory considered that "irreligious and absurd." Thus his treatise was his attempt to show why Christians affirm that God is one even while speaking of God as Father, Son and Holy Spirit.[9]

Gregory spoke about "the divine essence" as "Godhead." And it is this *ousia* or essence (sometimes translated as substance or nature) that is one. He followed Gregory of Nazianzus who earlier had said, "The three are

---

9. See Gregory of Nyssa, 223-326 in Hardy, ed., *Christology of the Later Fathers*, 256-57.

one in Godhead, and the one three in properties."[10] The analogy Gregory of Nyssa used is drawn from the human order, where we speak of a single humanity even though we can enumerate different persons, such as John, Mary and Ephraim. When we name the different persons, we are not claiming that they each have a different nature, said Gregory. Rather, "the nature is one, united in itself, a unit completely indivisible."[11] He goes on to note that it is a common but misleading habit to speak about humanity or "man" in the plural, because humanity is one, since all human beings have the same nature or essence. This mistaken habit should not be continued when speaking of God.

When we speak of the divine essence, the nature of the Godhead, said Gregory, we are encountering a reality that "cannot be named and is ineffable." However, although our language always falls short since the divine nature in itself is ineffable, we can see some of its attributes and operations. Indeed, Gregory argued, we should regard "Godhead" as "an operation and not a nature.[12]" It is that operation of "overseeing and beholding" that is as close as we can get to that divine nature. That "nature, said Gregory,

> is a unity in Father, Son, and Holy Spirit. It issues from the Father, as from a spring. It is actualized by the Son; and its grace is perfected by the power of the Holy Spirit . . . all providence, care and direction of everything, when in the sensible creation or of heavenly nature [is] one and not three . . . the preservation of what exists, the rectifying of what is amiss, the instruction of what is set right, is directed by the holy Trinity . . . it is not divided into three parts according to the number of the Persons acknowledged by the faith.[13]

It is, he continued, "the unity of operation" that "forbids the plural number" in relation to the unity of the Godhead. Again, even this term Godhead is inadequate, since the "divine nature is unlimited and incomprehensible;" it "entirely transcends every name for it and one of these names is 'Godhead.'" Thus, remembering that the reality of God knows no limitation, we can see that the term Godhead "*does not divide the unity into duality so as to call the Father and the Son two gods . . . The Father is God and the Son is God; and yet by the same affirmation God is one, because no distinction of nature or of operation is to be observed in the Godhead.*"[14]

---

10. Ibid., 199.
11. Ibid., 258.
12. Ibid., 259 and 261.
13. Ibid., 263.
14. Ibid., 264 and 266.

This is difficult going, as Gregory was well aware. And of course Gregory wanted to have it both ways: he wanted to affirm that God is one and yet that God is three persons, or hypostases, without falling into Greek polytheism. Did he succeed? Many of his contemporaries, and later generations, were persuaded that he did.

Gregory's writings were not limited to these highly complicated arguments concerning the divine trinity. He wrote many other things as well, including his *Making of Humanity* and his *Address on Religious Instruction*. In the *Address on Religious Instruction*, Gregory saw himself as threading "the mean between Judaism and Hellenism" in "our teaching on the knowledge of God." The task of religious instruction is, said Gregory, an "essential duty of the leaders" but it must be "adapted to the diversities" of one's audience. For the person of a "Jewish faith has certain presuppositions; a man reared in Hellenism, others" and one must put forward "reasonable propositions in each discussion so that the truth may finally emerge."[15] This sensitivity to his audience is striking in Gregory and helps to clarify who he was addressing in his writings.

Keeping the needs of his audience in mind, Gregory turned to expound the "doctrine of God and His Word," showing that "God's living Word is active and creative—a doctrine the Jew does not accept; and we admit no distinction in nature between the Word and Him from whom it comes." God then creates humanity "to participate in the divine goodness." Thus Gregory went on to say that creation can be summed up "in a single expression": humanity is created in the image of God. Furthermore, "our nature in its origin was good and set in the midst of goodness even though "human life is at present in an unnatural condition." Our present suffering is not an argument, said Gregory, against God or our creation in "a state of goodness." We must look elsewhere for the existence of evil. Where? Gregory said that when we were created in God's image, we were created with "the gift of liberty and free will." Evil arises "from within . . . it has its origin in the will, when the soul withdraws from the good." Gregory went on to explain:

> For as sight is an activity of nature and blindness is a privation . . . so virtue is in this way opposed to vice. For the origin of evil is not otherwise to be conceived than as the absence of virtue . . . God is not the cause of your present woes. For he made your nature independent and free. The cause is rather your thoughtlessness in choosing the worse instead of the better.[16]

---

15. Ibid., 273 and 269.
16. Ibid., 272, 276, 277-78.

Now the consequence is that we "became associated with evil [or] wickedness," which is "the privation of the good." Gregory then went to considerable length in trying to explain how our humanity, meant for goodness, comes to such a "pitiful and wretched state." He saw our original intelligent nature mixed with the sensible, our light dimmed by passion, our life marked by death, but he never gave up on our humanity created in the divine image. Rather, he saw that the solution is the Incarnation, which has its reason in "the love of man . . . a proper mark of the divine nature" and the "explanation . . . the reason for God's presence among men. Our nature was sick and needed a doctor. Man had fallen and needed someone to raise him up. He who had lost life needed someone to restore it."[17]

It is striking that Gregory saw the reason for the incarnation as the restoration of our humanity rather than the forgiveness of sins. In a remarkable passage, Gregory wrote,

> *There is no good reason for those who do not take too narrow a view of things to find anything strange in the fact that God assumed our nature. For when he considers the universe, can anyone be so simple-minded as not to believe that the Divine is present in everything, pervading, embracing, and penetrating it? For all things depend on him who is, and nothing can exist which does not have its being in him who is. If, then, all things exist in him and he exists in all things, why are they shocked at a scheme of revelation which teaches that God became man, when we believe that even now he is not external to man? For granted that God is not present in us in the same way as he was in the incarnation, it is at any rate admitted he is equally present in us in both instances. In the one case he is united to us in so far as he sustains existing things. In the other case he united himself with our nature, in order that by its union with the Divine it might become divine, being rescued from death and freed from the tyranny of the adversary. For with his return from death, our mortal race begins its return to immortal life.*[18]

Gregory's tone of sweet reasonableness in discussing the incarnation and the divinization of our humanity is disarming in its frankness and clarity. But that should not blind us to the astonishing claims he was making for the Christian revelation—claims concerning the incarnation, the omnipresence of God and the divinization of humanity. These claims are central themes for Eastern voices. Said Gregory, "This is the sort of teaching we derive from the mighty revelation of God's becoming man." And even Christ's

17. Ibid., 282, 291, 290–91.
18. Ibid., 302.

death on the cross is, for Gregory, part of God's assuming of our nature. It reveals the fullness of God's love for humanity so that "by the resurrection" our humanity was "exalted."[19]

Like Origen, Gregory was indebted to Greek philosophy, and he was unusually successful in keeping it in the service of his Christian faith. In some of his early homilies, Gregory employed the Platonic image of the ladder of ascent to the realm of the pure forms in speaking about the ascent of the soul to God. This ascent, according to Gregory, involves three stages. The first is freedom from the slavery of passion, the second is the stage of knowledge (gnosis in Greek) where one passes from the visible to the invisible, and the third is the stage of contemplation (theoria in Greek) of divine things. But for Gregory, we can never reach the essence of God, so we find ourselves in "divine darkness"—our contemplation of divine things is always limited. The idea of "divine darkness" is a theme later developed in Dionysius and found in other Eastern voices as well. But Gregory did not hide in the invisible. He returned to the Eucharist as the context for the fullness of the human relationship to God. His view of the Eucharist is striking as he argued that in "eating and drinking" Christ's "body and blood" we are incorporated into his transforming immortality.

This may seem a surprising turn. However, it illustrates the way Gregory saw the fullness of divine-human relations in the context of the liturgy and the Eucharist. In these, we have a glimpse of the kingdom of God. The Eucharist is not a mere rite but an occasion where humanity enters into a spiritual relationship with the divine. It is through the "body and blood of Christ" in the Eucharist, said Gregory, that we receive "life-giving grace," for when "the body which God made immortal enters ours, it entirely transforms it into itself." It is in the Eucharist that "the body of Christ [gives] life to all mankind." Thus in Gregory of Nyssa's writings, we can see clearly that, unlike later Protestant views, earlier Christian views of the Eucharist focused on its sacrificial character and made the Eucharist a life-transforming foretaste of the Kingdom of Heaven.[20]

With his works on Christology, on the Holy Spirit, against Arianism and so on, Gregory showed that he was the theoretician of the group. His work helped to pave the way for the councils of Ephesus and Chalcedon. He defined the language of *hypostasis* and clarified the terminology for speaking of the Trinity. He saw that there were two natures in Christ, one divine and one human, but that they were unified in essence. He contributed to the

---

19. Ibid., 304 and 310.
20. Ibid., 318-19.

merging of philosophy with the Christian faith. In many respects, it was the Cappadocian fathers who Christianized Hellenistic thought.

The Cappadocian's were noted for their stress on the view that humanity was made according to the image of God. Humanity is, in essence, the "imago dei," and no matter what human beings do, they remain essentially the image of God. Similarly, the incarnation is a rediscovery of the primordial humanity of Adam, his creation in God's image. The incarnation thus reconfirms the dignity of humanity. The Cappadocian fathers' view is very different from Augustine's. As a consequence, the whole notion of salvation took a very different direction in Eastern Christianity than in Western Christianity.

John of Damascus (674–749)

Perhaps the most remarkable Christian thinker between the fifth and the tenth century, John of Damascus made substantial contributions to the great conversation within Christianity. He lived in a time that saw the emergence of Islam, a dynamic new religion that spread from the Arabian Peninsula into the Middle East and across North Africa. Writing in the context of the changing Byzantine world after the emergence of this vital new religious movement, he was one of the first Christian thinkers to react to Islam. Muslims regarded Muhammad (570–632) as the last great prophet of Allah, the Arabic name for God. The cry of the Muslim was la illaha allah illah, "There is no God but Allah," followed by "Muhammad is his Messenger." Islam taught a radical and uncompromising monotheism that challenged Christian thinking with its now Trinitarian assumptions—Allah, says Islam, has no second or Son.

John of Damascus was a tax collector for a Muslim caliph, but he converted to Christianity and entered a monastery near Jerusalem where he lived and wrote until his death. Eastern Christian monasticism had been flourishing for several centuries by the time of John of Damascus. Centred in the western region of modern-day Syria and spreading up into southeastern Turkey and down into Israel, these monks had created distinctive patterns of life and, occasionally, lasting works of Christian thought. Simeon Stylites (c. fifth century) had come out of this corner of the Christian world and was famous for having spent much of his life on a raised platform in the Syrian desert. The monks often lived solitary lives, though hundreds of small cells may have dotted a particular valley or rock face in the desert. They gained reputations for sanctity and holiness and were often sought out for spiritual counsel while living—and for relics when they died. John of Damascus, who lived for years in a cell southwest of Jerusalem, was part of this often strange and peculiar world. His great work, the *Fount of Knowledge*, was in three parts.

After appreciating Aristotle and identifying more than 100 heresies of various kinds, John turned in the third volume to an exposition of the Orthodox way, especially focusing on the definition of the two natures of Christ.

John's account of Jesus Christ in the *Fount of Knowledge* is remarkable and impressive. It takes with absolute seriousness the Council of Chalcedon with its twin affirmations that Jesus Christ was "fully divine" and "fully human." John the Damascene, as he was known, wrote of Jesus Christ, we do not say that man became God, but that God became man. For while he was by nature perfect God, the same became by nature perfect man. He did not change his nature and neither did he just appear to become man. On the contrary, without confusion or alteration or division he became hypostatically united to the rationally and intellectually animated flesh which he had from the holy Virgin and which had its existence in him.[21]

In addition, he continued, "The natures were united to each other without change and without alteration." He underscored the importance of understanding the terms of the discussion of the nature of Christ and his relationship to God with intellectual precision as well as spiritual insight. He wrote, "we have repeatedly said that substance is one thing and person another, and that substance means the common species including the persons that belong to the same species—as for example, God, man—while person indicates an individual as Father, Son, Holy Spirit, Peter, Paul. One must furthermore know that the terms divinity and humanity are indicative of the substance or natures ... Since, then, in our Lord Jesus Christ we recognize two natures in one composite Person for both, when we are considering the natures, we call them divinity and humanity."[22]

In the Protestant world, which we will encounter later, Christian thinking about God is often thinking about Christ, and the focus is on the second person of the Trinity. But in the older, longer traditions, thinking about Christ is to lead us to think about God.

During the iconoclastic controversy of his time, John of Damascus wrote the most able defense of using icons and images. He wrote,

> Since not all know letters nor do all have leisure to read, the Fathers deemed it fit that these events [of Scripture] should be depicted as a sort of memorial and terse reminder. It certainly happens ... that we may see the image of his crucifixion and, being thus reminded of his saving Passion, fall down and adore. But it

---

21. See the selections on John of Damascus in Kerr, *Readings in Christian Thought*, 68-69.

22. Ibid., 69 and 71.

> is not the material we adopt, but that which is represented ... the
> honour paid to the image redounds to the original.[23]

At the Second Council of Nicea in 787, the veneration of icons was allowed while their worship was forbidden. The Council followed John's distinction that it was not the icon itself but that towards which it pointed that was being adored. This crucial distinction saved icons from destruction.

It is said that Thomas Aquinas had John's *Fount of Knowledge* close at hand six centuries later when he was writing his *Summa Theologica*. For John of Damascus, Christianity is the image of Christ. Christians are the ones who reflect the divine life on earth—that fullness of the image of God can now be depicted for you and me.

Gregory of Palamas: The Divine Energies

To conclude this chapter on Eastern voices, I now leap ahead to Gregory of Palamas (1296–1359), certainly the greatest Byzantine or Eastern thinker of medieval times. His work further developed the Eastern tradition and clarified the understanding of the spiritual quest characteristic of Eastern Christianity.

Gregory had grown up in the Byzantine court but abandoned court life and became a monk. He also persuaded the rest of his family—his mother, two sisters and two brothers—to do the same. He became a priest at thirty, in 1326, and the Archbishop of Thessalonica in 1347 after a highly turbulent and controversial life defending the Hesychast (contemplative prayer/quietness) movement.

The central themes of Eastern Christian thought—the incomprehensibility of God and the deification of humanity—were at the heart of Gregory's thinking as he dealt with issues arising in his own time. Central to his thinking was the notion of divine *energeiai*—divine energies and operations. He argued that while the divine essence—Father, Son and Holy Spirit in the Eastern tradition—remained inaccessible, there was an intermediate reality of divine *energeiai*, or divine love and light, between God and the creations of God: world, human beings and all creatures. Basil the Great had written nearly a thousand years earlier that it was "from his energeiai [that] we know our God," while God's essence remained inaccessible.

What are these divine energies and operations? They are God's love and light, and we grow towards God by participating in these divine energies and operations. It is by participating in the divine love that we grow

---

23. Ibid., 73.

towards God and are divinized or made one with God. Gregory used an analogy to describe these energies:

> *The divine and uncreated grace and energeiai of God is, being indivisibly divided, like the sun's ray, which warms and lightens and vivifies and increases its own splendour in what it enlightens, and shines forth in the eyes of its beholders.*[24]

Thus, Gregory filled the seeming gap between the incomprehensible God and the human task of deification by linking God to humanity through the divine energeiai. We move towards God as we participate in the divine light and love.

In Gregory's time, the Hesychast (hesychia means inward quiet or stillness) movement within the Greek monastic world came under fire. The monks of Mount Athos, the most famous of all Greek monastic centres, had for centuries claimed to experience the Uncreated Light, or divine energeiai, in their meditative practice. Earlier, Symeon the New Theologian (c. 1000) had written about the experience of the monks. So enthralled by his experience, Symeon had written that "those who have not seen this Light, have not seen God: for God is Light." Such views tended to limit "real" Christianity to those who had had such an experience, to an elite. The consequence was that some sought to dismiss the whole Hesychast movement, with its emphasis on the recitation of the Jesus prayer—"Lord Jesus Christ, have mercy on me . . . "—and breathing and meditative techniques. Gregory responded with his *Defense of Those Who Practise Sacred Quietude*, the most important of all his writings. It is, says John Meyendorff, "a major witness to the content and meaning of Christian experience."

While God remained transcendent for Gregory, as for the entire Orthodox tradition, it is essential that our humanity be in communion with God, since to be fully human is to be in communion with God. Gregory wrote that it is in Christ that we know our full humanity:

> *The Son of God, in his incomparable love for man, did not only unite His divine Hypostasis with our nature, by clothing Himself in a living body and soul . . . but also united himself . . . with the human hypostases themselves, in mingling himself with each of the faithful by communion with his Holy Body, and . . . becomes one single body with us . . . and makes us a temple of the undivided divinity . . . how should he not illuminate those who commune worthily with the divine ray of His Body which is within us, lightening our souls, as He illumined the very bodies of the disciples on Mount*

---

24. See Meyerdorff, *The Byzantine Legacy in the Orthodox Church*, especially the sections on Gregory Palamas and the Hesychasts, 167-94.

> *Tabor? . . . but now [Christ, the uncreated light] since it is mingled with us and exists in us, it illuminates the soul from within.*[25]

This explanation is difficult to follow, but it helps to see it as a defense of the Hesychasts and their experience of the transfiguring light of God. For the Hesychasts, it is our participation in the divine energies that brings us into communion with God. Thus our humanity is deified by its participation in Christ.

The two great traditions of Eastern and Western Christianity were estranged at the time, and these words were not heard in the West. However, in the East, the Orthodox tradition continued to develop, not as new or novel views, but as a deepening of the wisdom that had already been given in the writings of the early Fathers. The writings of Gregory of Palamas are laced with quotations from Basil the Great, Gregory of Nyssa, Maximus the Confessor (580–662), John of Damascus and many others who remain, in the East, the fountain of Christian wisdom and thinking.

Summary

The contributions of these Eastern voices to the great conversation of Christian thought are enormous. They provided not only some of the central terms for the articulation of Trinitarian thought, but also an exposition of the Christian faith that has remained foundational and normative for the Orthodox world. Characterized by a prayerful ethos centred on the majesty of the Creator, the miracle of the incarnation and the mystery of the divinization of humanity, the Eastern voices have endured. Orthodox thinkers turn time and time again to the early Fathers for direction in addressing issues that arise in later times. They are convinced that the wisdom found there is for the ages.

Review

1. Who were the "Cappadocian Fathers"?
2. What is the significance of "ousia" and "hypostasis" for Christian thinking?
3. Why is the *Fount of Knowledge* important in Christian thought?
4. What is the meaning of "hesychast"?

---

25. Meyendorff, *The Byzantine Legacy in the Orthodox Church*, 189 for this quote of Gregory Palamas.

Chapter 11

Benedict and the Rise of Monasticism, Boethius and the Via Positiva, Dionysius and the Via Negativa

OFTEN IN HISTORIES OF Christian thought, the 600-year period from Augustine to Anselm is passed over in silence. During that period, there is no large and important thinker like Augustine, a watershed figure in the history of Western Christian thought, or Anselm, the last great monastic thinker and a forerunner of the great schoolmen of the medieval world. While there were important developments during this period, they tend to be skipped over because they are not easily summarized in a particular outstanding theological figure. These developments happened slowly and over long periods of time. The first and most important was the rise of monasticism in the West. Benedict of Nursia (480-547) was crucial in this development.

Augustine died in 430 at a time when the Vandals were overtaking the city of Hippo, where he had been bishop for many, many years. In the centuries after his death, often referred to as the "Dark Ages," the Christian Church played a very large social role. The Church was the most developed institution in the Western world during this period, and the new institution of monasticism was central to its significant role.

There were Christian monks long before the time of Benedict—the Desert Fathers of Egypt, Syria and Judea—but Benedict is important because he fashioned the monastic rule that proved to be immensely successful in Western Christianity. He provided a structure that was able to sustain the monastic impulse while being adaptable enough to meet a variety of situations.

Monasticism is the quest for union with God through prayer and penance and separation from the world pursued by men or women sharing a communal life. Benedict is the founder of Western monasticism. His twin-sister, St. Scholastica, is considered the founder of the monastic orders for women in the West. Benedict was educated in Rome, where he was appalled by the vice in which his fellow students reveled. As a consequence, Benedict abandoned his studies and entered upon a single-minded quest for God. Initially the route that Benedict chose was one of solitude. Later on, as Benedict's reputation as a wise and spiritual man spread, he began to instruct others in the way of virtue.

It is said that when he became well known as a spiritual master, he was approached by some other solitary monks and invited to come and be their teacher and master. But Benedict said no. He wouldn't do it because they would not like his rule. However, they prevailed, and he did finally go and become their teacher and spiritual master. But, the legend continues, after a period of time some of the monks weren't happy with the rule he tried to impose on their life. One evening at supper, as Benedict lifted his cup to his mouth, it shattered. He was thus miraculously saved from being poisoned to death. He went away. But the monks later prevailed upon him to try again and the second time he was very successful. In his own life time and afterwards, the monastic movement grew very rapidly. It spread across Western Christianity largely on the basis of the rule that he formulated.

Christian monasticism is the quest for union with God. In pursuit of God, the earlier desert monks tended to live solitary lives. Benedict's great innovation was to generate a common life that became the context which could sustain this quest for union with God. He found a workable solution to handle both the individual and communal dimensions of the quest. Of course, the monastic life was to be pursued apart from and separated from the world, but wherever the monasteries were located there still needed to be some structure for the community. In the Benedictine Rule the heart of common life in the monastery was the Opus Dei—the Work of God.

The Opus Dei was a structured form of worship around which the whole day revolved. Eight periods of communal prayer would occur each and every day. The cycle began with Vigil at 2 a.m., followed by Lauds at daybreak (this is the summer schedule in Italy so around 4:30 a.m.), the service of Prime at 6 a.m. then Tierce at 9 a.m., Sext at noon, None at 3.p.m., Vespers at sundown and Compline at dark. One's life within the community was structured around these periods of formal prayer and communal worship. The aim was union with God, and to pursue that goal one lived within a community whose very life was structured in a way that would constantly redirect one's life towards this transcendent purpose. This daily structure of prayer helped to restructure the self and to organize the life of the community. It became the daily habit and pattern of one's life. Of course, this structure doesn't magically transform people, but it puts them in a context where they are constantly reminded that their purpose is union with God.

In addition to these daily hours of worship and spiritual work, manual labour was also very important in the Benedictine monasteries. The monk spent some part of everyday doing manual labour: working in the gardens or the kitchens, building or tending fields, caring for the animals. Every day involved some kind of manual labour. The third component of life within the Benedictine monastery was intellectual labour. Time was spent reading the Fathers, Christian writings and sometimes other writers. Later, work also included copying the manuscripts and in that way learning while preserving what had gone before and what other people had said about spiritual matters.

The Benedictine monasteries grew extremely rapidly, spreading through what is now Italy and then throughout the Western world in the centuries after Benedict's death. The rule that he gave was very successful because it was simple and adaptable. The rule was centred on a single virtue which was considered to lie at the heart of the monastic life: the virtue of obedience. Something has happened in modern cultures such that we don't think of obedience as a virtue any more. But for Benedict it was an essential virtue in attaining union with God. In Benedict's worldview, disorder and alienation from God came into the world as a result of disobedience—disobedience to the divine command in the Garden at humanity's beginning. In the prologue to the Rule, Benedict wrote, "Through the labour of obedience you may return to Him from whom you have withdrawn because of the laziness of disobedience."[1] It was, he argued, essential that humanity regain what had been lost. This source of disorder which was disobedience had to be rooted out and replaced with the virtue of obedience

Obedience to the Abbot is at the heart of the Benedictine order. The term Abbot comes from "Abba" or Father. It was the term that Jesus used to speak of God. In the monastery, the Abbot fulfilled this role. He was to be the beneficent father under whom one's life unfolded. This emphasis on the centrality of obedience is reflected in the opening words of Benedict's prologue to the Rule of St. Benedict:

> *Listen my son, and with your heart hear the principles of your Master. Readily accept and faithfully follow the advice of a loving Father, so that through the labour of obedience you may return to Him from whom you have withdrawn because of the laziness of disobedience.*

1. Benedict, *The Rule of St. Benedict*, 43.

> *My words are meant for you, whoever you are, who laying aside your own will, take up the all-powerful and righteous arms of obedience to figure under the true King, the Lord Jesus Christ."* [2]

What becomes obvious as he goes on is that for Benedict the source of humanity's misfortune lies in disobedience. Within Christian thinking there are differing understandings of the fall, but in Benedict's view the heart of the Christian doctrine of the fall is disobedience. Consequently, the reversal of that situation comes about by restoring obedience to the heart of the Christian life, or to the life of those who would seek perfection. Thus Benedict said,

> *Let us encompass ourselves with faith and the practice of good works, and guided by the Gospel, tread the path he has cleared for us. Thus may we deserve to see Him, who has called us into His Kingdom . . . If we wish to be sheltered in this Kingdom, it can be reached only through our good conduct.*[3]

This was Benedict's hope and vision. He continued,

> *We are about to open a school for God's service, in which we hope nothing harsh or oppressive will be detected . . . As our lives and faith progress, the heart expands and with the sweetness of love we move down the paths of God's commandments. Never departing from His guidance, remaining in the monastery until death, we patiently share in Christ's passion, so we may eventually enter into the Kingdom of God.*[4]

Here perfection is understood as union with God. Within the monastic community obedience is to Christ, the Master, and to God. But it is the Abbot who—in theory and often in actuality—exercises complete control over the life of the monks. Now the power given to the Abbot is not to be understood as mere despotism, as Benedict goes to great pains to point out. In giving the Abbot complete control over the life of the monks, he also makes the Abbot the one who is responsible for how the lives of the monks turn out. Benedict reminds abbots that at the Day of Judgement they will be held accountable not only for their own actions but also for what has happened to those under their charge. So, the Abbot is to exercise not mere control but control understood as the embodiment of the loving beneficence that characterizes the Divine Father. Benedict wrote,

---

2. Ibid.
3. Ibid., 44.
4. Ibid., 45.

> *To be qualified to govern a monastery as abbot he should always remember what he is called [Abba=Father] and carry out his high calling in his everyday life. In a monastery he is Christ's representative . . . the abbot should not command, teach or demand anything contrary to the way of the Lord . . . The Abbot should always remember that he will be held accountable on Judgement Day for his teaching and the obedience of his charges . . . The abbot shall not make distinction among the people in the monastery.*[5]

Within the context of the monastic community, the monks take the vows of obedience, poverty and chastity or celibacy. All are understood as spiritual disciplines which foster and assist in the quest for union with God. Through obedience one's will is remade in that one is taught to give up a self-will and instead heed the will of the Abbot who mediates to the monks the Divine will as it is reflected in Scripture. Benedict's Rule says, "The first degree of humility is prompt obedience." Chapter 4 of the Rule lists the "instruments of good works" that begin: "1 To love the Lord God with all our heart, soul, and strength, 2. To love one's neighbour as oneself . . . 8. to respect all men . . . 14 to comfort the poor . . . 28. to speak the truth with heart and lips . . . 47 to see death before one daily . . . 65. not to be jealous or envious . . . 70. to pray for one's enemies for the love of Christ." Monks take on the vow of poverty in order to wean themselves from the world and thereby place in the centre of their lives aspiration for a transcendent end or goal. Benedict says, "The vice of private ownership must be uprooted from the monastery. No one . . . shall dare give, receive or keep anything . . . nothing at all."[6] The vow of chastity or celibacy again signals the monks' separation from the human community and the possibility of family life so that they can devote themselves wholly to this transcendent quest.

The other distinctive mark of the monasteries that Benedict brought into being was that one became attached to a particular monastery for life. You became a monk only after a period of time in which it was determined if you were suitable for monastic life, but when that was determined and you took your final vows, then you were there for life. This of course gave the monasteries a remarkable degree of stability. In their earliest stages, monastic communities were small: small groups of men under Benedict and other abbots and small groups of women under his sister Scholastica and other abbesses. But as the monasteries and nunneries grew, they became much, much larger institutions. In the beginning membership ranged from

---

5. Ibid., 48.
6. Ibid., 52-54 and 76.

twelve to twenty people in a particular monastery, but later on membership in monasteries numbered in the hundreds.

Initially, the monasteries were always in the "wilderness." Only much later did some of them get established in urban centres. Benedict was in Italy and there is not much desert in Italy, but there are wilder places. Even when you drive through Italy today, you see the monasteries that were set high in the mountains so that traffic between them and the surrounding culture would be very difficult, or in out-of-the-way places. Ironically, the success of the monasteries tended to encourage settlement in those places, and sometimes small towns and even cities would grow up around the monasteries. In England the monasteries were sometimes established on swampy islands or remote islands along the coast. Ely was first a monastery in the fens in England that could be reached only by boat through marshy lands. But because of the success of the monastery in draining and farming the land, large areas of the fens became more easily occupied and towns grew up around the monasteries.

But the idea was to get away from the world, which was regarded as a place of temptation where all the other things that come into one's life would make it impossible to pursue the life of prayer and obedience. The monasteries were pretty much self-supporting and eventually produced a surplus. They often became centres for baking bread, milling grain, making wine, carding wool and curing cheese. These things were all important within the monks' own life in the monastery, but they also had more than they could use in their monastic life. The irony of these developments is that by pursuing their vows in a place apart, the monks ended up generating more wealth. The monasteries became centres of economic success and, later, of temporal power. There were periodic waves of reform in the history of monasticism as the monks tried to recapture the original ideal and find ways of divesting the community of the wealth and influence that it had achieved.

Within the monastery, there was an attempt to establish harmony and balance between the tasks of worship and work—understood as manual labour as well as spiritual and intellectual work. These were all aspects of one's quest for union with God. Augustine had denied the possibility of our achieving perfection in the larger society, but the drive for perfection was an important part of the monastic movement. It took root in these small communities of people who understood the quest for perfection as spiritual growth in terms of the capacity of the soul for union with God. The left the larger society or cultural sphere to other forces because they didn't believe that it was possible to bring a perfect social order into being. But within their small communities, they could attain a degree of perfection—inward and spiritual—that was not possible in the larger world.

The stress on intellectual activity as an aspect of work bore fruit in some surprising ways in subsequent centuries. The monasteries thus emerged as the central institution for the development of Christian thought over the next several hundred years. While the monasteries abhorred speculative thought, they nonetheless pursued an interiorizing of the spiritual writings of early Christianity. The monasteries became important centres of learning, in part because they copied the ancient manuscripts and in that way retained classical civilization and made it available to subsequent generations. And from time to time the monasteries produced some remarkable Christian thinkers, one of whom, Dionysius, we shall meet below.

It is also remarkable how quickly this new movement spread. Within a century of Benedict's death there were Benedictine monasteries across the Christian world. When they moved to the edges of the Roman world they flourished, but in somewhat different forms, in their contact with what has been called Celtic Christianity.

Three Lights in the Dark Ages

Boethius (480–525) a Roman Senator and Christian philosopher, the obscure Syrian monk whom we know as Dionysius (c. 500) and John Scotus Eriugena (800–877) reflected major tendencies in Christian thought during the period between Augustine and Anselm. These three men worked against the background of dark times in the history of Western civilization, though the Byzantine world of Eastern Christianity remained much stronger.

The Christian Church changed profoundly after Constantine made it the preferred religion of the Roman Empire, and it continued to change yet again after the fall of Rome in 430. Increasingly, much more than any other institution, it bore the idea of a universal civilization in the West and gave whatever substance there was to that notion. Or at least, that was the fantasy that lay hidden in its shadow.

Boethius (480–525)

Boethius was a contemporary of Benedict, perhaps born in the same year, but they don't have any relationship with each other. Boethius was born into a distinguished Roman family, and in his education was deeply influenced by the Neoplatonic tradition and knew the works of Plato and Aristotle. When Boethius became a Christian, he was coming into the community that was at the heart of the cultural life of his time. Because of his background in Greek philosophy, Boethius was responsible for giving a degree of clarity to much of the language of Christian thinking that was to loom so large later during the time of the schoolmen. Boethius examined the language of providence and fate, of person and nature, of desire and the good, of time and eternity and gave these terms clarity of definition and meaning. What is significant about him is how he understood the relationship between faith and reason—a perennial issue that would be returned to repeatedly throughout Christian thought.

For Boethius faith and reason are ultimately one. There is no contradiction or even, in the end, significant difference between them. This conviction is reflected in a famous text of Boethius's called *The Consolation of Philosophy*, written when he was in prison where he was very despondent and downhearted. He tells us that in the midst of that setting he was visited by a gorgeous lady, Lady Philosophy, who awakened him from his desolate slumber and led him to think about his situation and about some very fundamental questions, especially in relation to the notion of providence. Lady Philosophy promised to lead Boethius "to true happiness, to the goal your mind has dreamed of."[7]

The Consolation of Philosophy is in some ways a curious text, combining prose, poetry and dialogue in the exchange between Lady Philosophy, the embodiment of wisdom, and Boethius, the prisoner. It has puzzled scholars because there are hardly any explicit Christian images in this book. There is no reference to Christ, for example, though there is a great deal of talk about God. Some people see it as a text of philosophy not having much to do with Christian thought. But I think if we read it that way we miss the point. It is a book about the quest for human happiness, a happiness that is to be found in God, the Supreme Good. Even in the midst of human suffering, even—as Boethius found—in imprisonment, the highest end of humanity could be reached. For the highest good is not a matter of worldly success, fame or outward freedom, but the pursuit of wisdom and attaining God. In *The Consolation of Philosophy*, Boethius "acknowledges the truth of Philosophy's doctrine that true happiness and the perfect good are the same and are to be found only in God."[8] But it is not something that Boethius comes to easily, since he remains puzzled by the seeming injustice of the evil prospering while the good suffer. But Philosophy also addresses this point and, in the end, Boethius wins through to insight.

Boethius and many people of his time maintained the conviction that there was a single rational account of the universe and of a provident and omnipotent God. This was simply the true account of things that could be

---

7. Boethius, *The Consolation of Philosophy*, 42.
8. Ibid., 127.

approached either through faith or through reason. Boethius's approach is that of enlightened reason—of the mind responsive to the highest good which draws us to itself. Here the nature of the world and the nature of God is what it is—and through our minds we can apprehend the way things are and move towards the supreme good which is humanity's true end.

For Boethius, the way of coming at it is to allow the mind to be instructed by wisdom. The Consolation shows Boethius engaging in thought on things and moving by degrees to deeper understandings. For, Boethius remarks, "it would comfort me to understand things."[9] The process begins with the questions that one has and allowing those questions to be explored. The dialogue with wisdom then gives way to still deeper insight. The mind is capable of understanding reality, of moving towards its supreme good and goal. Protestant thinkers would later argue that the mind is so damaged by the fall that it is incapable of knowing the truth of God and the world. This was not Boethius's view. It is possible to know this truth. Boethius presupposed that the mind rises to God when it heeds its own internal dynamic. When a life of virtue and discipline are in place, the mind functions properly because it is fundamentally related to the very structure of reality. Or to say it another way, the same sort of structure that is inherent within the reality of all things is inherent within the mind. Faith and reason are, at most, different ways of moving towards the same end, but there is no fundamental conflict between the truth of faith and the truth of reason. And, as a matter of fact, our reason can bring us to that highest of all stages, which is the state of contemplation.

When Boethius first encountered Lady Philosophy, he "*lay there astonished, my eyes staring at the earth, silently waiting to see what she would do . . . When she noticed my grief-stricken, downcast face, she reproved my anxiety with song.*" It began, "*Alas, how this mind is dulled, drowned in the overwhelming depths. It wanders in outer darkness, deprived of its natural light.*" But, she later continued, "*it is time for medicine rather than complaint . . . you have forgotten yourself a little . . . I shall wipe the dark cloud of mortal things from your eyes.*" And Boethius "*was able to see the heavens again when the clouds of my sorrow were swept away; I recovered my judgement and recognized the face of my physician.*"[10]

Nevertheless, Boethius complains to her about his situation in prison, maintaining that he doesn't deserve imprisonment. Lady Philosophy, through a series of questions and statements, gets him to realize that his situation is a distraction. The fact that he is in prison doesn't really matter in

---

9. Ibid., 101.
10. Ibid., 5-7.

terms of what is highest and most important. That is to be gained through inner mental processes which lead the person, whether in prison or whatever other circumstances, to contemplate the higher things and to see things within the context of the providence of God. Once one sees this providential order of things, one realizes that the world of the temporal isn't that important. What is more important is the realm of eternity, which lies beyond the temporal and which the mind can to a certain degree approach and apprehend. By integrating the quest for the good with the quest for God, Boethius had a very large and lasting impact on Western Christian thinking. For Boethius, these were one and the same.

Dionysius (6th century)

Boethius's via positiva or positive way about how reason can bring us to God needs to be contrasted with the position that we find in Dionysius, the via negativa or negative way. Known throughout most of Christian history as Dionysius the Areopagite, this thinker was mistakenly identified with a figure in the book of Acts. Now it is thought that he was a monk from the Syrian tradition. His remarkable writings, including *Divine Names* and *On Celestial Hierarchy*, became the preeminent mystical texts in the West. Like Boethius, he seems to have been aware of and instructed by the Neoplatonic tradition, but he construed this tradition in a different way.

For Dionysius, God is above all attributes and qualities that the mind can discriminate and apprehend. This view was common among Eastern Christians. God is even, said Dionysius, "beyond being itself." He wrote,

> We must not dare to resort to words or conceptions concerning that hidden divinity which transcends being ... the unknowing of what is beyond being is something above and beyond speech, mind or being itself, one should ascribe to it an understanding beyond being. Let us therefore look as far upward as the light of sacred Scripture will allow, and, in our reverent awe of what is divine, let us be drawn together toward the divine splendour."[11]

God is an impenetrable mystery and therefore the mind doesn't ever get directly to God, nor are words or conceptions adequate to the reality of God. Instead, for Dionysius, the way of Christian thinking is a via negativa, a negative way. By our reflective contemplation, we know what God is not. At the same time, we are "drawn toward the divine splendour." Dionysius insisted,

11. See Dionysius, *The Complete Works*, 49.

> *We must not dare to apply words or conceptions to this hidden or transcendent God ... [yet] the Good is not absolutely incommunicable to everything. By itself it generously reveals a firm, transcendent beam, granting enlightenments proportionate to each being, and thereby draws the sacred mind upwards to its permitted contemplation, to participation, to becoming like it.*[12]

Thus, for Dionysius, a way of thinking that presumes to have captured the divine in its words and conceptions is rejected in favour of a "permitted contemplation, to participation," a knowing that is given by the divine subject to the longing mind. For Dionysius, the hidden God is "the Source of every source ... the Life of the Living, the being of beings, it is the Source and Cause of all life and of all being, for out of its goodness it commands all things and it keeps them going."[13] Such a reality cannot be captured in words and conceptions, but it can capture us, inwardly and mystically.

Our "knowing" is an "unknowing," a coming to know what God is not. But if we contemplate our unknowing aright, then it too points in the direction of the Divine. Our conceptions, no matter how refined or precise, are never adequate to the Divine Mystery. God is always beyond our conceptions. This is not an appeal for us to abandon talk of God, or thought of God. The goal is participation in the divine life, not conceptions of it. As Dionysius asserts,

> *We use whatever appropriate symbols we can for the things of God. With these analogies we are raised upward toward the truth of the mind's vision ... we must begin with a prayer before everything we do, but especially when we talk of God. We will not pull down to ourselves that power which is both everywhere and nowhere, but by divine reminders and invocations we can commend ourselves to it and be joined to it.*[14]

These views of Dionysius were represented in his works *On Divine Names*, *On Celestial Hierarchy* and *On Ecclesiastical Hierarchy*. Dionysius explored the names we give to God more than God's qualities, properties or nature. As he explained,

> *We cannot know God in his nature, since this is unknowable and is beyond the reach of mind or reason ... We therefore approach that which is beyond all as far as our capacities allow us and we pass by way of the denial and the transcendence of all*

12. Ibid., 50.
13. Ibid., 51.
14. Ibid., 59 and 69.

> things . . . God is therefore known in all things and as distinct from all things. He is known through knowledge and through unknowing . . . On the other hand, God cannot be understood, words cannot contain him, and no name can lay hold of him . . . This is the sort of language we must use about God.[15]

In his analysis of various categories we use concerning God—categories like being, eternal and omnipotent or all-powerful—he showed their ambiguities and their limitations. At the same time, he showed how various names of God—father, goodness—are also limited but point us towards God though they are only human constructions. They never contain or capture God. But in this reflection and contemplation our mind begins to rise towards the ineffable and hidden God that lies beyond these constructions. The point is "to praise the Transcendent One in a transcending way, namely, though the denial of all beings." For, in this way, he continued,

> My argument now rises from what is below up to the transcendent, and the more it climbs, the more language falters, and when it has passed up and beyond the ascent, it will turn silent completely, since it will finally be at one with him who is indescribable."[16]

For Dionysius, this is the real point of our thinking and contemplation, something he called the "ecstatic leap into the divine darkness and union in that darkness with God." Our union needs to be completed by mystical union, something that is beyond words. Dionysius remarked, "What is the divine darkness? . . . My advice to you is to leave behind you everything perceived and understandable, all that is not and all that is, and . . . to strive upward as much as you can toward union with him who is beyond all being and knowledge."[17] It is this ecstatic leap into the divine darkness that unites the soul of the believer with the divine. It is the unknowing knowing of participation.

Thus, as one reflects upon these things, God comes closer to our lives, our minds, and our souls and we realize the inadequacy of all of our conceptions and our thinking, so that these become ladders which we climb and which propel us beyond ourselves to this state of mystical union. The leap is something to which you are led by your reflection. You don't decide, "Oh well, this is no good—I'm going to jump off here." The via negativa or apophatic theology isn't anti-thinking— it just shows the limits of our

---

15. Dionysius, *Divine Names*, 108-9.
16. Dionysius, *Mystical Theology*, 108-9.
17. Ibid., 135.

thinking. We are brought to a state where we can let go of the conceptions and participate in the divine mystery.

John Scotus Eriugena: A Voice of Celtic Christianity

A later contributor to the via negativa was John Scotus Eriugena (800–877), one of the more original voices in the Carolingian intellectual and cultural renaissance of the ninth century. He was from Ireland, but we know him from his thirty years on the Continent in France. Surprisingly, he knew Greek and was familiar with Eastern Christian writers, including Dionysius the Areopagite and Gregory of Nyssa. He seems to have been shaped by and given voice to the older Celtic traditions of Christianity, as a recent study of his *Homily on the Prologue to the Gospel of John*—"In the beginning was the Word . . . "—suggests.

While Latin Christianity was dominant in the West, there was another accent to the Christianity developing in the lands of western Europe and the British Isles, where the Celtic languages were dominant. This was happening during a time when there was more regional variety in liturgy and practice in Western Christianity. .

Unlike the later medieval theologians who sharply differentiated between nature and the supernatural, Eriugena developed a cosmological perspective that saw the interpenetration of heaven and earth, God and nature, humanity and the cosmos. He saw creation as a "self-manifestation of the hidden transcendent." In creation itself, God is manifest in divine outpourings or theophanies. In the Celtic tradition the very rain, and sun and wind speak of God. It is a cosmology that testifies to a Living God present to and through nature. According to Eriugena, "God expresses Himself in creation and creation culminates in its return to the divine."

Eriugena held that God is the "beginning, middle, and end of all things." And nature or the living cosmos is the "totality of all things." That includes, said Eriugena, (a) nature which creates and is not created, (b) nature which creates and is created, (c) nature which is created and does not create and (d) nature which is neither created nor creates. It is this "totality of all things" that is in God and in which God is manifest.

In Eriugena there is a "thinness of the veil between heaven and earth, God and nature, humanity and the cosmos." That thinness means "the whole of creation . . . is a theophany, marvelously showing forth the divine while at the same time concealing it . . . God speaks through it."[18]

18. See Bamford, *The Voice of the Eagle: The Heart of Celtic Christianity*. It is a translation and commentary on Eriugena's *Homily on the Prologue to the Gospel of John*. See

A more modern expression of the sensibility we find in Eriugena is reflected in this Celtic prayer:

> *May the road rise up to meet you,*
> *May the wind be always at your back,*
> *May the sun shine warm upon your face,*
> *The rains fall soft upon you fields and until we meet again,*
> *May God hold you in the palm of His Hand.*

Eriugena was another voice that influenced his own time but then fell into eclipse. In more recent times there has been renewed interest in his thought.

The way of thinking typified by Dionysius and Eriugena, the via negativa as it is known in the West, is called the apophatic tradition in Eastern Christianity. This way of thinking has been influential down until our own time. For example, I was at a conference in the (1990s) where one of the participants, a Jesuit from Fordham University, kept telling us that we shouldn't put too much confidence in our words and conceptions and notions. It was a Dionysian approach to Christian thought, one that continually reminds us that there are limits to knowing God and that what is more crucial is participation in God, the mystical union that exceeds words and conceptions.

In the period after Augustine and throughout what are called the Dark Ages, much Christian thinking proceeds in this apophatic way. Those who follow the via negativa are just as rigorous in their thinking as those who follow the via positiva, but they understand the process of reflection in a radically different way. Like all Christian thinkers, they are engaging in thought about God. But they recognize that the reality of God always exceeds all our thoughts and can only be realized in that "mystical leap" into the "the divine darkness."

Between Christian thinkers like Boethius on the one hand and Dionysius and Eriugena on the other, there are differences of both methods and content. Boethius believed that through our reflection we are actually able to articulate some things that are true about God. Dionysius thought that what we say concerning God is always restricted by the limits of our words and conceptions—and that the truth of God is always beyond any and all of our conceptions. In terms of the history of Christian thought, the way of Boethius is more rationalistic and the way of Dionysius is more mystical. And often these different approaches to Christian thinking are set against each other. But are they really in opposition?

---

especially the chapter on *Theophany*, 152-61, 154.

When Boethius was trying to understand providence, he distinguished between providence and divine foreknowledge. This was an important distinction, because Boethius was also aware—as was Dionysius—that God exceeds our categories and that our words are not fully adequate to the truth of God. For Boethius, this was because God is of eternity and human thinking is of time. Thus we often get very confused when we talk about God's foreknowledge because we tend to ascribe to God the same temporal qualities that characterize human thinking. God is outside of the temporal process of past, present and future. God isn't subject to the temporal process in the way that all human thinking is. God is beyond the order of space and time, yet present to it. This, Boethius believed, tells us something that is true. The mind of God is not determined by temporal categories. Boethius would say this is true about God. You can, for Boethius, get to the point of recognizing, through thought, that God is beyond temporal categories, or that temporal categories are inadequate to the reality of God. But Boethius would also recognize that that reality which is eternity is beyond our capacity to fully or exhaustively articulate.

Dionysius started with the awareness that the reality of God always exceeds our categories and our words. Thus all our attempts to conceptualize the reality of God are bound to fail. Yet they also point us to something more or deeper or beyond and in that way we begin to glimpse something divine.

This division, if division it was, persisted through the Middle Ages. The highly rationalist medieval schoolmen—the Christian thinkers within the new institution, the university—saw the way to God as a via positiva. Meanwhile, others in this same period were centred on the journey of the soul to God in a via negativa or apophatic way. These medieval voices charted what I call the "grammar of the soul" or "grammar of the spiritual journey." Whether or not these two approaches can ultimately be harmonized is difficult to tell. Later figures like Anselm or Bonaventure attempted to synthesize these two tendencies. Whether they were successful is another question. I happen to believe that these two ways can be reconciled, but others think differently.

Perhaps what you see within the history of Christian thought is the presence of differences in temperament, different personality types that are predisposed to different modes of thinking—some more rationalistic, some more intuitive, some more moralistic, some more emotional. On a conceptual plane, it is sometimes difficult to understand exactly where the differences lie, but you know they are there. They are different orientations towards things that are difficult to express, but that you recognize in your dealings with people.

Charlemagne and the Holy Roman Empire

When Charlemagne (Charles the Great) was crowned Emperor of the Holy Roman Empire in 800, he issued a very important edict that was to have lasting significance for Western culture. In announcing his policy, he said, "It has seemed to us and our favourable councils . . . [that] without knowledge it is impossible to do good."[19] He brought about the beginnings of an educational system and the expansion of learning. Initially schools were associated with monasteries, and later with the cathedrals where the monks and clergy become the educators of a wider group within the society. These schools were the background for what emerged in the Middle Ages as the first universities. One of the important things here is the understanding of learning as one of the ways in which we love God that grows out of the monastic traditions. Charlemagne said that doubtless good works are better than knowledge, but without knowledge it is impossible to do good. This revealed a tension around this issue within the monastic communities. Some were worried that knowledge might lead people away from the love of God; others believed that knowledge is part of the love of God. This issue sometimes surfaced in questions about which texts from the past should be recopied: should pagan writings be copied or should they be left to turn to dust? Now as these new educational institutions began to emerge, the side that believed that it is possible to link learning and the love of God won out.

Later on, Bernard of Clairvaux (1090–1153), a medieval monk, argued that we should support education and encourage learning because knowledge is one of the ways we can be united with and joined to God. As we begin to move towards the medieval schoolmen, it is important to understand how this deep spiritual impulse was behind the rise of the great systems of Christian thought that emerged in the Middle Ages. In their work and in their learning, the schoolmen were simply seeking to express in the intellectual order the love of God. In our own time we tend to see learning as separate from and split off in a secular way from the love of God. This modern tendency to separate secular learning from religious learning –from that distinctive new medieval discipline of theology—is foreign to the medieval way of looking at things. In the Middle Ages the aspiration was to integrate and synthesize all of these various ways of knowing and various kinds of knowledge, to find their harmony with one another.

---

19. See Leclercq, *Love of Learning and the Desire for God*.

Summary

In the Rule fashioned by Benedict, Western monasticism found its way. His Rule proved to be enduring and gave to Christianity in the West a dynamic new institution. Centred on the Opus Dei—the eight periods of daily prayer—it became a life-transforming and stable environment for pursuing union with God. At the same time, there were other currents of thought, reflected in Boethius and Dionysius, that made lasting contributions to the great conversation.

Review

1. What is the "Opus Dei"?
2. Boethius is known for his contribution to the "via positiva." What is that? How does it contrast with the "via negativa" of Dionysius?
3. What was Benedict's view of "obedience/disobedience" in relation to monastic life?
4. What is the meaning of apophatic?
5. What distinguishes the Celtic Way in Christianity?

PART IV

Medieval Christian Thought: 1100–1500

THE CHAPTERS IN PART IV provides a glimpse into the rich and varied world of medieval Christian thought. Chapter 12 opens with attention to St. Anselm, a transitional figure between monastic-centred thought and the new world of the Schoolmen, Christian thinkers in the emerging new universities. Anselm saw Christian thinking as "faith seeking understanding." Anselm is widely known for his "ontological argument for the existence of God," as well as his thinking about the atonement. Anselm's view of the atonement was rejected by Abelard, who also charted a "new dialectical method" for Christian thinking. In Chapter 13, we explore what I call the "grammars of the spirit" as we look at the way figures like Bernard of Clairvaux, Hildegard of Bingen, Francis of Assisi, Bonaventure and Julian of Norwich articulate and chart the spiritual life. These figures address the mystical aspects of the Christian faith, often in surprising ways—as, for example, in Julian's notion of "God as our Mother." Chapter 14 centres on the figure of St. Thomas Aquinas, perhaps the greatest medieval thinker, and his magisterial *Summa Theologica*. Here we see the medieval aspiration for a synthesis of all knowledge. It was among the Schoolmen that "theology" as a "science of God" emerged, but in various forms. Towering intellectual as well as spiritual visions characterized this crucial era of Christian thought.

Chapter 12

On the Way to the Medieval Synthesis
Anselm's Faith Seeking Understanding and Abelard's New Dialectical Method

DURING THE LONG PERIOD between the fall of the Roman Empire in the fifth century and the flowering of medieval culture in the twelfth and thirteenth centuries, there were relatively few new voices, but as we saw in the preceding chapters, they included some that made lasting contributions to the great conversation. Christian thought had largely moved into a monastic context where its ends were internal—that is, for the sake of learning and interiorization. Consequently, Christian thinking unfolded in silence and away from the public sphere. As the monks copied ancient manuscripts and performed the daily *Opus Dei*, Christian thinking sought to shape the interior journey towards union with God. The monastery had become, as Benedict remarked, a "school in service of God."

There was a certain foreboding mixed with excitement that swept the Christian world as the first millennium of the Christian era ended. But the year 1000 passed without apocalyptic expectations being realized. However, the long-standing tensions between Eastern and Western Christianity led to mutual anathemas between the bishops of Constantinople and Rome and the resulting estrangement of East and West (c.1035). It was not a happy development. The first centuries of the new millennium were a time of transition and one of the early figures in that time of transition was Anselm.

Before I turn directly to Anselm I want to say a couple of words about new developments in Christian thought that are coming. In that transition between monastic thought of earlier centuries and the coming development of Scholasticism, Anselm was a crucial figure. He anticipated something of the approach to Christian thought and method that developed in the schoolmen and Scholasticism. This approach to the Christian faith first began to emerge in centres of learning and schools related to the cathedrals. They began to articulate the Christian faith in disciplined terms. The great achievement of Scholasticism was an exact theological vocabulary and method and the very discipline of *theology*, the science of God. All the terms of this new discipline of theology were subject to very precise definition. Protestants often caricature Scholasticism as a dead end, as people arguing about pointless issues like how many angels can dance on the head of a pin. Some of us find this is an interesting question. Especially, when we discover that the answer is an infinite number since angels do not occupy space. It could, however, be argued that this is taking the scholastic impulse to an extreme. Here we will look at some of the important ways in which the schoolmen contributed to the great conversation within Christianity.

The schoolmen and Scholasticism emerged within a culture that was largely Christian. This is very important to remember. In a sense, what we are seeing is an effort at internal clarification of what was held to be true within the wider culture. The schoolmen did not argue for the truth of Christianity vis-à-vis other ways of thinking because they were only aware to a very limited extent that there even were other ways of thinking. Some, like Thomas Aquinas, did come to know great Muslim thinkers like al-Ghazzali or Adquzel (1058–1111) and Averroes or Ibn Rushd (1126–1198) and the Jewish thinker Maimonides (1135–1204). He even mentions them approvingly. However, Christian thinkers were living in a culture that was fundamentally Christian in terms of its higher affirmations and ideals.

Anselm (1033–1109)

Anselm was one of the great monastic thinkers, though often wrongly identified, in my view, as an early Scholastic thinker. Anselm understood Christian thinking as "faith seeking understanding" *(fides quarens intellectum)*. Anselm's view of Christian thinking is often identified with that of Augustine, who argued that we must believe in order to understand. This is different from what we find in Anselm, who saw the purpose of Christian thinking as seeking to understand what is held to be true. Faith has a legitimacy and wholeness to it. Anselm simply assumes that faith is present in his audience; they were, after all, monks. However, the issue that arises for Anselm is that "aha moment" when faith realizes what it already knows. It is the moment of insight, the joy of realization.

Anselm was born in Italy, entered a monastery at Bec in France rose to become "novice master," then head of the monastery before becoming the Archbishop of Canterbury. In England, Anselm was in conflict with the King over a number of issues including the issue of slavery, which Anselm opposed. Because of his difficulties with the King, Anselm left England and returned to Italy for a number of years. He then returned to England to resume his office as Archbishop of Canterbury in the last years before his death. However, it was in the monastic context that Anselm made his greatest contributions to the great conversation concerning the Christian faith.

In Anselm's story, you can see that the Christian community was a transnational community. The divisions of the map that characterize our world as national states had yet to emerge. In the Middle Ages, membership in the Christian community allowed free movement across the different cultures, peoples, and languages across Europe. Thus, the pattern that you see in Anselm—born in Italy, in the monastery at Bec in France, Archbishop of Canterbury in England—is characteristic of the great Christian thinkers through the next centuries. The whole of Europe was their home territory rather than their being limited to a single national group.

Believing and Understanding

We begin our discussion of Anselm by looking at his argument—unfortunately often translated as "proof"—for the existence of God. We have to set it in context. The writing in which the argument is found was first called "Faith Seeking Understanding," but it was published as the *Proslogium* or discourse on the existence of God. It is here that Anselm first used this phrase—faith seeking understanding—to describe the purpose of Christian thinking. When we turn to his ontological argument, we have to remember that Anselm presupposed that we already believe in God. His argument was not aimed at making believers out of unbelievers but seeking to bring joy to believers by understanding what they already believe.

When Anselm discovered this argument and wrote many of his works, Anselm was a teacher of monks in the monastery of Bec. Even though the monastery is now small and the ancient buildings have disappeared, you can still walk, as I did, this beautiful valley not far from Rouen in western France. Anselm tells us in the opening of the *Proslogion* that, at the urging of his students, he had been trying for a long time to discover an argument that might satisfy the demands of reason to understand what faith already believes. He had long pondered this issue, trying to find a single argument that would require no other than itself alone. He thought and thought about this and had about given up on finding what he was seeking. It was at this point that the argument he presents occurred to him. One can sense in the preface to the *Proslogion* the delight Anselm experienced when he had finally discovered the argument.

He tells us in the *Proslogion* that he has written this little treatise "*in the person of one who strives to lift his mind to the contemplation of God and seeks to understand what he believes.*"[1] It is very important to keep this firmly in mind. Anselm already believed that God exists before he happened upon the argument. The argument did not change things in any external way. It did not create belief in God whereas before God's existence had been in doubt. It simply brought the joy of understanding to what is already held dear. The point of the argument is that it brings intellectual joy to the believer—that joy that comes with having discovered something sought for a long time, the intellectual joy of understanding. It becomes an aha moment, an occasion for insight.

The argument, at least in Anselm's mind and in the minds of many others was very powerful. At the very least, it allowed him to know that his belief was not nonsensical or irrational. Rather, there is a kind of intuitive logic to the belief that God is, and Anselm's argument demonstrated this logic. It allowed him to see that belief in God has intellectual credibility.

Prayer and Understanding

Before Anselm turns directly to his argument, he invites us to pray. Prayer becomes the indispensable context for even considering the argument. As he says in the first chapter: "*Enter the inner chamber of thy mind, shut out all thoughts save that of God and such as can aid thee in seeking Him. Close thy door and seek Him.*"[2] For Anselm, as for Augustine, the mind goes towards God. That is what the mind does. Anselm shared the Christian conviction that God created us in his image, which meant that we are creatures that can and should be mindful of the One who made us. We should love and contemplate God above all else. We should pray to prepare ourselves for the moment of insight; we have to adopt an attitude of prayerful inquiry.

Anselm shares the Christian belief that we are created in God's image, we are creatures whose mind desires to go to God. However, that longing for God is often bewildered and confused. It needs the practice and discipline

---

1. See Anselm, *Basic Writings*, 3.
2. Ibid., 8-9.

of prayer. Human beings need an inner awakening for the mind to recover its proper end: the contemplation of the divine. The way in which you begin to renovate the mind so that it can go towards its proper object is through the spiritual discipline of prayer. By and through prayer, we both focus our minds on these divine subjects and prepare our hearts to heed the spirit that moves within us and moves us towards this transcendent ground or God.

This is very important for Anselm. It is not the case that if you went up to just anyone walking around on the street and shared this argument with them, they would immediately be overwhelmed and persuaded. It does not work that way. Rather, it is set within the context of the spiritual disciplines that characterized life in the monastic community. That means, most centrally, the discipline of prayer, the Opus Dei. This is the proper context for thinking about God. In our thinking about God—and this is why Anselm is so excited—sometimes you can discover an argument for what you already believe. It is only in that context of prayerful searching that the argument works. As Anselm said, "*I acknowledge, O Lord, with thanksgiving that thou hast created this thy image in me . . . but I believe in order to understand.*" The last sentence before he turns to the argument: "*For this too I believe, that unless I believe, I shall not understand.*"[3] It is not an argument to make believers out of unbelievers. It is an argument to make believers more deeply understand what they already believe. That understanding gives intellectual joy.

The Ontological Argument

Anselm's argument is very simple. He had long puzzled over the words of the Psalmist concerning the fool who has said in his heart, "There is no God" (Psalm 14:1-3). He wondered what do we mean when we utter the word *God*. There are many associations in our mind around that term, but Anselm finally came to one thing entailed in the very word *God*. When we are speaking about God, we are speaking about "*that than which nothing greater can be conceived.*" Anselm was aware that there were other phrases like "God is love, God is the Creator, and God is spirit" that come from Scripture and from the tradition about God. However, Anselm argued, at least one of the things meant when we utter the word God is "*that than which nothing greater can be conceived.*" Moreover, if we remember that God is "*that than which nothing greater can be conceived*," then a curious thing happens: we cannot think of *that than which nothing greater can be conceived* as not existing.

3. See Kerr, *Selections from Anselm*, 84.

According to Anselm's definition of God, God cannot not exist. If we say that that than which nothing greater can be conceived does not exist, then we are not thinking of that than which nothing greater can be conceived. Anselm thought that was self-evident. Hence if "that than which nothing greater can be conceived" can be conceived not to exist, it is not "that than which nothing greater can be conceived." It is what later scholars call a wholly analytic argument. It just takes the term *God* and unpacks its own inner content. It looks at the demands of reason in relation to the word *God*. It does not appeal to anything outside of the very term itself for its force. It is a Christian *koan*.

There are two forms of the argument in the *Proslogium*; the first one is less convincing to me than the second argument. The less convincing argument makes the existence of God a predicate: it is better for God to exist in reality and the understanding than just in the understanding. The second, more persuasive argument (at least to me) is an internal analytic argument, but one where it is the intuitive mind that finally says "Yes." The rational mind remains caught in the web of logic.

When Anselm made this argument, another monk named Gaunilon was not impressed. He said he could think of a perfect island and that it would be perfect only if it existed than if it did not exist. What Anselm was doing was imaginative play, said Gaunilion, but this argument does not work. He objected more to the first form of the argument (it is better for something to exist in the understanding and in reality) than to the second argument (we cannot think of that than which nothing greater can be conceived as not existing). Thus, Anselm replied to Gaunilon that when you talk about perfect islands or any other perfect thing, you can see that wishing doesn't make it so. However, God is a special case. It is only God's existence, we discover, that is necessary, in the sense that in order for God to be God, God must be. All other existents are contingent and only God's existence is necessary. That means that only in relation to God do we find ourselves in logical contradiction when we say that God does not exist.

Anyway, that is the argument. Many people find it frustrating and unconvincing, and feel that Anselm has tricked us. That was my own reaction when I first heard the argument. Then, having taken Anselm's argument as my senior honours project, I spend a year trying to understand what the trick was. When I finally grasped what Anselm was trying to do, I found a delight I had not known before.

God and the Believer

Anselm did not think we wholly exhaust the reality of God in our thinking because God is always more than what we can grasp. For Anselm this is a little bit of light in the darkness. There is a whole tradition, the Neoplatonic tradition that stands behind him. That tradition assumes that the mind is in touch with reality: It is the microcosm within of the macrocosm without. In attending to the mind, we discover truths about reality. In modern thinking, the mind is not conceived as having this connection to reality. The mind is, in John Locke's terms, that blank slate on which experience writes, but it is not intrinsically related to what is. The world has to impress itself on this blank slate to generate sensations out of which we make up concepts and other mental constructs. This was not the view of the longer tradition within the West.

Anselm thought that the fool knows not what he is talking about when he uses the term *God* to deny the existence of God. For Anselm, the believer is the one more attuned to the way things are, or more faithful to the demands of intuition. He knew that this argument does not create faith in the believer, but he did want us to realize that one who speaks of God and says that God exists is not speaking foolishly. His arguments do not make people believers, but they do give insight to those who prayerfully seek

There are two dispositions that are crucial here. The first is whether we are open to persuasion, or not. If a person is not open to persuasion, then no argument, no matter how good, is going to persuade them. This happens all the time. Students sometimes ask teachers in religious studies, "Can you prove that God exists?" I always say, "Of course, but it all depends on what you will accept as a "valid argument or proof." Things usually end there because the only kind of argument or proof they will accept involves the empirical laboratory. One cannot give that kind of proof. However, if a person is open to persuasion by other kinds of considerations, arguments or exercises, then there are many "so-called arguments" found in Christian and other traditions. If people are open to persuasion by Anselm's argument, then it can be rather persuasive. Especially if the ground was prepared by prayerful contemplation.

The other condition presupposed in the argument is a disposition of the heart. If that disposition of the heart is not there—if one is not genuinely seeking the light or making an effort to know or to understand—then of course the argument is not going to be persuasive. Then the problem is not the argument, but rather the predisposition of those who encounter the argument.

Faith and Truth

The search for truth and the life of faith are one. For Anselm there is no contradiction. Faith seeks understanding. Faith is orientation towards the truth of things. When we gain the light of understanding then faith deepens and understanding grows.

How many ways are there to faith? How does one become a believing person? That is immensely complicated. I suppose it starts with how your mother and father took care of you when you were an infant and it goes from there to all the experiences of your life. Some come to have faith and others do not. In the generations after Anselm, some found Anselm's arguments persuasive and illuminating, while others did not. But what is critical here is to see the type of thinking that we encounter in Anselm—one that is rooted in a life of prayer yet seeks to understand what is given in the Christian faith.

Prayer precedes the argument. Prayer is the spiritual discipline that encourages the conditions that allow the hearer to hear the argument aright. However, there are all kinds of things that condition and shape and influence our believing or not believing over which the argument itself does not have any control. That we have objections to the argument should not be surprising since another feature of the mind is to raise questions about any proposition put before it. In addition, the extent to which we heed what the intellect demands—what intuitive logic requires in this case—is a very complicated issue. Anselm's way of acknowledging those things that surround the functioning of the mind is to invite us to a life of prayer as a way of setting conditions in us to consider the argument.

Of course, it is not required that one be persuaded by Anselm's argument. However, you should know the argument and the type of Christian thinking—faith seeking understanding—it represents. This kind of Christian thinking emerged in monastic traditions that revolved around the Opus Dei, or daily round of prayer. The great figures of the medieval period were all products of religious orders—Benedictine, Dominican, Franciscan, etc. Could there be a relationship between prayer and intuitive insight? I still puzzle over this question.[4]

---

4. Some years following my visit to Anselm's monastery at Bec in France, I spent three days at a monastery founded by Dogen (1200–253), a Soto Zen priest in Japan. It is Eiheiji or the Temple of Eternal Peace. While at Eiheiji, it dawned on me that meditative silence can lead to intuitive insight.

Cur Deus Homo?

Another of Anselm's contributions is contained in a book called *Cur Deus Homo or Why God Became Man*.[5] Here Anselm articulated the "objective theory" of the atonement, one of several different theories of the atonement within the history of Christian thought. Here Anselm offers one way of accounting for why God becomes man and from that an understanding of how Christ atones for human sin. In Anselm's view, God being the creator of all that is, it is only appropriate that creatures, since their life is not from themselves, return to God obedience appropriate to his honour and majesty. In terms of the Christian story, we know that rather than returning that obedience appropriate to God's honour and majesty humanity is now in a condition of sin or brokenness.

How do we restore the relationship between God and Humanity? Anselm argued that God could just wipe out the consequences of sin, mercifully forgive all, and in that way restore the relationship with humankind. However, in Anselm's view, that would violate the demands of justice, which requires that humanity repay the enormous debt owed to God. If God just ignored the sin of humanity, it would trivialize sin. It would be equivalent to God saying, "Well, it just doesn't matter that you sinned. Forget it, we will start over again." What justice requires, Anselm argued, is that man fulfills the requirements of obedience.

However, man cannot do this on his own because he already owes God everything. And now, after he has sinned, he owes God a double amount. The debt is enormous. The obligation is on man to rectify this situation and give to God what is his due. Man must atone for his own sin, but he is unable to. God could atone for man's sin, but he should not because it would contravene his justice. Therefore, Anselm's answer is the God-man, Jesus Christ. As man, he lives the life of perfect obedience, which is fulfilling what is required of all creatures. As God, Jesus Christ satisfies the requirements of justice because he pays the infinite debt. However, since Jesus Christ is perfect and does not sin he has, as it were, an extra reward coming—this is Anselm's language. He does not need it for himself and so he transfers this credit to sinful humankind. Thus, God's honour is maintained, man's sin is forgiven, and the relationship of humankind to God is restored. This is a wholly gracious gift of God mediated to us by Jesus, the God-man.

This is one of the influential accounts of how Jesus' death on the cross leads to a renewed relationship of God and humanity. Before the twelfth century, this renewed relationship between God and humanity was just

---

5. See Anselm, Basic Writings, for the *Proslogium*, 1-34, and for the *Cur Deus Homo*, 177-288.

asserted. Paul, for example, said that in Jesus Christ we are reconciled with God. Irenaeus argued that *"the Word became flesh . . . recapitulating the ancient creation of man in Himself, in order to slay sin, to remove death's sting, and restore man to life."*[6] Both of these views were without an account of the nature of the divine-human transaction. Anselm gave one—many have held it. However, not everyone found Anselm's account of how the death of Christ affects humanity's redemption at all persuasive. Indeed, some found it harsh and displeasing, as did many of my students over the years. One of the twelfth-century contemporaries who opposed Anselm was Abelard, to whom we turn next.

However, it is important to see in Anselm this new approach to Christian thinking, faith seeking understanding. The faith is given, but the reasons for those convictions concerning the existence of God, redemption in Christ Jesus, the procession of the Holy Spirit and other Christian doctrines are still awaiting discovery. It is as we take prayerful thought upon the teachings and doctrines of the faith that we can—at least sometimes, as Anselm well knew, from his own experience—discover something of the rationale and thinking that lies behind these convictions. With such discoveries comes the joy of understanding.

Abelard (1079-1142)

Abelard is best known for his love affair with Heloise (1090-1164), a scholar and later an Abbess. Abelard was Heloise's teacher, and they fell in love. The problem was that Abelard was a priest and when Heloise's guardian found out about the affair, he hired some men to castrate Abelard. Heloise was sent to a nunnery. Despite the prohibition of any contact between them, they continued to exchange letters. Theirs was one of the most talked about love affairs in the medieval world. Heloise went on to become an abbess, a notable figure in her own right.

Abelard was also a wonderful teacher. He taught at a new school near Paris, one that he had founded independent of the cathedral. His school is a forerunner of a new institution that was just emerging in his time: the university. Abelard taught near Paris and there he devised a new method for the study of the tradition of Christian thought. It was called *Sic et Non* or *Yes and No*, a dialectical method that differed from the method of memorization and interiorization which was common in the monasteries. It was a critical reading of the tradition of Christian thinking with arguments for

---

6. See Kerr, Selections from Irenaeus, 37.

and against the various assertions made by earlier Christian thinkers. Abelard was a remarkable example of the new schoolmen who were emerging.

Students flocked to his classes. Rather than having his students memorize and learn the teachings of earlier Christian thinkers, Abelard wanted his students to think critically. He felt that arguments for and against the claims of Christian thinkers should be marshalled. To use a term from our own time, his purpose was not to deconstruct the tradition of Christian thought. Rather, Abelard believed that this process would lead to a more penetrating and insightful view of the tradition. Later, Abelard's student Peter Lombard incorporated Abelard's method in his *Four Books of Sentences*; it became a standard text for students studying the new discipline of theology in the medieval university.

Another of his contributions was his theory of the atonement, written in opposition to Anselm. Abelard's view became known as the moral theory of the atonement. Abelard found Anselm's argument too rationalistic, too abstract, and rather gruesome. Whereas Anselm had made the atonement a matter of satisfying God's offended honour, Abelard made it a matter of compelling love. Abelard felt that the atonement is best understood in terms of the exemplary power of Christ's death on the cross. As Abelard says in the sketchy records that we have of his views on redemption,

> It seems to us that we have been justified by the blood of Christ and reconciled to God (Rom 3:24-25) in this way: through this unique act of grace manifested to us—in that his Son has taken upon himself our nature and persevered therein in teaching us by word and example even unto death - he has more fully bound us to himself by love with the result that our hearts should be enkindled by such a gift of divine grace, and true charity should not now shrink from enduring anything for him.[7]

For Abelard, the cross and the life of Christ is a shining and powerful example of God's love for humankind. It is an emblem of Divine Love. It is so powerful that it should kindle in our hearts a desire to emulate Christ in our lives:

> Everyone becomes more righteous—by which we mean a greater lover of the Lord—after the Passion of Christ than before, since a realized gift inspires greater love than one which is only hoped for."[8]

The atonement is not a transaction involving awkward concepts of satisfaction, honour, obedience and disobedience as in Anselm, but quite simply the transformative example of Christ and his redemptive suffering. For

---

7. See Kerr, the Selection from Abelard, 95.
8. Ibid., 94.

Abelard, what we are looking at when we look at Christ is so remarkable that it creates in us a desire to follow Christ, to exemplify and exhibit in our lives that same kind of loving obedience exemplified in his death. Abelard wrote,

> *Our redemption through Christ's suffering is that deeper affection in us which not only frees us from slavery to sin, but also wins for us the true liberty of sons of God, that we do all things out of love rather than fear—love to him who has shown us such grace that no greater can be found, as he himself asserts, saying, "Greater love than this no man hath, that a man lay down his life for his friends. (John 15:13)*

So, we are made one with God through this shining example, this exemplary act of love. Said, Abelard, *"He (Christ) came for the express purpose of spreading this true liberty of love amongst men."* Thus rather than the language of divine honour, obedience and justice that was central to Anselm's theory, Abelard spoke of the atonement in terms of redemptive love and grace.[9]

Summary

Anselm and Abelard are two important figures on the way to the great remaking of Western Christianity in the twelfth century. Under Pope Innocent III, the papacy would be centralized and remade as the church assumed responsibility for the shape of the whole of society. In the coming centuries, the universities would emerge, along with the beginnings of the rule of law. It would be a time of new patterns in the life of society and the spirit. It would also be a time of crusades, one of the darker sides of Christian history when crusaders ransacked Jerusalem and killed its inhabitants. Anselm's notion of faith seeking understanding would influence Christian thinking in the coming centuries. His argument for the existence of God would remain a challenge to those seeking to resolve the mind's quest to understand the reality of God. Abelard gave to the universities a new method of inquiry for Christian thinking as it came to be centred in these new institutions. He too would loom large, even though later thinkers would be more constructive in their efforts than Abelard had been. Similarly, Christian thinking would take a more rationalistic turn than Anselm had foreseen.

---

9. Ibid., 95-96.

Review

1. What is the meaning of "fides quarens intellectus?"
2. What is the relationship of prayer and understanding in Anselm?
3. What was Abelard's objection to Anselm's teaching about atonement

Chapter 13

Grammars of the Spirit

Bernard, Hildegard of Bingen, Francis of Assisi, Bonaventure and Julian of Norwich

THERE WERE TWO STRANDS of Christian thought throughout the Middle Ages. They are equally important in terms of the great conversation. One strand consisted of the articulation of Christian *spirituality*, while the other consisted of the development of Christian *theology*, the new "science of God" invented by the medieval thinkers. First, we focus on the attempts throughout the Middle Ages to clarify and develop an understanding of the way in which the spirit works in the life of human beings, and we begin by looking at Bernard of Clairvaux and his three-stage scheme of "purgative-illuminative-unitive," a characteristic form of medieval spirituality.

Bernard of Clairvaux (1090–1153)

Bernard was a monk who eventually became an abbot and was very influential in his time. Throughout his life, he often gave a series of sermons on the Song of Songs (Song of Solomon), a sensual love poem in the Hebrew Scriptures that many Christians found embarrassing. In these sermons, Bernard expressed this three-staged view of the spiritual life of the Christian. It begins with the purgative stage when the soul is cleansed—what he refers to as the stage of the first kiss. The penitent comes to Christ and places himself or herself at the feet of the Lord, a posture in which the soul lays down its sins and begins to strive for holiness. Thus, the soul is cleansed, purged of what leads away from God and turns towards God.[1]

The second stage that Bernard describes is the illuminative stage or the second kiss. In Bernard's words, the soul rises and kisses the hand of the Lord as one encounters the sanctifying grace of self-control and the fruits of penitence. At this stage, the soul is illuminated and gains deeper understanding. It is a period of growth in sanctity.

As important as this stage is, it is not the final stage, which for Bernard is the unitive stage or the third kiss. Here one enters into a direct relationship with the object of one's quest and stands, to use his imagery, mouth to mouth, with the Lord. Here there is a union between the soul of the believer and its divine object. Thus we have Bernard's scheme: a three staged view of the spiritual life:

1. Purgative stage or state of the "first kiss."
2. Illuminative stage or state of the "second kiss."
3. Unitive stage or state of the "third kiss."

The romantic language of Bernard's grammar of the spirit is noteworthy and is characteristic in the medieval world. It has its origin in the sensual language of the *Song of Songs/Song of Solomon* in the scriptures. This love poetry was understood allegorically in the Christian traditions as about the relationship of Christ and the beloved. We see it in Paul's hymn of the relationship between Christ and the Church as bride and bridegroom in Ephesians and in the Corinthian hymn to love. It is, however, surprising to see it here in the context of monastic accounts of the human journey among people who have taken vows of celibacy and eschewed marriage.

Now this unitive stage in Bernard's scheme involves contemplation of divine things. This stage is where the heart of the believer unites with God. This parallels the experience of beatitude or contemplation in the intellectual order. This connection between the pursuit of the spiritual life and the intellectual life will be more highly emphasized in the work of the great theologians of the Middle Ages such as St. Thomas Aquinas. For St. Thomas, as well as for the other medieval scholastics, the end of knowing is not knowledge per se but the union of the mind with the object of its quest, namely God, in the experience of contemplation of divine things.

In the modern world, we think of the end of knowledge as giving us mastery or control over the natural world. We understand the nature of things in such a way that we can translate this knowledge into a productive

---

1. For a Selection from Bernard of Clairvaux, see Kerr, *Selections from Anselm*, 96-99.

scheme or some kind of technology which allows us to gain mastery over the natural world and bring about some particular ends. For medieval thinkers, on the other hand, the point of our striving to know was to come to the stage where we can contemplate divine things and enjoy them for their own sake because they are worthy of our deepest aspirations. In the spiritual traditions that focus on the inner transformation of the human soul, many writers try to develop a grammar of the life of the spirit and the way it moves towards its transcendent end. Bernard was such a figure, but we also see this effort in important new movements such as the one that started around the life of Francis of Assisi in the late twelfth and early thirteenth centuries. Before we turn to Francis, we look at the remarkable contributions of a contemporary of Bernard's, Hildegard of Bingen.

Hildegard of Bingen (1098–1179)

Hildegard was German-born and entered a monastic community at the age of eight. After thirty years, she became abbess in her community at Bingen, and she remained in that position for nearly forty years until her death. Devout nun, writer, mystic, administrator, songwriter and visionary, she was a renaissance woman before the Renaissance. Known in her own time and influential in the flowering of the twelfth century, Hildegard was forgotten until the twentieth century when there was a revival of interest in her writings.

Her writings grew out of her visionary experience. This prompted Hildegard to write to Bernard of Clairvaux because she wondered whether her experience was of the devil or of God. Surprisingly, Bernard's response was very encouraging, and he urged her to publish her work, which she did in her *Book of Divine Works*. Here she presented her vision in the form of illustrations and then a written account of her vision followed by a kind of commentary or interpretation. We can see Hildegard's visionary Christian thinking in relation to her first vision, entitled "On the Origin of Life":

> I, the highest and fiery power, have kindled every spark of life ... With wisdom I have rightly put the universe in order. I, the fiery life of divine essence, am aflame beyond the beauty of the meadows, I gleam in the waters, and I burn in the sun, moon, and stars. With every breeze, as with invisible life that contains everything. I awaken everything to life. The air lives by turning green and being in bloom. The waters flow as if they were alive ... And thus I remain hidden in every kind of reality as a fiery power. For I am life. I am also Reason, which bears within itself the breath of the resounding Word, through which the whole of creation is

made. I breathe life into everything . . . For I am life, whole and entire . . . I am life that remains ever the same, without beginning and without end. For this life is God . . . [2]

There are still conflicting interpretations of Hildegard. Emilie zum Brunn, who taught at the Sorbonne, sees her thought as conventionally Augustinian and centred on the themes of sin and redemption. Another contemporary interpreter, the controversial Dominican (now Episcopalian) Matthew Fox, saw in her a remarkable departure from Augustinianism. For Fox, she was the proponent of what he calls a "creation-centred spirituality." This means that she gave a primary emphasis to God in creation—and the goodness of creation—as the foundation of Christian thinking. There is some evidence for this in the first vision which we looked at above, where she expressed a cosmic Christology which sees Christ as the "fiery power" present throughout creation and the inner dynamic in all things.

Book of Divine Works does give a primacy to creation that is quite significant. It (1) focuses on creation as the locus of divine presence and (2) sees an inner relationship between the human person and the cosmos. She was not a biblical thinker, nor did her thought unfold primarily as a reflection upon tradition. Rather, she was a visionary thinker, one whose thought grew out of her visions, which were then painted and reproduced in the books she later wrote. Her books are commentaries on her visionary experience. Her illustrations of her visions are reproduced in contemporary versions of her work. Her contributions to the grammar of the spiritual life and to the mystical literature of Christianity are considerable.

In speaking about the "The Fiery Life of Everything," which has "*kindled every spark of life*," Hildegard demonstrated a profound sense of the divine presence in everything. Although "*God cannot be seen directly*," she wrote, God "*is known through the divine creation*."[3] For Hildegard, the Christian vocation is to move the self into communion with the divine presence. The human person is enlivened by the soul, which she understands as "*the green life force of the flesh*." She often used biological images to speak of spiritual things, and regarded the whole creation as a sacrament.

Hildegard made many contributions to the developing conversation within Christianity, especially in seeing the link between cosmology and spirituality. Her Christic cosmology became the foundation for her spirituality. She challenged Popes and church officials. Nevertheless, Hildegard made many contributions to the great conversation. Thankfully, her voice has been recovered and restored to the longer narrative of Christian thought.

2. See Hildegard of Bingen, *Book of Divine Works*, 10-11.
3. Ibid., 220.

St. Francis of Assisi (1182–1226)

A century after Hildegard, Francis of Assisi gave voice to similar themes, although there is no evidence that he knew anything of Hildegard's writings. Francis too has a great sense of the wonder of God's creation, and he brought to the Christian faith an emphasis on simplicity that greatly touched the ordinary believer in his own time. He also founded a new lay monastic movement. St. Francis had an impact more through his life than through his writings, and his only known work is the prayer/poem called the "Canticle of Brother Sun."

Francis came from a well-to-do family in the town of Assisi in central Italy. When he was around twenty years of age, while praying at San Damiano just outside the walls of Assisi, he experienced a vision urging Francis to restore the Church. In heeding that call, he adopted a life of intense devotion to Lady Poverty. He immediately began to reconstruct the little church in which is received his vision, having taken the vision in very literal terms. Out of his life of fervent prayer, he came to realize that his call was not reconstructing churches but revitalizing the spiritual life of the Christian church, community and society.

He did this through a life of prayer that often involved extreme ascetic disciplines. He gathered around him a group of followers who travelled with him from place to place preaching his gospel. Francis, it was said, was so sweet that even the birds came to listen. In perhaps the most famous painting of Francis, by Giotto in the Church of San Francesco in Assisi, Francis has a bird perched on his shoulder. Francis's life became an emblem of the life of Christ, and later in life, Francis received the stigmata, the marks of the crucifixion, on his own flesh at La Verna in the Apennines north of his native Assisi, where he often went to pray. You can still visit the small cave below the rock face where he lived when he was there, sleeping on the stones.

This life of self-mortification stands in a curious—and to me unresolved— relationship to the outlook in his "Canticle to Brother Sun," the only writing we have that comes from Francis, and in the *Little Flowers*, sayings and stories of Francis gathered by his followers. The "Canticle to Brother Sun" is a beautiful hymn of praise to the Creator and his creation. It begins,

> *Most high, omnipotent, merciful Lord,*
> *the honour and the glory, and every benediction.*
>
> *To Thee alone are they confined*

to speak Thy name.

Praised be Thou, my Lord, with all Thy creatures,
Especially for Brother Sun.
gives us the light of day,
great splendor,
of Thee, most high, giving signification.

Praised be Thou, my Lord, for Sister Moon and the stars
Formed in the sky, clear, beautiful and fair.

It continues in a litany of praise to the different elements of creation, including Mother Earth:

Praised be Thou, my Lord, for Brother Wind . . .
Praised be Thou, my Lord, for Sister Water . . .
Praised be Thou, my Lord, for Brother Fire . . .
Praised be Thou, my Lord, for our Mother Earth/
Who sustains and rules us
and coloured flowers and herbs.

Then come two stanzas that praise God's forgiveness and love, as well as death *"from whom no living man can ever escape."* It concludes with this stanza:

Praise and bless my Lord, render thanks to Him
And serve Him with great humility.[4]

This poem reflects the kind of faith that surfaced in Francis of Assisi. It was also reflected in the monastic movement Francis founded. The members of this order are not restricted to a permanent monastic institution, as was the more typical pattern from the time of Benedict. The Franciscans adopted St. Francis's emphasis on living a life of extreme poverty, preaching and living the Gospel in the manner of Jesus and the Apostles. For a variety of reasons, this movement, unlike others from the same time, gained approval from Rome. Consequently, it spread very quickly during Francis's own lifetime and immediately after.

For St. Francis, a life lived hand in hand with Lady Poverty expresses the primary Christian work—not long discursive treatises on abstract theological topics. What is essential for Francis is a life of thanks and praise to

---

4. See Kerr, *Selections from Anselm*, 102.

the Creator, expressed in a form of spiritual life and spiritual practice shared with the Christian community. In his "Canticle," and in his life, we see a grammar of the spirit that begins with the conviction that the whole of creation is a sacrament of God to be lived in the simplicity of poverty. We see in Francis a sense of identification with the whole of creation—from Brother Sun through Sister Moon to Mother Earth and Death—that expresses the reality of God. We see creation aright when we see it as an expression of divine creativity, as a sacrament. We are to live a life of simplicity and poverty in this creation.

St. Bonaventure (1217–1274): The Soul's Journey

Bonaventure was nine when Francis died, but he was to walk in Francis's footsteps. Thirty years after Francis's death, Bonaventure would become the head of the Franciscans. He was also a professor and a cardinal and he died in the same year as St. Thomas Aquinas. He wrote an influential *Life of St. Francis* and produced one of the most impressive medieval grammars of the soul in his justly famous *The Soul's Journey into God*. In Bonaventure's view, the soul's journey to God proceeds through seven stages. It is a much richer and more diversified scheme than Bernard's three-staged view of purgative-illuminative-unitive. Rather than a first kiss which is a groveling at the feet of the Lord, it begins with "*a contemplation of God through his vestiges in creation.*" According to Bonaventure, God's vestiges are found throughout creation, in our humanity, and in our redemption too.

The seven stages of the spiritual life in Bonaventure's grammar of the soul are:

1. Contemplating God in His Vestiges in the Universe.
2. Contemplating God in His Vestiges in the Sense World.
3. Contemplating God in His Image Stamped on Our Natural Powers.
4. Contemplating God in His Image Reformed by the Gifts of Grace.
5. Contemplating the Divine Unity in its Primary Name that is Being.
6. Contemplating the Blessed Trinity in its Name that is the Good.
7. Spiritual and Mystical Ecstasy: When through Ecstasy Our Mind Passes Over into God.

These are, for Bonaventure, *"the steps of the ascent into God."* In order to proceed along *"the path of God, we must enter into our soul, which is God's image, everlasting, spiritual and within us."*[5]

Some of these deserve a further word of explanation in order to understand the proposal that Bonaventure is making, one that offers a profoundly different grammar of the soul from that of Bernard of Clairvaux, we need to look more closely at some of these stages. Consider, for example, stage one or contemplating God through His vestiges in creation. Notice the different starting point: here we begin with the contemplation of creation, rather than Bernard's purgative beginning point. For Bonaventure, the universe itself is full of vestiges of the Creator. We are invited, wrote Bonaventure, *"to consider the origin, magnitude, beauty, fullness, activity and order of all things"* since these are the categories to see the vestiges of God in creation. They were so obvious to Bonaventure that he concluded that we *"wonder at God's power, wisdom and benevolence"*:

> ... Whoever, therefore, is not enlightened by such splendor of created things is blind; whoever is not awakened by such outcries is deaf; whoever does not praise God because of all these effects is dumb.

But Bonaventure went on to see these vestiges in the sense world—*which has the character of ... a sacrament* —and our own minds—*in which the image of the most blessed trinity shines in splendor*, namely, the powers of memory, choice and intellect. Bonaventure also saw God in the way the image of God, *imago dei*, is restored and reformed in redemption as well as in the contemplation of God's name as being—a very contemporary way of thinking of God—and in contemplating the Trinity. All these stages lead finally to the stage of "spiritual and mystical ecstasy." [6]

The movement in Bonaventure's journey is from the external to the internal and from the temporal to the eternal. We can, said Bonaventure, *"contemplate God not only outside us (creation) and within us (the mind) but also above us."* The fifth through the seventh stages deal with the God above us. Just as we are led to beauty and harmony and wonder by contemplating God's vestiges in creation, we are now led back to God as their *"fountain source."* God is present throughout creation and is the underlying principle that informs all creation. This is Bonaventure's explanation of Jesus as *"the Way, the Truth, and the Life."*

In the *Soul's Journey*, Bonaventure continued the Augustinian tradition, which believes that God is immediately present and knowable to the

---

5. See Bonaventure, *The Soul's Journey into God*, 60.

6. Ibid., 65, 67, 77 and 79.

soul or mind and that knowledge of God precedes all other knowledge. As Bonaventure said,

> We can contemplate God not only outside us and within us but also above us; outside us through his vestiges, within through his image and above through the light which shines upon our minds, which is the light of Eternal truth since our mind itself is formed immediately by Truth itself.[7]

For Bonaventure the journey to God through his vestiges, his image, and his light is a journey to realize what is already, and always, the case, that we are connected to God. It begins where we are in the world since God is present to the whole creation and precedes through the "*three perceptual orientations*" of the mind towards God their transcendent end. It is a vision of the journey to God reflected in the great cathedrals of the Medieval Age.

Julian of Norwich (1342–1423): The Living Trinity

We know little of the person or history of Julian of Norwich. Her name comes from the fact that she attached a small "anchorage" to the cathedral church in Norwich, England, and there lived out her long life. Such a long life is not what Julian expected. Indeed, it was in the midst of a very severe illness that she had the experiences that were to lead to her only book, *Showings* (often translated as *Revelations of Divine Love*)—and what a remarkable book it is.

It is regarded by some as "the most profound and difficult of all medieval mystical writings." It contains Julian's experiences and visions and her reflections upon or interpretations of those experiences. This process of reflection went on over decades and consequently there are two versions of her *Showings*—a longer version, which we will look at here, and a shorter one. Julian's voice, like that of women generally in the history of Christian thought, did not receive the attention it deserved in her own time. However, her book was known to smaller circles within the Christian world, it came to enjoy renewed interest in the twentieth century.

Today, Julian is widely known for her use of the term *Mother* in speaking of God. This occurs in connection with Julian's discussion of the connection of the spiritual life to the Divine Trinity. In the crucial text Julian wrote,

> I contemplated the world of all the blessed Trinity, in which contemplation I saw and understood these three properties: the property of the fatherhood, the property of the motherhood, and

---

7. Ibid., 94.

> *the property of the lordship in one God. In our almighty Father, we have our protection and our bliss ... which is ours by our creation ... and in the second person, in knowledge and wisdom we have ... our restoration and our salvation, for he is our Mother, brother and saviour; and in our great Lord the Holy Spirit we have our reward and gift for our living and our labour ... surpassing all that we desire in his marvelous courtesy ... his great plentiful grace. For all our life consists of three: In the first, we have our being, in the second, we have our increasing, and in the third, we have our fulfillment. This first is nature, the second is mercy, and the third is grace.*[8]

Thus, we have this remarkable linkage in Julian between God the Creator and our being, between God the Mother and our re-making, and between God the Spirit and our fulfillment. Notice the pronouns and the names: Father, Mother, and Lord. Julian always spoke of the Mother as "he" because she was speaking of the second person of the Trinity, the Redeemer who remakes us, Jesus Christ. He embodies the principle of motherhood. Julian explained in the following words:

> *... I saw and understood that the high might of the Trinity is our Father, and the deep wisdom of the Trinity is our Mother, and the great love of the Trinity is our Lord ... And furthermore, I saw ... [That] the second person of the Trinity is our Mother, in ... our substantial creation, in whom we are founded and rooted, and he is our Mother of mercy ... And so our Mother is working on us in various ways ... For in our Mother Christ we profit and increase, and in mercy he reforms and restores us, and by the power of his Passion, his death, and his Resurrection he unites us to our substance. So our Mother works in mercy on all his beloved children.*[9]

Each of the dimensions of human life—our being, our remaking and our fulfillment—are thus linked with a person of the Trinity, so that Julian could say,

> *Thus in our Father, God almighty, we have our being, and in our Mother of mercy we have our reforming and our restoring ... and through the rewards and the gifts of grace of the Holy Spirit we are fulfilled ... As truly as God is our Father, so truly is God our Mother ...* [10]

8. Julian of Norwich, *Showings*, 293-94.
9. Ibid., 294.
10. Ibid., 127-29.

In Julian, then, we have this remarkable correspondence between human life and the Trinitarian structure of divine life: Being and Creation, Remaking and Redemption, Fulfillment and Consummation. Here God is no distant reality. Rather, God is in our life as our being, remaking and fulfillment.

Moreover, for Julian "God is our Mother." Julian develops this language of God as Mother more than anyone else in the traditions of Christian thought. However, what a close reading of her stunning book reveals is that the term *Mother* has little or nothing to do with gender. Though the term "mother" is surrounded by all kinds of gender associations and is specifically linked to the female in ordinary usage that is not how Julian uses it. In relation to God, it seems, the term transcends gender. This is equally true for the term *Father* that is not, in Julian, a gendered term. What is it? For Julian the terms *Father* and *Mother* refer to "properties of the divine trinity," not gender. God is a God who creates and secures our bliss (fatherhood), remakes and redeems our humanity (motherhood) and brings us to fulfillment (lord-hood). It is these properties of the divine trinity that we know in our lives as human beings who are daily made, remade and fulfilled.

Hidden in the text is Julian's inclusive universalism when she says, "for all mankind will be saved by the Sweet Incarnation and the Passion of Christ, all is Christ's humanity . . . and we are his members."[11]

This text of Julian's deserves much more attention than we can give it here. Julian's invaluable contribution to the great conversation of Christian thought teaches us how we can speak of God as Mother. The language of "Mother" is decoupled from gender and related to qualities of caring, renewing, nurturing, helping, remaking and redeeming. It is a way of speaking of those dimensions of human life—our being remade in the crucible of life itself—where we know the divine Mother who cares for all His children. Few Christian thinkers have seen the interior connection between the life of human beings and divine life as profoundly as Julian of Norwich. For Julian, our very being is connected to the Maker, our being remade to the Redeemer and our fulfillment to the Glorifier.

Summary

Earlier, in the chapter on Eastern Voices, we discussed the work of Gregory of Palamas, who died in 1359. His work, like those discussed here, contributed to the grammar of the spiritual life, an essential dimension of the great

---

11. Ibid., 276.

conversation within Christian thought. These Christian thinkers exhibit the importance of vision and experience in Christian thought.

Each of these thinkers has contributed, in their own distinctive ways, to the Christian Grammar of the Spiritual Life. Like other Christian thinkers, they affirm that human life is from-God, in-God and to-God. However, this is not a static reality or condition. Rather, as these figures have shown, it is a dynamic reality as human beings pass through various conditions and stages on their journey to God. They seek to chart the dynamics and order of the spiritual life to guide the Christian seeker after God. While some see that journey to God as a threefold process, others identify as many as seven stages in the journey. All agree that there are stages to the spiritual life and that it is much more complicated than the unsaved/saved or unconverted/converted dichotomies of much evangelical fundamentalist thinking of our own time. Here we see that some saw the journey as beginning with an awareness of sin while others saw its beginning in the wonder of creation. Some saw the renovation of the human interior as a reforming of one's inner life, while others saw it more as a reawakening to or recovery of what is already there. Some saw many different stages along the way to a mystical marriage of the soul with God, while others saw the end as transcending description, characterized by ecstasy. They all agreed that the end of humanity is God.

Review

1. What are Bernard's three stages of the spiritual life?
2. Who defined the soul as "a green life force"?
3. What connection did Julian make between the Trinity and our experience of life? What did she mean when she spoke of God as "Mother"?
4. How did Bonaventure view the stages of the spiritual life?
5. What was Francis's view of creation?

Chapter 14

The Quest for Synthesis and the Emergence of Theology as the Science of God in Medieval Christian Thought

Thomas Aquinas and the Summa Theologica

Thomas Aquinas died on March 7, 1274, the same year as Bonaventure, whom we encountered earlier. They had been friends, as each had defended his order—the Dominicans for Thomas and the Franciscans for Bonaventure—against those who challenged the presence of the religious orders in the universities. This friendship stood despite the differences in their thinking about "sacred doctrine." Bonaventure sought to chart the soul's journey to God, while Thomas sought to summarize the whole of our knowledge of God.

Thomas stands as a pivotal figure in the history of Christian thought because he articulated his understanding of Christianity on a new philosophical foundation. That new foundation arose from the recovery in the West of one of the great ancient philosophers, Aristotle. From early Christianity until St. Thomas's time, Aristotle had not received a great deal of attention in the West, and in many respects, his work had been virtually lost to the Western tradition of Christian thinking. The philosophical assumptions of Plato and the neo-Platonic traditions had very much dominated Christian thought in the West. That began to change in Thomas's time. Muslim scholars, philosophers, and theologians in Spain had long known Aristotle's works, and now Aristotle was re-introduced into the life of medieval Europe. Following his teacher Albert the Great at the University of Paris, Thomas was among the first in the Christian world to take the philosophy of Aristotle seriously. The overall effect of the recovery of Aristotle was complex, but it is fair to say that, in part, it led to a new appreciation of the created world.

You may recall that in the Platonic tradition a fundamental distinction is between appearance and reality. Thus, what we see with our eyes and touch with our hands is a part of the realm of appearances and not the ideal world, which stands behind this world of appearances. The world we see is a dim reflection of what truly is. In contrast, in the Aristotelian tradition, the world that we see is reality. The sensible world is much more highly valued in the Aristotelian tradition than in the Platonic tradition, and what arises from this is a different understanding of the way the mind works, especially in terms of the relation of the mind to the sensible external world. For Aristotle, rationality and thinking arise in relation to making sense out of what is given to us in our experience of the world. While for Anselm or Augustine, God is immediately present to the human mind. In the Aristotelian tradition as interpreted by St. Thomas, the things of God are present to the mind through the sensible world. Thomas remarks: "*all our knowledge originates from the senses.*"[1]

Thus, as we reflect upon that world that is given to us "from the senses," we can come to understand the causes that lie behind things. For Aquinas this appreciation of the natural world is not naturalism since "in all creatures there is found the trace of the Trinity" and in our reflection on what is given through the sensible world, we can come to understand the deeper sources and causes of things. Indeed, the greatest of those causes is, in Aristotelian terms, the "Unmoved Mover" which stands at the very origin of things. This is one of the ways that Aquinas, following Aristotle, comes to speak about God. For this reality is, as Aquinas says, *"a first mover, put in motion by no other; and this everyone understands to be God."* God as *Being Itself* is the formal cause of everything that is. In addition, we can know that God exists through our analysis of and reflection upon the sensible world. This is one of the most important consequences of this shift from more Platonic philosophical assumptions to more Aristotelian assumptions.

This shift in sensibility we can see in Aquinas's arguments—there are five of them—for the existence of God. Aquinas rejected Anselm's ontological argument, but offered his own arguments on different grounds. When we look at Aquinas's arguments, we will see that they all begin with the world that we see and know: the world of motion, the world of contingency and so on.[2]

1. Aquinas, *The Summa Theologica*, 9.
2. Ibid., 248 and 13 and for Thomas' arguments for the existence of God see Kerr,

The Young Aquinas

Before pursuing some aspects of his contributions to the story of Christian thought, first let us look briefly at who Thomas Aquinas was. He was born into a titled family and sent to a school run by Benedictines when he was five. His family expected that he would eventually become a member of this Benedictine order and rise to a position of some prominence in the order. The Benedictines were the most prestigious order in the Catholic tradition at the time. In 1240, when he was 15, Thomas went to school in Naples, where he did the equivalent of university work. While he was in Naples, he became attracted to a new religious order that had just emerged: the Dominicans. Founded by Dominic, a Spanish monk, the Dominicans were the street preachers of Aquinas's day. Their order did not lead a secluded monastic life, but rather sought to bring the Christian message to the people. The Dominicans were always out teaching, preaching and propagating the Christian faith.

Thomas's interest in the Dominicans provoked a great crisis within his family. They were much opposed to his becoming associated with this new order. The Dominicans were not that highly regarded and did not represent a way into positions of power and influence. His family was embarrassed by his interest in the Dominicans. They tried unsuccessfully to dissuade Thomas from becoming a Dominican. Finally, they kidnapped him and held him prisoner for fifteen months hoping to bring him to his senses. However, Thomas persisted in his conviction that his life lay with the Dominicans, and finally his family relented and allowed him to enter the Dominican order.

He then went on to further study from 1245 to 1248 at the brand new University of Paris. There he came under the influence of Albert the Great, a fine teacher and a champion of the renewed interest in Aristotle. Under Albert's influence and impact as a teacher, Thomas came to appreciate Aristotle and began to work out the implications of these new philosophical assumptions for articulating the Christian faith.

Later, Aquinas became known as the "Angelic Doctor," but in his own time, he was known as the "Ox" for what were seen as his stubborn qualities. He also had a remarkable capacity to organize vast amounts of material and present it in a very systematic way. There are stories of how Thomas, later in his life, had built for himself a table in the form of a half-circle. Five or six scribes would sit around the table, and he would dictate to the scribes different sections of different books that he was writing simultaneously. This great

---

Selections from Thomas Aquinas, 110-115.

capacity for the systematic organization of Christian thinking is reflected in his writings, and especially in his *Summa Theologica*.

Summa Theologica

What was Thomas trying to do in the *Summa*? He said in his prologue that it is a book "*suited to the instruction of beginners*" and designed "*to set forth whatever is included in sacred doctrine as briefly and as clearly as the matter itself may allow.*" Thomas's suggestion that it is a book for "beginners" makes me smile, since it is a very difficult text. More important is his claim to comprehensiveness: "*to set forth whatever is included in sacred doctrine.*" This effort to be comprehensive points us to why Thomas is so important in the history of Christian thought. Partly his significance lies in his aim: to provide a comprehensive account of Christian thinking and to order all knowledge properly. One slogan that is often associated with Thomas is "Everything in its place and a place for everything." For Thomas, as for others in his time, knowledge was ultimately one, and the problem was that knowledge was scattered, not integrated and ordered. Thomas felt that we needed a scheme to integrate all knowledge. That meant a scheme of thinking which places "theology," the "queen of the sciences," at the apex of a great arch where all forms of knowing—the philosophical sciences, the moral sciences and the sciences of nature—had their proper place. The problem for St. Thomas—and others within the new universities of his time as well as the wider society—was that there was no systematic vision of the whole. Thomas set out to redress that lack. A comprehensive account of things that would put all aspects of our knowing into their proper place was Thomas's aim.[3]

The second reason for the significance of Thomas's work is that it employs a new philosophical foundation—an Aristotelian one—to articulate the Christian faith. Therefore, in Thomas's work we have a version of the Christian faith in terms drawn from Aristotle, or as Thomas calls him in the *Summa*, the Philosopher. These twin purposes—a systematic and a comprehensive account—came together in the new science that Thomas and the other schoolmen were creating; they called it theology, the science of God (*theos*, God, plus *ology*, science). In Thomas's view, theology was the primary knowing, the "queen of the sciences." Theology stands first because it relates things of God and provides us with knowledge of our human end. With this knowledge, then, we can see how all knowledge—the *philosophical sciences built up by human reason*—fits in with our knowledge of God.

3. Ibid., 1, 3.

This "sacred doctrine" is, says Thomas, a "*science.*" It is both "*speculative and practical,*" and "*God is truly the subject of this science.*"[4]

Two Sources of Knowing God

According to Thomas, there are two sources of our knowledge of God: reason and revelation. "*There is,*" says Thomas, "a *twofold mode of truth in what we profess about God.*" It is important to distinguish the proper sphere of reason from that of revelation. The sphere of reason is the natural order:

> *Beginning with sensible things, our intellect is led to the point of knowing about God that He exists, and other such characteristics that must be attributed to the First Principle. There are, consequently, some intelligible truths about God that are open to the human reason.*

And of course, the philosophical sciences provide us with other kinds of knowing too, as for example when "*the astronomer and the physicist both prove the same conclusion—that the earth, for instance, is round.*" But, Thomas continued, "*There are others that absolutely surpass its power*" and this is the sphere of revelation or the supernatural order. For Thomas, it was possible for human beings to know something of God apart from revelation. Thomas believed that we could know that God is, that God is one, and a number of other things.[5]

However, the sphere of revelation was another order. To know some further things about God, God had to make them known to us. Thomas insisted that "*it was necessary for man's salvation that there should be knowledge revealed by God besides the philosophical sciences built up by human reason.*" This further knowledge, given in revelation, included the mysteries of the Incarnation and of the Trinity. In light of the two sources of knowledge of God (even if the knowledge given in revelation could not be known by reason alone), there can be a great deal of co-operation between the theologian and the philosopher, between the Christian and the natural knower. However, even though there are "*truths about God which human reason can discover,*" they would "*only be known by a few.*" Thus, "*it was necessary that [we, the many] should be taught divine truths by divine revelation.*"[6]

For Thomas, then, there was no fundamental conflict between reason and revelation. Though revelation takes one significantly beyond natural

---

4. Ibid., 3-5 and 7.
5. Kerr, Selections from Thomas Aquinas, 107-10, and 4.
6. Ibid., 3.

reason, it is not contrary to reason. The issue is one of coming to understand the true end of human beings, which is "to know God." It is this *"vision of the divine essence"* which is *"the final and perfect happiness"* of humanity.[7] With clarity about the end of humanity as related to God, then we can see other knowing in relation to God, and there is some possibility that we can find the proper place for what we know through the philosophical sciences as well as through this science based in revelation. Confusion abounds when things get out of their proper place.

Thomas argued that:

> ... there is a twofold mode of truth in what we profess about God. Some truths about God exceed all the ability of the human reason. Such is the truth that God is triune. But there are some truths that the natural reason also is able to reach. Such are that God exists, that He is one, and the like."

St. Thomas sought to reconcile reason and revelation in this way. He understood that the final purpose of reason was to contemplate divine things. How does this reason come to know whatever it knows? Every science, says Aquinas, *"proceeds from principles"*—and in this case from those principles given by revelation. The human mind works in relation to the external world and here knowledge arises from and through the sensible world. The knowledge of God does not come primarily from the mind's direct connection to God, as had been earlier believed. Rather, knowledge comes through the sensible and external world. We can see this when we look at Thomas's arguments for the existence of God.

Arguments for the Existence of God

Aquinas rejected Anselm's ontological argument for the existence of God and instead offered five arguments of his own. Because knowledge arises through the sensible world for Thomas, his argument proceeds in a very different way from Anselm. Anselm proceeded not by looking at the external world as the place that we come to know that God exists, but rather through an internal examination of the term *God* itself. We see, in Anselm, the intuitive logic and power of his argument that we cannot think of God, as *that than which nothing greater can be conceived*, as not existing, and in that way we gain some certitude about God's existence. For Thomas, however, Anselm's self-evident argument does not establish that God "actually exists."

---

7. Aquinas, *Summa Theologica*, 629.

Thomas's own thinking can demonstrate God's existence *"from those of His effects which are known to us."*

For Thomas, reason works in a very different way. He offered five *"demonstrations"* of the existence of God. See how his arguments work. The first is Thomas's argument from motion. He said that this is the *"first and more manifest way . . .* [since] *it is certain, and evident to our senses, that in this world some things are in motion."* He continued, *"Now whatever is in motion is put in motion by another,"* and explained what he meant by motion: the movement from *potency to act*. Moreover, *"if that by which it is moved be itself moved, then this must also be moved by another."* However *"this cannot go on to infinity, because then there would be no first mover."* Therefore, Aquinas concluded, *"it is necessary to arrive at a first mover which is moved by no other. And this everyone understands to be God."* This is his argument. It begins with the familiar and sensible world and moves inductively to what lies behind motion: a first mover that is itself not moved by another. Moreover, it is obvious to Aquinas that this is God. The argument goes back and back and back. As we do this, Aquinas said, we come to a notion of a first mover that *"everyone understands to be God."* Well, perhaps not everyone. However, when we look at his five arguments they all unfold in a similar way.

Thomas's second argument is an argument from efficient cause. Similarly, in considering efficient causes we are led *"to a first efficient cause . . . to which everyone gives the name of God."* What is important to see here is that Aquinas was thinking inductively from our experience of the world and that leads us back to the first efficient cause to which everyone gives the name of God. The third argument is the argument from contingency, the fourth from graduation and the fifth from the governance of the world. The perfect reality that is the cause of all things is, in one way or another, God. These are the arguments that Aquinas offers for the existence of God.[8]

For Aquinas, Christian thinking is thinking about God. His manner of proceeding—seen above in his arguments for the existence of God—is typical throughout the *Summa*. He begins with a question: for example, whether the existence of God is self-evident. Then he presents the *objections* to the claim, and then gives the *contrary* before providing his answer, which always begin *"I answer that . . . "* It is a difficult but remarkably precise text, as Aquinas defines terms, clarifies the issues and, in conversation with others in the tradition, offers his solution.

Something similar to what we have seen above is found in how Aquinas stated the relationship of nature and grace. You will recall that the issue of nature and grace was addressed by Augustine in his debate with Pelagius.

---

8. See Ibid., 12-13 and 110-15.

Nature & Grace

For Thomas, *every being that is in any way is from God . . . who is Being itself*," or, "*it is necessary to say that all things were created by God.*" Moreover, Thomas affirms that, "*every being, as being, is good.*" The issue of nature and grace in Aquinas can be characterized in this way: grace does not contradict nature but perfects and fulfills nature. You can see this issue backward in relation to Augustine and forward in relation to the reformers who quarreled with Aquinas's understanding of this relationship of grace and nature. For Aquinas, grace is already present in our created nature and comes into the soul to perfect and bring to completion those capacities and powers that are already in the soul, in what God has given us in nature. This means that for Thomas there is not as radical a doctrine of sin as we see in Augustine or in the reformers. The question that arises concerns the impact on human nature of the Fall? In Thomas's view, the Fall wounds human nature but it is not destroyed or altered. Calvin, on the other hand, will argue that the Fall results in a "hereditary depravity and corruption of nature." For Thomas, grace enables nature to come to perfection, to complete itself, to be fulfilled.[9]

Moreover, grace and nature do not stand in opposition to each other. For Thomas, nature is already graced since human beings, like all creation and all creatures, were "*created in grace.*" Grace is the love of God and embedded in creation itself, since creation arises from the love of God. A general grace pervades creation and marks all created natures. There is also, in Thomas, special grace and divine mercy that come into play following the Fall: "*for more things . . . for the remission of sin, and for the support of his weakness.*" But here again, grace is not opposed to nature or created beings, but enables created beings to reach their proper end and fulfillment in God. As Thomas remarked, "*faith presupposes natural knowledge, even as grace presupposes nature, and perfection supposes something that can be perfected.*"[10]

This is very central to Aquinas's thinking. We have already seen a similar principle at work in how he understands reason and revelation. He evaluates reason so highly because he does not see it as destroyed by the fall of man. Given in creation, reason is fundamentally intact, though diminished by sin.

This is reflected in a section in the *Summa Theologica* called "The Effects of Sin." Here Thomas asked the question of whether the entire good of man can be destroyed by sin. "*He performs actions in accord with reason,*

---

9. See Ibid., 238, 243, and 25.

10. See Ibid., 506, 509, and 12; See also Kerr, *Selection of Aquinas on Effects of Sin*, 115-18.

which is to act virtuously. Now sin cannot entirely take away from man the fact that he is a rational being, for then he would no longer be capable of sin. Wherefore it is not possible for this good of nature to be destroyed entirely." The form of his statement is very important. "*The good of nature . . . is the natural inclination to virtue*," and that natural inclination to virtue has not been diminished by sin. Later John Calvin will argue that the image of God in man is wholly destroyed by the Fall, and therefore without grace we can do nothing. That tradition is very pervasive within Protestant Christianity. However, in Thomas, while the natural inclination to virtue is diminished, it is still intact. Thus, we can appeal to this capacity within human beings and expect them to do the good. We can expect that to a very significant degree. Human capacities have not been destroyed by sin. This is true in relation to the other powers of the human being as well.[11]

The fact that we are rational beings means that we can appeal to reason and expect that others will hear us and heed us as long as we are speaking rationally and coherently. This underlying assumption permeates the whole of Aquinas's work. It is one of the reasons that there arises out of the Thomistic tradition a form of Christian humanism, a capacity and ability reflected in institutions in this tradition working in close co-operation with the humanistic traditions in philosophy in particular. For Thomas, we can remedy the difficulties that we experience within our life and work through more effort on our part, and that effort is made through God's enticing and enabling grace, which allows that nature which God gives in creation to simply achieve its proper ends and perfect itself.

Consider these matters very closely when looking at Aquinas, for they are very important not only in their own right but also for the larger project that Aquinas undertook, which was both to "instruct the beginner" and also to "*set forth whatever is included in sacred doctrine*." Curiously, but importantly, Thomas's work in the *Summa Theologica* remained uncompleted. In 1273, while Thomas was saying Mass he experienced a vision. It led Thomas to say that compared to the vision "*all of his work was straw*." The last year of his life was spent in prayer and contemplation. En route from Italy to France for a church council that he had been asked to attend, he became ill and died. It was 1274.

There was a great deal of controversy around Thomas's work in his own time. He was accused of heresy. His notion of God as pure act was strongly criticized and some articles of his Christian thinking were rejected by the larger scholastic and Catholic community of his own time. However, within 50 years of his death, his works were regarded as theologically sound and

---

11. See Kerr, *Selections of Aquinas on Effects of Sin*, 115.

he came to occupy a very large and central place in the Catholic theological tradition. In the nineteenth century, at the First Vatican Council (1869-70) St. Thomas became the official theologian of the Catholic tradition. Within his time—and in centuries after—many other voices were contributing to the great conversation. Some of those voices rivalled Thomas, and some stood in opposition to views that Thomas had held and had articulated in such a profoundly significant way.

I do not think that if you pick up the *Summa Theologica*, you will find it the most exciting work you will have ever laid hands on. What is impressive is Thomas's knowledge of the long tradition of Christian thinking and his organizational power. In dealing with each particular teaching/doctrine, he summarized what earlier teachers in Christian thought had said and, from that, tried to draw out two or three major positions. Then he went on to list all of the objections raised against each of these positions and responds to all of these objections. At the end of this process, he finally states his own summary understanding of this particular teaching or issue or doctrinal question. There are few questions that Aquinas failed to address in the *Summa*. That in itself is a remarkable achievement, even if one disagrees with his particular conclusions.

John Duns Scotus (1265-1308)

Among the schoolmen, there was a range of understandings of the Christian faith. One of the critics of Aquinas who emerged at the end of Aquinas' life and held an alternative view was a Franciscan named John Duns Scotus.

Duns Scotus was a Franciscan who was educated at Oxford and later in Cologne in Germany. He is often regarded as the most important or authoritative thinker among the Franciscans. Even though that distinction might arguably belong to Bonaventure, Scotus came to have a position among Franciscans parallel to the position Thomas held among the Dominicans.

The heart of the disagreement between Scotus and Aquinas concerns their conception of the basic category for understanding God—and human beings. According to Thomas, God's "essence is His being" and "good and being are really the same." Further, Aquinas said that "truth is convertible with the good" and that "man excels all animals by his reason and intelligence . . . which are incorporeal, that is . . . the image of God." Thus, for Thomas, the universe is essentially intelligible and knowable, because the essence of God and humanity is essentially intelligible and knowable. Scotus did not see this intelligibility at the heart of things: he saw an inscrutable sovereign will. This is a very complicated distinction, and I will summarize it briefly and draw out some of its implications.[12]

For Aquinas, God creates because He sees that it is good. Thus, there is a fundamental harmony between God and reason, because God creates in accordance with what is good, and what is good is what is reasonable. Hence, there is a basic harmony between God's purposes and the intelligible or rational nature of things.

Scotus felt that Aquinas's understanding of God was too rationalistic, and argued that we have to think about God in terms that are different from the ones Aquinas proposed. In Scotus's view, things are good because God created them. On the surface this looks more or less the same as Aquinas's view, but what Scotus was getting at is that, as he saw it, the essence of God is his will, and things are good by virtue of God's willing them to be so. Hence, there is no inherent reason or intelligibility to things. The world is as God, in his sovereign will, wills them to be. If God had made the world in some other way, it would be equally good, because whatever God wills is good. By contrast, Thomas aimed to see a fundamental harmony between divine willing and reason, which gives the primary role in God to intelligence rather than the will. When we act, we act in accordance with our reason, and our action is good because it is in accordance with our reason.

For Thomas, the universe has *logos* or reason at its heart. For Scotus, the universe has will or divine sovereignty at its heart. For Scotus, when we speak about God then we should realize that things are good simply because God wills them, and we are obliged to heed them whether we can see any reason for them or not. They are simply good by virtue of their coming from God.

This difference has some important consequences for the Christian life. We could say that Aquinas's view tends to heighten the Christian's reliance upon his or her natural faculties, whereas the tradition that grows out of Scotus tends to heighten reliance upon authority, because God reveals his will in Scripture and to the Church. So how are we to know what God wills? If we follow Aquinas, then we can take thought upon things and we come to know God's will because it is built into the order of things. If we follow Scotus, then we know God's will by turning to authority or to Scripture and the Church. It is there that we are instructed in God's will and purposes, because the claims which faith makes upon the human person are beyond rational demonstration. Thomas was convinced that all the important things that we should know and should guide our action could be known by taking thought upon them (although it was still necessary to be schooled). Arguments and rational demonstrations could establish the truth of fundamental

---

12. See Aquinas, *Summa Theologica*, 17, 23, 15.

Christian claims, though Aquinas recognized that there were things known only through revelation (Scripture). However, once known through revelation, we can see that they too are not unreasonable.

For Scotus, the truth of the Christian claims had to be accepted on the basis of authority, and we had to bring our will into conformity with that authority. He did not agree with Thomas's assertion that rational demonstrations could be provided for the truth of the claims of the Christian faith. Even in the oversimplified form in which I've presented the complex issues that separated Scotus and Aquinas, the difference between them signifies a growing rift within medieval Christianity. Some thinkers were still deeply committed to the scholastic approach of offering a comprehensive account of things that would be both consistent with the Christian faith and rationally persuasive, while others were not. We find quite precise and subtle thinkers like Scotus who no longer thought that the approach to Christian thinking exemplified by Thomas was possible, and who saw a much greater divergence between faith and reason. This divergence would play a very large role at the time of the Reformation.

Summary

Among the many and diverse Christian thinkers of the medieval period, here we have focused on Thomas Aquinas as representative of the best of Christian thought in that period. Thomas gave us a remarkably comprehensive account of the "sacred doctrine" of the Christian faith. In doing so he drew upon "the Philosopher"—Aristotle—but not, in my view, in ways that overwhelm faith. Rather they bring it into a new form, which draws upon the longer tradition of Christian thinking. In some ways, his *Summa* is a summary of Christian thinking, as Aquinas continually incorporated the views of early Christian thinkers into his thought. It is laced with references to Augustine and Dionysius, for example, and it is said that he always had John of Damascus's works on Christ before him while writing the *Summa*. His contributions to the great conversation are many and varied, and his achievements in the *Summa* are remarkable. The vision of the Christian faith that emerged from his great work—revolving around his conviction that grace fulfills and perfects nature as it leads humanity toward its highest end, the vision of God—has been enduring.

Review

1. What, according to Thomas, are the two sources of our knowledge of God?
2. How did Thomas understand the relationship between reason and revelation?
3. Why was the recovery of Aristotle important for Christian thought?
4. What is the nature of the divergence between Thomas Aquinas and Duns Scotus?

PART V

Reforming Christian Thought: 1500–1780

THE SIXTEENTH CENTURY WAS a period of reform across the Western Christian traditions. Chapter 15 focuses on the great Protestant reformers: Martin Luther and John Calvin. Luther, an Augustinian monk, came to a spiritual crisis in his life and protested the practice of indulgences in his Catholic world. In the resulting conflict, Luther, with the support of some German Princes, broke with the Catholic Church. This led to the emergence of the Protestant traditions, in which "justification by faith alone" and "Scripture alone" as the foundation of Christian life and authority in the life of a Christian became central ideas. John Calvin was a Protestant thinker who focused on the sovereignty of God and offered an impressive presentation of Protestant principles in his *Institutes of the Christian Religion*. Not all of the Protestant reformers agreed among themselves. We will see this in Chapter 16 when we look at Anabaptist (Menno Simons) and Anglican (Richard Hooker) figures. However, reform was not limited to the newly emergent Protestant traditions: it was also present across the Catholic world, as we see in Chapter 17. Here we look at Desiderius Erasmus, who was initially sympathetic to Luther but finally opposed him because Erasmus wanted to preserve the unity of the Catholic tradition. Moreover, two Spanish Catholics, Teresa of Avila and Ignatius of Loyola, initiated spiritual reforms that were to have a great impact on Christian thinking and life. Teresa's *Interior Castle* renewed the Carmelites and Ignatius's *Spiritual Exercises* was central to the founding of the Jesuits. Chapter 18 looks at the further "reforming of the reformers" by examining reform movements within the Protestant world that would make significant contributions to the Great Conversation: Puritans, Pietists and Methodists. The final chapter in this section looks at Christian thought in the new world, especially the work of Bartolomé de Las Casas, who critiqued the treatment of the indigenous peoples of the new world by the Spanish, and the ideas of Jonathan Edwards, one of the American colonies' most influential thinkers. This chapter also touches on Canadian developments.

Chapter 15

Protestant Reformers
Luther, Calvin and Zwingli

BETWEEN THE THIRTEENTH AND sixteenth centuries, much had happened within the Christian world of the West. The great synthesis between reason and revelation that had been achieved in the work of St. Thomas began to break down after Thomas's death. One element of that breakdown was the rise of Nominalism, the view that universals are neither "real nor ideal" but mere "puffs of air" or words. Another element of that breakdown was reflected in the controversy between Scotus and Thomas over the question of the nature of God and the primacy of the will versus the primacy of reason within the Divine. Increasingly, the view associated with Scotus that the will took precedence over reason led to a greater emphasis on the church as the institution that we need to rely upon to know the truth of God.

A part of the Middle Ages achieved a synthesis not only in the intellectual order but also in the social order; here the church came to play a dominant role in all aspects of social life. At the heart of medieval culture stood the sacramental system of the Church as the means by which grace is mediated to the hearts and lives of human beings. This understanding of the Church is important background for looking at the reform movement that came to expression in the sixteenth century. The period of the Reformation is often thought of in terms of the great division that entered into Western Christianity between the Catholic and Protestant traditions. We should rather speak of the sixteenth century as a period of reform across the whole of the Western Christian world, although those reforms were different in different parts of that world. During this century, the Catholic tradition underwent its own reform, while other reforms resulted in the emergence of a series of new churches and communities: Lutheran, Calvinist, Anabaptist and so on. Reform cut across the whole of Western Christendom but had different expressions in different contexts.

Martin Luther & the Protestant Reformation

The central figure in the emergence of the Protestant Reformation was the German Augustinian monk Martin Luther (1483-1546). There were, to be sure, anticipations of the reform movement Luther initiated, which are important to note to undercut any notion of a wholly static Catholic tradition. Indeed, the history of Christian thought is a story of continuous change and development, even though it contains periods of institutional stability. Two of the more significant antecedents of Luther were John Wycliffe (c.1320-1384) and Jan Hus (1369-1415). Already in the fourteenth century, Wycliffe attempted to raise the place of Scripture within the Christian life and translated the Bible into vernacular English. Luther later championed the view of "sola scriptura" or "Scripture alone" in his conflict with the larger Catholic tradition, and translated the Bible into German. Likewise, Jan Hus in early fifteenth-century Bohemia sought to reform Christian life by challenging the authority of the church and by initiating "communion in both kinds," that is, a sharing of both the bread and the wine during communion. Luther too would challenge the church and initiate changes in ecclesiastical practice, although this was not at the heart of his reforms.

Luther's reform movement grew out of his own personal struggle to find resolution to his inward sense of unease, bad conscience and guilt. Luther was deeply troubled by the question of how human beings stood vis-à-vis God. Were they condemned, judged, accepted or loved? Luther felt judged (he would later see this as "living by works"), and he worked his way to feeling and believing that he, like all humanity, was loved by God (what he would later see as "living by faith"). In this process, Luther articulated a version of the Christian faith that would alter the religious landscape of Western Christianity. Moreover, his views were caught up in the socio-political—like rising nationalism—and cultural elements that were simmering in the world of his time.

Luther was born in Germany in 1483. His father was a miner, and when Luther went off to university, the family hoped that their son would become a lawyer. He went to study at Wittenberg, a new university in Saxony. In 1505, while travelling between his home and his university, he got caught in the middle of a lightning storm. He was terribly frightened by the storm and is reported to have called out, "St. Anne, save me; I will become a monk." Later, historians would learn that Luther had been struggling with vocational issues for some time. When he returned to Wittenberg, he left the university and entered an Augustinian monastery. Here Luther did exceedingly well, and he was ordained in 1507. He was a very able student and soon came to be a teacher within the university where he had initially studied. His early teaching assignments were in the study of Scripture. He knew the original languages of Scripture and embraced some of new approaches to it then emerging in humanist scholarship of his time. Over these next years, Luther served as a university lecturer, and was asked to do many important things within his own Augustinian order. Those included a trip to Rome in 1510-11 on Augustinian business. To all outward appearances, Luther was very successful. He had become a priest, a university lecturer, and was highly regarded within his religious order.

The Inner Journey & Breakthrough

But inwardly, however, Luther remained an immensely troubled human being. He felt that he was a very sinful person; he seemed to feel constantly under judgment rather than loved. His was an uneasy conscience. He sought in vain to find resolution for his inward unease within the sacramental system of his church and time—specifically through the sacrament of penance. He believed that if one was inwardly troubled by one's sins, then one could go to a priest to make confession of those sins, receive absolution and then walk in some newness of life.

But this did not work for Luther. It seems that he was constantly troubled by his own inward sense that there were many sins—tiny and even unconscious ones—that he had not confessed. He felt that failure to confess them meant that he remained under the judgment of God, abandoned, alone. In the monastery, we would later learn, Luther would spend hours in confession. His spiritual advisor and close friend within the Augustinians was a man named Johann von Staupitz (1460-1524), who became exasperated with Luther when the troubled monk spent hours and hours sorting through all of the sins that he had committed so that he could confess them and stand in a righteous way in relation with God. Go away, Staupitz would tell Luther: get on with your life, do not be so scrupulous. It did not work. Luther remained inwardly tormented.

This was Luther's problem: he just could not find the resolution to this inward sense of being under judgment within the sacramental system of the church. Luther experienced God as being against him, rejecting him and condemning him.

Luther's journey towards some change in his inward sense of things relates to his study of Scripture, on which he lectured in the university. His early lectures on the Psalms were important ones in Luther's development because he very much identified with the anguish of the existential turmoil present in the Psalms. And when he comes upon the words where the Psalmist expresses his sense of being forsaken by God, words repeated at Christ's crucifixion—"My God, my God, why hast thou forsaken me (Psalm 22:1)—Luther felt that these words marked his situation too.

Luther later turned his attention to the Pauline writings, especially the Book of Romans. It was in Paul's writings that Luther encountered anew something that had always been part of the Christian tradition: the Pauline doctrine of justification. When Luther read in Paul that "all have sinned and fall short of the Glory of God, they are justified by his grace as a gift through the redemption which is Christ Jesus" (Romans 3:23–24), or that "a man is justified by faith apart from the works of law" (3:28), or that "since we are justified by faith, we may have peace with God through our Lord Jesus Christ" (5:1), he was hearing words he had not understood before. In words like these from Paul, Luther achieved a crucial existential breakthrough. He finally realized that God has already acted decisively in Jesus Christ. He saw that in Jesus Christ God has reconciled us to God—"we were reconciled to God by the death of his Son" (5:10). Here God has announced his love for humankind. These teachings of Paul came to Luther as a revelation. Was not this the answer to his angst, his inner anxiety? Was not Paul teaching us that it is not our effort but Christ's work that reconciles us to God? This was, for Luther, the good news of the gospel: we are saved by the grace of God, not by any human works. What this meant for Luther was that he did not need to be anxious about his relationship with God since in Jesus Christ God has announced his love for humankind. We needed only to realize this, to accept it.

Later, Luther would write of the Apostle Paul's letter to the Romans that "*it is in truth the most important document in the New Testament, the gospel in its purest expression.*" However, we "*must learn what Paul means by such words as law, sin, grace, faith, righteousness ... and the like.*" Luther explained that, for example, "*you must not understand the term 'law' in its everyday sense [as] acts permitted or forbidden*"; rather, you must understand it in a spiritual sense. It is the demand of God that we inwardly and lovingly fulfill God's will, but that is something human beings cannot do on their own. Faith, Luther explains, is not mere belief, but a "*living and unshakeable confidence in the grace of God.*" It is faith that gives rise to "*peace, joy, love* to God and all mankind... When faith is at home it is joined by all things of this kind because of the overflowing goodwill which God shows us in Christ."[1]

Of course, this Pauline doctrine of justification had always been part of the longer Christian tradition, but it came to Luther as a powerful answer to his inward quest. Paul says that "we are justified by grace through faith," and these words took on a special life, vitality, and meaning for Luther. Luther heard them as saying that the human situation vis-à-vis God was not one determined by human effort or human works. Rather, what he felt he had discovered was that God has already graciously forgiven us, accepted us, and bestowed a status on us, not because of anything we do but out of God's own gracious goodness. Later, Luther would call this "alien righteousness" or "the righteousness of another, instilled from without."

He would further explain:

> ... He who trusts in Christ exists in Christ; he is one with Christ... This righteousness is primary; it is the basis, the cause, the source of all our own actual righteousness. For this is the righteousness given in place of the original righteousness lost in Adam... It is in this sense that we are to understand the prayer in Psalm 31... "In thee, O Lord, do I seek refuge... in thy righteousness deliver me!" It does not say "in my" but "in thy righteousness," that is, in the righteousness of Christ my God which becomes ours through faith and by the grace and mercy of God.[2]

One of Luther's slogans that emerges from the Reformation is that we are "justified by faith alone," meaning that we stand before God on the foundation of what Christ has done for humanity. This was Luther's view of the heart of the Christian gospel.

Faith as Trust

For Luther, the scholastic tradition had misunderstood the nature of faith. Faith was not consent to propositions, consent to truths about the nature or being of God. Rather, faith was the radical experience of trust, the experience of trusting in the promises of God. What God has done most centrally in the life of Jesus is to disclose to us his forgiveness and his willingness to accept us, not for what we have done but through what Christ accomplishes. Thus, the human heart can achieve a certain inward rest and peace by simply

---

1. See Dillenberger, *Martin Luther*, 19, 20, 24, 28. For an illuminating study of the young Luther, see Erikson, *Young Man Luther*.
2. Dillenberger, *Martin Luther*, 155-57.

trusting in what God has already accomplished and what God has already given to us: God's redemptive love accepts us, loves us and reconciles us to God through Christ. It is here alone that the restlessness within Luther came to a resolution. It is here that one gains a good conscience. It is here that one overcomes and transforms the sense of desolation and being apart from God. God graciously comes into our life and renews our life, not because of anything that we do other than receive, in an attitude of trust, the gracious movement of God towards human beings. For Luther this was the heart of the Christian life: the experience of justification by grace alone received through faith.

These changes in Luther's understanding of the Christian faith had occurred over a period of years punctuated by moments of great insight. Those insights are to be found in some of his early writings before 1517 and in his commentaries on biblical material, but they had not really come to public notice. This was soon to change, even though the occasion would not be related to what we have discussed thus far.

1517: Indulgences and the 95 Theses

Luther's views became public in relation to the late medieval practice of selling indulgences. The practice of indulgences had to do with how one receives release of a soul from purgatory so that it might go to the heavenly realm. In the late Middle Ages, someone came up with the idea of selling indulgences to raise money for church projects. Many people literally believed that through the payment of a certain amount of money one could receive an indulgence for a departed soul that would free them from purgatory. This was going on in Wittenberg, the city in which Luther was teaching. When Luther heard about it, he became very upset. He felt that such a practice was obscuring the primary problem, the inward existential question of how we can stand before a seemingly demanding God. He had come to realize that the answer lies in what God has done for us. This was something received freely in faith. Luther felt it was nonsense to believe that one could buy a soul's release from purgatory. However, Luther did not state his opposition to this practice directly. Rather, he proceeded in a way more appropriate to his scholarly position.

In 1517, Luther posted on the Wittenberg Church door the famous 95 Theses—more properly his "*Disputation on the Power and Efficacy of Indulgences*"—statements that he put forward for theological debate and discussion. Growing up in the Lutheran tradition, I remember seeing films about Luther shattering the Catholic tradition as he nailed these 95 Theses to the church door. I was later to learn that in the sixteenth century a church door was a community bulletin board. When Luther put his 95 *Theses* on the church door, he was simply following the practice common in university towns. You put up your theses as a way of announcing that you wanted debate on these issues.

> "*Out of love and concern for the truth . . . ,*" the document began, "*the following heads will be the subject of a public discussion at Wittenberg under the presidency of the reverend father, Martin Luther.*" The first thesis stated, "*When our Lord and Master, Jesus Christ, said, 'Repent' He called for the entire life of believers to be one of penitence.*" The theses then proceeded. Thesis #6: "*The pope himself cannot remit guilt, but only declare and confirm what is remitted by God.*" Thesis #16: "*there seems to be the same difference between hell, purgatory, and heaven as between despair, uncertainty, and assurance.*" Thesis #32 read: "*all those who believe themselves certain of their own salvation by means of letters of indulgence, will be eternally damned, together with their teachers.*"[3]

We have to see what Luther was doing in the context of his own time: simply raising some questions about a practice within the church of his own day. He was not intending either to split the church or to leave it. It was only later that he realized that the consequences of his actions would be a split within the church.

Shortly after Luther's 95 *Theses* was posted, they were translated into German and printed up by the hundreds on the new printing press of his time. Suddenly his criticism of church practice became widely known. He had moved into the public arena.

There were many things going on around Luther at this particular historical moment that his work indirectly addressed. The fact that he wrote in German, for example, touched the latent nationalistic sentiments of his time. There was also considerable tension between the German princes and the central government of the Holy Roman Empire, as well as a certain antagonism towards Rome. Wittenberg was also an aspiring intellectual and political centre. Other younger scholars at Wittenberg were, in different ways, critical of the church, although not necessarily on the same basis as Luther. Within the university there were those calling for new humanistic reforms, some of which Luther also supported. These scholarly reforms had come out of the Renaissance and involved the recovery of ancient languages. Thus, learning Greek and Hebrew was

---

3. Ibid., 490 ff. The # indicates the number of the 95 Theses quoted.

integral to the study of Scripture. Frederick the Wise, who had established the new university at Wittenberg, was an important figure within the Holy Roman Empire and one of the German princes who was trying to expand his political influence and the significance of the German territories within the Empire. Some regarded Luther as a spokesman for this emergent nationalistic spirit. All of these things came together around the 95 *Theses* and favoured their wider circulation.

So suddenly, Luther who had seen himself as simply doing his academic and theological work now found himself thrown onto a much larger public stage. Reactions to the publication of the 95 *Theses* were immediate and very strong. Luther was ordered to Rome in 1518, but he did not go. A year later, he held a public debate in Leipzig with a very able defender of the Catholic Church, John Eck. In these debates, Eck managed to get Luther to admit that councils, the collective gathering of the Church, could err, as could popes. It was during this debate that Luther was driven to say that Scripture alone could not err. All other authorities within the Christian life were subject to error.

Authority and Sola Scriptura

One of the issues that emerged as this process unfolded was the whole question of authority within Christian life. There were two major traditions within the Catholic Church at this time: one that would have vested authority in councils, and another that vested authority in the papacy. When Eck got Luther to acknowledge that councils could err, he was identifying Luther with earlier reformers, especially figures like Jan Hus, who had been condemned as a heretic and subsequently burned at the stake (1415), as Hus was at the Council of Constance. To identify Luther with this tradition was to identify him with the "bad guys."

Luther, whose concerns grew out of the inward existential and personal crisis that he had experienced, now found himself drawn into a much larger conflict. Initially, Luther believed and expected that his concerns about the selling of indulgences would be addressed. He thought that once brought to the attention of the authorities, the issues Luther identified in relation to the selling of indulgences would lead to internal reform in church. However, by 1518-19, it became evident to Luther that what he had begun was going to issue in splitting the church. An increasing number of people were turning to Luther and his views. Monks and nuns were leaving their religious orders in response to Luther's criticisms of church practice and thought, and many of them turned to Luther and other reformers of his time for direction. For

Luther, however, all this turmoil was based on the existential religious issue of how we are to understand the relationship between God and human beings and how we as human beings stand in relation to God.

The Reformation slogan *sola scriptura* grew out of this conflict as a way of addressing the issue of authority within Christian life. Luther felt driven to this principle by events, and it came to be increasingly central to Luther's teaching.

Faith versus Works

Luther came to contrast his way—that of faith—with what he felt was the Catholic way—that of works. For Luther, we stand before God on the foundation of what God has done in Jesus Christ, which we receive as the promise of God to humanity. This is the way of faith. In the Catholic tradition, said Luther, we stand before God on the foundation of our own human works. By *works,* he meant the view that human beings are made righteous before God through our own capacity to do and act in a virtuous way. This is the way of works. Luther felt that that was an impossible way because it never managed to address this question of our inward spiritual disorder, our incapacity to do, as Paul said, the "good that we should." It was a view of the Christian way that, according to Luther, led to self-glorification and failed to address the moral dilemma that all human beings faced vis-à-vis God: our inability to save ourselves. He contrasted this view with his own view based on faith, where we simply cling to the promises of God. In this attitude of radical trust in the gracious movement of God towards human beings—a movement that forgives and in that forgiveness transforms the human heart and makes human beings acceptable to God—we find our redemption. This attempt to shift the primary focus of the relationship between God and human beings to one based on faith rather than works, led Luther to a much broader criticism of the Catholic tradition.

So in 1521, when Luther was called to meet the leading ecclesiastical and political authorities at the Diet of Worms (an imperial assembly in a city in Germany and not an austere monastic meal), the die was largely cast. It was here that Luther was asked to recant his views. He attempted to respond to the criticisms made against him, but he finally said, "*Here I stand,*" he could not, and would not recant these views, unless "*persuaded by Scripture and reason.*" Obviously, Luther was not persuaded. Luther was excommunicated.

By this time, Luther had grown very sharp in his condemnation of the church at Rome. In the year prior to the meeting at Worms, he had published his treatise entitled *The Babylonian Captivity of the Church*, in which he argued that the church had become anti-Christ. The lines were drawn. It was not Luther's own little debate any more. If it had not been for the actions of some political figures and his close associates, Luther would have been arrested at Worms, and probably put to death as had happened to the Czech reformer Jan Hus in 1415. However, Luther was spirited out of the city and taken away to the Wartburg Castle, where he remained in seclusion for several months. Here he translated the Bible into German. This must have been frantic or inspired activity. He translated the entire Scripture, Old and New Testaments, in a few months, and his translation still ranks as a classic. Luther's translation of the Bible was published and the Bible in German came into people's hands.

Luther had come to the view that we stand before God on the basis of God's work in Christ, not human effort. This was, for Luther, the heart of the Christian Gospel. He renounced his monastic vows, left the monastery and eventually married. Many other people also abandoned their monastic vocations in response to this new understanding of the Gospel. For Luther, the only authority that was binding on Christians was the authority of Scripture, and consequently he made a large distinction between Scripture and tradition. Scripture is the word of God and tradition is the mere word of fallible human beings. On the basis of a sharp distinction between Scripture and tradition, Luther articulated his critique of the Catholic tradition. He also became involved in the formation of a new Protestant ecclesial tradition, a task that occupied the remainder of his life.

One of the major crises that occurred in relation to the Lutheran reforms was the Peasants' War of 1524–25. Some people heard what Luther was preaching as a call for the wholesale overturning not only of church structures but of social and political structures as well. Some German peasants began to rise up against political authority. Luther first addressed himself to the princes, calling for them to respond to some of the demands for reform. Later, when the princes did not respond and the war became more widespread, he supported the princes in calling out the armies to put down these "murdering and thieving hordes." There was no clear theoretical answer to the question of how the church reform movement related to larger social and political questions. This relationship emerged in response to events. Luther felt that what was happening in the Peasants' War threatened the very fabric of society. His conservative reaction also revealed Luther's ties to the ruling princes of the German states.

The Peasants' War well illustrates the variety of ways in which Luther was heard and understood in his own time. When we speak about a Protestant Reformation and identify the two central slogans of "faith alone" and

"Scripture alone" as characteristic of all of the reformers, we need to understand that their meaning varied from one reformer to another. One place we can see some of these differences is in relation to the reform movements that emerged in Switzerland in the 1520s.

Ulrich Zwingli (1484–1531)

The reform movement in Germany influenced Ulrich Zwingli, a priest in Zurich in Switzerland, as had the tradition of Renaissance humanism. Zwingli's central question was not the same as Luther's question. Rather than the question of how one can stand before God, Zwingli focused on the authority of Scripture as the ruling principle for governing the life of society. For Zwingli, the Christian's primary loyalty was to God as mediated through Scripture. Zwingli sought to initiate a reform movement in Zurich that would affect both church and society. He came to dominate the civil government in the city. Under Zwingli's leadership, the civil government attempted to work out town laws based on Scripture, in an effort to create a truly Christian society. A very rapid change took place in Zurich over the years 1522–24, change that transformed church life and the life of the canton.

Zwingli was iInfluenced by Renaissance humanism, Zwingli was very interested in the study of Scripture using the ancient languages. He was also a rationalist in his reading of Scripture. He understood the Christian message as a criticism against practices that had developed within Christendom. Zwingli therefore sought to cleanse and purify the Church by restoring a simpler form of worship and eliminating elements that had permeated Christian piety, such as the veneration of relics and the role of the saints. Zwingli regarded these practices as superstitions that needed to be expunged from Christian life as quickly as possible.

For Zwingli, the central issue was obedience to the will of God as mediated in Scripture. This has an impact upon one's life in the Church and in the world. In 1525 Conrad Grebel, Felix Manz and George Blaurock broke with Zwingli over the issue of "Believers' Baptism." They were re-baptized as adults in accordance with their reading of Scripture that, they argued, did not mention infant baptism. It was the beginning of what came to be known as "Believers' Baptism." Proponents of Believers' Baptism rejected the practice of infant baptism as inconsistent with Scripture and hence not a "true baptism." Zwingli disagreed, as did the Zurich Council that was then under the control of reformed elements. Felix Manz was arrested and—to mock the practice of adult baptism—put to death by drowning. George Blaurock was expelled from Zurich, and later burned at the stake in another town. Conrad Grebel left Zurich but died young.

These three men stand as martyrs to the wing of the reform movement known as Anabaptism. We discuss this movement more fully in Chapter 16, but now it is important to note that all the reformers took up the slogans of "faith alone" and "Scripture alone," but understood them in very different ways.

John Calvin (1509–1564) and the Sovereignty of God

The major systematic voice of the Protestant Reformation was that of John Calvin. He was born in Noyon, France. Calvin went to Paris for his education when he was fourteen. Initially, his father, Gérard Cauvin, had hoped that John would become a priest, but conflict with the cathedral chapter at Noyon led Gérard to send John to Orléans to study law in 1528. Calvin already had his master's degree in philosophy. However, he was a dutiful son and he eventually received a degree in law. After his father's death, Calvin returned to humanistic studies and the study of ancient languages. In 1532, he published a treatise on Seneca, the Stoic philosopher of ancient Rome. Throughout this period of his studies, Calvin showed little interest in the reformers, though they had long called for a break with Rome.

Suddenly in 1533, Calvin identified himself with the Protestant cause. In 1534, he fled France because of his association with the French Protestants. Initially he went to Basel to pursue his studies, and was on his way to Strasbourg when a detour led him to Geneva and an encounter with William Farel, the spiritual head of the reform movement in Geneva. Farel persuaded Calvin to remain. He became a Professor and a "Reader in Holy Scripture to the Church in Geneva." At the age of twenty-six, only two years after his conversion to the Protestant cause, he would become Geneva's most important reformer and preacher. He later wrote,

> *Whilst I remained so obstinately addicted to the superstitions of the Papacy that it would have been hard indeed to have pulled me out of so deep a quagmire by sudden conversion, God subdued and made teachable a heart which was . . . far too hardened in such matters. Having thus received some foretaste and knowledge of true piety, I was straightway inflamed with such a great desire to profit by it."*[4]

---

4. See Wendel, *Calvin*, 37.

What is central in Calvin's description of his conversion is the sense that now he had become "teachable." This spirit in Calvin was different from what we found in Luther, for whom the burning religious question was how one stands in relation to God. While Calvin accepted Luther's insights, there was not the same kind of emotional passion around the issue of justification that we find in Luther. For Calvin, the emphasis was on having *knowledge of God*. Calvin's *Institutes of the Christian Religion* reflects this concern for what he called "knowledge of God and of ourselves." He began working on the *Institutes* shortly after the time of his conversion. The *Institutes* first edition was first published in 1535. He continued to revise and expand the *Institutes* over the course of his lifetime until his death in 1564. It was Calvin's effort to offer a systematic presentation of Protestant and biblical teachings.

Institutes of the Christian Religion

In the *Institutes* Calvin wrote that "*the entire sum of our wisdom . . . may be said to consist of two parts: namely, the knowledge of God and of ourselves.*"[5] Unlike Thomas Aquinas, he recognized only one source for our knowledge of God and ourselves: the revelation given in Scripture. In Calvin's view there is, after the Fall, no natural knowledge of God available to human beings. Thus, the *Institutes* seek to present a systematic account of what is given in revelation. For Calvin, that meant what is found in scripture. What did Calvin find? The revelation given in Scripture discloses how things stand between God and humanity.

As noted above, the *Institutes* went through a number of revisions and editions. In its first form (1535–36), it was a catechetical work introducing the main elements of the Christian religion. In its mature form (1559), the *Institutes* is divided into four major sections: the first on the knowledge of God the Creator, the second on the knowledge of God the Redeemer, the third on the manner of receiving the grace of Christ and the fourth on the external means or aids by which God calls us into communion with Christ. It is the major systematic exposition of the new Protestant version of the Christian faith. Each of its sections requires further attention.

Knowing God

How do we gain knowledge of God and ourselves? Earlier Anselm had proposed that we could know God through prayerful thought and an interior

---

5. Calvin, *Institutes of the Christian Religion*, 35.

journey. Aquinas believed that there were two sources for knowing God: reason and revelation. The starting point for Calvin is very different. Calvin's belief, shared with some other Reformed and Protestant thinkers, was that man's original ability to know God has been wholly lost. Before the Fall, humanity had a natural capacity to know God, but after the Fall, that capacity was wholly destroyed by sin. It is from this belief that we get the radical doctrine of sin that characterizes Calvin. He understood original sin as "*a hereditary depravity and corruption of nature diffused through all parts of the soul.*"[6]

This notion of sin stands in contrast to the much milder doctrine of original sin that we find, for example, in Thomas Aquinas. For Thomas, humanity was weakened by sin, but not radically depraved and corrupt as in Calvin's teaching. Here the original ability to know God is wiped away by sin. As Calvin saw it, for us to know God, God must have made himself known to us. Since we have no natural capacity to know God, the place where God has made himself known to us is in Scripture. It is to Scripture that we must turn to regain our knowledge of God, God's purposes and way of salvation. Revelation alone is the source of knowledge of God.

This is an important point in terms of the history of Christian thought. Christian thinking, for Calvin, is thinking about Scripture. It is biblical theology, an attempt to summarize the teachings of Scripture under various heads and in that way recover some of the lost knowledge of God that we cannot find on our own through the exercise of our fallen natural capacities. Unlike the medieval Catholic tradition, Calvin maintained that reason must be subordinate to Scripture. Reason thus functions in a wholly instrumental way in relation to the guidelines and parameters that are determined by the revelation found in Scripture.

Scripture: Seeing Things Aright

Given this perspective, it is not surprising that for Calvin, as for many Reformation figures, the only authority that is binding on the Christian is the authority of Scripture. For Calvin this means that we must understand Scripture in its totality. We cannot pick and choose a few texts from here or there. Rather, we have to grasp Scripture as a whole so that we can see things aright.

Calvin believed that Scripture is a remarkable narrative. It begins in Genesis with creation by a sovereign God. It then moves on to the tragic Fall of humanity and God's covenant with Israel until we reach the turning point

---

6. See Kerr, *Selections from Calvin*, 167.

of God's redemption of humanity and re-creation in Christ. The narrative then continues in the ongoing movement towards the consummation of God's purposes in what the Book of Revelation calls the "new heavens and new earth." This is the narrative, the structure of revelation; it is the main story of Scripture. When we grasp Scripture as a whole, then we see that God's purpose in creation is one of bringing human life back into communion with God. If we ask Calvin what God is doing in creation, the answer is that God is restoring the whole creation to Himself. The life and person of Jesus Christ discloses and reveals this divine purpose.. There we see how God is restoring creation to Himself. Thus, Part II of the *Institutes* deals with our knowledge of God the Redeemer, and Parts III and IV deal with the "manner of receiving the grace of Christ" and "the external means by which God calls us into communion with Christ."

One of Calvin's phrases for talking about Scripture is that Scripture becomes the lens, the glasses, that we can put on to see the world aright. Because of sin, we have lost our natural capacity and we are dependent upon revelation to know God's purposes at all. Scripture understood in its totality, understood in its revelatory narrative, gives us the lens through which we can perceive the word and world aright.

The affirmation that our knowledge of God is limited to what God has revealed to us means, on the other side, that Calvin was very much against vain speculation. There are many questions about what God is doing and how God's redemption unfolds that are not revealed in the scriptural narrative. These questions are unanswerable and we have to take care not to let reason bewitch us into pursuing these questions, for which there are no answers. This sense of the limited power of reason is very important in understanding what Calvin was trying to do in the *Institutes*. He was trying to present the major teachings of Scripture in as systematic a form as possible and, at the same time, to warn us against the dangers of unrestricted speculation about God and his purposes.

The Sovereign God

The only point in relation to God of which we can be certain is that whatever unfolds in creation and in time and history unfolds under the sovereignty of God. Whatever happens, we might say, happens in the providence of God, but for Calvin that does not mean that we can know what that providence is in every particular case. Oftentimes, God's purposes remain incomprehensible to us. We do not know them in any detail, but we still affirm that whatever happens, it happens in the sovereignty of God. This was very crucial for Calvin, who many have described as the Protestant theologian of the sovereignty of God. Sovereignty is the central category of Calvin's *Institutes*. He sought to show how the sovereign God is ordering creation, redemption and consummation.

Church & Society

Calvin was persuaded to stay in Geneva and assist William Farel in reforming the city because in Switzerland the Protestant reforms moved in a somewhat different way than they had in Germany. In Switzerland a small territory, often a city and surrounding lands, a canton, would come into the hands of either a Protestant or a Catholic majority. Within that territory, the dominant and/or leading figure attempted to initiate a reform that affected the life not only of the church but of the whole canton. It is often said that Calvin attempted to establish a theocracy in Geneva. This is not correct, since Calvin maintained the historic distinction between the church and civil authorities. However, he did seek to have both the civil and ecclesial orders acknowledge the centrality of scripture. In those efforts he was sometimes successful and sometimes not. He hoped to see both the church and the life of the society reformed. This became one of the distinctive marks of the Calvinist reformers.

For Luther the sphere of society remained ambiguous, under the sway of dark—even demonic—forces as well as the providence of God. In society the law, according to Luther, functions primarily in order to restrain evil, but within the sphere of the Church and the Christian community the law of grace prevails. The Calvinists did not hold to this "two kingdom" theory: they saw the relationship between the two as more co-operative, at least theoretically. In Calvin's view, the 'visible saints' should play a leading role in both spheres. This is a very important shift and one of the significant differences between Lutheran and Calvinist reformers. It bore fruit both in the Swiss context and in other territories influenced by Calvinism, particularly Scotland and later North America. A wing of the Calvinist movement, Puritanism, played a central role in the formation of life in the United States in particular.

When Calvin went to Geneva, he was persuaded by William Farel to stay and so he began the task of trying to reform Geneva. A couple of years later the city kicked both Calvin and William Farel (1489-1565) out and Calvin then went to Strasbourg. Three years later, in 1541, the citizens of Geneva asked Calvin to return and Calvin remained in Geneva until his death in 1564.

External Means of Communion

You will recall that Calvin had studied law. One of the major innovations in Calvin's *Institutes of the Christian Church* occurred in Section IV, which deals with the external means or aids by which God calls us into communion with Christ. Under this heading, one would normally speak of the means of grace, primarily the Church and the sacraments. Calvin, however, rejected the notion of sacraments, though he did approve of the memorial of the Lord's Supper. Instead, Calvin discusses the nature of civil society and specifically the role of the magistrate under this heading on the how God calls us into communion with God. For Calvin, civil society and government became one of the means of grace or one of the ways in which God calls us into communion with Christ. Unlike Luther, Calvin did not leave civil society to the side, but accorded it an important place in his theological vision.

Rather than falling into the old error of Marcion and denying the revelatory status of the Hebrew scripture and much of the New Testament, Calvin sees the Scripture whole. Consequently, Calvin takes take seriously the history of Israel and attempts to establish a form of civil society and civil government (Kingship). For Calvin, such institutions are one of the ways in which God is working to restore the creation to Himself. The primary functions of government are twofold: (1) to establish and allow for the exercise of the Christian religion and (2) to provide positive regulation of moral life. Again, this view contrasted with Luther's doctrine of the two kingdoms, the state on one side and the church on the other. According to Luther's teaching, one is under the law in society, whose primary function is to restrain sin, but one also lives in the Church where love is to prevail and dominate. The law of love is to shape our face-to-face relations with other members of the Christian community and the wider society. As Luther said, "we are to be Christ's to one another." Then faith active in love can dominate. However, Luther had little hope and little expectation that the state could play any reforming role in the lives of Christians.

Law and Gospel/Gospel and Law

Unlike Luther, Calvin offered a view that sees civil society—and the state—in a more positive light. He placed a high value on the role of civil society and governing authorities in God's providence, and saw them playing a positive role in reforming social life. While the first task of civil society is to permit and promote the practice of the Christian religion, civil governance is called to act to transform society and bring its life more in line with moral teaching and providence. For Calvin, the way that is accomplished is through the *visible saints*. Within society, the visible saints are to play a leading—indeed exemplary—role in the exercise of their vocations or callings, including that of magistrate.

Such a reformist view of government is evidenced in Calvin's threefold view of the law. For the reformers, Scripture is about Law or God's commandments and the Gospel, or God's Good News. How one understood each of these terms, and the relationship between them, was crucial. Luther had primarily two uses of the law, while Calvin had three. The first use of the law—which includes the Ten Commandments and some of the teachings of Jesus, especially those of the Sermon on the Mount—is that it shows forth the righteousness of God. The law's second use is as a mirror in which we become aware of our sinfulness and our need for Christ's mercy. When we measure ourselves against the law and the demands of the law, both Luther and Calvin argued, we discover how far short we fall of what God demands of us. Whom looking at themselves carefully in the mirror of the law, can find themselves blameless? According to both Luther and Calvin, we find ourselves full of blame, guilty and consequently in need of Christ's mercy.

Luther stopped after approving this second use of the Law, but in Calvin's teaching, there is a third use of the law. For Calvin, the law now becomes a guide for the redeemed, as it points to the ways that make for holiness. The law does not save humanity, but the law in this third use functions positively to point us in the way ahead. This tradition is very important to subsequent generations and affects the understanding of governance in jurisdictions influenced by the Calvinist tradition.

Vocation: Serving God and the Neighbour

It is also important to clarify Calvin's teaching on the visible saints and on vocation. In Calvin's Geneva, the saints were the members of the Church and specifically that meant the Protestant Church in Geneva. The mark of the saint was an exemplary moral or public life, especially in the exercise of your vocation or calling. In the longer Christian tradition, there were two vocations: marriage and the religious life.

The test, as it were, of whether you were among the redeemed was your public life and the extent to which it exhibited love of God and your neighbour. It was not that difficult to know who the Saints were, at least in a general way. Calvin felt that the saints could be easily distinguished. This is related to the question of vocation, an important issue for the Protestant reformers.

Luther was both an Augustinian monk and a Catholic priest, and while Calvin never became a monk or a priest in the Catholic tradition, he was originally headed in that direction. Both Luther and Calvin rejected an understanding of vocation that limits "callings" or "vocations" to the religious life. Instead, they argued that every believer was his or her own intercessor with God—the "priesthood of all believers"—and that "all social roles are callings or vocations." Throughout medieval times, emphasis was placed on those who had vocations as priests and as members of monastic and religious orders. The rest of us have jobs. We have things that we need to do to maintain our life and the life of the larger society. However, these are not roles in which we act, as does the priest, as mediators between God and humanity, or in which we serve God and our neighbour.

But one innovation that came in the Protestant traditions was an expansion of the notion of vocation to include every social office and task. All the many callings that exist in society have a religious significance to them. You exercise your vocation as fathers and mothers. You exercise your vocation as clergy and laity. We have vocations as magistrates, merchants, teachers and professors and, as the nursery rhyme says, as butchers, bakers and candlestick makers. There is no social role or task, in the Protestant view that does not have this kind of moral and spiritual significance. Every calling is a vocation in which you are called to serve God and the neighbour.

As a matter of fact, Luther, and to a lesser extent Calvin, strongly attacked the religious orders. The monk shifted from being the highest calling to the lowest calling. Luther comes to view the monastic life—wrongly in my view—as a flight from life. Men and women began to leave their vocations after hearing Luther's message, just as Luther himself had. Luther often counselled them after they left and arranged marriages for them. Indeed, Luther's own marriage came about when he could not find a mate for Catherine, so he married her himself. It was to be a long and happy marriage, though Catholic antagonists saw this as evidence of Luther's inability to maintain his vows and control his own sexuality. The special status given to those with religious callings in the Catholic world changed in the Protestant Reformation. Ones calling to the social roles one fulfills—as a spouse, parent, church member, citizen, and worker—is every bit as significant as the religious callings had been.

You can see that for Calvin this would be a very important teaching in the context of the overall thrust of his view that through the exercise of God's sovereign providence in all things, God is *restoring this fallen creation to Himself*. One of the ways that God is doing that is through worldly vocations in which God is transforming the life of society, through people fulfilling their callings as fathers and mothers, as butchers, bakers and candlestick makers. Luther remarks that "God is milking the cows through the hands of the milkmaid."

In Calvin's discussion of the magistrate, he also speaks of the magistrate's obligation to oppose the king/ruler if they act contrary to God's Law. This was an important difference between Luther and Calvin as it underscores the prophetic dimension of vocation. If the ruler, the boss, the owner, the leader fails to fulfill their vocation to love God and the neighbour than one is called to speak out.

North American societies trivialize this important doctrine of vocation as the "Protestant work ethic," where success and money rather than service to God and the neighbor become marks of a fulfilled vocation. In fact, it is a very profound teaching and an important contribution to the great conversation concerning the Christian faith. The notion of vocation is one important means by which the Church, as the priesthood of all believers, is visible in the life of society.

Providence and Predestination in Calvin

A final topic that comes up in relation to Calvin is predestination. It is generally seen in very negative terms as a terrible teaching, that God, as the great puppet master, assigns us to be either among the redeemed or among the reprobate.

It certainly is true that Calvin, like all of his contemporaries, had a doctrine of predestination, but we need to look at what it means to speak about election and predestination. In the *Institutes of the Christian Religion*, Calvin made it clear that, in his view, everything unfolds in the providence of God—nothing happens outside God's sovereign providence. However, why things happen in one way rather than another is something that we do not know. There is a general affirmation about providence, but we do not have what we might call positive knowledge in relation to all cases. Calvin believed that God who created the world is also sovereign over the world and disposes his creation towards certain ends. However, Calvin said we do not know how that providence works in specific cases, and things appear to us to be fortuitous. It is in this context that we can consider the specific question of whether God elects and predestines the saints.

This is a more particular aspect of Calvin's general doctrine of divine providence. When we look at the *Institutes* for this teaching, it is important to note that it comes up not in section one (on knowledge of God as creator), nor section two (on knowledge of God as redeemer), but rather in section three, where Calvin discussed how we come into communion with Christ. Calvin understood the doctrine of election and predestination as a word of comfort to the believer.

Calvin wrote the *Institutes* for the Christian community. His goal was not to answer the objections of the critics of Christianity, but simply to explicate what Christians affirm based on Scripture. From Scripture, Calvin derived his notion of predestination. It is a reflection of the experience of the Christian that one's life and one's participation in the Christian community is not wholly a function of one's own individual will. Calvin is aware that forces beyond our control are at work in one's life and influence one's spiritual journey. Calvin used the terms *election* and *predestination* to express this aspect of Christian experience. When Calvin discussed election and predestination, he actually listed all the normal objections to these doctrines and said that "election and predestination" were among the most confusing and even dangerous of all Christian teachings. They were dangerous and confusing for precisely the reasons that people often articulate in opposition to these doctrines: they encourage inattention or resignation or passivity in relation to one's own salvation. If everything is in God's hands and in His election and predestination, then I do not have to do anything: I can just go on with my life. If I am predestined to be a part of the elect, I will be. If I am not, then I cannot do anything about it. If that is your understanding, Calvin said, you have misunderstood what I have tried to say. As Calvin remarked, "God helps only those who walk in his Ways, that is, in his calling."[7]

What positive function was in Calvin's mind? For Calvin, election and predestination means that we should relax a bit about the question of our salvation. His teaching was a comfort to those overly exercised about whether or not they are in communion with Christ. Calvin said, in effect, that such people should quit worrying because that is in God's hands, and get on with their Christian life. Do not constantly worry this question to death; just do what you have to do and trust in the providence of God.

After Calvin, the discussion of election and predestination became part of Calvinist doctrines of God, rather than how we come into communion with Christ. This made God the seemingly arbitrary agent of one's salvation. Later Calvinist traditions contained a very strict and harsh doctrine of election and predestination, which in part falls into those very worries that Calvin expressed in his *Institutes*. Calvin felt very strongly

---

7. Calvin, *Institutes of the Christian Religion*, 406.

about the dangers of speculation in relation to predestination: "*Human curiosity renders the discussion of predestination, already somewhat difficult of itself, very confusing and even dangerous.*" At the same time, he insisted that the doctrine had its place within the Christian faith: "*There are others who, wishing to cure this evil, all but require that every mention of predestination be buried; indeed, they teach us to avoid any question of it as we would a reef.*"[8] So, Calvin was trying to walk a fine line between those who are overly curious about this doctrine and those who want to dismiss it out of hand. He saw the doctrine as an account of a certain part of the Christian experience, namely, that there are things over which we do not exercise control. He also wanted to emphasize that being part of the community of faith does not simply reflect our efforts, but tells us something of the graciousness of God.

Summary

The sixteenth century saw some profound shifts in Christian thought. Martin Luther did not initially intend to break the unity of the Church, but a combination of factors, many of them having little to do with Christian thinking and most of them beyond Luther's control, led to the formation of new Protestant churches. Although there is a remarkable diversity of thought in Christian history, Luther came to believe that his view of Christianity centering on justification by faith was contrary to the teaching of the longer Catholic tradition. John Calvin, the great French Protestant thinker, contributed a remarkable systematic—though Calvin saw it as biblical—account of the Protestant vision, focused on the sovereignty of God rather than Luther's justification by faith alone. It would be centuries for these ruptures within the body of Christendom to be healed. Yet there are still many today who continue to caricature and denigrate those in Christian Churches/Communities other than one's own. Moreover, there were significant differences between Luther's and Calvin's Christian thought, especially on the issue of the relationship between the church and the governing authorities of the wider society.

---

8. See Kerr, *Selections from Calvin*, 170.

Review

1. What event launched the Protestant Reformation?
2. What did Luther mean by "justification by grace through faith"?
3. Was Zwingli's reform the same as Luther's reform?
4. Why is Calvin called the theologian of "the sovereignty of God"?

Chapter 16

Anabaptist and Anglican Reformers
Menno Simons (1496–1561)

MENNO SIMONS WAS AN important figure in the left wing of the Reformation, the Anabaptist tradition. Simons was a Dutch parish priest who renounced his connection with the Catholic Church in 1536, joined the Anabaptists and played a very important role in the small and scattered Anabaptist communities for the rest of his life. While Simons is a Reformation figure, it is important to understand that his questions were not either Luther's or Calvin's questions. The issue that arose for Menno Simons was "Am I living as a Christian, a follower of Christ?" There was a strong moral element in Simons' eventual decision to leave the priesthood and become part of the Anabaptist community.

While yet a Catholic priest, Simons became aware of Anabaptist figures. They made a deep and troubling impression on him. He wrote that while a young priest, he had questioned the doctrine of transubstantiation. However, it did not lead him to question his priestly calling, nor, finally, his allegiance to the Church. Simons admits that he was not taking the deeper dimensions of his priestly ordination very seriously. Indeed, he, with other young priests, would "*spend our time emptily in playing cards together, drinking and in diversions.*" It was in this context that he begins to hear stories about these quite remarkable people, who were more God-fearing and pious than he was and who practiced adult baptism. They were so committed to adult or believer's baptism that some of them even suffered death rather than give up their commitment to it. These stories are what moved Simons "*to examine the New Testament diligently.*"[1] His study of the

---

1. See Simons, *The Complete Works of Menno Simons*, 686.

New Testament initially led Simons to becoming an "evangelical preacher" within the context of his Catholic parish.

However, stories of the Anabaptists continued to trouble Simons. He later wrote about a man named Sicke Snijder who was martyred near where Menno Simons was serving as a priest. It inwardly troubled Simons so deeply that it led him to study Scripture in order to see if there was anything to the Anabaptist claims that Scripture supported adult rather than infant baptism. As Simons studied the Bible, he came to doubt the Catholic practice of infant baptism. Then Simons turned to the writings of some of the reformers. He looked at Luther and Martin Bucer (1491-1551) on the question of baptism, but their writings were not persuasive. He eventually came to the view that Scripture taught adult baptism. As he wrote, *"I obtained a view of baptism and the Lord's Supper through the illumination of the Holy Ghost, through much reading and pondering of the Scriptures, and by the gracious favour and gift of God."*[2] In 1536, Simons broke with the Catholic tradition and joined a local Anabaptist community.

Simons realized that the practice of adult baptism led the Anabaptists to view the "church" as a community of those who made a public profession of their faith and a willingness to live as followers of Christ. This and other things about the Anabaptists impressed Simons. He wrote that he pondered *"these things ... which I have obtained."* As he did so, the question that became central for him, as it was for the Anabaptists, was how one lives agreeably with the word of the Lord. He certainly agreed with the other reformers that Scripture comes first in the Christian life and stands higher than tradition in determining what one should do and how one should live. There is relatively little discussion in Menno Simons about the doctrine of justification by faith alone, which did not play as big a role in his thinking as it did for others. He did hold, however, to the view of "Scripture alone." It was precisely this commitment to following Scripture—plainly written and understood—that led him to abandon his priestly vocation and cast his lot with the Anabaptists.

Menno Simons is a representative figure of the left wing of the Reformation. He spoke of his conversion as centred on the issue of living in fidelity to the teachings of Jesus. A number of very important differences between the left-wing reformers on the one hand and both the larger Catholic tradition and the new Protestant communities of his time on the other emerged. Central here were the issues of baptism and discipleship. Simons viewed baptism as an event that follows a sense of inward conviction of the necessity to follow Christ's teaching. As he wrote, the Christian is first

---

2. Ibid., 669.

*"baptized inwardly with the Spirit and fire, and externally with water."*³ This is why he understood adult baptism—and not infant baptism as practiced for centuries in the Catholic tradition and retained in other Protestant traditions—as consistent with the New Testament teaching.

Now in the sixteenth century the issue of baptism was important not only as a part of Christian practice, but also in relation to the definition of the Christian community. In medieval Christian culture and society, baptism was a sign of communion with the Church and membership in Christendom. It was a way of marking one's entrance simultaneously into the Christian community and into the wider society. The emphasis in infant baptism was on God's prevenient grace: grace given to human beings prior to their response to that grace. Grace marks one's life and places the infant under the horizon of God's gracious benevolence towards human beings. For Simons, this view missed the point. Simons saw baptism as outward sign of an inward change; it marked those who take up the Cross and follow the non-violent Way of Jesus.

The dissent from the more traditional practice not only had repercussions within the Church but also signaled the Anabaptists' dissent from the larger project of creating a Christian culture in which the boundaries of the Church would be coterminous with the boundaries of the whole society. Within Anabaptist circles, the Church is a community of believers who exhibit their regenerated state in their relationships with other members of the Christian community, and separation from the wider society. Behind this lies a sense that the larger culture and the larger society are not under God's sway, but are really under the power of dark forces. For Simons, a Christian is a person called out from that larger society to participate in a smaller community of those baptized: "inwardly by fire and the Spirit" and "outwardly by water." This action symbolizes a believer's promise to forsake an earlier life and follow the new law of love disclosed in Jesus' life and teachings.

The Church was to be a dynamic fellowship of believers and the emphasis was much more on the interpersonal aspects of Christian life and witness to the larger society. Simons wrote that the Christian Church was *"an assembly of the righteous, and a community of the saints."*⁴ The Anabaptists were unlike Protestants and Catholics by their emphasis on the visible Church in which the outward life should be lived as closely as possible to the inner spirit and teachings of Jesus. They refused to take oaths, and to serve in the army. In some respects their view of the Church is closer to

---

3. See Kerr, *Selections from Menno Simons*, 186.
4. Simons, *Complete Works*, 234.

Calvinist than Lutheran views. For Luther, the Christian remained always simultaneously a saint and sinner, or better, remained simultaneously justified and yet a sinner: *simul justus eppacator*. For the Anabaptists, there is a movement from being an unbeliever to being a believer, which is a matter of following Christ. This is the real making of the Christian, for here one passes from one way of life into another. There is none of this Lutheran talk about *simul justus eppacator*, or just while yet a sinner.

Anabaptists also differ from other Protestant reformers in their understanding of the nature of sin. Menno Simons distinguishes four different types of sin: original sin, actual sin, human frailties and willful sinning. In the traditions that practiced infant baptism, the baptized person is welcomed into the Church freed from the stain of original sin, but other types of sin remain in the life of the Christian. For Simons, original sin is overcome in baptism, and there is a much greater emphasis on our capacity to avoid what he called "*actual sin, human frailties and willful sinning*," the kind of sin that arises in adult life and is unpardonable unless repented.[5] In part, the Christian community becomes a community which assists and nurtures within the believers and followers of Christ a capacity to be watchful about their lives and overcome sinning—something that is possible for the regenerate.

From this view, a strong conviction arises in the Anabaptist tradition for a radical separation of church and state. The state is under the sway of evil powers and only the Christian community is committed to living a disciplined and exemplary life in conformity to Christ's teachings. The Anabaptists rejected the role of magistrates and the possibility of Christians serving as magistrates in the larger society. They refused to take oaths since they had pledged themselves to following Christ alone. They refused to serve in the army and came to practice non-violence, again in conformity to their understanding of Christ's teaching. The Church then becomes an exemplary community where brotherly love is expressed daily and visibly.

One of the things that characterize the Reformation and post-Reformation era, from the sixteenth century on, is an intra-Christian polemic of a sort unseen since the early Christian battles over who was heretical and who was not. Increasingly, every strand of the Christian communion partly defined itself over against other parts of the larger Christian tradition. Lutherans attacked Anabaptists, Calvinists criticized Lutherans and attacked Anabaptists, and all of them stood against Catholics. Meanwhile, Catholics stood against Protestants and Anabaptists. This polemical element permeates many of the writings that began to emerge in the post-Reformation era. The Anabaptists in many respects got the short end of the stick, because

---

5. Ibid. 563–65.

they were the least powerful of the groups that emerged after the Reformation. What happened to the Anabaptists, persecuted both by Catholic majorities and by Protestant majorities, is a very sad story, exemplified by Menno Simons' constant flight from one place to another, always a step ahead of arrest and imprisonment. Many Anabaptists end up imprisoned or martyred by Protestant princes or by Catholic kings and rulers.

The witness of the Anabaptists is an important contribution to the great conversation and a perpetual challenge to those strands of Christian thought that collapse the distinction between Christian teaching and the dominant culture.

Reform in England: The English Reformation of the 1530s

The reform movement that emerged in England took a very different, indeed opposite, path from that of the Anabaptists. In the English Reformation in the early 1530s, Henry VIII came into conflict with the Catholic Church over the issue of an annulment, which would allow him to remarry. When he could not persuade Church officials to allow this to happen, he simply put through Parliament in 1534 an Act of Supremacy that made the monarch the head of the church. Henry made some nods in the direction of Luther and the other continental reformers, but the role they actually played in the English Reformation was tiny. Neither the issue of doctrine, which was the focus of the Lutheran reform, nor baptism, the chief concern of the Anabaptists, received much attention in the English reform. Instead, it focused on changes in the authority structure of the church and the reform of the liturgy. One of the great monuments to that reform is the English *Book of Common Prayer*; it became the book for worship within the Anglican Church. It remained unchanged down to the twentieth century. For this tradition, at the heart of the Christian faith is the experience of worship. Rather than right doctrine or right living, right worship is central to the English reforms.

Richard Hooker and the Middle Way (1554–1600)

One of the finest and most important voices to emerge in the Anglican tradition in the sixteenth century was Richard Hooker. In his work *Of the Laws of Ecclesiastical Polity*, Hooker attempted to chart a middle course between the Catholic tradition and the new Protestant movement, especially as this movement came to be expressed in Calvinism on the Continent and Puritanism and Non-Conformity in England. He gave an enduring defense of the fledgling reforms in England. For Hooker, three elements bind members of the Christian community to one another: Scripture, tradition and reason. Protestants tended to elevate Scripture above tradition and see the Christian life and the Christian community as under the authority of Scripture. The Catholic tradition set tradition over Scripture in the sense that tradition interprets Scripture and the Church precedes Scripture.[6] Many Catholic thinkers also attributed an important role to reason in the Christian life. Hooker tried to bind these three elements into his Christian understanding of authority.

The reason, argues Hooker that you cannot follow the Protestant tradition of Scripture alone is it makes the individual supreme in the interpretation of Scripture. In other words, the problem that arises is that everyone becomes his or her own authority. This is what Hooker saw when he looked at the Protestants, especially the Puritans in England. He pointed out that everyone was claiming that their actions were most in accord with Scripture. The consequence was instability and continual controversy in the Christian community and confusion in understanding what is authoritative in the Christian life. Every Christian reads Scripture differently, so that appeal to Scripture, by itself, is a disruptive and schismatic principle. In Hooker's time, there was already considerable evidence for his view. He saw the fragmentation that began in the Protestant world and would become more pronounced later on. He acknowledged the Puritan view that there were practices within the Anglican tradition that are not found in Scripture, but have the warrant of tradition.

On the other hand, according to Hooker, the Catholics' view of the preeminence of tradition in their understanding of authority did not give enough place to Scripture and tended to have Scripture mediated only through ecclesiastical authority. Neither of those options commended itself to Hooker. One of the reasons that the Anglican tradition is often described as a *via media* or middle way is that it attempts to chart a middle course that does not fall into either extreme.

---

6. The point here about Scripture, Tradition, and which takes precedence is complicated. The Scripture over tradition position of Protestants assumes that Scripture was complete at the time Christianity began, and the Catholic position recognizes that Tradition was there prior to the completing of the Christian Scripture, so Tradition precedes Scripture. Orthodox argue that we should read Scripture through the lens of the Creeds and Tradition. This matter is more complicated than these simple formulas suggest.

Hooker also brought back into the reformed world that he was championing in England the positive role of reason. For Hooker, one of the great gifts that God gives to us creatures is the capacity to reason and to discern the truth or law that is in things. Thus, for Hooker, there is a threefold view of authority within Christianity and the goal is to bring all three of these elements into fruitful harmony with one another within the Christian community. The Anglican way, centred on the worshipping community, then includes respect for Scripture (the Protestant element) which goes hand in hand with respect for tradition (the Catholic element) and the mediating role of reason.

In his work, Hooker attempts to show that we need not rely solely on scriptural authority since God has given us other sources of knowledge and other ways of discovering God's laws and will. Those are the ways of tradition and of reason. Indeed, reason, for Hooker, is a means by which God supplements revelation, just as tradition, understood as the *"general and perpetual voice of men . . . as the sentence of God Himself,"* discloses laws by which God regulates the world. The first of these laws is *"the law whereby the Eternal himself doth work. Proceeding from hence to the law, first of Nature, then of Scripture, we shall have the easier access to those things that come after."* Hooker understood law as *"that which doth appoint the form and measure of working, the same we term a Law."* Unlike the Puritans—and earlier Duns Scotus—who emphasized the sovereignty of God's will, Hooker believed that God always acts in accord with reason, even though we *"are not able to discern . . . the proper and certain reason that is of every finite work of God."*[7]

God's *"eternal law"* is not only the law of God, but God is also the *"author and guide of nature,"* through God's natural law, or *"that manner of working which God hath set for each created thing to keep."* The law of nature is known through right reason and is for the sake of *"a happy life."* one *"wherein all virtue is exercised."* Hooker also discussed the *"laws of nations"* before turning to *"laws for the maintenance of communion"* among nations and for *"one church . . . all having one Lord, one faith and one baptism."* These Hooker called *"supernatural laws,"* and *"the Church being both a society and a society supernatural"* is subject to *"the selfsame original grounds which other politic societies have, namely, the natural inclination . . . unto sociable life"* as well as this supernatural dimension. Thus, he sought to hold together the threads of reason, tradition and revelation in his view of things.[8]

---

7 Hooker, *Of the Laws of Ecclesiastical Polity*, 150-53. See also the Selection of Hooker entitled *"Church and State as One"* 178-79.

8. Ibid. 154-55, 188, 198, 200, 210, 221.

For Hooker, one of the major accomplishments of the English Reformation was the way in which they hold together the church and state as one. For Hooker, the Church is a society that is, first, organized as a public or civil government and, second, distinguished from other societies by the exercise of the Christian religion. In Protestant discussions about the Church, much was made of the distinction between the visible and invisible Church. Hooker started at a much more common sense view. When he talked about the Church, he meant that assembly and building right across the street where people gather every day and every week. It is a public or civil reality. The Church is that public institution where people gather and they gather in relation to an order of common prayer. That is what he meant by a public or civil government: it is a body of people coming together and regulating their lives with certain rules and order. What distinguishes this community and institution from other states is that in this public realm, Christian worship is performed and practiced. This reflected his commitment to worship and liturgy as being at the heart of the Christian life.

Now in England, he said, a unique situation exists. Here in England, everyone who is a member of the Church of England is a member of the larger Commonwealth; and everyone who is a member of the larger Commonwealth is a member of the Church of England. As in the longer medieval Catholic tradition, there is an attempt in the Church of England to make the boundaries of the church coterminous with the boundaries of the larger society. Membership in the church is just one side of membership in English society: one is a simultaneously a member of both the church and the commonwealth. For Hooker, these are two ways of looking at a single thing. The relationship of the church and the commonwealth is like the relationship of the two sides and base of the triangle: the same line can be both a side and the bottom. There is a distinction between church and state, and yet the same group is both church and state. No one who is a member of the church, can be prevented from being a member of the state and vice versa. Hooker's view is an apology for a parish system of church government and his view of Scripture is unique.

This Anglican view of the Church is profoundly different from the view of someone like Menno Simons, for whom what is crucial is a believer's voluntary decision to unite his or her life with Christ. For Hooker, everyone in society is a member of the Church and the Commonwealth. Participation in the ecclesial community is manifest in their coming together in public worship.

Summary

The period of the reforms is immensely important to the great conversation. There is diversity of opinion among the reformers on very fundamental issues: the nature of justification, the role of Scripture and especially on the nature of the Church or Christian community. The two ends of the spectrum of views of the Church are represented in the thinking of Menno Simons, who came to be so important to the Anabaptists, and that of Richard Hooker, who provided a rationale and defense for the Anglicans. Heretofore, different views of the Christian faith had been held within one overarching ecclesiastical structure, as can be seen in the diversity of Benedictines, Franciscans and Dominicans during the Medieval period. In the sixteenth century, difference led to division. It led to a polemical element within Christian thought. Each Christian thinker arguing for his or her version of Christianity against views held by other Christians. It was a tendency that would persist down to the twentieth century.

Review

1. How did Menno Simons view baptism?
2. How did Richard Hooker understand the Church?
3. Contrast the views of Simons and Hooker on the Church and tradition.

Chapter 17

Reform in the Catholic World
Erasmus, Ignatius of Loyola and Teresa of Avila

THE SIXTEENTH CENTURY WAS a period of reform across the Western Christian world. In addition to the reforms that led to the emergence of the Protestant traditions, there were developments and changes within the Catholic world that served to reform it as well. The Council of Trent (1545-1563) debated and codified the changes and challenges in the Catholic world and redefined the Catholic tradition. The Council of Trent is the Council of the "Counter-Reformation."

Earlier in the century, one of the leaders of an Augustinian order, Giles of Viterbo, called for reform within the Catholic tradition. He argued that the needed reform was one in which human beings are "changed by religion," rather than human beings "seeking to change religion." Religion changes people Viterbo argued. Hence, reform efforts are best directed to the ways in which the Catholic religion can change human beings. He opposed getting into the business of changing the religion, especially in ways that would destroy the unity of the Church.

In this view, religion remains intact, while efforts at renewal focused on changes in its effects. How can our beliefs, our rituals, our convictions move more directly into people's lives? In a sense, that notion was shared earlier by Erasmus, a leading figures in the new humanistic scholarship of the times.

Erasmus (1469-1536) the Learned Voice

Erasmus was a great scholar; influenced by the humanist movement emerging from the Renaissance. He was well trained in classical languages and involved in historical criticism of earlier traditions. When Luther came along, Erasmus was very open to Luther's call for reform; he felt that everyone should be engaged in this effort. However, he soon realized that what Luther was calling for would destroy the unity of the Church. When he saw that this was going to be the consequence of the reforms, he began to back away from them. For Erasmus, who was a model of the rational, calculating and cool-minded humanist, the reforms that needed to take place in the Church were primarily moral reforms: not doctrinal or ecclesiastical reforms but reform in the moral order. He did not see a need to change the teaching of the Church especially in relation to indulgences and justification as Luther had called for. For Erasmus, the heart of the Christian faith was its moral component. His issue was bringing the lives of people in the Church more deeply into line with the moral teachings of the Church.

Erasmus' most famous writing is his ironic, often satirical; *Praise of Folly*, written in 1509, and dedicated to Thomas More in England. In the end, it outlines the Christian ideals he shared with other renaissance humanists. The *Folly* ironically praised the moral teachings of Christ. However, an earlier text by Erasmus, written before Luther, the Protestant reformer, appeared on the scene, presents his exposition of the virtues of the Christian way of life. Erasmus called his book the *Enchiridion* or *Handbook of the Militant Christian*. Here Erasmus presents the basic rule for the Christian life in a very clear and intelligible way. Erasmus called it a "method of living which might help you achieve a character acceptable to Christ." Aiming at what it meant to be a true Christian, he emphasized Christian holiness as something lived in the world. "Life," he said, "is nothing but a kind of perpetual warfare." Thus it was necessary, Erasmus sought to show, that the Christian should "always be armed with prayer and with knowledge," as well as with the Christian virtues of faith, hope and charity. These virtues, Erasmus argued, should govern the Christian's life—and the life of the Christian community.[1]

Erasmus then outlined twenty-two rules for the Christian. They range from "Faith," the first rule as the antidote to ignorance, through "Trust not Yourself but Christ" (the eleventh rule) and "The Nobility of Man" (the eighteenth) to "The Impermanence of Life," (the twenty-first). Taken together, they "point out the road that leads directly to Christ." Erasmus concluded

---

1. Himlick, *The Enchiridion of Erasmus*, 37, 38, 47.

with the prayer that Christ consent "to favor your sound beginning" and "increase His grace and make it perfect in transforming you, so that you may swiftly grow strong in Him." Ever the reasonable Christian humanist, Erasmus did not offer the ringing challenges of the reformers who would come, but rather the voice of one who urged the cultivation of the best in our nature.[2]

Although Erasmus, like other Renaissance humanists, sought to move beyond medieval Christianity, he did follow Aquinas' teaching that humanity was wounded — not ruined by the Fall—as some Reformers would argue. Jesus is the example for people to follow. In their Christian life, they must be on guard against all temptations and seductions that lead to idolatry. At the same time, Erasmus reminded his readers that the sacraments, gives one the grace needed to follow in Christ's way.

Erasmus' *Enchiridion* is well argued and reasoned. He pushed for moral reform, seeking to make Christian teaching more accessible to people and emphasizing its moral component. Later on, when Luther came on the scene, there were exchanges between them on the question of the freedom of the will—an issue central to Erasmus and, in a different way, important to Luther as well. While Erasmus championed the freedom of the will, Luther maintained that Erasmus failed to understand how deeply human life had been damaged by the fall and by sin. Consequently, Luther argues that the sweet reasonableness that Erasmus puts forward is not a human capability. Life is not a simple matter of choosing to do what is right. Luther's response to Erasmus was passionate, even bombastic, as he argued for "the bondage of the will." For Luther, the gift of God's grace in Jesus Christ heals our fallen humanity.

This exchange demonstrates the differences of character and temperament between Luther and Erasmus as well as their doctrinal differences. Erasmus is reasonable and controlled, Luther more passionate and explosive. For Luther, the problem is that our will is bound; we are not free to do what we will. Human beings can gain the freedom promised to the Christian through the transforming act of justification. Luther insisted that we have to see how central this is to the Christian life. He argues that we need to recognize that Christian freedom does not arise from something that we do, but because of what is given to us in Christ. Thus we will be able to exercise Christian liberty. Erasmus obviously felt very differently on this issue. In his view, human beings confronted with choices can freely make those choices and in that way live a more Christian life. Thus, when Erasmus saw that Luther was breaking the unity of the Church, he

---

2. Ibid., 200.

moved away from the German reformer. However, he continued through his scholarship and writings to encourage a more reasoned and moderate reform of Christian life.

Ignatius of Loyola (1491–1556): The Emergence of the Jesuits

A Spanish thinker of the period, Ignatius of Loyola, deeply influenced the entire Catholic world. Spain had emerged in the late fifteenth century as a major global power and as the champion of the Catholic faith. In 1492—the same year Columbus sailed from Spain to discover the New World, populated for millennia by native peoples of the Americas—Ferdinand and Isabella, the country's Catholic monarchs, expelled the Jews from Spain. Spanish Catholicism, which developed such unique institutions as the Inquisition, was immensely hostile to the Protestant reforms. In the midst of all this piety and treachery, some very important figures were emerging.

One of those important Catholic figures from this time is Ignatius of Loyola. For Ignatius, the problem confronting the Church was a lack of spirituality and depth of spiritual life. Born into a Basque family, Ignatius received a military education. Wounded in a battle, Ignatius underwent a profound conversion that radically transformed his life. During his convalescence in 1521–1522 he read two popular medieval religious works, Ludolph of Saxony's *Life of Christ* and the collection of saints' lives known as *The Golden Legend*, compiled by Jacobus de Voragine. These works had a profound influence on Ignatius; they opened up for him the vision of another kind of life that led him to reorient his life. He came "to recognize the differences between the spirits that agitated him, one from the demon, and the other from God," and resolved to "forsake his worldly desires and ambitions." Some months later, "he saw clearly an image of Our Lady with the holy child Jesus," which, he felt, confirmed the changes he had been going through and his intention to devote his life to serving God. Thus began the way ahead for Ignatius.[3]

In the following year, he went to the shrine of Our Lady at Montserrat in Catalonia and the nearby town of Manresa. It was here that he became "a soldier of Christ." After nearly a year in Manresa, he set out for Jerusalem. Although he made it to Jerusalem, he encountered opposition and returned to Italy. He then studied in France and Spain in further pursuit of his vocation. He began to gather followers around him and to teach them his "exercises."

---

3. See O'Callaghan, *The Autobiography of St. Ignatius Loyola*, 24, 5, 24.

Out of his own experience and his education, Ignatius developed a set of spiritual exercises that he taught to those he encountered. They took written form as *The Spiritual Exercises* in the early 1540s, and were at the heart of the Society of Jesus or Jesuits, the new religious order he founded in 1539. The new Jesuit Order spread very quickly. Jesuits often became the most able opponents of the Protestant reforms; they played important roles at the Council of Trent and helped to redefine Catholic teaching. John Olin remarks, "In all these events Ignatius and the Jesuits . . . became perhaps the most important agents of Catholic revival in this troubled age."[4]

Ignatius of Loyola made an important contribution to the efforts to unfold a grammar of the spiritual life, a contribution that marks a departure from what had emerged in the medieval period. *The Spiritual Exercises* become very influential within the Catholic world of his day and continue to be so down to the present day. In the late twentieth century, the Spiritual Exercises became more broadly accessible to lay Catholics and other Christians. Ignatius sought revitalize the Church from within. His emphasis on this new spirituality is in some ways simply a revival of the spiritual traditions within the Catholic Church, but put in a very effective package and form. In other respects, Ignatian spirituality constituted a new initiative, with its emphasis on "contemplatio in actione," contemplation in action.

The point of the Exercises is to bring one into a dynamic spiritual life of obedience and discipline, which is at the heart of the spirituality Ignatius championed. A central theme is the kingdom of Christ. The Exercises take place over a four-week period, with each week designed to lead one through a set of interior actions that remake one's interior life. The outcome should be deepened self-understanding of who one is in the context of a deepened commitment to the kingdom of Christ.

In the first week of retreat on the Spiritual Exercises, the focus is on contemplation of one's sins in order to begin the process of purifying oneself inwardly. The second week focuses on the kingdom of Christ, the third week on the Passion and the fourth week on the resurrection of Christ. As Ignatius conceived the Exercises, one did them with the assistance of a spiritual director who helps one to understand the spiritual dynamics present in one's life and how they are understood. You should not do this on your own because it is important to understand—and understand aright—the spiritual dynamics that are set in motion. That requires the assistance of a director, someone with whom you can speak about what is happening. Over time, the individually directed Exercises gave way to the "preached retreat," where the retreat director addressed the group of exercitants several times

---

4. See Olin, *The Catholic Reformation*, 9.

a day. However, the individually directed Exercises have enjoyed a revival since the 1950s.

Two principles underlie the *Spiritual Exercises*. The first is that nothing can be done except through the Holy Spirit. One of the ways to bring oneself in contact with the Divine Spirit is by examining one's own life in the light of Christ's life: first an awareness of sin, followed by the call to the kingdom, and then identification with Christ's passion and with the resurrection. As one brings one's life into relationship with these dimensions of Christ's life, the Spirit has an opportunity to work in one's life.

The second principle is that the Spirit of Christ demands the co-operation of the human soul. This principle was especially abhorrent to the Protestant reformers of the sixteenth century, who rejected the idea of co-operation between the human soul and divine life. For Ignatius, bringing our soul into voluntary and willful co-operation with God's spirit is precisely what lies at the heart of Christian spirituality, and in this co-operation, a transformed life can emerge.[5]

The innovative spirituality arising from the *Spiritual Exercises* was extremely effective and transforming. The impact of this new spirituality extended well beyond the Jesuit order and was a source of considerable renewal within the Catholic tradition.

Matteo Ricci (1552–1610), a Jesuit in Confucian China

In addition to influencing the Council of Trent, the Jesuits also pioneered the expansion of Christianity into the cultures of the East and South, and—along with the Franciscans and Dominicans—into the Americas. No one was as innovative as the remarkable Jesuit Matteo Ricci would prove to be.

Christianity had come to China as early as 587 in the form of Eastern Nestorian Christianity from ancient Persia. Known as "Light from the West," the Tang Dynasty rulers welcomed Christianity. The astonishing writings of what some contemporary authors' call 'Taoist Christians,'[6] which only recently have come to light, had long been lost when Ricci arrived in Macau in 1582 and joined other Jesuits who had preceded him. The ancient Chinese culture and the learned Confucians he encountered impressed Ricci. His first task was to learn Mandarin, and when he learned Mandarin, he began to dress in the mode of the Confucian scholars.

---

5. See Teresa of Avila, *The Spiritual Exercises of St. Ignatius*.
6. See Palmer, *The Jesus Sutras*.

Matteo's way was not easy, as the Chinese regarded all foreigners with suspicion. However, his knowledge of mathematics, the new cartography and sciences emerging in the West attracted the attention of the authorities. Invited to settle in Zhao Qing in mainland China in 1583, it was not until 1595 that he reached Nanjing, the southern capital, and three years later, he reached Beijing, site of the Forbidden City and the Imperial Court.

Basic to Ricci's encounter with Confucianism was the notion of *Tien*, translated as Heaven, signifying the transcendent celestial order, and what Western thinkers often called "ancestor worship." Ricci understood the Christian God as the "Lord of Heaven," and argued that veneration of the ancestors is compatible with the Christian faith. During these years, Ricci wrote his account of "the Lord of Heaven," arguing that Christianity is the completion and fulfilment of Confucianism.

It was not his interpretation of Confucian and Christian teaching that interested the Imperial Court. It was his scientific knowledge; and the Imperial Court invited Ricci in 1601 to become an advisor in matters of cartography and mathematics. He was the first Westerner invited into the Forbidden City.

Ricci was given permission to build what became the Cathedral of the Immaculate Conception in Beijing and he began to gain some converts among the Confucian scholars. By the time of his death in 1610, there was a community of more than a thousand Confucian Christians. Remarkably, the Emperor allowed Ricci's burial in a Buddhist temple in Beijing, the first foreigner so allowed.

Matteo Ricci charted a novel way into other cultural and religious traditions, one that respected indigenous ways. Ricci and others acknowledged Confucian values and argued that the veneration of ancestors was not contrary to Catholic teachings. Known as the "Rites Controversy," in 1645 the Vatican rejected Ricci's approach to Chinese culture and Confucian teaching. Over the centuries, this matter has been on a roller-coaster ride. It was approved in 1656, then banned again in 1704, then again approved in 1939. When I visited the Cathedral in 2011, the liturgy sounded, "Like it was sung by angels."

Ricci's approach to Chinese traditions was a pioneering way that would resurface in the twentieth century when Vatican II (1962–65) urged "dialogue and collaboration" with other religious traditions.

Teresa of Avila (1515–1582): The Interior Life

The walled medieval city of Avila still stands in the high plains of central Spain, as I discovered when I went to visit the places associated with the fascinating woman who lived there, Teresa of Avila. Avila is an hour and a half from Madrid on modern roads, but in Teresa's time, it was a more rural setting. A part of her nunnery still stands, although it has been subject to renovation over the years.

Teresa may have come from a "Converso" family, that is, a Jewish family that converted to Christianity in the period leading up to the expulsion of the Jews from Spain in 1492. Her development as a contemplative—and a reformer within her monastic world—came later in her career. Avila had another famous resident during Teresa's time, John of the Cross (1542–1591). Although he was much younger than Teresa was, they were close friends and had a deep impact on each other.

Teresa is the author of her *Interior Castle*, a work written at the encouragement of her own spiritual director. It is a work written by a woman for other women, for purposes of instruction and spiritual direction in her own community. Teresa wrote,

> *I was told . . . that the nuns of these convents of Our Lady of Carmel need someone to solve their difficulties concerning prayer, and as . . . women best understand each other's language and in view of their love for me, anything I might say would be particularly useful to them.*[7]

The Interior Castle is intended to be practical and to aid Teresa's sister contemplatives in their own spiritual journeys. It compares the spiritual life to a series of rooms within that lead to the innermost chamber and the soul's "spiritual marriage or union with God." The "Interior Castle" is the inner life of the spirit. This castle contains many rooms, many dimensions, Teresa said. It also includes different stages and states as we enter it and make our way to God. We proceed through it in a series of stages as we enter the different rooms in the castle of the self.

Now Teresa knew that insight in spiritual matters does not come easily. If it does come, she noted in her opening chapter, we should regard it as a gift—a gift about the most important thing of all: the relationship of the soul to God. Teresa, like others, saw that there were different states of the soul, different stages in the journey towards God. Teresa characterized these different states and stages of the soul as the "Seven Mansions" of the Interior Castle.

---

7. Teresa of Avila, *Interior Castle*, 24.

Teresa made many contributions to the grammar of the spirit, and we can see some of them as we follow her through the Interior Castle. If we ask about God's intention and purpose for the human being, then Teresa said that we should "be perfect and one with Him." What is the way to that goal? Teresa said that it is "the love of God and the neighbour" cultivated on the interior front by prayer and meditation. Prayer and meditation open us to the interior castle and guide us to its innermost chambers. The "Seven Mansions" of that interior way are:

1. *Entry into the interior castle*: The first stage in Teresa's grammar of the soul is—surprisingly—an awareness of oneself as a child of God coupled with—not surprisingly—an awareness of sin. Actually, the awareness of oneself as created in the image of God is the stronger emphasis as she describes "the great dignity and beauty" of the human soul. For Teresa, as we become aware of our status as children of God created in God's own image, we gain a more realistic appraisal of ourselves, and an awareness that we are not all we should be. The distinctive prayer of this stage is the "prayer of humility." Such prayer and meditation lead one into the spiritual life and mark its beginning: our entry into "our beautiful and delightful castle." Thus, it is both a state and a stage. Teresa insisted that "self-knowledge" is essential to this stage and to the entire spiritual journey. She remarked, "Self-knowledge is so important that, even if you are raised right up to heaven, I should like you never to relax your cultivation of it." One must be aware of oneself as created in the image of God, even though the bright crystal of the soul be darkened by sin.[8]

2. *Persevering State and Stage*: The second mansion in Teresa's Interior Castle is the room of persevering. The life of prayer and meditation has its vicissitudes. Teresa knew this and encouraged her readers to persevere in their practice of the interior journey. It takes time to cultivate an inner disposition of quiet and peacefulness. It is not a one-day or one-month or one-year thing, but a practice pursued in order to develop a habit, an enduring and persistent awareness of oneself in relation to God. As one encounters these vicissitudes, one must simply persist. During these times we must "embrace the cross . . . which is ours to carry too." Teresa reminds us of the importance of persevering in the life of prayer. When we get discouraged we have to remember that God is faithful, always there, always available to our efforts.[9]

---

8. Ibid., 29, 31, 19.
9. Ibid., 50.

3. *Walking in Fear*: Teresa's account of the spiritual life does not characterize the journey as moving from triumph to triumph. Nor does it exclude the difficult, terrifying and troubling moments from the journey itself. Thus, the room "walking in fear" is a stage and state that is within the interior castle. This is part of the story of the soul's journey to God. "Walking in fear" is a condition that one encounters while moving along the difficult path of self-knowledge and perseverance. Here one finds one afraid, alone, and full of fear, but this is not a reason to abandon the journey. Rather, one needs to recognize it as part of the journey.

4. *Understanding in the House of Consolation*: A fourth part of the soul's journey is what Teresa called "understanding" in the "house of consolation." Here we begin to gain "understandings that exceed mere concepts." It is crucial to understand Teresa aright here. The Way of prayer and meditation that she is counselling is not to be confused with an intellectual or conceptual journey of understanding. Here understanding is something deeper than the conceptual: it is spiritual, intuitive, and contemplative. As Teresa remarked, "we cannot express" the understandings or "consolations" that begin to come "adequately in rational terms." These consolations are the "spiritual gifts" that come, Teresa pointed out, when we "rest in God rather than our own efforts." This is a central paradox of the spiritual journey and spiritual life. Although the way of prayer and meditation does involve effort, striving, seeking, it is also about letting go, receiving, resting not in our own efforts but in God. In Teresa's terms, we will then have achieved disinterestedness in our spiritual life, a state where love is uncorrupted by self-interest. Her advice is especially directed to those who "suffer greatly from distractions during prayer." Here Teresa encouraged prayer as recollection as the way into this crucial stage and state in the spiritual journey.[10]

5. *Uniting with the Will of God*: The fifth room in the interior castle is what Teresa called the room where we begin to unite our will with God's will. Strikingly, the image and analogy that Teresa used to speak about this moment in the spiritual journey is marriage. It is in marriage, she argued, that we see two wills unite in a love relationship. This is precisely what we are moving towards in the life of prayer and meditation, a state where our will, our heart, our love is united with God's will, God's love. Such union is only possible in a loving relationship—and that is what is always there in the relationship of God to the

---

10. See Teresa of Avila, *Interior Castle*, 72.

human soul. However, from the human side we have to make our way through all kinds of obstacles, fears, distractions and misunderstandings to realize the nature of our relationship with God. This, again, is a difficult but possible stage to achieve. Just as in marriage, not everyone achieves this union of wills or hearts, but it is by analogy a fitting image for this stage. Though this is not the final stage, the final state, or the final room, this is life made whole and moving towards perfection.

6. *Stage of Greatest Favours and Greatest Trials*: Now, just when we might think we have arrived, Teresa says we have reached the point of both the "greatest favours" and the "greatest trials." Here we are closest to the goal yet most fearful that all will be lost. The language here is important, for it underscores the fragility and terror of the spiritual life as well as its glory and joy. Here Teresa seems to be talking about that moment that her colleague, John of the Cross, described as "the dark night of the soul." Perhaps, John learned of this dark moment from Teresa. What is significant is that this state is part of the interior castle: it is not something to be ashamed of or to make one feel that one has failed. It is integral to the journey of the soul.

7. *Spiritual Marriage*: The deepest room in the interior castle, the highest stage of the soul's journey to God is what Teresa called a "spiritual marriage" or "divine marriage." This is Teresa at her controversial best. She acknowledged that this stage exceeds easy description—indeed any description. She was insistent that the "the soul is made one with God." This union of the soul with God should not be confused with "our senses, our faculties, or our passions" having attained union. This is something deeper, more spiritual, beyond our capacity to describe. In this relationship of "spiritual marriage," unlike spiritual betrothal or even spiritual union, Theresa wrote,

> He has been pleased to unite Himself with His creature in such a way that they have become like two who cannot be separated from one another: even so, He will not separate Himself from her.

Here one has attained the goal of the way of prayer and meditation. Moreover, when realized it is recognized as a gift from above and not a reward for our striving.[11]

Teresa's work was to result in a transformed Carmelite order. Her remarkable contributions to understanding the soul's journey to God are among the most profound in the history of Christian thought.

---

11. Ibid. pp. 207-08 and 214.

Summary

While the ecclesiastical unity of the Christian way in the West was broken in the sixteenth century, it was also a time of reform, renewal and retrenchment across Western Christianity. Within the Catholic world elements of reform were centred on the reform of the moral and spiritual life, while in the emergent Protestant world the reforms were doctrinal and ecclesiastical. Representatives of the new humanistic learning, like Erasmus, had an impact on Christian thought, as did the important Spanish religious, Ignatius of Loyola and Teresa of Avila. At the same time, the Council of Trent presented itself as a retrenchment and reaffirmation of traditional Catholic teaching against the Protestant critique of the Catholic tradition, even though it involved real reform.

Review

1. Reform spread across the Christian world in the late fifteenth and sixteenth centuries. How would you describe those reforms in the Catholic world?
2. Describe the stages/rooms of Theresa's "interior castle." Do you find any resonance with your experience of prayer and the inner life?
3. Ignatius of Loyola, the founder of the Jesuits, pioneered a new spirituality. Identify and discuss the key features of his Spiritual Exercises.
4. Why was Matteo Ricchi an important figure?

Chapter 18

Reforming the Reformers
Three Protestant Movements: Pietists, Puritans, and Methodists

WITH THE REFORMATION, THE development of Western Christian thought within the context of a single ecclesiastical tradition ended. This was not the first division within Christianity. A half-millennium earlier we had seen the division into the Orthodox and Western Catholic traditions, and a half-millennium before that, after the councils of Ephesus and Chalcedon, the Church of the East or Nestorian Christianity had gone its own way. However, after the Reformation, Christian thought increasingly fragmented. Now Christian thinking took place against the background of a multiplicity of denominations, new creeds, and in relation to a variety of national cultural and political contexts. Attempts to cover the story of Christian thought over these remaining centuries becomes much more difficult.

In the sixteenth and seventeenth centuries, virtually all of the new denominations developed their own creeds and creedal statements. The Lutherans affirm the Augsburg Confession of 1530 and later the Book of Concord (1580s), the Anglican tradition develops its Thirty-nine Articles of 1563, the Reformed traditions the 2nd Helvetic Confession of 1566 and the Westminster Confession in 1646, the Anabaptists the confessions of Schleitheim (1527) and Dordrecht (1632) and so on. Many of these creeds also include an affirmation of the Nicene Creed. They are a new overlay on the earlier creed. In this period in Western Christianity, there was a dramatic revival of the creedal impulse that had no parallel since the end of the great ecumenical councils of the early Church. Those creedal statements became benchmarks for Christian thinking in their respective traditions.

In addition, after the period of the Reformation, the attempt to establish a synthesis of faith and reason or of Christian faith and culture began to break down or was limited to national and regional cultures. Within Western societies, there was a growing desire to be free of the tutelage of the Church, a desire that flowered later during the Enlightenment and was manifest in the nationalist sentiments that are stirring after 1500. The desire to be free of the tutelage of the Church is evident in the greater autonomy of the philosophical traditions, the new empirical sciences, and the desire to find new configurations of church and state.

For more than 1,200 years, Christian theology had largely developed hand in glove with philosophy in the West. Greek philosophy, especially Platonic and Neo-platonic and, more recently, Aristotelian thought had been part of the conversation. Thus, many of the great Christian thinkers of earlier periods were philosophers as well as theologians. After the Reformation period, these ways of thinking developed in much greater autonomy from each other. That growing division between Christian thinking and philosophy—or faith and reason—often entailed an increasing separation of Christian faith from the wider sphere of culture and society.

A third factor was the rise of nationalism in Europe. As the Reformation period proceeded, the Holy Roman Empire declined and new national states begin to emerge. When we speak about Europe, we must increasingly speak about France, Spain, Portugal, England, the Netherlands, Sweden and Italian city-states. The emergence of these new spirits of nationalism then national political units also had an impact on Christian thinking. What happens when Christian thinkers think of themselves not simply as citizens of the Church or as part of a Christian culture, but instead as Christian thinkers within denominations and as members of particular national units? These developments should be remembered as we explore the great conversation in more recent centuries. Confronted as we are with so many new voices we are even more selective than in previous centuries.

We should also note the pattern emerging within each of these particular traditions. First, there is the creative moment of the reform leaders, who articulate their new understandings of the Christian faith. An attempt to systematize and integrate the insights of the reform figures follows, sometimes resulting in new creeds for each of the denominations, as well as new patterns of Christian life. Some important Christian thinking goes on as a new generation clarifies and amplifies the terms and perspectives that have emerged as foundational or thematic to a denomination or tradition. For example, justification by faith becomes the central theme among Lutheran thinkers, the sovereignty of God among Reformed thinkers, the worship of God among Anglican thinkers, discipleship among Anabaptists

There is also these efforts, especially among Protestants, to revitalize the tradition and find patterns of what we might call "lay spirituality." One of the contributions of the Reformation period to the great conversation is the notion of the priesthood of all believers. This view rejects the distinction that had so long obtained in Christianity between the priest and the laity, between the ecclesiastical hierarchy and the ordinary members of the Church. When Protestants affirm this principal—as they do to varying degrees—then one of the problems that arises is the issue of authority and maintaining the unity of the Church. This notion also leads to different understandings of the community of faith, the Church.

Thus, Christian thinking turns again in a more practical direction, one aimed at lay spirituality. One of the reforms that attempts to revitalize denominational life through developing patterns of lay spirituality is Pietism that is especially important within the context of the Lutheran traditions. In another context, we see the rise of Puritanism, which grows up against the background of Calvinist and Reformed thinking. It too wants to understand the Christian faith in ways that will touch the laity. Later, John Wesley initiated a reform movement in the Anglican tradition that eventuated, despite Wesley's efforts to find a place for this new movement within his own tradition, in another new denomination: Methodism.

Philip Jacob Spener (1635–1705), the Founder of Pietism

We look at the first attempt to revitalize the Lutheran tradition that we find in the life of Philip Jacob Spener, the founder of Pietism.

Spener was born into a devout Protestant home and studied history and philosophy at the University in Strasbourg. He later studied and lived for a period in Switzerland, where he had contact with some of the more radical Anabaptist communities that had grown out of the Reformation. Consequently, Spener's own religious self-understanding began to move in a direction that increasingly emphasized the personal and interior character of the Christian faith. He became a Lutheran minister and served in a congregation in Frankfurt. It was here that he began to develop a particular form of congregational and lay life known as the "Collegia Pietatis." Groups met weekly to study the Bible and pray together and, Spener hoped, in this way to revitalize life within the Lutheran community. In the background of Spener's concern was the recent Thirty Years' War, a period of intense religious conflict that had devastated Europe. The Peace of Westphalia, which had ended the war in 1648, established the rule that the religion of the ruler would be the religion of a given territory.

The other factor in the background was the shift that had taken place in the understanding of faith within the Lutheran tradition. Luther spoke about faith as trust: "trusting in the promises of God" was the vital heart of faith. This lively and transforming faith had its center in the conviction that God in Jesus Christ has justified and accepted humanity. Spener felt that in the interval between Luther and his own time, a shift had taken place. Faith had come to be understood as assent to certain propositions. He saw this as having a debilitating effect on the life of the congregation. He sought a pattern of lay spirituality that could revive the life of the Church as the priesthood of all believers. Spener eventually expressed his views in a book called *Pia Desideria* or Pious Desires. This book is the source of the name Pietism for the movement Spener initiated.

His basic concern was to find ways to revitalize lay Christian life. In a 1669 sermon he remarked,

> *How much good it would do if good friends would come together on a Sunday and instead of getting our glasses, cards, or dice would take up a book and read from it for the edification of all . . . if they would speak with one another about the divine mysteries, and the one who received most from God would try to instruct his weaker brethren . . . by virtue of their universal Christian priesthood . . . to work with and under us to correct and reform as much in their neighbours as they are able.*[1]

Later, in his *Pia Desideria*, he would offer six recommendations towards this end. The first proposal was for "a more extensive use of the Word of God among us." Here he urged "diligent reading of the Holy Scriptures" at home and meetings of members of congregations that "take up the Holy Scriptures, read aloud from them, and fraternally discuss each verse in order to discover its simple meaning and whatever may be useful for the edification of all." This intensified study of the Bible, Spener believed, would lead to enhanced personal devotion and piety. These are practices many Protestants take for granted. However, in Spener's time, these were innovations.[2]

Second, Spener called for an enhanced role for the laity in "the diligent exercise of the spiritual priesthood." This meant that rather than relying wholly on the leadership of the clergy, the laity within the Church had to assume responsibility for one another's spiritual welfare and growth. Thus, people were to gather in small groups around the study of Scripture and

---

1. See Spener, *Pia Desideria* translated by Theodore Tappert.
2. Ibid., 87-89.

relate the study of Scripture to their own personal life. Rather than depending upon a pastor to guide and correct their understanding of Scripture, and what it meant for their daily life, they should rely upon one another. It was the function of the group to interpret Scripture, to hear the living word. As people laid out their problems about what a particular passage of Scripture meant to them, other lay members should enter into the discussion and help them come to a deeper insight.[3]

The way that Spener understood Scripture needs further comment. For Spener and the Pietists, Scripture was the "living Word of God." It was not a historical text that one had to study by historical means to find out what it meant. Nor was it a book to be interpreted by clergy or learned people. Now available in vernacular languages and widespread by the printing press, it was a moveable text, a living word. For Spener, the Bible was a living text that belonged in the hands of laypeople. It was a book in which God spoke directly to the believer. If you came to the Bible with a pure heart, then God could address you in a living and immediate way through the words of Scripture. Thus, as the group came together and presented to Scripture their concerns and questions, Scripture could address them in a living way.

Third, Spener asserted that Christianity consists not in knowledge, but in practice. This shift in emphasis from abstract knowledge to practice is a reaction against Lutheran scholasticism. It is, as Spener said, "by no means enough to have knowledge of the Christian faith, for Christianity consists rather of practice."[4] It is a matter of living the Christian life.

Fourth, Spener counselled a greater emphasis on charity in religious controversy. After the recent religious conflict of the Thirty Years' War, Spener felt that one of the sources of conflict that led to open warfare was the spirit that governed Christians' exchanges with one another. People were often arguing for their version of the Christian faith over against that version found in another strand of Christianity. Spener felt that was inconsistent with religious faith: "we must beware of how we conduct ourselves in religious controversies." We should conduct ourselves with the spirit of Christian charity. A sense of affection should be the first mark of how controversies between Christians—and with unbelievers—should be conducted. As Spener laments,

> "If only we Evangelicals would make it our serious business to offer God the fruits of his truth in fervent love . . . and show this in unalloyed love of our neighbours.[5]

3. Ibid., 92.
4. Ibid., 95.
5. Ibid., 97 and 102.

Fifth, Spener called for the reorganization of theological studies at the university and the establishment of higher standards of religious life among both teachers and students. Spener supported an educated clergy; they would lead the way in the reform of the church that he was calling for. Spener felt that there was too much emphasis on acquisition of abstract knowledge within theological schools. Spener wanted more emphasis placed on the centre of education, the "practice of faith and love."[6]

Specifically, that meant there should be an emphasis on holiness, piety and building Christian character. For that to happen, it was going to be necessary for the teachers and students to exhibit a much higher standard of religious life than they previously had. Teachers were to set an example, primarily conveyed through their moral character. This concern was to take priority over abstract knowledge or mere notional learning. Spener was not against those things, but it was a matter of where the emphasis was to fall and the primary point of theological education. In part, what Spener was trying to get at is the reform of the clergy, through the reform of their education to include spiritual formation.

The sixth proposal involved the reform of preaching within the churches. Preaching, Spener argued, aims at the edification of the hearers, rather than at demonstrating the scholarship of the pastor. The pastor should bend his preaching and his efforts to edifying his congregation. As Spener said,

> *Our whole Christian religion consists of the inner man or the new man, whose soul is faith and whose expressions are the fruits of life and all sermons should be aimed at this.*[7]

These reforms and responded positively to what Spener was suggesting. There was also considerable opposition to his suggestions, especially among the clergy who saw these reforms as threatening to their position and place within the church. That perception was partly correct. Although Spener envisaged the clergy as leading these reforms, the movement was rooted in the very bosom of the Protestant traditions and its emphasis on the priesthood of all believers. In the Catholic tradition, the priest participates in the priestly role of Christ. However, in the Lutheran tradition, clergy within the life of the church fulfill certain functions—teaching, preaching, the administration of the sacraments, leading in worship—for the sake of good order within the church. The status of the clergy had thus become ambiguous, since theoretically anyone in the "priesthood of all believers" could fulfill the role of minister. However, for the sake of good order, you

---

6. Ibid., 105.
7. Ibid., 116.

select one person or another to do it. Consequently, when movements came along that reemphasized the priestly character of all members of the congregations; the clergy often received them with some unease.

There were, however, grounds for genuine concern. Within the churches where Spener's reforms took hold, there was a tendency for the new groups that began to form to consider themselves the "true Church" as opposed to the rest of the congregation that did not participate in the reforms. Those who did not participate in these new reforms were called "mere professors"—that is, people who professed but did not live the Christian life. Though Spener was concerned about this spirit emerging within the "Collegia Pietatis," it remained a problem for the churches to address. Oftentimes it led to the splitting of congregations, as those who were involved in this form of lay spirituality became so critical of the minister and the congregation that they abandoned the church and set up their own community.

Pietism was important not only in reviving congregational life but also in leading to some new social institutions, including orphanages and mission work. Hospitals and numerous educational institutions formed around Spener's ideas for fostering a revived Christian faith. Pietism was centered in Lutheran churches but spread across the Protestant world. Elements of its impact on Christian life can be seen today. For example, in my university I regularly see notices for people to gather for Bible study. In most of these groups, the purpose is not to study a book written long ago but to encounter the Living Word, an approach to Scripture that comes from Pietism. Spener also contributed to an understanding of the Christian faith as a vital inward reality, a view that has come increasingly to dominate large sections of modern Christian thought.

Puritanism: Reforming the World

The second reform movement is especially important in North America: Puritanism. It takes its inspiration from Calvin, the great reformer of Geneva. The term "Puritan" is the name of a party that emerged in the Parliament in England in the late sixteenth and early seventeenth centuries. This party sought to expand the reform in that country beyond what had taken place within the Church of England. For the Puritans, the reform movement involved not only the reform of the Church but also the reform of the world. Hence, the Puritans are "Worldly Reformers." They felt that, especially in the context of England, the reforms initiated under Archbishop Thomas Cranmer in the early sixteenth century and later defended by Richard Hooker simply did not go far enough. In their view these reforms, which stopped at the reform of the liturgy, were minor reforms that left the Catholic tradition intact. Puritans advocate reforms based on a commitment to Scripture as the Word of God. Scripture is sufficiently clear to serve to regulate all aspects of Christian life—in relation not only to the Church but also to the world.

In the early period of Puritanism, scripture was mediated to the larger community by the learned Saints. They were those who experienced a personal conversion that followed the classic pattern. This pattern had four elements. First, under the impact of the preaching of the Word, a person experienced a conviction of sin. Second, convinced that there was nothing in himself or herself that was adequate to overcome sin, the person experienced a conviction of the need for a redeemer. Third, the person experienced the assurance of salvation—some inward conviction that he or she was among the redeemed. Fourth, the person exhibited evidence of a Christian life—the experience of one's inward conversion and transformation is manifest in one's outward life in the world. Moreover, many of the early Puritans knew and studied the languages of the Bible: Hebrew and Greek.

The Puritan movement was extremely problematic within the context of English life. The Puritans were a disruptive force within the larger society, and consequently, many of them left England and went to the Netherlands and Europe. Later, they became the first immigrants to England's North American colonies, where they had their greatest success. In the American colonies, they had an opportunity to live out their vision of the Christian life in ways that were simply not possible within the context of English national life. At the same time, they had a great impact in England. In the Great Rebellion of the 1640s under Oliver Cromwell, the Puritan forces, who were quite diverse, eventually overthrew King Charles I, becoming the first group in Europe to behead a king. After the Kings' death, a parliamentary system established under Cromwell, transformed England's social and political life and had a deep effect upon its religious life as well.

When I was in England many years ago, I visited the great cathedral at Ely about forty minutes from Cambridge. There is a chapel, and in it are many beautiful statues, except they do not have any heads. The heads were all whacked off during the Great Rebellion, as the Puritans tried to cleanse these churches and rid them of their "superstitious" elements. Many of the statues on the outer walls of cathedrals were pulled down and had their heads whacked off. This says something about the passion with which the Puritans sought to purify the Church and ecclesiastical and civil life. Did it go too far? Was it misguided? I leave those questions open as we pick up the story of the Puritans' emigration to the American colonies, where they had their greatest impact.

The first Puritans who came to North America settled in the Plymouth Colony in 1620 and then in the Massachusetts Bay Colony in 1630. On their way to the Massachusetts Bay Colony, John Winthrop, aboard the Arabella, described the vision that motivated the Puritans: they were to establish "the city set upon a hill," an exemplary Christian society, all of whose parts would be subject to the rule of Scripture and the saints. In the first period of colonization in Massachusetts, it was clear who the saints were—the people who had gone through the kind of conversion experience described earlier. The Puritans were also very clear about what they were against, namely, what they considered the corrupt social life that they had known in England.

The Puritans who came to North America were mostly "non-separating Congregationalists." That means that they had a congregational form of church polity—an ecclesiology that places a great deal of emphasis on the congregation, rather than bishops, as the primary authority within the life of the church. They were non-separating in that they wanted the rule of the saints to extend to other spheres of cultural and social life. Both civil and church life should be lived under the clear word of Scripture, which provided the basic outlines of how things should be in social as well as personal life. The form of social life the Puritans saw in Scripture was a theocracy—a society in which God rules through Scripture and through the saints.

The early Puritans were certainly not democrats. They suppressed dissent, even as they were suppressed in England, where they were considered a dissenting community. In the early 1630s Ann Hutchinson, who heard inner voices and promptings of the Spirit, was tried in Boston and convicted of holding heretical beliefs. Roger Williams (1603-1683) was expelled from the colony (1635) and eventually went to Rhode Island where he established a new colony. The non-separating Puritans wanted an integrated society, and one in which they would not tolerate a great deal of deviance from the established theology and the rule of the saints.

The problem that occurred in the Bay Colony was that as more and more people came to the colony, and as those who originally came had children, the numbers of saints began to dwindle. When you were in "nasty" English society, there was a clear sense of what you were saying no to and what you were joining when you became a member of this dissident group, the Puritans. However, in the colonies, that rejected option—the world as it was—was gone. Presumably one was living in a society which was already, in its main lines, Christian according to Puritan lights. Born into and grown up in a reformed society, the need for a personal experience of conversion diminished. In fact, people were not going through the traditional conversion experience. Meanwhile, the saints were getting older and dying off. How were you going to continue to have a society led by the saints?

One solution that emerged in the Bay Colony was the "Half-Way Covenant," often associated with an important early American Puritan named Solomon Stoddard (1643 -1729). Later, we will meet his grandson, Jonathan Edwards, arguably the greatest of American Christian thinkers. First, however, we will focus on the question of what happened under Stoddard's Half-Way Covenant.

The purpose of the Half-Way Covenant was to redress the declining number of visible saints. Stoddard's Half-Way Covenant stipulated that the children and grandchildren of the visible saints—the full members of the Church—could be baptized and made members of the church on the strength of their parents' and grandparents' piety. They could be admitted to the church as "half-members." It was hoped that the experience of conversion might come later. This marked a significant change as the understanding of the visible saint shifted from an inward experience of conversion to an outward form of moral behaviour.

Everyone in the Bay Colony was obliged to participate in church life. That meant everyone was to go to meeting on Sunday for three hours in the morning and a couple of hours in the afternoon. You then met on Wednesday evening, and very often participate in other events as well. Rarely has there been a more theologically literate culture, and the sermons of the great ministers, which constituted daily or weekly fare, were astonishingly sophisticated and difficult. But this whole social system was increasingly under a great deal of pressure internally as the saints who had constituted the heart of the society dwindled and growing numbers of people who were not particularly religious or caught up in the Puritan ethos immigrated to the Massachusetts Bay Colony.

Puritanism was an attempt to create a form of lay spirituality that could involve all members of society. It understood the Christian faith as open not just to a small group of people but in principle to everyone. While this effort in North America came under greater and greater stress because things didn't work out as envisaged, it is still important to understand what the Puritans were trying to do: to become the "city set upon a hill." In the next Chapter, we examine the next stage in these developments as we look at the figure of Jonathan Edwards (1703–1758), but first we turn our attention to another founder of a reform movement, John Wesley.

John Wesley (1703-1791) and Methodism

Methodism is the third movement we are considering here. John Wesley initiated and guided the movement until his death in 1791. This movement in English religious life was partly a reaction against what Wesley judged to be the failings of the Anglican tradition—its tendencies towards ritualism and, in his view, rationalism. Wesley's father was an Anglican rector who did battle with "nonconformists," while his mother came from a dissenting family. This remarkable woman had nineteen children, many of whom did not survive very long. She educated all of her children at home. A strict disciplinarian, they all learned Latin and Greek.

John Wesley went on to study at Oxford, and while there was deeply influenced by the writings of Bishop Jeremy Taylor especially *The Rule and Exercises of Holy Living*, *The Rule* and *Exercises of Holy Dying*, Thomas à Kempis, *The Imitation of Christ*, and William Law, *A Serious Call to a Devout and Holy Life*. These books led to his devoting his life to the "love of God and neighbour."[8] Later, John and his brother Charles founded what their student critics called the "Holy Society," a term they eventually took for themselves. The "Holy Society" was a student group within the university who met for Bible study, mutual discipline in devotion and frequent communion, along with the reading of spiritual literature. In this context, they pursued a quest for perfection and holiness—a form of disciplined love exhibited in their daily life.

His college experience was certainly important to Wesley, but even more decisive for him was hearing a Moravian preacher in 1738 preach on Luther's doctrine of justification by faith alone. In response to that sermon, Wesley had a deep conversion experience. He said that he felt "my heart strangely warmed. I felt I did trust in Christ, Christ alone for salvation; and an assurance was given me that he had taken away my sins."[9]

After this time Wesley, who was an ordained an Anglican priest, took up a life of itinerant ministry and preached throughout the highways and byways of England. If you want to read an exhausting autobiography, read Wesley's. He had incredible energy to work, go, preach, and talk for years and years and years—right down to the end of his very long life. Throughout that long life, he sought to revitalize faith within the Anglican Communion and more generally within English society. Hundreds would gather as Wesley preached in open-air settings—frowned upon as unseemly by his Anglican superiors and fellow clergy. Around these meetings, battles would

---

8. See Outler, *John Wesley*, 7.
9. Ibid., 68.

sometimes erupt. Wesley was pelted with stones and bottles on more than one occasion.

For Wesley the focus was not on doctrine in a formal sense, but rather on the Christian life. For Wesley, Christian life is rooted in the experience of justification by faith alone—a Reformation formula that Wesley frequently used. He wrote of the testimony of the Spirit as:

> *an inward impression on the soul, whereby the Spirit of God immediately and directly witnesses to my spirit, that I am a child of God; that Jesus Christ hath loved me, and given Himself for me; that all my sins are blotted out, and I, even I, am reconciled to God.*[10]

But this experience marked the first moment in the Christian life and was not, as it was for Luther, the whole of Christian experience. Wesley's writing and preaching came to focus more and more on the issue of sanctification. How is it that, growing out of the experience of justification, the life of the believer is inwardly transformed? As he wrote,

> *The distinguishing marks of a Methodist are not his opinion of any sort. His assenting to this or that scheme of religion, his espousing the judgment or one man or of another, are all quite wide of the mark . . . What then is the mark? . . . A Methodist is one who has "the love of God shed abroad in his heart by the Holy Ghost given unto him;" one who "loves the Lord his God with all his heart, and with all his soul, and with all his mind, and with all his strength . . .*
>
> *. . . The plain, old Christianity that I teach . . . and whatsoever I preach [are] . . . the common fundamental principles of Christianity . . . He is a Christian, not in name only, but in heart and in life . . . [who] is inwardly and outwardly conformed to the will of God . . . his soul is renewed after the image of God in righteousness and in all true holiness.*[11]

It is a commonplace of the reform movements within the Protestant traditions to see themselves as returning to an earlier form of Christian life and practice. They said they were teaching an earlier, simpler, lay-centred Christianity, even though such a time never existed. In reality, the version of Christianity that Wesley championed is marked by distinctive convictions. He did in fact hold to a definite scheme of religion—eventually realized in the Methodist Way, even though he long sought to remain within the Church of England. While reformers sometimes cloaked the innovation of

---

10. See Kerr, *Selections from John Wesley*, 195.
11. Ibid., 195-96.

their views in the use of biblical language; Wesley's reading of the Christian faith was innovative.

That innovation is particularly noticeable in Wesley's view of Christian perfection, which he saw as another name for holiness. For Wesley, this is what distinguished the Methodist. While notions of any sort, or assenting to this or that scheme of religion, are secondary, what is primary is the inward experience of the spirit of God indwelling the believer. Convincing the believer that he or she is a child of God; and being inwardly transformed, and made "perfect." This is one of Wesley's most controversial teachings.

Wesley's innovations can be seen by looking back to some of the major reform figures he drew upon in his preaching. You will remember that for Luther the Christian always remains simultaneously justified and a sinner, so that a fundamental ambiguity permeates the Christian life. If you look back further in the Catholic tradition, you find a distinction made between the priestly or religious life as followed rigorously in the context of a vocation and the general Christian life of a layperson as expressed through participation in the sacramental life of the Church.

Given Wesley's Reformation orientation and his belief in the priesthood of all believers, the central issue for him was the spirituality of the ordinary Christian. Was the Christian transformed by the work of the spirit? Wesley did not share Luther's idea that in justification God declares us just, but inwardly we remain what we were—that we are not changed, but God looks at us as if we were different. Wesley said we have to take this much further and show how it is possible for the ordinary believer to attain a life of holiness or what he called "Christian perfection." When in faith a believer unites with the love of God through the Holy Spirit, this action inwardly renovates and transforms the believer so that he or she becomes in one sense holy or perfect.

When Wesley spoke about Christian perfection, he was very careful to say that he did not mean to suggest that Christians are perfect in knowledge, or even necessarily in behaviour. Rather, he was speaking about an inward transformation of the human heart, which for Wesley meant a transformation of motive, so that all of the Christian's life and action could flow from a genuine love of God. "Everyone," wrote Wesley,

> ... *that hath Christ in him, the hope of glory, purifieth himself, even as He is pure. He is purified from pride; for Christ was lowly of heart. He is pure from self-will of desire; for Christ desired only to do the will of His Father, and to finish His work. And he is pure from anger.*"[12]

12. Ibid., 199.

Pride, self-will and anger are, in Wesley's view, the primary evidence of human disorder or human sin. Sin, for Wesley, is not identified with certain types of behaviour. Rather, sin is rooted in an inward disorder of the human personality, manifest in attitudes, dispositions and motives that are prideful, self-willing and angry. These features of the human heart can be overcome, in Wesley's view, so that we are free of anger, free of self-will and free of pride. They can be wholly rooted out and displaced by the Christian virtues that can be—and often were—summarized in the idea of Christian love.

The transforming and perfecting love mediated to us through Christ is effective in our lives through the indwelling of the Spirit. As Wesley wrote,

> "Everyone that has Christ in him . . . and is pure from anger . . . for Christ was meek and gentle . . . Thus does Jesus 'save his people from their sins,' and not only from outward sins, but from the sins of their hearts, from evil thoughts, and from evil tempers." [13]

For Wesley, Christ so inwardly dwelt within the heart that the things that characterized fallen humanity—pride, self-will, and anger—could be overcome. The Christian could attain inward perfection in this spiritual sense, and that would be manifest in outward behaviour. Wesley was one of the great democratizers of Christian spirituality.

Wesley also had a method for accomplishing this inward renewal. It became known as the "Methodist Way." When Wesley went around preaching and teaching, he set up little cells of twelve Christians—analogous to what we find in some Pietistic movements -- who met together and monitored one another's spiritual life and growth. Through these groups of twelve—a very biblical number, reminiscent of the twelve disciples—Christ was made the reality of one's interior life. While classic Reformation doctrine emphasized the forgiveness of sins, for Wesley the emphasis always fell upon overcoming the disorder within the heart that gives rise to sin so that it can be eliminated—something that was not true for Luther or Calvin.

The Christian can attain perfection such that his or her life becomes "sinless" because sin, for Wesley, has to do with motivation. You may still make mistakes in your actions, but that is a different matter. The Methodist groups (like the Holy Society that he and his brother founded) engaged in the reading of Scripture, the life of prayer, the mutual discipline of the members of the small group—all of these were external aids for the internal transformation. Here was a post-Reformation grammar of spiritual life available to all.

---

13. Ibid., 195.

It is interesting that Wesley, while clearly standing within the Protestant traditions, read many classic Anglo-Catholic and Catholic spiritual writers. But he reinterpreted them or reoriented their work in a lay direction. As we get closer to our time, the contributions to Christian thought become more familiar since they are an ongoing part of the Christian denominations we know. In the context of their own time, they were controversial. Wesley hoped to revitalize the life of his own Anglican communion and bring back something that he regarded as missing within the Anglican tradition. He tried very hard to keep his movement within the Anglican tradition and not have it lead to schism, but it finally resulted in a new denomination. This fracturing of the Christian community is one of the problems that afflicted the Protestant churches. If you imagine Wesley in a twelfth century setting, he would have been the founder of a new religious order, but in the eighteenth century, he became the father of a new Protestant denomination.[14]

Wesley provided a nice summary statement of the Methodist view when he wrote about the "Character of a Methodist." A Methodist, wrote Wesley, is one who has

> the love of God shed abroad in his heart by the Holy Ghost given unto him; one who "loves the Lord his God with all his heart, and with all his soul, and with all his mind, and with all his strength" . . . Dost thou love and serve God? It is enough. I give thee the right hand of fellowship.[15]

Here Wesley sought to shift the focus towards Christian life and away from doctrine. He felt that the significant part was not doctrine but the transforming work of the Spirit in the heart of the believer that brings us back to the basics. He believed that what he was championing was New Testament Christianity.

Summary

These three patterns of lay spirituality—Pietism, Puritanism and Methodism—all had a significant impact on Christian thought, an impact that is still vital within world Christianity. They contribute to the great conversation by

---

14. This fracturing of Methodist life continued until in the 20th century there were literally dozens of Methodist denominations in the US, each have their own distinctive take on the Methodist Way. This was also true for the Lutheran Church in the USA where every Lutheran group that immigrated to the USA founded its own Lutheran denomination. It was only towards the end of the 20th century that most of the 50 Lutheran denominations merged into one Evangelical Lutheran Church in the USA.

15. See Kerr, *Selections from John Wesley*, 196-97.

unfolding the significance of the Christian faith for the priesthood of believers in terms of their life in the world. It is worth noting that the focus in each of these movements is the Holy Spirit, the third article of the Creed. The first article of the creed deals with creation, the second with redemption and the third with sanctification. One of the things that characterize these movements is renewed attention to sanctification and consummation, or how the Holy Spirit works in the lives of people to renew and make all things new. While this is not the sole issue addressed in these movements, it is near the centre of each even though they deal with the issue in very different ways. Out of Wesley, for example, comes a widespread interest, especially in American Christianity, in Christian perfection or "holiness." Heretofore, this issue was confined to the monastic traditions of Christianity, but now it is explored in relation to the lay Christian's life in the world.

Review

1. Did these "reforms of the reformers" really move Christian thinking beyond the initial reformers? Alternatively, did they signal a retreat from the reformers' doctrinal reforms?
2. What was Spener's view of Scripture?
3. What was Wesley's view of "Christian Perfection"?
4. Why are Puritans known as "worldly reformers"?

Chapter 19

Christian Thought in the Americas

IN 1492, COLUMBUS SET sail in search of the Indies of the East, but instead found the lands of the new world, the Americas. It was, however, a "new" world only for Europeans. For the millions of indigenous people of the Americas it was their homeland, and had been for millennia. It included a diversity of peoples that stretched from the mountains of Patagonia in the south through the remarkable Inca cities of the Andes and the Mayan and Aztec cities of Mesoamerica to the villages of the North American plains and the icy settlements of the far north. Everywhere there were people. It was an encounter with fateful consequences for the indigenous peoples. Within a century of the appearance of the Europeans, at least 60 per cent of the indigenous population had died from European diseases. Ronald Wright in his *Stolen Continents: The Americas Through Indian Eyes since 1492* estimates that ninety per cent of the native people died.[1]

With the conquest of the Americas came Christianity. First, there was Spanish Christianity as it spread from the Caribbean into Central America then south into the lands of the Incas and north into the lands of the Mayans and Aztecs, and into what is now the southern United States. Then there was French Christianity, stemming from the settlements in Atlantic Canada and along the St. Lawrence into the Great Lakes region. Finally there was the spread of a special brand of English Christianity in the Massachusetts Bay Colony and other American colonies. These developments are too many and too diverse to cover in any detail here. Rather, we will have to content ourselves with a very selective account of a few voices that contributed to the great conversation of Christian thought in the Americas.

---

1. See Wrights, *Stolen Continents*.

Bartolomé de Las Casas and the Spanish Conquest

With the Spanish conquistadores came missionaries and priests to Christianize the so-called, heathen. By 1520, Hernán Cortés's forces had captured and killed the Aztec ruler Moctezuma in Mexico, and by 1532, Francisco Pizarro's forces had captured and killed Atahualpa, the Inca ruler. Cortés and Pizarro had their hearts set on gold rather than God, but the indigenous population died of disease and enslavement. Dominicans in the Caribbean, Franciscans in Mexico and Jesuits in Peru sought to make converts of these new peoples. Their methods were appalling.

One voice that was raised in opposition to these developments was that of the Spaniard Bartolomé de Las Casas. His merchant father, Pedro de Las Casas, returned from the new world in 1497 bringing an Indian companion, Juanico, to his son. The de las Casas family was granted lands in Cuba, where enslaved indigenous peoples worked the fields. Bartolomé was in Hispaniola from 1502 until 1506, where he learned more about the indigenous people and participated in military actions against them. In 1507, he became a priest and in 1510, he returned to the new world, where in addition to his priestly functions he oversaw family lands. He was troubled about his treatment of the native people and reformed his own practice. In 1534, he wrote an important volume entitled *The Only Way*, a learned and moving plea for reform of Spanish practice in relation to the native peoples.

Unlike most of his contemporaries, Las Casas saw the "humanity of the Indians." Indeed, he continued, "there exist extraordinary kingdoms among our Indians" and "their society is the equal of that of many nations . . . they surpass many . . . they are inferior to none." He quoted Thomas Aquinas approvingly to the effect that

> ". . . no king, no emperor, not the Roman Church itself, can make war on them [pagans who have not heard the gospel] for the purpose of occupying their territory or subjecting them to temporal rule. There is no just cause for such a war."

And Las Casas saw what was unfolding in the New World as making war on the Indian peoples.[2]

However, Casas did believe that it was appropriate to seek the conversion of Indians since it was "the will and work of Christ . . . that God's chosen should be called . . . from every race, every tribe, every language, and every corner of the world." However, what was happening in the New World was not part of this authentic calling. *The Only Way* is a treatise on the appropriate way of calling—of seeking conversion among the Indian peoples.

2. See Parish, *Bartolome de las Casas: The Only Way*, 63, 64-65, and 67.

That way is the one that "Christ Himself... fashioned and prescribed... the method He first used." It is "preaching a living faith" that "wins the mind with reasons, wins the will gently, by attraction, by graciousness."[3] Las Casas offered his vision of authentic conversion when he wrote,

> "We were to invite people to a wedding feast, that of Christ, the Son of God. We were to invite them to recognize that this world Savior, the Savior of humankind, was God, was truly God, one with the Father and the Holy Spirit. Anyone who knows this ... opts for eternal life. 'It is eternal life ... to know you, true God ... and Jesus Christ whom you sent to us ... Go teach people everywhere to keep the commandments I gave you."

Biblical texts require of us, de las Casas continued, both faith and works...

> I am speaking about the way Divine Providence proposed to draw people toward Christ. It was to be attuned to the souls of those approached. It was to breathe peace and love and kindness. It was the fittest means for God's purpose, the conversion, the salvation of humankind, a means steeped in love, grace, charm, humanity, joy, a means worthy of anyone's choice.[4]

Las Casas was like a voice crying in the wilderness, as few heard his plea. Across the New World, Las Casas said, most "continued the practice of subjecting pagans to Christian political power by the awful engines of war." This was "the utter opposite of the natural... way" that, for Las Casas, was the only way to relate to the remarkable peoples of these new lands. Although he was able to reverse the treatment of the Indians on his own lands in Cuba, the war against the indigenous peoples of the Americas continued. Later, as a Dominican and then as a bishop, he was able to shape missionary activity along the lines he had outlined in *The Only Way*. Las Casas spent the rest of his life working for the rights of the Indians, including the restoration of their lands, and against the methods of the Conquest. It is said that when Las Casas died in Madrid in 1566, he had nearly persuaded the Spanish crown to restore Peru to the Incas.

Jonathan Edwards (1703-1758)

While the Spanish Catholic missionaries were working in Mexico, and what became the southwestern states of the USA, the Puritans of New England

---

3. Ibid., 63 and 71.
4. Ibid., 116.

were central to the formation of Christianity in England's American colonies. Perhaps the greatest voice to emerge among Christians during colonial times was Jonathan Edwards from Northampton in New England. Educated at the new school of Yale in New Haven, Edwards was a very scholarly man. He went to Yale when he was fifteen, received his bachelor's and master's degrees and was a tutor there before he came to Northampton in the late 1720s as the assistant pastor under his grandfather, Solomon Stoddard, who had framed the Halfway Covenant. By 1730, Edwards had succeeded his grandfather as pastor. Although towards the frontier, Northampton was an important centre lying up the Connecticut River from New Haven and a day from Boston by horseback.

The Connecticut River Valley Awakening

In 1733–34, some quite extraordinary things began to happen in Edwards's church and throughout the Connecticut River Valley. A remarkable outpouring of religious enthusiasm spread throughout his congregation and others in the valley. This outpouring, that historians call the Connecticut River Valley Awakening, took Edwards and everyone else by surprise. It was an important new religious phenomenon peculiar to the Protestant and Puritan world. Suddenly, everyone, Edwards wrote, was caught up in a revival spirit. Even though a series of sermons by Edwards on "justification by faith alone" was the occasion for the outbreak of this revival spirit in Northampton, he was as surprised as everyone else was. He understood these events as an outpouring of the Divine Spirit. There were times when Edwards had to counsel his parishioners that even in the midst of their "enthusiasm for the things of religion," they had to take care of the harvest and business. Edwards wrote an account of the revival: *The Faithful Narrative on the Surprising Work of God in Northampton*. Edwards describes how suddenly and surprisingly individuals and the life of the community changed by this outpouring of God's Holy Spirit. John Wesley read and was inspired by Edwards' *Faithful Narrative*.[5]

The Awakening came to a sudden end after the suicide of a parishioner. However, when the revivals reemerged in the 1740s, they had a profound impact on American religious and cultural life. The events of the 1740s became known as the Great Awakening.

---

5. See C.C. Goen, *The Great Awakening*. It includes Edwards' *The Faithful Narrative on the Surprising Work of God in Northampton*.

The Great Awakening: Revival & Renewal?

Edwards initially felt that in these revivals one could discern that presence of the Spirit of God making all things new. It was there in the experience of "new birth"—the phrase used to speak of the conversion experience—and in the renewal of congregational life and in its impact on the larger society, all consequences of the revival. During the Great Awakening of the 1740s, the revival phenomenon spread throughout the American colonies. The Christian experience of new birth was extending to the whole population. An estimated one-fifth of the population of Puritan New England directly experienced the inward work of the Spirit through the revivals. There was virtually no household in New England left untouched by these revivals and they greatly added to the membership of the churches in this period.

As indicated before, Edwards saw the Connecticut River Valley revivals of the 1730s as a surprising work of God and not the consequence of his preaching. In the 1800s, revival preachers were persuaded that a revival was something that evangelists could create and manage. This was not Edwards' thinking: he understood the revivals as a special outpouring of God's Holy Spirit. When the revivals again broke out in the 1740s, Edwards was initially one of their most articulate defenders. What he suspected might be happening in these events was the beginning of a new age, the longed-for coming of the millennium. Edwards seems to have believed that through this special outpouring of God's Spirit the life of the world would be transformed. First, the hearts of people would be transformed, making them new creatures through new birth. Then these newly awakened people could come together and renovate the life of society because God was now working directly in the hearts of people through the indwelling of the Holy Spirit.

New Birth and Religious Affections

Later, Edwards came to be very critical of the revivals, and it was in his criticism of the Awakening that Edwards made his most enduring contributions to the great conversation. We can see those contributions in his *Religious Affections*. Compelled by the Great Awakening to look again at "the nature of true religion," Edwards directed the reader's attention to "the distinguishing marks of the Spirit of God." True religion, Edwards said, consists in large part in holy affections. As Edwards wrote,

> *The author of human nature has not only given affections to men, but has made them very much the spring of men's actions. As the affections not only necessarily belong to human nature, but are a*

> *very great part of it; so holy affections do not only belong to true religion, but are a very great part of it . . . . affections are very much the spring of man's action, this also shows, that true religion must consist very much in the affections.*
>
> *Such is man's nature, that he is very inactive, any otherwise than he is influenced by some affection, either love or hatred, desire, hope, fear or some other. These affections we see to be the springs that set men agoing, in all the affairs of life, and engage them in all their pursuits . . .* [6]

Here Edwards distinguished the "affections" from "emotions." Affections are not to be confused with the transitory fluctuations in one's emotional life, but are rather what Edwards called the "deep abiding dispositions" or enduring states of consciousness in a person, which shape the person's basic orientation towards life. Edwards called the basic dispositions that shape our entire outlook on life "holy" affections. For Edwards, "holy affections" can remake one's life.

The issue for Edwards was the linkage between the affections and right belief that leads to rightly ordering the self in relation to God and divine things. Here belief, as deep and abiding states of consciousness or affections, becomes a matter of the renovation of the self. That transformation comes about through the displacement of affections that turn one away from God to affections that are centred on God. God-centred affections, rather than the self-centered emotions of the Awakening, are the mark of the Spirit of God.

For Edwards, the chief of all affections is love. Love is the main characteristic of the abiding disposition that characterizes the life of the Christian. Edwards saw that love in contrast to lives ruled primarily by fear. That was the main contrast for Edwards—between love and fear. Genuine love is a deep and abiding disposition, centred in God that transforms the whole life of the person. As Edwards remarked,

> *God has given mankind affections for the same purpose which he has given all the faculties and principles of the human soul, namely, that they might be subservient to man's chief end, and the great business for which God created him, that is the business of religion . . . The Scriptures place religion very much in the affection of love, in love to God, and the Lord Jesus Christ, and love to the people of God, and to mankind.* [7]

6. Smith, *Jonathan Edwards*, 100-101.
7. Ibid., 103.

Edwards initially affirmed the revivals as an outpouring of the Spirit of God, but then saw that they had become compromised by "hubris or pride," too mixed with "self-love rather than the love of God." This led him to attempt to develop a deeper understanding of the sensibility or affection that should characterize the Christian life. He wanted to rescue an understanding of the affections for religion from what he regarded as the more trivial and passing aspects of the revivals. People tended to interpret any kind of raised emotion as a sign of the presence of the Holy Spirit. In his *Religious Affections*, Edwards went through twelve signs that he said do not count one way or another as sure signs that you have these godly or holy affections. Those signs include "that religious affections are very great or raised high," "that they have great effects on the body," "that they cause one to be fluent, fervent, and abundant in talking of things of religion," or "that you praise or glorify God." Such things are not sure signs.

Then, in the second half of the *Religious Affections*, he turned to twelve signs that show what constitutes truly gracious and holy affections. For Edwards, affections that are "truly spiritual and gracious" have a "supernatural and divine origin," and their first ground in the human personality is some sense of the "transcendently excellent and amiable nature of divine things." His commentary on this first sign runs to more than 30 pages as he seeks to distinguish this sign from its counterfeits. In other words, in the authentic Christian, the affections are not rooted in any self-interested disposition but in God alone.[8]

Agreeing with his Calvinist forebearers that the experience of redemption brings one into relationship with God, Edwards was trying to establish connections between that experience and those abiding dispositions or affections, that shape our being and doing in life. Central here is Edwards's formula for talking about how the Christian loves God for Himself rather than some conceived relation to self-interest. Seeking holy affections to avoid some imagined terrible thing is, for Edwards, a sign of self-interest. It is not disinterested, and therefore not a sure sign that these affections are truly holy affections.

In his discussion of the last of these sure and distinguishing signs of holy and gracious affections, Edwards argued that they have their exercise and fruit in Christian practice. For Edwards, we are reconciled to God through Christ, but that work becomes efficacious in the life of human beings through the work of the Holy Spirit. This is the meaning of the transforming work of the Spirit, the sign that these affections are truly gracious and from God. For Edwards the new birth is not a momentary emotional

---

8. See also Kerr, *Selections from Jonathan Edwards*, 203-05.

high but a practice that exemplifies having placed at the centre of our life the holy affection of love.

American Christianity & the Republic

The revivals also provided an answer to the perplexing question that had troubled the Puritan experiment in the new world: the problem of the decline of the number of saints, which emerged in the late seventeenth and early eighteenth centuries and led Solomon Stoddard to formulate the Halfway Covenant. Here in the revivals the number of saints was dramatically expanding again. This shift was very important because it in a sense democratized the experience of Christian sainthood. Now, rather than being the experience of one person here and one there individually and in isolation, it was the great masses of people who were coming into the Christian fold through the medium of the revival. These events were very significant in the formation of Christianity in the American colonies. They bequeathed to American Christianity an evangelical emphasis on new birth and conversion as well as the social horizon of becoming the city set upon a hill.

These events contributed to a characteristic American self-understanding. Many scholars have drawn lines from the Great Awakening to the American Revolution. For example, the great American cultural historian Perry Miller talked about the American Revolution as a revival that had the good fortune to succeed. It was an outpouring of the revival spirit. The legacy of the Great Awakening also stands behind the well-known American sense of being part of a society that has no precedent historically. While it does not turn out to be the beginning of the millennium, the social vision that took hold in the colonies does turn out to be a new society, the American Republic. There is an abiding confusion in the American psyche between the hope for the millennial age or God's Kingdom and this new society that is emerging.

Of course, there were also secular factors that led to the American Revolution, but it is important to see how ideas and developments in Christian thought had an impact on the formation of cultural traditions. Here among the Puritan thinkers of colonial America, we can discover the sources for that ethos of American exceptionalism —"we are like no other and have a unique God-given destiny to fulfill"—that is so striking in American life.

However, Jonathan Edwards became a critic of what he had earlier helped to spawn. In his critique of the Great Awakening, he spied the danger of pride in its midst, as people confused their own impulses with God's purposes. He would also later write an important critique of the idea of the will as self-determining in his *Freedom of the Will*. However, here again, Colonial America did not heed Edwards and have continued to believe that the will is self-determining. His last great work, *The History of Redemption* remained unfinished when Edwards died shortly after becoming president of Princeton, the new college in New Jersey. In the emerging Christianity of the new world, Edwards was an important figure. He not only articulated some of its enduring themes but was an important critic of some elements of the emerging culture as well.

Christianity in Canada

In Canada, initially explored by French voyageurs and trappers, the first Christianity was Catholic. By 1763, Canada was under the control of the British. Not long afterward, because of the American Revolution, thousands of Loyalists came to Canada. With the possible exception of the Jesuit Bernard Lonergan (1904-1984) and Gregory Baum (1923-2017), Canada has not produced Christian thinkers who have contributed, enduringly, to the great conversation. Here we will look briefly at a couple of figures who helped to shape English Canadian Christianity. Both of these figures played a large role in the formation of life in Upper Canada (Ontario). They saw the Christian faith as relevant to the formation of public order, in contrast with the American emphasis on conversion and the freedom of the believer. We also briefly review some religious developments in French Catholic Quebec.

Bishop John Strachan, Champion of Establishment (1778-1867)

John Strachan arrived in Kingston, Upper Canada, from Scotland in 1799 to become a tutor for the children of a colonial family. It was here that he established his first school. A few years later, Strachan was encouraged to seek ordination in the Church of England. As he grew in his new vocation, he also began to articulate a forceful apology for the establishment of the Church of England as the official church of the new lands of Upper Canada. Strachan was not deterred by the religious diversity of the population. He treated other denominations with scorn as he assumed the mantle of the champion of establishment.

In Strachan's view, society builds on the institutions of church, state and school. Thus, Strachan wrote,

> *It is the duty of every Christian government to support such a religious establishment as may best secure the benefits of this revelation to all their subjects . . . this revelation is intended to promote among all . . . true morality and purity of life, to become the mother of good works and our cordial in affliction and comfort in death, to bring us daily into the presence of God and our Saviour.*[9]

Strachan viewed with alarm what had unfolded in the American Revolution, and he had worked tirelessly in York, now Toronto, to comfort those wounded in the War of 1812. He considered the emphasis on religious liberty, voluntary churches and the free movement of the Spirit in revivals as distasteful and disruptive of society. Strachan's vision of Christianity centred on "true morality and purity of life," and was socially conservative and focused on loyalty as a central virtue. It was a view of Christianity that saw priests as "public teachers of righteousness."[10] Strachan believed, like most Anglicans, that the collective and accumulated wisdom of generations is embodied in the institutions of church and state, so much so, that they are viewed as means of salvation.

Thus, for Strachan, much was at stake in the issue of establishment—it was not simply a matter of the self-interest of the clergy. The establishment of religion was, for Strachan, the foundation of an ordered society. For, he wrote, "a parish priest is an integral part of God's visible church on earth, and essential to the spreading of moral and religious truth and feeling . . . to society."[11] The church was an institution that would form the moral character of new generations. The aims of church and state came together in the concern with inculcating moral virtues. Strachan held to a moderate doctrine of the Fall in which the children of Adam were redeemed through participation in the life of the church.

Strachan also championed schools and education. He established a school in Kingston, later transferred to Toronto, where it became integral to the new University of Toronto in the middle of the nineteenth century. The benefits of British institutions of government and society were so obvious to Strachan that any other way was inconceivable. Thus, throughout his long life, Strachan carried the torch for establishment in Upper Canada: it was the linchpin of an ordered and stable society. Although Strachan was not successful and Canada would not have an established church, his forceful personality and his views set an agenda that would influence Christianity in

---

9. Henderson, *John Strachan*, 91.
10. Ibid., 92.
11. Ibid., 112.

Canada, one that would take seriously its public responsibilities. Strachan died in 1867, the year the Dominion of Canada was established.

Egerton Ryerson Champion of Public Education (1803–1882)

Throughout much of Strachan's life, one of his most able opponents was Egerton Ryerson. A quarter century younger than Strachan, he championed the opposite view on the issues of establishment and religious liberty. Ryerson was a Methodist, one of those "foolish sectaries" against whom Strachan had railed. However, he came from a United Empire Loyalist family, one of the families that left the American colonies at the time of the Revolution and came to Canada. Ryerson's family credentials belied Strachan's attempts to link "sectaries" and "social sedition."

Ryerson experienced a conversion as a young man. This event in 1825 was the beginning of his sense of ministry. He wrote in his journal "I consider it a divine requisition that my whole course of life, both in political and social life, should be governed by the infallible precepts of revelation."[12] When, a year later, Ryerson was invited to leave his Methodist group and become an Anglican priest, it provoked some introspection:

> *"Shall I leave a Church through whose faithful instruction I have been brought to know God, for any advantage that the entrance to another might afford me? No, far be it from me, as I received the Lord Jesus, so I will walk in him . . . my heart is united with the Methodists."* [13]

Ryerson's long life would show his fidelity to his early vow. He became a Methodist minister, often riding great distances to preach. In the 1820s and 1830s, he became a champion of religious liberty: that is, the rights of smaller Christian groups, like his own Methodists, to practise freely their religion. Ryerson challenged Strachan and criticized his view of those who followed other Protestant ways in Upper Canada. Methodists, Congregationalists, Presbyterians, Quakers and Baptists should be allowed to pursue their ways rather than the established views of the Anglicans. Moreover, despite what Strachan said, Ryerson saw his Methodism as emphasizing both conversion and social responsibility. Ryerson offered

---

12. Ryerson, *The Story of My Life*, 37.
13. Ibid., 41.

> "*the first defiant defense of the Methodists and of the equal and civil rights of all religious persuasions . . . and against the erection of a dominant church establishment . . . in Upper Canada.*"[14]

In 1844, Ryerson became the superintendent of schools for Upper Canada, a position he would hold under various political regimes for more than thirty years. Once again, he took to his horse as a circuit rider, but this time in the cause of a public educational system. Ryerson visited virtually all of the small villages across Upper Canada, preaching in favor of the new educational system. In his efforts, Ryerson was successful; he became the architect of the public school system in Upper Canada. The aims of education were the acquisition of knowledge, the building of character and a sense of duty to civil society. For Ryerson, the public school system that he laboured so long and hard to create was an expression of his socially responsible Christian faith.

Towards the end of his career as superintendent of schools, he was troubled by what he perceived as a growing secularity in Canadian life and a diminished knowledge of the Christian faith. Thus, one of his final tasks was to introduce explicit religious and moral education into the school system. Thus, even though Ryerson found himself in conflict with Strachan over freedom of religion and the notion of establishment, they did share the conviction that Christianity should contribute to the public life of society. Indeed, one of the contributions that Canadian Christianity makes to the great conversation is this emphasis on the role of Christianity in the formation of a public life and society.

Quebec & Catholic Christianity

The French founded Quebec and Catholic Christianity shaped its life and development until the "Quiet Revolution" of the 1960s. The Séminaire de Québec, the predecessor to Laval University, was founded in 1663, one of the first institutions of higher learning in the Americas. The conflict between the French and the English for dominance in North America grew as the eighteenth century progressed, culminating in the defeat of the French troops led by the Marquis de Montcalm by the British forces led by General James Wolfe on the Plains of Abraham in Quebec City in 1759. Surprisingly, the Treaty of Paris in 1763 gave the right of the inhabitants to maintain their Catholic religion in Quebec– a provision that was to play a large role in Quebec's educational future. In the nineteenth century, the Ultramontane

---

14. Ibid., 49.

tendency—a very conservative brand of Catholicism that looked across the mountains to the Vatican for guidance—became dominant in the Catholic Church in Quebec. It would remain so well into the twentieth century. During my studies at Harvard in the 1960s, the renowned sociologist Talcott Parsons held up Quebec as an example of a traditional society that had resisted the liberalizing forces of modernity.

However, that was changing. In the 1940s and 1950s, an authoritarian Premier Maurice Duplessis and his Union Nationale machine dominated Quebec politically; but other social forces were percolating. A strong union movement led the resistance to Duplessis, the hegemony of the Catholic Church in the field of education was being challenged, a revitalized Quebec nationalism sought to restore French as the language of Quebec, and new ideas were emerging within the church itself. Duplessis died in 1959, and in the election of 1960, the Liberals under Jean Lesage took power, winning 51 seats to 43 for the Union Nationale. The Lesage government moved quickly to establish a public hospital network, institute a ministry of cultural affairs, nationalize the private hydroelectric companies and transform the educational system in Quebec. It was the beginning of what came to be known as the "Quiet Revolution."

A year later, Pierre Elliott Trudeau, a Quebecer who had been a leading figure in the opposition to Duplessis, became the new Canadian Prime Minister. One measure of the dramatic changes was attendance at Sunday Mass: from 90% in the forties and fifties it had fallen to under 30% by 1970. The Second Vatican Council (1962–65) had also opened its doors to the winds of change. However, the resistance of the Catholic Church in Quebec to the changes in Catholic teaching was surprisingly muted. A newly secularized Quebec had emerged.

Summary

Christianity came to be the dominant religion of the Americas. Protestant forms of Christianity were dominant in the United States, although Catholic Christianity became numerically the largest single denomination by the late twentieth century. American Christianity became denominational Christianity. It was initially characterized by its evangelical emphasis on the transformation of the individual and the coming Kingdom of God. However, this begin to shift with the emergence of American Fundamentalism in the early twentieth century, along with the Pentecostal movement. As we enter the third millennium, there is a shrinking of the mainline Protestant Churches and a growing Pentecostal movement. There is a growing Latino and Charismatic Catholic stream, along with an Evangelical world that ranges widely from alt-right to socially conscious.

Canadian Christianity divides between Catholic and Protestant forms and is more centred on the social and ordered aspects of the Christian faith. However, church going has dramatically declined among Catholics in Quebec, as has membership in the mainline Protestant churches across Canada. Throughout Latin America, the Catholic tradition was dominant and remains so today. Some streams of the Catholic tradition incorporated and transformed elements of the indigenous religious ways they encountered in the Americas, as, for example, in the veneration of Our Lady of Guadalupe in Mexico. In the 1960s, the birth of liberation theology with its "preferential option for the poor" dramatically shifted the role of the Catholic Church in the life of Latin American societies. Beginning in the early twentieth century, a new form of Christianity known as Pentecostal Christianity began to emerge. In the early twenty-first century, it is the fastest growing form of Christianity throughout the Americas, and has grown especially rapidly in Latin America in recent decades.

Review

1. How did Las Casas describe the peoples of the new world?
2. What was Jonathan Edwards's view of the "religious affections"?
3. Characterize some of the differences between Strachan and Ryerson in relation to Canadian Christianity.

PART VI

The Enlightenment and Beyond: 1780–1914

THE ENLIGHTENMENT OF THE eighteenth century marks a watershed in the history of Western thought. However, even prior to the Enlightenment, new sciences based on observation and empirical methods were on the rise. Though these new sciences are often regarded as hostile to Christian thought, our attention to Galileo and others in Chapter 20 presents a different picture. A gradual hostility to religion did emerge, as can be seen in the French mathematician Pierre-Simon Laplace's statement that the "hypothesis of God is unnecessary for science." In the Enlightenment, then, a worldview emerged that did not assume the reality of God, and this had implications for Christian thinkers.

In Europe, Immanuel Kant sought to limit religion to the sphere of morality, and later Friedrich Schleiermacher, often called the father of modern theology, sought to relocate religion in the realm of "feeling." Modern Christian thinkers often found themselves on the defensive as they strove to establish anew the very bases of Christian thought, challenged by the "eclipse of transcendence" in the Enlightenment worldview.

In the United States, the 2nd Great Awakening spawned a number of new religious movements like the Mormons and the Disciples of Christ. We also saw the international emergence of social movements like the Women's movement and the Abolitionists, opposing slavery. There was also opposition to these changing times among those who sought to reassert conservative modes of Christian self-understanding. In the midst of this time of transition, many thinkers made important contributions to the Great Conversation. Here we will just focus on three nineteenth-century figures: Søren Kierkegaard, Cardinal John Henry Newman and Walter Rauschenbush.

Kierkegaard, a Danish Lutheran thinker, credited with initiating an "existentialist" form of Christian thought, and Cardinal Newman recognized the role of development in Christian thinking. Walter Rauschenbush was one of the articulate proponents of the "Social Gospel" movement that paid more attention to the problems of the modern industrial world.

Chapter 20

The Rise of Modern Science, the European Enlightenment, And the Beginnings of Modern Christian Thought

God and the Rise of Modern Science

A DEVELOPMENT IN THE Western world that began in the time of the Renaissance and extended through the Reformation would deeply affect Christian thinking over the coming centuries: the rise of the modern sciences. We often think about the rise of science as the emergence of an impulse within Western civilization that is fundamentally hostile to the religious traditions, but this is at best a half-truth. It is more part of the propaganda of a later scientism that is hostile to Christianity than an accurate reflection of the historical developments that gave rise to the modern empirical sciences.

Consider, for example, Galileo Galilei (1564–1642), one of the first great modern scientists. Galileo did not see his own science as hostile to the Christian faith, though many in the Catholic world did see it that way. Those who opposed Galileo did so under the guise of an older Aristotelian and deductive science as much as a wooden version of the Christian faith. We often overdramatize the story of Galileo's conflict with the Catholic Church and make this incident the whole story of the rise of modern science. Other of the early modern scientists did not have problems with ecclesiastical authorities: Nicolaus Copernicus was a Catholic priest; Robert Boyle was an Anglican; and ecclesiastical authorities in the Netherlands, England and many of the newly Protestant jurisdictions were very positive towards the new sciences. Moreover, in our haste to see Christian authorities as the "bad guys," we forget to ask about Galileo's own views of science and their relation to his understanding of God.

Galileo's self-understanding was that God works in relation to the cosmos and we know Him in two different ways. For Galileo, we know God through the book of Scripture and through the book of nature. In Galileo's understanding, his scientific endeavours were explorations to know God as he discloses Himself in the orderliness of the natural world.[1] Thus, for Galileo, the discoveries of the new science were not hostile to religion. So what was the problem? The problem was that Galileo's science, based on observation, was hostile to the deductive science upheld by many within the Catholic tradition of his time. This science, which had grown out of Aristotelian assumptions, was not experimental in nature but rather theoretical and deductive. Galileo wanted a new science based on observation of the natural order. Through looking at the natural order, one would begin to discover those patterns and orderly and regular features of the universe God had placed there; and which human beings, through their new methods, could come to discern. For Galileo it was not an issue of science versus religion, but one of a new observational science versus an older deductive science.

Of course, there were those who saw Galileo as championing a Copernican view of the world that they considered "contrary to the Bible." In 1615, Galileo wrote a letter to Christina, the Grand Duchess of Tuscany outlining his views "concerning the use of biblical quotations in matters of science." Galileo acknowledged that he held "the sun to be situated motionless in the centre of the revolution of the celestial orbs while the earth rotates on its axis and revolves about the sun." He also said, "the Bible can never speak untruth—whenever its true meaning is understood." Thus he dismissed some of the objections to his view of the physical universe as resting on misunderstandings of "the true meaning" of scriptural texts. For, Galileo noted, Scripture is "often very abstruse" and its "primary purpose" is "the service of God and the salvation of souls." It is in such matters that the authority of Scripture resides. However, Galileo continued,

> *"In discussion of physical problems we ought not begin from the authority of scriptural passages, but from sense-experiences and necessary demonstration; for the holy Bible and the phenomena of nature proceed alike from the divine Word."*

---

1. I don't think that Aquinas with his affirmation of two sources of knowledge would have found Galileo's views troubling.

Galileo cited Augustine, Jerome, Dionysius and many others to support his view that there is no necessary contradiction between these admittedly new understandings of the physical world and the Bible.[2]

While it was necessary for the Bible "to be accommodated to the understanding of everyman" and thus "to speak many things which appear to differ from the absolute truth," science is to be conformed to nature which is "inexorable and immutable." Moreover, God is not "any less excellently revealed in Nature's actions than in the sacred statements of the Bible." Here he quoted Tertullian with approval: "God is known first through nature and then again, more particularly, by doctrine; by nature in His works, and by doctrine in His revealed word."[3] For Galileo, the citing of biblical texts—erroneously and out of context in his view—against his science came to nothing. Rather than opposing the new sciences, the Catholic Church should embrace them for the truth they give us about the physical world. However, it was not to be. In 1633, after some of his supporters in the Catholic Church had died; Galileo was placed under house arrest. Despite these developments, his new methods of observation and science were to persist and flourish.

In his *Religious Origins of Modern Science*, Eugene Klaaren argued that the belief in an ordered creation, coming from God, very much set the context in which the new sciences emerged. Without that prior assumption of an ordered creation, there would be no expectation that observation of the natural world would lead to the recognition of pattern and order. The notion of an ordered creation was an inheritance from earlier times that provided the background for the rise of modern science.[4]

Isaac Newton: God & Gravity

We can see views similar to those of Galileo in the life and work of Sir Isaac Newton (1642-1727). For Newton too, the admirable order of the universe bespeaks of a Creator. When he discovered his laws of gravity, Newton was convinced that he had discovered the way in which God, spiritually through the forces of gravity, holds together the whole created order. This did not lead to a diminution of Newton's faith. Rather, he was uncovering

---

2. See Drake, *Discoveries and Opinions of Galileo*, 177, 181-82. and 182.

3. Ibid., 183.

4. See Klaaren, *Religious Origins of Modern Science*. Klaaren gives much attention to Robert Boyle (1627-1691). I am aware of how contested these matters of science and religion are, but wanted my students to be aware of a strand of thinking that moves beyond an easy opposition between religion and science.

those divine tracks that God had left in the universe for the human mind to uncover and make explicit. Indeed, Newton wrote several commentaries on the *Book of Revelation*, and he felt that these, rather than his scientific discoveries, might well be his most lasting contribution. How wrong could he be? We would all forget his commentaries, but we all remember his great contributions to science. Indeed, these were the discoveries—the laws of gravity, energy and motion, the calculus—that would give rise to an understanding of a mechanical and determined universe. Newton's universe would first be challenged—then replaced—by later developments in the sciences, including Einstein's theory of relativity in the twentieth century.

In Newton's own time, and after, a view of God began to emerge that gradually led to the separation of science from faith. This is Deism, the belief that God originally created the universe in an orderly way, but then, as it were, retired from the scene of his creation. God allows the universe to unfold according to the unchangeable laws of nature that God had built into the creation God made. Thus, God is understood in impersonal terms as the principle of origin of this intricately vast mechanism we know as the universe. This is the context for one of the liveliest questions of Christian thinking in the eighteenth century: the question of miracles. Some within the religious world championed the notion that God is unfolding creation and part of that continual making of the creation is through his miraculous intervention. Thus, while God has created an orderly universe, God can continue to intervene in creation in ways that seemingly overturn the laws that God has created. The overturning of those laws in these miraculous events is evidence of God's continuing sovereignty over this creation. The Deist and rationalist opponents of this view wanted to abandon belief in miracles—understood as violations of natural law—as in conflict with what we now know about the orderliness of nature.

It was only in the eighteenth century that science began to be explicit about the conviction that the "hypothesis of God" or a Creator is, in the words of the "French Newton," Pierre-Simon Laplace, "unnecessary for science." Science does not answer the why questions of the universe, but simply looks at how things work in the material world and how things unfold. For this kind of investigation of the world, the hypothesis of God is not necessary. Earlier, as we have seen, the notion of God was very important for many of the major figures in the founding of science.

The Enlightenment

The major watershed event that determined what is here called "modern" Christian thinking was the emergence of the Enlightenment worldview in the mid-eighteenth century and afterwards. That outlook was presaged by John Locke (1632–1704) in England, reflected in the life of people like Voltaire (1694-1778) in France, and Immanuel Kant in Germany (1724-1804). In the Enlightenment, we see the emergence of outlooks on life that are in some ways hostile to traditional Christian thought. Voltaire viewed all religion as "superstition," as "smoke and mirrors, and something humanity should move beyond. We need a new order, one that begins to dawn as reason puts flight to the superstition of the past and leads to the progressive enlightenment of our life as human beings and as members of new societies. In this way, Enlightenment is linked to the new sciences. Some now saw the new empirical sciences as a complete account of the universe, and science slid over into scientism.

As I have already suggested, the decisive shift occurred when God was viewed an unnecessary hypothesis for science. It signals the emergent conviction that human and social life, as well as the life of the universe, can be seen in relation to itself and does not need to refer to transcendence as its source or origin. The conviction that the orders of nature and society can understood wholly in relation to themselves and not in relation to some transcendent order is a key aspect of the modern Enlightenment worldview. Out of this conviction came naturalism—the belief that the order of nature is a self-contained dynamic system—and materialism—the conviction that the material is all there is. Here we do not need the divine or transcendent to understand nature or society. Human social orders are the products of human social contracts or compacts. They reflect the will of human beings to create and maintain societies. Before the Enlightenment, it was assumed that societies, like nature, were seen in relation to some transcendent reality, but now they could be viewed as autonomous. This same urge towards autonomy is present in many different spheres of life and thought. It is present in the increased autonomy of philosophy from the theological disciplines, of the individual from tradition, of society from the Church and of nature from God. These developments were profoundly different from what had been commonplace in Western societies for many centuries.

As the Enlightenment begins to develop in ways that were hostile to Christianity, Christian thinking was confronted with a new set of challenges. Some Christian thinkers attempted to restate the nature of Christian faith to create a better fit with this Enlightenment mentality.

Immanuel Kant: Religion Within the Limits of Reason (1724–1784)

One of the people who sought to reformulate what Christianity is all about was Immanuel Kant, a great German philosopher of the age of Enlightenment. In his famous essay "What is Enlightenment?" Kant responded to the fateful question: "Are we now living in an enlightened age?" His answer was "No, but we live in an age of enlightenment." In his view, the age of enlightenment would unfold as humanity discovered the courage "to use one's own mind without direction from another." Humanity was in transition, on the way from immaturity to maturity, from dependence upon tradition to "autonomy." Reason and freedom were the twin virtues that would give rise to this new age. Indeed, Kant was so confident of "man's emergence from his self-imposed tutelage," that he stridently asserted that if the public "is only given freedom, enlightenment is almost inevitable."[5]

Kant's immensely difficult philosophical argument, found in his *Critique of Pure Reason* and *Critique of Practical Reason*, was important for new ways of understanding the world. Kant distinguished between the "noumenal" (things as they are in themselves) and "phenomenal" (things as they appear to us) worlds. We only know, said Kant, the world as it appears to us. We cannot know things in themselves. His Critiques remain influential down to the present day despite their metaphysical density. Then in his last major work, Kant attempted to unfold his understanding of religion in the light of the new sciences and his own new philosophical vision that came to be called "Transcendental Idealism." According to Kant, it was not the supernatural or metaphysical elements of religion that were important or at the heart of Christianity.

Rather, he argued in *Religion within the Limits of Reason Alone*, it was the ethical dimension. Religion, for Kant, was "ethics writ large." He maintains that "man himself must make or have made himself into whatever, in a moral sense . . . he is or is to become . . . It is an effect of his free choice." Kant rejected the widespread assumption in earlier Christian thinking that human beings need to conform to the moral order that is given in things as well as in Scripture. For Kant, we cannot have knowledge of the way things are in themselves. Rather, humanity makes itself moral—or evil?—through its ethical/moral choices. The supreme historical example of this struggle to make ourselves good is Jesus Christ, our model and archetype. "It is," said Kant, "our universal duty as men to elevate ourselves to this ideal of moral perfection." "Moral religion . . . that is to be established." Such a religion

---

5. See Beck, *Foundations of the Metaphysics of Morals*, 85-86.

centred on "the heart's disposition to fulfill all human duties as divine commands" and not "dogmas or rites"—is not grounded in "miracles" but must be "engraved upon the heart of man through reason." This is religion within the limits of reason, and it had an enormous impact on thinking beyond Kant. It is a religion shorn of theological and metaphysical intuition, shorn of rite and ritual, but centred wholly in the struggle to become a good human being. This is Kant's understanding of what constitutes the heart of Christianity.[6]

According to Kant, this new age of enlightenment required that Christian thought redefine itself. For Kant, this meant that Christianity—when Kant wrote of "religion," he meant Christianity—must find itself within the new views of reason. This certainly challenged the longer Christian tradition, which saw the human as not wholly autonomous but within the context of a divinely grounded given. Moreover, while the longer tradition had seen reason in different ways, from Justin Martyr's "Logos" to Anselm's "Understanding" to Bonaventure's "Leap," all those differing views all assumed that reason, or the light within, was an intimation of the Light Without that is the Transcendent itself or God. Now, figures like Kant were arguing that we have no access to that Light Without since things in themselves are not available to us. All our knowing is, for Kant, bound to the realm of the phenomenal, to the way things appear to us.

Thus, during and after the Enlightenment, Christian thought increasingly found itself in a situation where it had to articulate itself over against a worldview that saw itself as autonomous from the Christian tradition. It was critical of many aspects of that longer theological and religious tradition (Voltaire and others saw Christianity as superstition against which reason fought) and, in some cases, explicitly rejected the longer Christian tradition. One of the responses of Christian thinkers to this situation was to identify anew the nature of religion and its place in the human journey. What aspects of human life does the Christian faith most centrally address.

The response of Immanuel Kant's response was to locate religion in the ethical sphere. Religion is humanity's moral duty writ large. That morality is not rooted in the way things are since the world of values lies in human choices and decision. Kant attempted to reduce the metaphysical aspects of the Christian theological tradition for the sake of emphasizing its moral character and teaching. In the context of Kant's work, Jesus Christ is the model and archetype for an ideal humanity, as Kant said in his *Religion Within the Limits of Reason Alone*. Kant argues that "man himself must make or have made himself into whatever, in a moral sense, whether good

---

6. See Kerr, *Readings in Christian Thought*, 213-14.

or evil, he is or is to become." Hence, what is at the centre of human life is our capacity for choice and determining whether we move in a direction that is good or evil, right or wrong, for human beings make themselves through their choices. Jesus, then, is viewed by Kant as the example of the virtuous person, the fully ethical and realized human being. While God remains important in Kant's thought, it is as the guarantor of moral order in the universe. However, that universe is the domain of facts, and morality is the domain of values that are rooted in the human will.

The philosophical complexity of Kant's thought as seen in his *Critique of Pure Reason* is beyond our scope here, but it gave rise to the facts/values dichotomy that became so commonplace in much of modern thought.

Friedrich Schleiermacher (1768–1834) and "Absolute Dependence"

Another view that attempted to give religion a new place in the modern paradigm is found in the work of Friedrich Schleiermacher, often regarded as the father of modern theology. For Schleiermacher, the essence of religion is not to found in the ethical or intellectual sphere. Schleiermacher argued that it is in a sphere that is prior to both our doing and our knowing and underlies them both. That is the realm of feeling or those determinate dispositions of human life. In his famous *Speeches on Religion*, Schleiermacher argued that what is essential to religion is human feeling—the emotional and affective dimensions. When we come to explore religion, what we have to pay most attention to is not what people do or think, but how all their doing and thinking arises out of this deeper sphere of human life, the sphere of feeling. In his *Speeches*, Schleiermacher asked that we "turn from everything usually reckoned religion, and fix our regard on the inward emotions and dispositions."[7] His focus on the feeling dimension—as fundamental to religion—arose, in the view of some observers, from his familial and youthful connections to the Moravians. Others wonder if his conviction that the heart of religion is "the feeling of absolute dependence" came from his work as a hospital chaplain. Still others see it as connected to the romanticism of his times.

The reason Schleiermacher is called the "father of modern theology" is that in his great systematic theological treatise *The Christian Faith*, published in 1830, he forged a new way of articulating the faith. In that work, Schleiermacher attempted to follow a "method of correlation." That is, he sought to correlate Christian doctrine with determinate "states of human

---

7. Ibid., 219.

consciousness," which was his phrase for speaking about this realm of feeling, or "*gefuhl.*" Schleiermacher came to the view that religion, if we analyze it closely, is grounded in a particular feeling that he called the feeling of absolute dependence. We might call this the universal dimension of religion. For Christians, this feeling of absolute dependence is mediated to humanity through the person of Jesus Christ.

For Schleiermacher, Jesus Christ is truly human and divine, a man in whom this feeling of absolute dependence, or powerful God-consciousness, is perfectly realized. The source of that feeling is God—the divine "whence" of human life, the source of human life and everything that is. If we can penetrate deeply enough into the faith of Christians, we discover this feeling of absolute dependence. Then we can see the way in which that feeling is mediated to the Christian through their historical continuity with the unique figure of Jesus Christ, who in all of his life and in all of his actions and thinking perfectly embodies this feeling of absolute dependence, this "God-consciousness."

All of what Jesus does and thinks—as he is presented in Scripture and mediated through the tradition of Christianity—involves us in this God-consciousness, in realizing in ourselves the feeling of absolute dependence. The heart of Christianity, we might say, is a distinctive spirituality or a distinctive form of human consciousness. That is what is fundamental to the Christian faith. When theologians try to articulate the Christian faith in their systematic theologies and religious writings, what they are trying to do is unfold these feeling-states that lie at the heart of religious life.

Theology for Schleiermacher is not thinking about thinking or beliefs or actions but thinking about feeling. It is also urging and encouraging in people the way of living a life in awareness and consciousness of the divine source of all life. The doctrine of sin, and especially the doctrine of redemption, if we are to understand it aright, should not be seen as a set of ideas that we can play around with in one abstraction or another. Rather, we should see how these words and ideas are an attempt to communicate to the hearer an awareness that the source of renewal in human life lies in recognizing the absolute dependent character of life. God is realized in the realm of our inward states, dispositions, and consciousness. This method of correlation constitutes a major innovation in theology. When we examine Schleiermacher's *Christian Faith*, we can see that he attempts to summarize the Christian faith as faith in Jesus Christ. What that faith entails is the way in which Jesus Christ mediates to us the experience of redemption, which is an experience of becoming aware of our absolute dependence upon a divine source for our lives.

In the *Christian Faith*, Schleiermacher wrote about the person and work of Christ in these terms: "The peculiar activity and the exclusive dignity of the Redeemer imply each other, and are inseparably one in the self-consciousness of believers."[8] He was trying to emphasize the inextricable link between the person of Jesus Christ, what was distinctive about Him, and the historic community and self-consciousness that emerges. They are inseparable. All of those who come after Him have enlarged in them this sense of our absolute dependence. We have to go through all the doctrines of the Christian faith and show what they mean—not abstractly but in terms of the state of consciousness that is implicit within them.

In relation to the doctrine of sin, for example, what we are talking about in the story of Adam and Eve in the Garden of Eden is not thinking wrong thoughts or a failure to do this or that. For Schleiermacher this is not the issue. What is important is a consciousness in people of being alienated, of being out of touch with the foundations of their own life. It is that state or disposition or consciousness that Schleiermacher says is the real significance of talk about sin. When we explore this doctrine, we have to follow it back and see how it is rooted in the life and experience of people in the world—that is where its significance is centred.

Likewise, when we talk about grace or redemption, we again have to show what that teaching relates to and what it means in terms of human consciousness. The experience of redemption is, in a general way, an experience of inward reconciling of elements within the human personality, and that is the content of Christ's redemption or reconciling work. Further, what that involves is a reordering of a person's inner life of in relation to the feeling of absolute dependence.

Thus, Schleiermacher allows us to think about the person of Christ in a new way. One reads the Gospel story trying to see what Jesus' words and actions imply in terms of what life means for a human being who has God-consciousness, who is aware of the presence of God in all moments in his life. That, according to Schleiermacher, is where the real distinctiveness of Jesus lies: in his God-consciousness. In the *Christian Faith*, Schleiermacher wrote,

> *"The Redeemer, then, is like all men in virtue of the identity of human nature, but distinguished from all by the constant potency of his God-consciousness."*[9]

---

8. See Kerr, *Readings in Christian Thought*, 222.
9. Ibid. 225.

The Redeemer is like all other human beings, but distinguished from them by the vitality of his God-consciousness, which is the veritable existence of God in him. Jesus, unlike other human beings, is continually aware of God in all moments in his life. Moreover, Jesus, as the Risen Christ, communicates that God-consciousness to others historically through the practices, preaching and life of the Church. Schleiermacher is very impressed by the continuity of the Christian tradition's capacity to mediate this sense of God to his followers over time. Schleiermacher is probably the most important Christian thinker between the reformers and the twentieth century. His significance lies in his attempt to establish a new theological method and turn theology in a new direction.

G. W. F. Hegel (1770–1831) & the Infinite/Geist in Time

In his lifetime, of course, Schleiermacher had his rivals, and other people had different ideas about where the heart of Christianity was located. One of those figures was Hegel. Hegel and Schleiermacher taught in Berlin at the same time, but they did not have a positive relationship. Hegel was dismissive of Schleiermacher's emphasis on "feeling" in religion. Neither Kant's attempt to locate religion in ethics, nor Schleiermacher's attempt to locate it in feeling was adequate in Hegel's view. Instead, Hegel sought to locate the centre of the Christian religion in the Spirit/Geist realizing itself in the order of history—this view is part of his significance for the history of Christian thought. At the heart of Christian faith is a commitment to the historical process, through which God or the *Geist*, the Spirit, the Whole, in Hegel's terms, is realizing itself. For Hegel, the Absolute is coming to expression in the dialectic of the historical process. This takes place through a process of what he calls "thesis" and "antithesis," which come to "synthesis." That synthesis then becomes the ground for a new thesis, which generates its own antithesis, and the results in a new synthesis, and so on and on. This process goes on continuously until the Spirit realizes or completes itself at the end of time. For Hegel this secret lies behind the Christian faith. He articulated his views in philosophical terms, and his *Phenomenology of Mind* is exceedingly abstruse and difficult. Consider, for example, these words on "the life of spirit":

> ... These three moments constitute the life of spirit. Its resolution in imaginative thought consists in its taking on a determinative mode of being ... its detailed process thus consists in spreading its nature out in each of its moments as in an element in which it lives; and in so far as each of these spheres completes itself in

itself, this reflection into itself is at the same time the transition into another sphere of its being . . . the third stage is the return from this presentation and from that otherness; in other words, it is the element of self-consciousness itself.[10]

He concludes his *Phenomenology* with these words:

The goal, which is Absolute Knowledge or Spirit knowing itself as Spirit, finds its pathway in the recollection of spiritual forms (Geister) as they are in themselves and as they accomplish the organization of their spiritual kingdom. Their conservation, looked at from the side of their free existence appearing in the form of contingency is History . . . looked at from the side of their intellectually comprehended organization, it is the Science of the ways in which knowledge appears. Both together . . . form at once the recollection and the Golgotha of Absolute Spirit, the reality, the truth, the certainty of its throne, without which it were lifeless, solitary, and alone. Only "the chalice of this realm of spirits/foams forth to God His own Infinitude."[11]

His *Lectures on the Philosophy of History* are slightly more accessible. Here Hegel argues that we should move beyond the discourse or language of theology. If we look over the broad sweep of the unfolding of the Spirit in the order of time, then we notice a three-fold movement. It began back in earliest times when the Spirit realized itself in and through the realm of myth and magic. That stage of historical life finally gave way to a stage that Hegel characterized as centred in religion and theology. Here Christianity played a central role in that during this epoch the Absolute realized itself primarily in the Christian religious and theological traditions. Now, Hegel said, a new era was emerging. While we take into ourselves the accomplishments of the earlier stages, we are moving into a stage that will be dominated by clarity and philosophy. We can state the truth of what was achieved in earlier historical epochs, but without the disadvantages that come from religious and theological language—tendencies towards anthropomorphism in talking about God and problems of superstition in religious life. Now we have to turn our attention away from these unfortunate aspects of the religious and theological tradition and towards the realm of history, because it is in history that the Divine Spirit, the Absolute, is realizing itself.

Still, in Hegel's view, Jesus Christ plays a very central role. For Hegel, Jesus stands as an anticipation of the end towards which the historical process is moving. Standing at the centre of history, he is an embodiment of

10. See Hegel, *Phenomenology of Mind*, 765.
11. Ibid., 808.

the Infinite particularly actualized in the finite. In Hegel's terms, this is a coincidence of opposites—that which is Infinite is realized in a finite human being. The significance of Jesus is not in terms of his particularity but that he is an embodiment of a universal truth. As the embodiment of a universal truth, he is what is potentially and essentially true of every human being. In the unfolding of the historical process, the Absolute Spirit has made itself known in this figure Jesus, and his significance lies in the fact that what is possible for every human being is disclosed.

Summary

In this chapter, we have covered an extremely important and complex period in a too brief a manner. Indeed, several volumes could be– and have been—written about the twists and turns of Christian thought in this period. We have sought to find our way through the writings of Christian thinkers in this time by noting the emergence of an outlook that is, in many respects, strikingly novel in the history of human thought: the Enlightenment view that the world as known to human beings can be seen in relation to itself and not as funded by Transcendence. The Enlightenment worldview poses a continuing challenge to Christian thought that believes that human life is rooted in something beyond itself: in God, the creator of heaven and earth.

Review

1. What are the "Book of Scripture" and the "Book of Nature" in Galileo?
2. What was the "Enlightenment?" Why was it a challenge to Christian thought?
3. What did Schleiermacher mean by "feeling of absolute dependence"?
4. How did Kant conceive of "religion within the limits of reason"?
5. Where did Hegel locate the Eternal/Spirit?

Chapter 21

Three Movements of the Nineteenth Century

Existentialism, the Oxford Movement and the Social Gospel

Søren Kierkegaard (1813–1855): Existential Christianity

SØREN KIERKEGAARD IS ONE of the most curious figures in the history of Christian thought. A product of Lutheran Denmark, Kierkegaard lived in Copenhagen. He is remembered as the melancholy Dane. Kierkegaard reacted very sharply against Hegel. The heart of his response is disclosed in the following story. Kierkegaard likened Hegel's accomplishments to the construction of a magnificent glass castle. This vast unfolding of the Absolute in time and history is being realized through those stages of thesis, antithesis and synthesis as it moves relentlessly through vast sweeps of time towards its end. It is magnificent in every respect, save one. Kierkegaard said that human beings do not live in this castle. Human beings do not live in the world Hegel constructed, but rather, as it were, in a hovel outside of this magnificent achievement.

What Hegel ignored was the human being, the solitary individual who does not recognize himself in these vast schemes. Instead, the human being is struggling with existential angst, inward suffering, meaninglessness, dread and despair. What we need, Kierkegaard thought, are ways of speaking about this messy human existence, about particular human beings in their existential anxiety, trying to make their way through life. Here is where the attention of Christian thinkers should be focused. And not, on Hegel's vast historical schemes, or on morality as Kant proposed, or on feeling as Schleiermacher would have it.

Suppose," said Kierkegaard, "that Christianity is subjectivity, an inner transformation, an actualization of inwardness." Then we would have to deal with it differently, since it "would be a mistake for the observer to be objective."[1] Instead, of the way of the "speculative philosopher," Kierkegaard argued, Christian thought has to return again to deal with the "individual subject," the one who is struggling between a life of faith and lack of faith, the human being who is in a sense contending with God on the landscape of his or her own inner life.

Kierkegaard is a very unusual figure, and in his own time was not widely recognized. He was a nineteenth-century figure who came into his own in the twentieth century, when after the First World War many thinkers within the Christian tradition found a resonance with his emphases. For Kierkegaard, the human problem is the problem of faith—faith as the antidote to despair and anxiety and inward dread. The titles of some of Kierkegaard's writings are suggestive: Sickness Unto Death, Fear and Trembling, Either Or. For Kierkegaard, we have to focus our attention on the problems of what he called "existence"—the existence of the solitary individual. Because of his emphasis on the problems of existence, Kierkegaard is regarded as one of the sources of the movement known as existentialism. This movement is very important within Christian thinking, though there are forms of existentialism that are outside the Christian circle.

Fear and Trembling, Kierkegaard turned to an existential analysis of Abraham, the father of faith. This analysis gets to the heart of the issue: faith as the most difficult thing in the world. Abraham is the father of faith and the father of Isaac—and these two conditions (Abraham's faith and being the Father of Isaac) are intimately related to each other in Kierkegaard's Fear and Trembling. You will remember how God had promised Abraham that he would be the father of a race of people that would number more than the sands on the shore. Yet as Abraham and Sarah aged, it seemed that none of God's promises would be realized. So you can imagine—as Kierkegaard did—the kind of inner turmoil that Abraham must have gone through: "Did I hear Him right? Is God lying to me? What is God doing?" The human life situation is, for Kierkegaard, at the center of Christian thinking.

Abraham, Late in Abraham's life, his wife Sarah, long beyond her child-bearing years, finally gives birth to a son. The son, Isaac, grows up and

---

1. See Kerr, *Selections from Kierkegaard*, 276.

becomes a young man. Then there comes the terrible moment when God commands Abraham to sacrifice his son. Kierkegaard analyzed this story in existential terms. In Kierkegaard's marvelous book, he drew out several scenarios of Abraham making his journey with Isaac to the mountain where he is to sacrifice his son. What could Abraham have been thinking or feeling? Kierkegaard portrayed Abraham as inwardly burdened with this terrible command to sacrifice his son, the one he and Sarah had waited for all these years. You just walk with Abraham and Isaac on the way to the mountain.

What Kierkegaard did in retelling this story was to show us what is at stake in the religious life of faith. Faith, said Kierkegaard, is "the paradox of life and existence."[2] If we can speak about faith at all, we have to speak about it in the language of paradox. We have to speak about it in terms of a process of inwardness. We have to speak about it in terms of men and women daily confronting anxiety, despair—on the verge of abandoning it all. Christianity is not easy, said Kierkegaard. It is the most difficult thing in the world. No one can be born a Christian. That is ridiculous. It is something we can only become and we become it through this intense inward drama and struggle. We cannot say it is simply outward conformity to some ethical laws.

In the case of Abraham, God tells Abraham that the most important thing he can do is to slay his son. What kind of God is this? It is a God beyond all of our ethical categories. What is all this Hegelian talk about looking at history and seeing how the divine Absolute realizes itself in the historical process? That is not where the life of human beings is lived. This Hegelian scheme of thesis, antithesis and synthesis—what is that? How does that answer any sort of significant human question? In the end, it is the solitary individual that is confronted with the truth of God, and all of these schemes are ways to block us from dealing with the fundamental questions of life. In speaking of Abraham, Kierkegaard remarked,

> *A paradoxical and humble courage is required to grasp the whole of the temporal by virtue of the absurd and that is the courage of faith. By faith, Abraham did not renounce his claim upon Isaac, but by faith he got Isaac.*[3]

The faith of Abraham is not a cheap faith, but one that leads through his anguished interior. Kierkegaard said that if he were to speak of Abraham, "I would first depict the pain of his trial."[4]

2. See Kierkegaard, *Fear and Trembling*, 267.
3. Ibid., 59.
4. Ibid., 63.

In his analysis of the story of Abraham, Kierkegaard explored what he calls "the teleological suspension of the ethical." As this story makes obvious, God calls Abraham to do things that from any ethical point of view appear to be absolutely mad. The God with whom Christians must reckon just does not fit any of our neat moral categories. When we realize this we get closer to what is central—or what should be central—to Christian thinking. We get closer by getting more in touch with the inward struggle to come to faith and, in Kierkegaard's famous phrase, "to take that leap of faith"—that leap beyond the realm of what is functional as articulated in rational or conventional ethical schemes. That faith is not merely conformity to conventional mores or to what appears to be the best thinking of our age—it is much more than that. It is to live the paradox of faith in Jesus Christ, the God-Man, who is "God Incognito." It is to cultivate inwardness. It is daily to do battle with the anxiety and despair and the various threats of meaninglessness that characterize the life of the solitary individual. As Kierkegaard remarked of Abraham,

> ... *Abraham is the representative of faith, and that faith is normally expressed in him whose life is not merely the most paradoxical that can be thought, but so paradoxical that it cannot be thought at all. He acts by virtue of the absurd, for it is precisely absurd that he as the particular is higher than the universal. This paradox cannot be mediated.*[5]

For Kierkegaard, Abraham is the "father of faith" precisely because his faith cannot be reduced to an instance of reasoned or ethical behaviour. It moves in a different order: he acts "by virtue of the absurd."

In Kierkegaard's own life, which was a brief one, he was a person who—as he said of himself—never knew childhood. Rather, he was burdened by his father's cursing of God, which hung over him pervasively throughout his life. He became engaged to be married, but finally broke off his engagement, feeling that the life to which he was called would not allow him to settle into any kind of marriage relationship. His was a very solitary life. In a dozen years he produced thirty volumes under different names—he employed a whole list of pseudonyms, publishing very little under the name of Søren Kierkegaard—all trying to get at the basic problem of how one becomes a Christian and what is at stake in being a Christian. This meant that Kierkegaard not only attacked the great systems of his day and the prevailing philosophy of Hegel. He was also highly critical of the Church and especially of any notion of Christendom.

---

5. Ibid., 67.

For Kierkegaard, what was preached in the churches of his day had nothing to do with Christianity. In speaking of the "religious situation in our country [Denmark] . . . Christianity does not exist." The religious situation was, according to Kierkegaard, polite, functional, neat, and nice. It encourages people to live their lives in the illusion that they are already Christians, rather than realizing that this is the most difficult task of all.[6]

What Christian faith really involves is *becoming contemporaneous with Christ* who suffered, was persecuted, who died and rose again. This was "God incognito" the God-Man Jesus Christ in whom we have the merging of the Infinite and the finite. This is not something that we can articulate in an easy, rational way. It is the supreme paradox of the Christian faith that here in a particular human life, God is present. For Kierkegaard that is sheer paradox—beyond understanding, but true. We cannot easily speak about it. It is something you have to approach inwardly, subjectively, until you come to make this leap of faith and live a life of faith. It is, in one of Kierkegaard's images, to live a life of treading water in 10,000 fathoms. There is nothing there to hold you up. It is a life of total risk. At any moment, you may be swallowed up in the great sea, but you continue to stay afloat through a divine graciousness that you cleave to inwardly, deeply. Kierkegaard said that one could never say, "I have arrived. I am a Christian." When you make that statement, you know you have not arrived.

Kierkegaard was constantly in conflict with every part of his society. While some saw Kierkegaard's harsh criticism of Christendom as prophetic, it ensured that his contemporaries would not look kindly on his voice. When, in the early twentieth century, Europe was devastated by "the war to end all wars" and most of a generation lay dead in the trenches, many found in Kierkegaard a voice that spoke to their anguish and suffering. Suddenly Kierkegaard was "discovered," and his work gave rise to an existential Christianity that was important to twentieth-century Christian thought. His criticism of a self-satisfied Christianity and his incisive analysis of inwardness and subjectivity were to make significant contributions to the great conversation.

The Oxford Movement and Cardinal Newman

In England in the nineteenth century, a very different development was occurring in the context of the Anglican tradition. In comparison with Protestant traditions, Anglicanism had always maintained a higher degree of

---

6. See Kerr, *Selections from Kierkegaard*, 282-84. For "God Incognito" see ibid., 279-82.

continuity with the longer Catholic tradition. At Oxford between 1833 and 1845, a number of Anglican thinkers led by John Klebe, Edward Pusey and John Henry Newman (1801-1890) began to explore that longer "catholic" tradition in relation to both thought and liturgy. Over those years, they published a series of tracts or essays on a variety of historical, liturgical and doctrinal subjects. Newman was, arguably, the most eloquent representative for "Tractarianism," as it came to be known. His studies of early Christianity led him to question his own Anglican tradition on several important doctrinal issues. Consequently, Newman eventually found his way back into the Roman Catholic tradition where he was ordained a priest and eventually became a cardinal.

In his famous *Essay on the Development of Christian Doctrine*, Newman saw early Christian thought in a different way from many Protestants (including the early Newman himself) who believed it was an accretion on—and often a corruption of—a pristine biblical and apostolic era. Newman, however, now saw the development of doctrine as an unfolding of latent possibilities inherent in early Christian faith. Rather than "a series of developments" that some regarded as "corruptions," Newman saw a Church that "wrought out the one and only consistent theory which might be taken." According to Newman, the "integrity of the Catholic developments is still more evident when they are viewed in contrast with the history of other doctrinal systems." Newman's view of the development of Christian doctrine and dogma was exceedingly positive—and equally controversial. He regarded "dogmatism" in an affirmative way as "a religion's profession of its own reality as contrasted with other systems." Thus, he became well known for his views on the development of doctrine. For Newman, there is no genuine "development" that is not the further unfolding of what was always there is the beginning.[7]

Not only did these views lead Newman back into the Catholic Church, they began to establish his reputation as a Catholic apologist in an "age of agnosticism." His *Apologia Pro Vita Sua* is a bold account of his life and the development of his thought that led to his entering the Catholic tradition, for which he became one of the most eloquent voices in the nineteenth century. He also published his *Idea of the University*, which became a classic as it argued for Catholic education in a wise and expansive way. Other "Tractarians" remained Anglican and greatly contributed to the recovery of the earlier traditions of Christian thought within the Anglican world.

What is crucial to notice here is the inexhaustible character of the early traditions of Christian thought: their ability to speak across time and

---

7. See Kerr, *Selections from John Henry Newman*, 243.

re-inspire a generation centuries later, to be a continual contribution to the great conversation within Christianity. Orthodox Christianity most consistently, generation after generation, turns to the "early fathers" for insight and guidance. Orthodox Christians dissent from the widespread modern notion that the crucial mark of thought is innovation and novelty. The Orthodox tradition prefers what is given in the wisdom of the past.

Walter Rauschenbusch (1861–1918) and the Social Gospel

Known as the foremost proponent of the Social Gospel movement in America, Walter Rauschenbusch was an American Baptist who early in his life worked as a pastor in an area of New York City known as Hell's Kitchen. It was in this context that he encountered those who were most adversely affected by the Industrial Revolution. Deeply affected by his experience, Rauschenbusch sought to recast the Christian faith in ways that could address the emerging social reality and social problems of the late nineteenth century.

For Rauschenbusch the centre of the Christian faith was its teaching on the Kingdom of God. For Rauschenbusch, the Kingdom of God was at the heart of the prophetic strand of the Old Testament and central to the life of Jesus. This teaching had in Rauschenbusch's view, come to be neglected in the more recent history of Christianity and especially within the Protestant traditions. Rauschenbusch's critique of Christianity in his own day was that it had too narrowly focused on the personal dimensions of salvation. In contrast, he felt that the centre of the prophetic tradition and of Jesus' teaching, the doctrine of the Kingdom of God, was an inherently social conception of the Gospel. As Rauschenbusch wrote,

> *Individualistic Christianity has almost lost sight of the great idea of the kingdom of God, which was the inspiration and center of the thought of Jesus. Social Christianity would once more enable us to understand the purpose and thought of Jesus, and take the veil from our eyes when we read the synoptic gospels.*[8]

Consequently, we needed to refocus our theological efforts to bring the social dimensions of the Gospel more to the fore and to relate Christian faith to the problems of industrial society. According to Rauschenbusch,

---

8. Rauschenbusch, *A Theology for the Social Gospel*, 267.

> "The industrial and commercial life of today is dominated by principles antagonistic to the fundamental principles of Christianity."[9]

For Rauschenbusch, sin was not only personal but also social. He recognized that sin in its social sense was selfishness embedded in the life of institutions. Thus, there is a kingdom of evil that stands in contrast to and over against the kingdom of God. That kingdom of evil is inherent within social institutions that encourage and legitimate selfishness. Just as sin is social, redemption is social, involving the redemption of the social order.

Rauschenbusch was one of the first figures in the history of theology to take the new social sciences seriously. He was conversant with the Marxist tradition of his own time and the new efforts of others to give an account of our life in time as structured by social institutions. Rauschenbusch said that if we look back historically, we can see now with greater clarity than in the past how Jesus' own life and ministry of fidelity to the Kingdom of God brought him into conflict with the social forces of his own day. The Kingdom of God, said Rauschenbusch, is "humanity organized according to the will of God." Christians must broaden their understanding of the Kingdom and how that Kingdom relates to the social structures in which they live.

In his *Theology of the Social Gospel*, Rauschenbusch laid out eight marks of the Kingdom of God, which summarize the teachings of the Social Gospel. For Rauschenbusch, the Kingdom of God is "divine in its origin, progress and consummation." It contains "the teleology of the Christian religion"—in other words, it is the goal of Christianity. Surprisingly, Rauschenbusch concluded:

> "the kingdom of God is not confined within the limits of the church and its activities. It embraces the whole of human life. It is the Christian transfiguration of the social order."[10]

This is a social Gospel.

Rauschenbusch sought to emphasize that rather than looking for the Kingdom of God and its realization in some other realm, we should look to see it realized in the historical order. In his view, the realization of the Kingdom of God is progress in history. There has been movement in history that is divine in origin, and this movement reflects the creation of social institutions and forms of social life that are overcoming the social dimensions of sin. For Rauschenbusch, not only persons need redemption. Social institutions and whole societies are also in need of redemption.

---

9. Ibid. 267.
10. Ibid. 269 and 269-70.

The second point is that the Kingdom of God contains *the teleology of the Christian religion*. The end or goal of what Christians are striving for is not doctrines or rights or some narrow religious realm but for the transformation of the social order.

Third, Rauschenbusch argued that since God is in it, the Kingdom of God is always both present and future. In both the present and the future, we have some evidence of its effectiveness within the life of human beings in society, and yet we should not ever think that the Kingdom of God has wholly arrived. It is always still ahead of us, but it impinges upon our present order of time and is always calling us to realize higher degrees of justice than those that have been attained in the present moment.

Fourth, even before Christ, people of God saw the Kingdom of God as the great end to which all divine leadings were pointing. Rauschenbusch saw the unity of the Old and New Testaments. He also realized that there are initiatives outside Christianity that are inspired by and look towards the coming of the kingdom.

Fifth, Rauschenbusch's definition of the Kingdom of God was *humanity organized according to the will of God*. Under this heading, he developed three points to make this definition a little more concrete. Thus, he argued that (1) what Christ revealed was the divine worth of life and personality, and so Christians at every point historically are to be sensitive to and concerned with the welfare of particular lives and people's personalities. When we see social forces that are blocking the full development of particular human lives, we should see that as an offence against God's purposes. In addition, Rauschenbusch said that (2) since love is a supreme law of Christ, the Kingdom of God implies a progressive reign of love in human affairs. What Christians should do in terms of society is (3) attempt to create social forms and institutions that are more in conformity with the notion of love. This involves the redemption of society from political and economic oligarchies, the substitution of redemptive for vindictive penology, the abolition of constraint through hunger and the abolition of war. He saw these as things that Christians should seek to bring into being, social forms that are more grounded in love.

Here he argued that since the highest expression of love is the free surrender of our own life, property, and rights, no social group or organization that draws on the efforts of others for its own ease or enhancement could claim to be within the Kingdom of God. Here he was arguing against the form of capitalist society of his time, which he said has participated in the Kingdom of Evil by giving precedence to profit and the exploitation of others in the normal workings of the economic system.

Sixth, Rauschenbusch says the Kingdom is the supreme end of God. Hence, the Church exists for this purpose. The point of the Kingdom of God is not the Church but humanity organized according to the will of God. This was an implicit criticism of the Church's preoccupations. The Church is for the sake of the coming of the Kingdom. If its preoccupations are only self-directed, it is not doing its job.

Seventh, since the Kingdom is the supreme end, all issues of personal salvation need to be re-thought or reconfigured from the point of view of the Kingdom. Again, Rauschenbusch was making the general point that the Kingdom of God is at the heart of the Social Gospel. The Kingdom of God has implications for all aspects of the Christian faith. For him, that meant that we had to turn our attention much more to the social matrix within which lives unfold and be concerned with its transformation more than just on issues of personal salvation.

Eighth, the Kingdom of God is not confined within the limits of the Church and its activities. It embraces the whole of human/social life.

Through these eight points Rauschenbusch expressed his conviction that Christianity is realizing itself in its attempts to transfigure and redeem the social order and that it is in those efforts, and not just within the narrow sphere of the Church, that Christianity achieves its fullest expression.

One of the things often forgotten about Rauschenbusch is his strong support of the temperance movement. Here his social analysis of the issue comes into view. Alcohol is not just an individual moral problem. It is a social and institutional one. Beyond the individual, the negative consequences of alcoholism affect the lives of families and unfold within a social context. So Christians should not only try to assist people who have problems with alcohol but also try to change the social network that surrounds this practice, and in that way create a social condition where alcohol becomes less and less of a problem.

The Social Gospel movement was very influential throughout North America in the late 1800s and early 1900s. It was one of the most dynamic elements in Protestant life in the late nineteenth century. However, this movement was challenged by the outbreak of the First World War. The war exposed the optimistic and progressive underpinnings of the Social Gospel—its implicit view that things were getting better and better. This view was reflected in the founding in 1900 of a new journal called *The Christian Century*, which expressed the belief that in the twentieth century Christianity would achieve its fulfillment in its effect upon the whole of civilization and usher in a glorious new age. Of course, when the terrible war erupted, it generated a crisis of faith for those many deeply influenced by the Social

Gospel. Nevertheless, the Social Gospel continues to be a major strand in North American Christianity, down to the present day.

Summary

Existentialism, the Oxford Movement, and the Social Gospel made important contributions to the great conversation within Christianity. They again disclose the diversity within the history of Christian thought, as these movements reveal widely differing understandings of the Christian faith and its primary focus and direction. While the existentialist thought of Søren Kierkegaard focuses on the solitary individual in his or her own struggle towards faith, the Social Gospel turned to the reform of society and the social dimensions of faith. It was through the study of the history of Christian doctrine that John Henry Newman was led back into the Catholic tradition. Newman's view of the development of doctrine as an unfolding of what was already implicit in the earliest strata of the Christian faith was an important response to the emerging historical consciousness of the nineteenth century. Others saw more discontinuity in Christian thinking than Newman did—that is a perennial issue in Christian thought on which there is no unanimity.

Review

1. What is existential Christianity?
2. How did Newman understand the "development of doctrine"?
3. What was Rauschenbusch's view of the Kingdom of God?

PART VII

Contemporary Christian Thought:
1920-2017

IN THE FIRST OF the three chapters that end our study, we identify some of the important voices in Christian thinking in the twenty-first century. The "Great War," World War I, marked the end of an era. This epochal change is reflected in the work of the figures reviewed here.

Karl Barth was a Swiss thinker who initiated a way of Christian thinking that moved beyond the 'liberal traditions' of the nineteenth century. He was crucial to the movement of 'neo-orthodoxy' premised on the insight of Kierkegaard concerning the "infinite qualitative difference" between God and humanity and the conviction that God moves towards humanity in Jesus Christ to redeem and renew humanity. Barth's multivolume *Church Dogmatics* was a major undertaking. Pierre Teilhard de Chardin, who served as a stretcher-bearer during the war, was a visionary Catholic thinker who sought to reconcile evolutionary thought and the Christian faith. Eugen Rosenstock-Huessy had been profoundly shaken by the war, and his *Out of Revolution: Autobiography of Western Man* was "a hand stretched out . . . for the survival of humankind." He sought to retell the Western story and saw the need for a "third Christianity of hope" that would be "incognito" as it attempted to incarnate itself in the midst of suffering humanity. While Barth was a more traditional theological thinker, Teilhard de Chardin was a scientist and Rosenstock-Huessy was a Christian social thinker. Paul Tillich had served as a chaplain in World War I and sought to offer a fresh statement of the Christian faith, one that would correlate the existential situation of contemporary humanity with the Christian message.

The early twentieth century also saw the emergence of the Fundamentalist movement within American Christianity. It was rooted in a view of an inerrant Scripture, fixed, unchanging views of redemption, the Virgin Birth, a rejection of other forms of Christianity, and secular humanism. It also had an impact on the newly emergent Pentecostal movement that became a worldwide movement in the twentieth century.

The next chapter focuses on Catholic developments, looking first at thinkers whose efforts were redefining Catholic thought in the early and mid–twentieth century. Yves Congar was only 10 when WWI broke out. He became a Dominican and already in the 1930s called for a new ecumenism. His theological work moved beyond the neo-Scholasticism of his time. Likewise, Hans Urs von Balthasar, a Jesuit, charted his own way and created "a symphony of Catholic Thought." Similarly, Karl Rahner began publishing his studies in the mid-thirties, spent the war years as a parish priest, and came under some suspicion in the mid-1950s. When Pope John XXIII announced Vatican II, Congar and Rahner were invited to contribute to the new initiative. Their work bore fruit in the Second Vatican Council, which sought to "open the doors" and let a fresh spirit into the Catholic world. The Council sparked some new directions in Catholic thought that worried the more conservative Catholics. The liberation theology of Gustavo Gutiérrez, a Latin American, sought to shift the focus of Catholic thought to social transformation. Dom Henri LeSaux, better known by his adopted Indian name, Abhishiktananda, called the Church to engage in interfaith dialogue with the Hindu world. Fresh breezes were indeed blowing through the Catholic world.

Our final chapter sees Christian thought poised on the beginning of a new millennium in which it will face new challenges as it continues the Great Conversation into the future. Those challenges include the place of women in the Christian/Catholic world, interfaith dialogue with the great world religions: Hindu, Buddhist, Muslim, Daoist, Confucian and others, the environmental movement, and most recently, Climate Change. These challenges call for the best there is within the Great Conversation that is not only the history of Christian Thought, but its future as well. Our new postscript focuses on *Laudato Si*.

Chapter 22

The War to End All Wars and the Beginnings of Contemporary Christian Thought

When I began my own study of religion in 1960, the figures discussed in this chapter were all living or had recently died. Now, in the early twenty-first century, we are beginning to gain some historical perspective on their work and contributions. I realized while teaching the history of Christian thought, that the Christian thinkers here were not figures known to today's students. Nevertheless, World War I constitutes a watershed event that had a profound impact on Christian thinking. Here it marks the beginning of the contemporary era. Since it is not possible in this overview of Christian thought to offer a reading of this era that is either comprehensive or encyclopedic, we have been selective in order to illuminate some features of the contemporary contribution to the great conversation. I begin with a Swiss thinker, Karl Barth.

Karl Barth (1886–1962)

In the midst of World War I, a Swiss pastor mounted the steps of his pulpit one Sunday morning and found he had nothing to say. His name was Karl Barth, and he was to become one of the most influential Christian thinkers of the twentieth century. World War I was the deadliest war in the history of humankind up to that point, killing more people than any previous war. In the trenches of Verdun, the average life expectancy of a battlefield officer measured in hours. Millions died here. Although mostly fought in Europe, it affected the whole world and left the human landscape—and Christian thought—profoundly altered.

Barth was educated in Germany and had been educated in that hopeful and progressive liberal theology of the nineteenth century that had some of its roots in figures like Schleiermacher. Later in the century, liberal Christian thinkers had taken very seriously the beginnings of the historically critical study of Scripture. In his *Essence of Christianity*, the great German historian Adolf von Harnack (1851-1930) had come to summarize the Christian faith in terms of the twin affirmations of "the fatherhood of God and the brotherhood of man" (obviously, there weren't many feminist theologians around in those days). This summary of the essence of Christianity as "the fatherhood of God and the brotherhood of man" was linked to a progressive understanding of history as moving straight towards the Kingdom of God.

It was in this tradition that Barth had been educated and it was this outlook that he carried with him into the pulpit on that fateful day during the World War. Barth tells us how he suddenly found himself in a quandary on a Sunday morning: he did not have anything to say to his congregation in the face of the terrible events unfolding in the war. He felt as if his liberal and optimistic faith had been found wanting in the face of these events. In that situation, Barth turned once again to the study of Scripture, and out of his studies, he wrote a commentary on *The Epistle to the Romans*. Published right at the end of the war, it was a real bombshell. In that volume and in his understanding of Paul, Barth articulated a number of themes that have come to loom very large in contemporary Christian thought.

The Epistle to the Romans

Drawing upon Kierkegaard, the first thing Barth did in his *Epistle to the Romans* was to reassert the infinite qualitative difference between God and humanity. For Barth, liberal theology had tended to obscure this infinite qualitative difference. This can be seen, for example, in the writings of Albrecht Ritschl (1822-1889), a German Lutheran theologian and in Walter Rauschenbusch, the American theologian. In their writings, there is a close connection between human effort and divine purpose. Humanity and divine purpose work hand in glove in the task of transforming humanity as it moves towards the Kingdom of God. Barth rejected this optimistic view. Insisting that we had to recognize the infinite qualitative difference between God and humanity, he drew the implication that the relationship between God and humanity was confused if not reversed in much modern theology. In Barth's view, rather than understanding the relationship between God and humanity as a movement from God's side towards the human side in the person of Jesus Christ, modern Christian thought had turned things on their head and seen humankind moving towards God. For Barth, this was a primary expression of human idolatry. Consequently, Barth offered a devastating critique of religion as an attempt to storm the heavens.

Religion, in Barth's view, is the human attempt to go to God—an attempt to build ladders and bridges through liturgies and institutions as a way for human life to get to God. For Barth, this is idolatry. Christianity, in his view, is to be distinguished from every other and all religion. Instead, Barth spoke about the Christian faith, which he contrasted with notions of the Christian religion. Here he meant that the basic movement within the Christian faith is a movement from God's side towards humanity. What Barth felt he was rediscovering in his encounter with Paul's writing to the Romans, or what he called—"the strange and the wonderful world of the Bible"—was the story of how God relates to humanity.[1] God, according to Barth, redeems and reconciles humanity to God, not vice versa. God does this despite all the human efforts to avoid God, to move away from God, to hide in religiousness or in other human creations. God comes to overturn all of our human efforts and cultural creations, and chief among them is our very religiosity. Religion for Barth is oftentimes a way of avoiding an encounter with God rather than coming to God.

For Barth, then, the heart of the Christian faith is the person of Jesus Christ, who reconciles us to God. Reconciliation, for Barth, has to be the focus of Christian thinking and reflection. As he wrote,

> *Between God and man there stands the person of Jesus Christ, Himself God and Himself man, and so mediating between the two. In Him God reveals himself to man. In Him man sees and knows God. In Him, God stands before man and man stands before God . . . in Him God's plan for man is disclosed . . . God's deliverance of man accomplished . . . In Him God has joined Himself to man.*[2]

All we can do or all we should do in our Christian thinking is to witness to this miraculous event in and through which we are restored to communion with God. Barth's theological position came to be known as neo-orthodoxy, a new orthodoxy that attempts to recapture many of the older emphases within the Christian tradition and articulate them in a powerful new way.

1. See Barth, *The Epistle to the Romans*.
2. See Kerr, *Selections from Karl Barth*, 297.

The Church Dogmatics

The fullest expression of Barth's neo-orthodoxy is his unfinished work *Church Dogmatics*, which he began in the late 1920s and worked on for the rest of his life. His first volume appeared in 1927 and was revised in 1932, and then other masterful volumes were to come over the years. The first volume became Volume I, Part 1, followed by Volume I, Part 2 and Volume I, Part 3, then Volume II, Part 1 and so on. Each volume ran to over 500 pages and, even though he never finished it, the whole work comprises more than 7,500 pages (sometimes footnotes would run on for twenty pages of fine print). You can get your whole education in the history of Christianity by reading these books. The goal of Barth's efforts, and the slogan that came to be associated with them, was to refocus the theological task back on the issue of God. Barth repeatedly insisted that what theologians had to do was to let God be God. Instead of confusing their efforts with God, they needed to see that the best that we can do is simply point towards the transcendent source of our life, our redemption and our consummation. It is impossible to do justice here to Barth and the impact he had upon Christian thinking, except to say that his work was the most influential contribution to the great conversation in the twentieth century.

Two Visionary Christian Thinkers: Teilhard de Chardin & Rosenstock-Huessy

Some thinkers who emerged in the twentieth century were not theologians in the traditional sense, but added some new dimensions to the unfolding great conversation. Here we look at two such figures: Pierre Teilhard de Chardin, a French Jesuit and paleontologist who sought to reconcile science and religion, and Eugen Rosenstock-Huessy, a Christian who offered a new vision of the story of the West and the future of the Church as well as a social grammar that illuminated the life of society.

Pierre Teilhard de Chardin (1881–1955)

A Jesuit, paleontologist, philosopher and theologian, de Chardin was a visionary Catholic thinker who sought to reconcile evolutionary thought and the Christian faith. Teilhard was born in Orcines, France, the fourth of eleven children. His father was an amateur naturalist, his mother a devout Catholic. He went to a Jesuit school when he was twelve and earned degrees in mathematics and philosophy that allowed him to pursue a university education. In 1899, he entered the Jesuit novitiate and continued his studies in science and philosophy. He taught physics and chemistry in a Jesuit school in Cairo from 1905 to 1908. It was here that he had his first glimpses of the Eastern world, and it dazzled him.

He went to England to study theology. Here the young Teilhard encountered the work of his fellow Frenchman, the philosopher Henri Bergson (1859-1941), and especially Bergson's book *Creative Evolution*. In Bergson, Teilhard encountered the notion of an élan vital (vital impulse) that drives evolution. It opposed mechanistic views of evolution, and it would have a profound impact on Teilhard's life and work. Following his theological studies, Teilhard worked in paleontology at the Museum of Natural History in Paris (1912-14).

When World War I began, Teilhard was called into military service and he served as a stretcher-bearer during the war. He received the Legion of Honour and during the war wrote his first essay, "La vie cosmique" (Cosmic Life). It signaled the direction of his thought. He concluded his essay with these words: "There is a communion with God, and a communion with the earth, and a communion with God through the earth."[3] The last would become Teilhard's way. He took his solemn vows as a Jesuit in 1918 and after the war continued his studies in the natural sciences at the Sorbonne in Paris, receiving his doctorate in 1922.

In 1923, he went on a geological expedition to China with Father Émile Licent (1876-1952), a fellow Jesuit and scientist who de Chardin had collaborated with at the Paris Museum of Natural History. While in the Ordos Desert in Mongolia, Teilhard wrote his remarkable Mass on the World. Back in France in 1925, he got into difficulty with Catholic authorities for an essay that some viewed as questioning St. Augustine's views of original sin.

Consequently, Teilhard returned to China in 1926 to continue his geological studies. With intervals in Europe and geological expeditions and studies in India and Africa, Teilhard was primarily in China between 1926 and 1946. Five geological expeditions to different areas of China allowed him to provide a general geological survey of China. In the mid-1930s, de Chardin wrote his *Divine Milieu*, claiming that

> "God reveals himself everywhere ... as a universal milieu, only because he is the ultimate point upon which all realities converge ... In the divine milieu all the elements of the universe touch each other by that which is most inward and ultimate in them."[4]

---

3. See Teilhard de Chardin, *Writings in a Time of War*, 14. It was originally entitled, *La vie Cosmique* and written in 1916.

4. See Teilhard de Chardin, *The Divine Milieu*.

Teilhard had established himself as an internationally known paleontologist—one who studies how physical changes of geology, geography and climate have affected the evolution of life. He was appointed Director of the Laboratory of Advanced Studies in Geology and Paleontology in Paris in 1938. However, the outbreak of war in Europe kept him in China. By 1938, he had also completed the manuscript of Le phenomène humain (*The Phenomenon of Man* or *The Human Phenomenon*). When he returned to France after the war, Teilhard discovered that Church authorities had forbidden him to publish his work. After his death, his works were published and many Catholic thinkers—including the future Pope Benedict—wrote in support of de Chardin.

In the preface to *The Phenomenon of Man*, Teilhard wrote that it must be read "purely and simply as a scientific treatise." It is an attempt to "develop a homogeneous and coherent perspective of our general extended experience of man . . . a whole which unfolds." In a word, the human phenomenon, Teilhard argued, must be seen in a Bergsonian evolutionary perspective. This was a perspective "within the scope of the requirements and methods of science." However, he acknowledged that his study "may appear" to have larger implications—and it does.

The study is divided into four parts: "Before Life Came," "Life," "Thought," and "Survival." The first part deals with elemental matter and the vital within of things or spiritual energy. The second unfolds the advent, expansion and complexification of life. At the end of the second part, there is a crucial transition when Teilhard argues that complexification leads to the birth of thought or consciousness in the human phenomenon. Part three of the book then explores this transition, the deployment of the noosphere—his term for the sphere of mind—and the modern earth. In the final section of the book, he deals with the confluence of thought, the hyper-personal and the ultimate earth, including the conjunction of science and religion.

In the epilogue to *The Phenomenon of Man*, he explores the Christian phenomenon. Here Teilhard is more speculative as he sees the evolutionary trajectory of life as moving towards an Omega point, the cosmic divine. Already in 1920, Teilhard had written of "the universal Christ, the organic centre of the entire universe . . . the centre on which even every natural development is ultimately physically dependent,"[5] but here the Omega point is articulated in physical and mathematical terms. While his *Phenomenon of Man* is offered as a scientific treatise, it included his conviction that the evolutionary process moves in a spiritual direction. Its outcome is what Teilhard called the Omega point or the Cosmic Christ. Teilhard thus wove

---

5. See Teilhard de Chardin, *Science and Christ*, 14.

his science and his faith into a sweeping unitary vision of the universe. Here are his words:

> What makes the world in which we live specifically modern is our discovery in it and around it of evolution . . . what disconcerts the modern world at its very roots is not being sure . . . that there is . . . a suitable outcome to that evolution.
>
> We have seen and admitted that evolution is an ascent towards consciousness. That is no longer contested even by the most materialist . . . of humanitarians. Therefore, it should culminate forward in some sort of supreme consciousness.
>
> Because it contains and engenders consciousness, space-time is necessarily of a convergent nature. Accordingly its enormous laws, followed in the right direction, must somewhere ahead become involuted to a point, which we might call Omega, which fuses and consumes them integrally in itself . . . In the perspective of a noogenesis, time and space become truly humanized, or rather super-humanized . . . the Universal and Personal (that is to say centred) grow in the same direction and culminate simultaneously in each other . . . at the Omega Point."[6]
>
> By the Universal Christ, I mean Christ the organic centre of the entire universe . . . that is to say the centre on which every even natural development is ultimately physically dependent . . . Of the entire universe, again, that is to say, the centre not only of moral and religious effort, but also of all . . . physical and spiritual growth."[7]

When his books were published beginning in the late 1950s, they gained a large following, especially among Catholic intellectuals. Many within the scientific community dismissed his work, but others, including the evolutionary biologist Julian Huxley (1887–1975) gave it guarded approval.[8] Teilhard de Chardin societies sprang up around the world.

Eugen Rosenstock-Huessy (1888 -1973)

Another important—though little-known—Christian thinker was Eugen Rosenstock-Huessy. Born into a cultured and assimilated Jewish family in Berlin, he entered the Christian community as a teenager. He was trained in law and became a professor of law in a German university when only

---

6. Teilhard de Chardin, *The Phenomenon of Man*, 252 and 284-86.

7. Teilhard de Chardin, *Science and Christ*, 14.

8. See the edition of the *Phenomenon of Man* published in London by Collins in 1965 for Julian Huxley's positive view.

twenty-three years of age. In the German army in World War I, he served at Verdun where he witnessed the incredible carnage of the war. Left profoundly shaken by these events, Rosenstock-Huessy's subsequent life and writings addressed the transformed human landscape left by the war.

It was at Verdun, Rosenstock-Huessy later wrote, that he had the vision that led to his great work, *Out of Revolution: The Autobiography of Western Man*. His response to the tragedy of World War I was an attempt to see the story of Western life as the making of humanity in the forge of revolution. For Rosenstock-Huessy the making of humanity—*anthropurgy* is the word from early Christian thinkers—is the divine imperative that calls every generation from the beginning to the end of time. It is this insight that informs his retelling of the autobiography of Western humanity. It assumes the unity of humankind in our origin and our destiny, but this unity is not uniformity. It is rather a multiform and differentiated humanity in which all nations, peoples, and cultures contribute to the whole. Our destiny unfolds in the midst of revolution and tumult stretching from Lenin to Luther—this was Rosenstock-Huessy's way of identifying Part I of *Out of Revolution*—and back through the clerical revolutions of the preceding half-millennium. He thus revealed our history as the story of our interdependence and unity. His account of "Western man" is informed throughout by his Christian faith.

After the war, he returned to Germany where he refused to go back to the university, work on the constitution for the new Weimar Republic or become an editor of a religious journal, *Hochland*. He felt that the war was the consequence of the failure of these institutions—state, university and church—to keep the peace. He went to work in an automobile factory and began to organize adult education programs and work camps that could rebuild society from the ground up. Later in the 1920's he went back to teaching in the university, but when Hitler came to power, he was one of the first to resign his position in protest. He left Germany and went to the United States, where he taught at Harvard for three years and then at Dartmouth until his retirement. George Morgan called him "one of the most original thinkers of the twentieth century."[9]

It is difficult to summarize his thought since he was, as he indicated in the title of one of his last books, an "impure thinker." He wrote widely, but across the disciplinary lines of modern thought and across the boundaries that often separate Protestant from Catholic and religious from secular. His was an effort to chart a vision of Christianity that could retain what was essential from the tradition yet be responsive to the future.

---

9. See Morgan, *Speech and Society*.

In his 1946 book *The Christian Future or the Modern Mind Outrun*, he said that he had never doubted the Creed but understood it as "a record and promise of life."[10] He saw that Christianity was the keeper of the secret that "life was stronger than death" and that it had continually reinvented itself throughout history, in faithfulness to its own secret. In this dawning third age of Christianity, Rosenstock-Huessy argued, we needed a fresh penetration of the Cross, into the suffering of our time. He believed that "the wearing out of the old names, the old words, the old language, is the most widely and deeply felt fact in the crisis through which Christianity is passing." "Modern man is crucified already," Rosenstock-Huessy, wrote, by the trenches of Verdun, the horrors of Hiroshima, the mechanization of modern life.

> "*The salvation he [modern man] needs is inspiration for his daily toil and leisure . . . Finding Christian and pagan . . . no longer separate from each other as at first, but side by side within every soul, we are challenged to achieve a further innovation in the evolution of Christianity.*"

We need a Christianity that would be "incognito" as it incarnates itself amidst the suffering and displacements of modern life. It would be a Christianity that knew the secret of losing itself, as the way to the future:

> "*A third Christianity, the Christianity of Hope, is beginning . . . Though I believe that the Church is a divine creation and that the Creed is true, I also believe that in the future, Church and Creed can be given a new lease on life only in services that are nameless or incognito. The inspirations of the Holy Spirit will not remain inside the walls of the visible or preaching Church. A third form, the listening Church, will have to unburden the older modes of worship by assembling the faithful to live out their hopes through working and suffering together . . . thereby to wait and listen for the in-break of a new consolation that shall redeem modern life from its curse of disintegration and mechanization.*" [11]

In this way, we could "outrun the modern mind" and move into a renewed and re-inspired contemporary world.

The task of the coming millennium, wrote Rosenstock-Huessy, was "to reveal God in society." The way to approach that task was through a new dialogical social science. In *Speech and Reality*, Rosenstock-Huessy outlined this new method, which focused on "speech as the life blood of society." It

---

10. See Rosenstock-Huessy, *The Christian Future*, 98.
11. Ibid., 129 and 127-28. See also Eugen Rosenstock-Huessy, *Out of Revolution*.

rested on a new grammar that one of his students, Clinton Gardner, characterized as follows:

1. First, imperative (or vocative) speech toward the future, addresses us as thou. Parents and teachers, religious leaders, and politicians, often address us this way.
2. Second, the subjective speech of our inner self, our I, arises when we consider our possible reply to an imperative.
3. Third, historical speech, records what we did in response to imperatives. Such speech preserves the past, telling how we and other people formed and maintained institutions, as we.
4. Fourth, objective speech can look at what happened in the first three stages of any complete experience—and provide an analysis of them. It considers how we affected the world, or persons, around us. Now we see things as it; persons as he, she, or they.[12]

That summary shows us that the Cross of Reality—Eugen Rosenstock-Huessy's way of characterizing the human situation—is not a static image. It depicts the process through which we become and remain human. It is a way that challenges those social scientific methods that reduce social reality to objects and numbers. Could it be a new social grammar?

Teilhard de Chardin and Rosenstock-Huessy contributed, each in his own way, to enlarging the great conversation in relation to the world of science and the life of society.

Paul Tillich (1886–1965) and the Way of Correlation

Born and educated in Germany, Paul Tillich served as a chaplain in World War I. He came to the United States in 1933, shortly after Hitler's rise to power. He taught at Union Theological Seminary in New York City where he was a colleague of Reinhold Niebuhr (1892-1971), another distinguished Christian thinker. Tillich is known for his method of correlation: correlating the questions that emerge in human existence with the answers found in the Christian faith. Deeply influenced by existentialism—a philosophy and sensibility that looked deeply into the human condition—he was often characterized as an existential thinker.

Tillich's three-volume *Systematic Theology*, published beginning in the 1950s, saw itself as an attempt "to understand the Christian message as the

---

12. See Rosenstock-Huessy, *Speech and Society*, 9-44. See also Clinton C. Gardner, *Beyond Belief*, 44-47 and 76-82 for a fuller account of ERH's social grammar.

answer to the questions implied in . . . every human situation." For Tillich "theology is necessarily existential" since the theologian is "involved with the whole of his existence, with his finitude and anxiety . . . with the healing forces in him and in his social situation." The theological project is a task carried out in relation to philosophy since; Tillich argued, philosophy also asks, "the question of the structure of being." While the philosopher, like the theologian, is concerned about being in general, the Christian thinker

> . . . must look where that which concerns him ultimately [Tillich's definition of religion is "ultimate concern] is manifest, and he must stand where its manifestation reaches and grasps him. The source of his knowledge is . . . the Logos "who became flesh," that is, the logos manifesting itself in a particular historical event.

Proceeding, then, through an analysis of human existence characterized by the poles of individuation and participation, dynamics and form, freedom and destiny, Tillich concluded that "'God' is the answer to the question implied in man's finitude; he is the name for that which concerns man ultimately," God is "being itself . . . or the ground of being." Tillich argued, like early Christian thinkers, that all our views of God are symbolic and that the reality of God always exceeds our grasp. As symbols, they are useful pointers towards what Tillich called "the God beyond God."[13]

The correlation of the Christian message and the realities of human existence led Tillich to see Christ as "the bearer of new being," the Logos made Flesh in whom we are healed or made whole—the literal meaning of "salvation." Tillich said that "Christianity was born . . . in the moment in which one of his followers was driven to say to him, 'Thou art the Christ.'" In making this affirmation, Tillich explained, one is affirming that Jesus as the Christ is "he who brings the new state of things, the New Being." Tillich went on to explain that in affirming Jesus as the Christ, one is embracing

> the basic Christian assertion that Essential God-Manhood has appeared within existence and subjected itself to the conditions of existence without being conquered by them. If there were no personal life in which existential estrangement had been overcome, the New Being would have remained a quest and an expectation . . . Only if existence is conquered in one point—a personal life, representing existence as a whole—is it conquered in principle, which means "in beginning and in power.

Tillich's language for speaking of the Christ drew upon contemporary existentialist thought. Humanity is characterized by existential estrangement

---

13. Tillich, *Systematic Theology*, 8, 22, 20, 23,177, 211, and 235.

or Fallenness. Moreover, human life unfolds within the polar of freedom and destiny, dynamics and form, individuation and participation. Moreover, it is "the Christ who brings the New Being, who saves men from the old being, that is, from existential estrangement and its self-destructive consequences." "New Being" is the phrase that Tillich used to speak of "salvation." Its primary meaning is "healing," which "means reuniting that which is estranged, giving a centre to what is split, overcoming the split between God and man, man and his world, man and himself . . . the fulfillment of the ultimate meaning of one's existence."[14]

After he came to the United States—and especially after World War II—Tillich became a popular figure with a wide following. Books like his *Courage to Be* and his sermons were widely read. The existential cast he gave to Christian thought seemed to address a pervasive angst and search for the meaning of our living and longing in the twentieth century.

Tillich's contribution to the great conversation lies in his recognition of the perpetual need to renew Christian thought in every generation. He also shows us the power of Christian thought to illuminate the human condition when he understands "unbelief" as the human being's tendency to "remove his center from the divine center" and "hubris" as making "himself . . . the center of his world."[15] Christ as the bearer of the New Being, said Tillich, heals such estrangement and returns humanity to its fullness of being. His existential reading of the Christian faith contributed to an engagement with the meaninglessness that haunted many in the war-torn twentieth century.

Summary

Barth, de Chardin, Rosenstock-Huessy and Tillich reflected the profound impact that the "War to End all Wars," which saw more deaths than any war in human history up to that point, had on Christian thought. World War I was only the precursor to an even larger war twenty years later. World War II was truly global, with conflict that stretched from Europe across the Soviet Union to Japan and from Indonesia to North Africa. During this war, great numbers died not only in battle but also in the Nazi concentration camps and elsewhere. The end of the war revealed the horrendous truth that nearly six million Jews were executed by the Nazis, along with other non-combatants in other arenas of the war. These events unfolded in the midst of an unprecedented growth in science and technology that was rapidly transforming the shape of the world. The automobile and the airplane reshaped our relationship to space,

---

14. Tillich, *Systematic Theology*, 97, 98, 150, 166.
15. Ibid., 51.

our landscape and our air. The world began to shrink. Radio and television reworked our relationships with one another and within society through new electronic media that reached across vast distances instantaneously.

Following World War II, Europe came back to life with the help of the Marshall Plan that laid the foundations of the European Union. Devastated Japan began to remake itself as a major economic power. The great colonial empires collapsed or slowly disintegrated as countries from East Asia to India to Africa regained their independence. British India was partitioned into the two independent countries of India and Pakistan in 1947. Israel declared itself independent in 1948. Mao entered Beijing to found the People's Republic of China in 1949.

An ecumenical landmark signaled change within the Christian world when the long-awaited World Council of Churches was founded in 1948. In 1959, Pope John XXIII would announce a 2nd Vatican Council that would profoundly shift the teachings of Roman Catholic Church.

New threats and tensions emerged as nuclear-armed Eastern and Western blocs faced off in a Cold War. The struggle for civil rights began in the United States. Canada's placidity was shaken by a newly assertive Quebec and young people throughout the Western world proclaimed their dissatisfaction with the status quo—all against the backdrop of a destructive and unpopular war in Vietnam. Affluence in the West grew, but so did the gap between rich and poor nations, the stuffed and the hungry. The feminist and environmental movements, which loomed large in the late twentieth century and pose a major challenge to Christian churches, experienced their first stirrings. The world was a-changing.

Review

1. What is Barth's approach to Christian thought?
2. What is the "Omega Point" in the thought of Teilhard de Chardin?
3. What is the "Christianity of Hope" in Eugen Rosenstock-Huessy?
4. How does Paul Tillich understand the task of theology?

Chapter 23

The War to End All Wars and Contemporary Catholic Thought

WITHIN THE WHIRLWIND OF change that was the world after 1945, the Roman Catholic Church appeared for a time to be an island of stability. Underneath the surface, new currents were emerging. These currents burst into the open when a new pope, John XXXIII, called an ecumenical council. The Second Vatican Council or Vatican II (1962–65) would profoundly change both the official teaching and the lived experience of the Catholic world.

Catholic Thought in the Twentieth Century

The revival of medieval scholasticism in the Catholic world in the middle of the nineteenth century became known as Neo-Scholasticism. It was hostile to the currents of the modern world and sought to revivify the thought of the great medieval thinker St. Thomas Aquinas (1225–1274). Early in the twentieth century figures like Étienne Gilson (1884–1978) and Jacques Maritain (1882–1973) offered interpretations of Aquinas that moved beyond the constraints of Neo-Scholasticism. Even more dramatic was the emergence of the "Nouvelle Théologie" or "New Theology" that called for:

- a return to the sources, that is Scripture and the early Fathers;
- a critical attitude towards Neo-Scholasticism; and
- a recognition of the place of history in theological explorations.

Here I will just mention three of the most important figures in this current were the Dominican Yves Congar and the Jesuits Hans Urs von Balthasar and Karl Rahner.

Yves Congar (1904-1995)

Yves Congar was born in the French Ardennes. He was ten when World War I broke out. His father was deported and Yves felt called to become a preacher to end the misery that war brought. He joined the Dominican order. In the early 1930s, he was teaching at Saulchoir, the Dominican House of Studies. He was influenced by his fellow Dominican, Thomas Aquinas, but not in the direction of Neo-Scholasticism. Instead, Congar saw Thomas as responsive to the needs of his time. In 1937, Congar published his *Divided Christendom: A Catholic Study of the Problem of Reunion*. He was an early advocate of ecumenism and drew upon Orthodox and Protestant sources as well as Catholic ones in his study. He initiated *Unam Sanctam* (One Holy), an ecumenical journal, and he supported Young Christian Workers. From 1940-1945 he was held a prisoner in German prison camps.

Following the war, he returned to teaching. In 1950, he published *True and False Reform in the Church*. The church hierarchy had been suspicious of his work for some time, and in the 1950's he was silenced, partly for his writings and partly for his support of the worker-priest movement in France. Pope John XXIII lifted the ban and, in 1960, invited him to work on the "preparatory theological commission" for Vatican II. He became a major influence at the Council, but he felt that the Council did not go far enough on many issues. He continued to work on those issues. Late in life, Pope John Paul II made Congar a cardinal. He charted many ways to the future Church.

Hans Urs von Balthasar (1905-1988)

Hans Urs von Balthasar, a Swiss theologian and Catholic priest, was another figure who challenged Neo-Scholasticism. Trained as a Jesuit, von Balthasar was drawn to early Fathers like Gregory of Nyssa (c.335-395). He immersed himself in their thought, seeking to bring their "mystical warmth and rhetorical power" into contemporary Catholic theology. In the 1930's he published his *Apocalypse of the German Soul*, a study of German literature, theology and philosophy in the modern period. In Basel in the 1940s, von Balthasar met Adrienne von Speyr (1902-1967), a Protestant medical doctor and mystic. She had sought out von Balthasar as a spiritual director and he led her into the Catholic Church. Together they formed the Community of St. John for men and women. Balthasar recorded and published sixty volumes of von Speyr's mystical visions and scriptural commentaries arising from her contemplation. In the 1950s, von Balthasar published his Theology of *Karl Barth: Exposition and Interpretation*, an analysis of the noted Protestant theologian's work. Barth said it was the best book on his theology.

Under something of a cloud for his association with Adrienne von Speyr, he was passed over for inclusion on the theological commission for Vatican II. Beginning in the 1960s and concluding in 1985, von Balthasar wrote a Trilogy that consisted of fourteen volumes. Part I contained seven volumes on *The Glory of the Lord: A Theological Aesthetics*. The next five volumes, entitled *Theo-Drama*, focused on soteriology, Christology and eschatology. The final three volumes were entitled *Theo-Logic* and addressed the relationship between Christology and ontology.

Unlike some of the other New Theologians, von Balthasar was critical of modernity. He made an enduring contribution for his largeness of spirit, his respect for the gifts of others, his refusal to fall into any camp and, in the words of his fellow Jesuit Henri de Lubac, his "symphony of Catholic thought." He died in 1988, on the day before Pope John Paul II announced he had made him a Cardinal.

Karl Rahner (1904–1984)

Karl Rahner was born in Freiburg, Germany. Upon graduation he entered the Society of Jesus (the Jesuits), as had his older brother Hugo. Rahner's novitiate in the 1920s involved an immersion in the Spiritual Exercises of St. Ignatius. This Jesuit spirituality had a profound impact on Rahner and it remained the touchstone of his life and thought. In the late 1920s, he studied the early Fathers and contemporary Thomists like the Belgian Jesuit Joseph Maréchal (1878–1944).

In 1934, he returned to Freiburg to do a doctorate in philosophy. One of his teachers was the controversial philosopher Martin Heidegger (1889–1976), the author of *Being and Time*, who offered an existential phenomenology that challenged traditional philosophies of being. Heidegger understood the human being as Dasein or "being-there" characterized by care. Some felt Heidegger's views had too great an influence on Rahner's dissertation on *Geist in Welt* (*Spirit in the World*). Unlike Heidegger, however, Rahner felt that human being opened out into the mystery of Transcendence. He also considered Thomas Aquinas, rather than Heidegger, the major influence on his thinking. The University of Innsbruck rejected Rahner's dissertation though it was later published as *Geist in Welt/Spirit in the World* in 1939. Years later, he received an honorary doctorate from the University of Innsbruck. It was a belated recognition of his earlier dissertation. Already in the 1930s, Rahner was publishing ten to twenty essays a year on the early Fathers and the mystics of Christianity.

After he spending two years as a lecturer in theology at Innsbruck, the outbreak of World War II in 1939 led to Rahner's moving to the Pastoral Institute in Vienna, where he would remain until 1949. He was an active parish priest but continued his intellectual work. The themes that began to emerge in his writings were rooted in "the incomprehensible mystery of God." Yet God "communicates God's own reality" and makes "grace" a "constitutive element of the human and the fulfillment of the creature." Like other contemporary Christian thinkers, Rahner sought to disclose the correlation of existential questions with theological answers, but he did so in his own distinctive way and vocabulary. Rahner would later assert that all human beings have a "'transcendental experience' that orients them to God."[1] This ground-tone of his theology became more obvious after he returned to the theological faculty at the University of Innsbruck. Now he began to publish his *Theological Investigations*. Rahner's Investigations were later gathered and published as books. Over the coming decades, Rahner published a *Lexicon for Theology and Church* that ran to ten volumes. His *Sacramentum Mundi* was a six-volume encyclopedia. His complete bibliography encompasses 3,500 articles, books and encyclopedias.

However, in the fall of 1962, his superiors ordered him to stop publishing and told him that his work was under suspicion. This order was quickly forgotten, when two months later Pope John XXIII named Karl Rahner a *peritus* or expert advisor for Vatican II. Many commentators see Rahner's influence on Vatican II as pervasive, especially in the declaration known as *Lumen Gentium* (Light of the Nations). *Lumen Gentium* deals with the church, defined as the "People of God" on pilgrimage towards the Kingdom of God.

Towards the end of his life, Rahner published his *Foundations of the Christian Faith: An Introduction to the Idea of Christianity*. Aimed not at the theological specialist but at the beginner, it is Rahner's most accessible book. It outlines the major themes of Christianity and affirms "our transcendence, responsibility, and freedom, our orientation to the incomprehensible mystery, our being in history and the world, and our social nature. We are those beings 'bequeathed an endlessness of meaning.' This makes each of us pure

---

1. See Wesley Wildman on Karl Rahner in the Boston Collaborative Encyclopedia of Western Theology at people.bu.edu/WWildman/bce/rahner.htm.

openness... to mystery." It is not easy going, but it is worth the effort. The Stanford scholar Thomas Sheehan remarked that Rahner's gift was that "he revolutionized the way the Church understands its message."[2]

Pope John XXIII (1881–1963): Letting the Wind Blow Through

In 1958, the Roman Catholic Church named Angelo Giuseppe Roncalli as its new pope. Already in his seventies at the time of his elevation to the papacy, Roncalli, who took the name John XXIII, surprised the church and the world in 1959 by calling for a new ecumenical council. Known as the Second Vatican Council, it brought a fresh spirit into the life of the largest church in the Christian world. Pope John XXIII was a remarkable figure, known for his "daring simplicity, so wholly evangelical in its nature that it demands and obtains universal respect and edifies many."[3] He became known as "the good Pope" or "everyone's Pope," and was canonized as a saint in 2014.

Pope John XXIII presided over the opening session of the Second Vatican Council in 1962 and announced that "the Council now beginning rises in the Church like daybreak, a forerunner of most splendid light." He was to die before the Council concluded, but the Council continued under his successor Pope Paul VI and its declarations brought a new spirit and many new views into the Catholic world. In the declaration on the church, *Lumen Gentium*, the church is characterized as "the whole people of God" on pilgrimage to the Kingdom of God. The understanding of the Eucharist shifted from "sacrifice" to an anticipation of the Messianic Banquet. In addition, and most importantly to my mind, the Second Vatican Council acknowledged what was "true and valid" in other religious traditions and called for dialogue with people of other faiths. In its *Declaration on the Relationship of the Church to the Non-Christian Religions, Nostra Aetate*, we read these words:

> *Men look to the various religions for answers to those profound mysteries of the human condition which, today even as in olden times, deeply stir the human heart:... What is the meaning and purpose of our life? What is goodness and what is sin?... Where lies the path to true happiness?... What, finally, is that ultimate and unutterable mystery which engulfs our being...?*

---

2. See Rahner, *The Foundations of Christian Faith*.
3. Pope John XXIII, *Journal of a Soul*, xviii.

> Religions . . . have struggled to reply to these same questions . . . Thus in Hinduism men contemplate the divine mystery . . . they seek release from the anguish of our condition through ascetical practices . . . Buddhism in its multiple forms . . . teaches a path by which men . . . can . . . attain supreme enlightenment . . . Upon the Moslems, too, the Church looks with esteem. They adore one God, living and enduring, merciful and all-powerful, Maker of heaven and earth . . . The Church repudiates all persecutions . . . and displays of anti-Semitism directed against the Jews . . .
>
> The Catholic Church rejects nothing that is true and holy in these religions . . . The Church therefore has this exhortation for her sons: prudently and lovingly, through dialogue and collaboration with the followers of other religions, and in witness of Christian faith and life, acknowledge, preserve and promote the spiritual and moral goods found . . . as well as the values of their society and culture.[4]

There were critics of *Nostra Aetate* who felt it was a mistake even to acknowledge other faiths. There were other critics, who felt that the statement did not go far enough, especially in relation to the Jewish community. This declaration was historic and far-reaching. It was the first time in a Christian ecumenical council that other faiths were acknowledged and spoken of positively. It at least opened up the possibility of new dialogical and collaborative relations with people of the non-Christian faiths. This is among the most significant contributions of the Second Vatican Council to that great conversation that continues to explore the meaning of the Christ for every time—including our own.

Gustavo Gutiérrez and the Theology of Liberation

Two other Catholic figures represent post-colonial developments in the great conversation. One is the Peruvian thinker Gustavo Gutiérrez, whose work *A Theology of Liberation* was an important of example of liberation theology. This movement began in Latin America in the 1960s and attempted to reformulate the Christian vision in relation to the impoverished masses of Latin American societies. As Gutiérrez wrote, "many in Latin America have started along the path of a commitment to liberation" and that commitment means "solidarity with the oppressed."

---

4. See Abbott, ed., *The Documents of Vatican II*, 718, 666-67.

Liberation theology saw the task of Christian thinking as the sociopolitical liberation of humanity from the historical structures of underdevelopment. It was deeply rooted in the "*comunidades de base*," or "base communities" struggling to overcome impoverishment and oppression. The goal of this "theology of liberation," wrote Gutiérrez, is "to reconsider the great themes of the Christian life within this radically changed perspective." Here the horizon of Christian thinking has been historicized and focused on the issue of sociopolitical transformation, with the goal being to transform "the oppressed and exploited land of Latin America." Gutiérrez wrote that "the struggle to construct a just and fraternal society where people can live with dignity and be the agents of their own destiny" is the issue of our times. He also saw that this focus on social liberation raised "a question about the very meaning of Christianity and about the mission of the Church."[5] In its Latin American context, liberation theology challenged the long-standing relationship of the Catholic Church to Latin American societies. The church had been present to the conquest of the lands of the Americas, including Peru, mostly serving the interests of the conquering European power. Over the centuries, the Catholic Church continued to work with the ruling elites to maintain power over the indigenous peoples and the poor. Liberation theology challenged that history and argued that authentic Christianity—or what Gutiérrez called "liberation centered in the salvific work of Christ"—involved turning Christianity upside down and identifying with the poor. Gutiérrez said that the "theology of the signs of the times" that had been called for "since John XXIII and Vatican Council II" involved "a call to pastoral activity, to commitment, and to service." Here theology was not an abstract science of God as Thomas Aquinas had imagined but rather, said Gutiérrez, "critical reflection on praxis." According to Gutiérrez,

> *It is becoming more evident that the Latin American peoples will not emerge from their present status except by means of a profound transformation, a social revolution, which will radically and qualitatively change the conditions in which they now live . . . But in order for this liberation to be authentic and complete, it must be undertaken by the oppressed people themselves . . . The Church feels compelled to address itself directly to the oppressed . . . calling on them to assume control of their own destiny, committing itself to support their demands.*[6]

This agenda and perspective placed the Christian faith firmly with the forces for socio-political revolution; it was a radical refocusing of the

---

5. Gutiérrez, *A Theology of Liberation*, ix, x, xi
6. Ibid., xi, 18, 84, 91, 114.

Christian faith. Critics of liberation theology quickly charged liberation theologians with being Marxists in disguise for incorporating into their theological reflection Marxist notions of class struggle and social revolution. Even though it was true that they employed Marxist categories of social analysis, liberation theologians did not see it that way. They more often pointed to figures like Dom Helder Camara, a remarkable Catholic bishop of Recife and Olinda in northeast Brazil, who urged solidarity with the oppressed. However, Camara rejected violent social revolution and was deeply committed to non-violence in the tradition of Gandhi in India and Martin Luther King, Jr. in the USA, while some liberation theologians called for a violent social revolution. Camillo Torres (1929-1966), a Catholic priest, joined a guerrilla movement in Colombia and died fighting against government forces.

The earlier Cuban revolution that brought Fidel Castro to power in 1959 and the ill-fated socialist Chilean government of Salvador Allende (1970-73) were events in Latin America that had fueled this widespread desire for social change. The question that faced Christian thinkers was how these events stood in relation to the Kingdom of God. Gutiérrez felt that the "prophetic task of the Church is both constructive and critical." It should "point out those elements within a revolutionary process which are truly humanizing . . . " and also "point out the dehumanizing elements to be found in a process of change."[7] This prophetic task is undertaken within a church that is committed to such change because of its identification with the oppressed.

There were parallel developments in Christian communities in Africa with "contextual theology," in Korea with "minjung theology" and in India with its own form of liberation theology. Across the so-called Third World, Christian thinkers emerged who wanted an indigenized form of Christian thinking rather than the European Christianity of Western missionaries.

Dom Henri LeSaux (1910-1973) and the Dialogue of Religions

At the same time that liberation theology emerged in Latin America, a second development in contemporary Christian thought was beginning to unfold in India. Instead of the turn towards social justice in liberation theology, the new developments in India sought to renew the contemplative traditions of Christianity through dialogue with the great traditions of the East. The initial focus of these developments was the encounter with Hindu

7. Ibid., 115-16.

spirituality, especially the non-dual or Vedanta teachings of the Hindu Way. However, they would broaden out to include the other great traditions of the East.

Vatican II (1962–65) was enormously important for global Christianity, especially in its call for "dialogue and collaboration" with the "non-Christian religions." However, prior to Vatican II, pioneering figures like Father Henri Le Saux had seriously begun to engage the great traditions of Indian spirituality. Le Saux was a French Benedictine monk who had come to India hoping to establish a contemplative tradition that took seriously an encounter with Hindu spirituality. He had first experienced a "call to India" in the 1930s, but it was not until 1948 that he set foot on Indian soil.

Father Jules Monchanin (1895–1957) had come to India in 1939 and, together with Le Saux, founded Saccidananda Ashram in Tamil Nadu in 1950. It was the "Ashram of the Holy Trinity"—or, in Indian terms, sat (being), cit (consciousness) and ananda (bliss). Here Monchanin and Le Saux began to forge a renewed contemplative tradition that incorporated elements of Indian spirituality into their life and practice. They wore the saffron robes of the renunciate, the way of sannyasa. They adopted Hindu names: Le Saux became Swami Abhishiktananda (Bliss of the Anointed Lord) and Monchanin became known as Swami Paramarubyananda (Bliss of the Supreme Formless One). They incorporated Indian texts and terms into their liturgy. It was the beginning of a profound encounter with Hindu spirituality.

Already in 1949, Abhishiktananda went to Arunachala, a holy mountain in South India where the ashram of Sri Ramana Maharshi (1879–1950) was located. Sri Ramana Maharshi was widely regarded as a "realized soul," one of the great sages of India. This visit had a profound impact on Le Saux. He later recounted something of his experience in *The Secret of Arunachala: A Christian Monk on Shiva's Holy Mountain*: "In the sage of Arunachala . . . I discerned the unique Sage of the eternal India . . . it was as if the very soul of Indian penetrated to the very depths of my own soul."[8] This encounter with the non-dual spirituality of the Hindu Way would set the course of Le Saux's quest and would be at the heart of Le Saux's spiritual journey. He wondered how this non-dual experience of the divine, which he sensed in Ramana Maharshi and which the Upanishads, the sacred writings of the rishis, bore witness to, related to the deep truths of Christianity. Le Saux wanted to answer this question not theoretically but existentially.

In the 1950s, Le Saux continued his exploration of the Hindu Way. Though based in Saccidananda, he returned often to Arunachala. There he learned much from Sri Harilal Poonja, a disciple of Ramana Maharshi. In

---

8. Abhishiktananda, *The Secret of Arunachala*.

the mid-fifties, he became a disciple of Sri Gnanananda Giri. In *Guru and Disciple*, published after his death, Abhishiktananda would write of this encounter.⁹ The encounter with Sri Gnanananda was all part of an interior journey—and struggle—that lasted through much of his life.

In the early 1960s, he brought together a group of Christians to explore the Hindu and Christian experience of the "mystery beyond all names." This involved a contemplative exploration of the sacred literature of Christians and Hindus, reflection on what they heard, and periods of silence, meditation and prayer. From these meetings, in which the participants explored the meaning of the Upanishads to gain some insight into the non-dual or Advaitic experience of the ultimate mystery and turned to the Bible to discover how this experience relates to the Christian revelation, Abhishiktananda later published *Hindu-Christian Meeting Point: Within the Cave of the Heart*. Sara Grant, the volume's translator, noted Abhishiktananda's conviction that "only in the cave of the heart can true dialogue between Christianity and Hinduism take place."¹⁰ This was an ongoing interior dialogue. Throughout his life in India, Abhishiktananda struggled to reconcile these two paths to the sacred heart of things.

From 1950 until 1968, his journey was linked to Saccidananda Ashram. In 1968 he turned the Ashram over to Father Bede Griffiths (1906–1993), who would also become a pioneering figure in interreligious encounter and dialogue. Abhishiktananda took up residence in a small hermitage/kutiya built on the banks of the Bhagirathi River near Uttarkashi high in the Himalayas. Here he spent six to eight months in contemplative solitude each year. He also wrote some of his most enduring works during this period. When I visited Uttarkashi in the 1990s, I met a family that lived nearby and they reported that they "often heard the 'click, click' of his typewriter."

Abhishiktananda also continued to have wide contact with a circle of friends, both Hindu and Christian, around India. He played, for example, an important role in the National Seminar on the Church in India held in Bangalore in 1969. He worked on preparations for the National Seminar and throughout championed the contemplative way and a deeper engagement with Indian spirituality. He was also involved in a reworking of the liturgy. Though the outcome of the seminar was not all he had hoped for, he felt it was a moment of awakening for the church in India.

In 1971, he had his first written exchanges with Marc Chaduc, a French Catholic seminarian, who subsequently became his disciple. In July 1973,

---

9. See Abhishiktananda, *Guru and Disciple*. A glimpse of Abhishiktananda's inner struggle can be found in James Stuart, ed. Abhishiktananda: *His Life Told Through His Letters*, and Panikkar, ed. *Ascent to the Depth of the Heart*.

10. See Abhishiktananda, *Hindu-Christian Meeting Point*, viii.

while preparing for a retreat with Chaduc, Abhishiktananda suffered a heart attack. It also proved to be his final awakening. As he wrote to his longtime friend Murray Rodgers,

> ... a door opened in heaven when I was lying on the pavement. But a heaven which was not opposite to earth, something which was neither life nor death, but simply "being," "awakening" ... beyond all myths and symbols.[11]

And he wrote,

> I have found the Grail. And that is what I keep saying and writing to anyone who can grasp the figure of speech. The quest for the Grail is basically nothing else than the quest for the Self ... It is yourself that you are seeking through everything.[12]

On December 7, 1973, he died. Everyone who saw him between his attack/awakening and his death was struck by the joy that he radiated.

His spiritual diary, published in 1998 and entitled *Ascent to the Depth of the Heart*, is a moving account of his struggles and experiences in his search for an authentic spirituality that could acknowledge the profound depths of both the Hindu and the Christian Way.

Abhishiktananda was a pioneer in interfaith encounter and dialogue prior to Vatican II and the call in *Nostra Aetate* (Declaration on the Relation of the Church to non-Christian Religions) for all Catholics to engage other traditions in "dialogue and collaboration." Thus, he saw that Vatican II "gave an unexpected impetus to the renewal of Christianity ... the necessity for Christians to enter into dialogue with all men of good will has now, he said, become a commonplace."[13] While prophetic, his words come as a surprise to many. These words were the fruit of his quarter-century encounter with Hindu spirituality.

Out of that encounter, Abhishiktananda came to a more inclusive understanding of what some would call "the wider ecumenism." As he wrote,

> The time is ripe ... for followers of Christ and the great world religions ... to understand each other in a profound spirit of humility, sincerity, and charity. Each will be aware of the irresistible attraction of the unfathomable mystery of God in the depths of his own being and will recognize that the religious beliefs and practices of his neighbor are the outward signs of an awareness of that Presence and of a desire to respond ...

11. See du Boulay, *The Cave of the Heart*, 234.
12. Ibid., 236.
13. See Abhishiktananda, *Saccidananda*, xi.

However, he was also sensitive to the significantly different way that the great traditions of the East had articulated and practiced that "unfathomable mystery" that they had known:

> *The Oriental world, however, whether Hindu, Buddhist, or Taoist, seems to have reacted to that experience of the indwelling Mystery which lies at the root of all genuine religions quite differently from the cultural and religious world of the Mediterranean.*[14]

Thus, it was not at the level of concepts, doctrines or words but at the level of experience and in silence—what Swami Abhishiktananda called the "cave of the heart"—that the encounter and meeting would occur. As he wrote at the end of his life,

> *Behind the external dialogue, there will necessarily be a silent interior dialogue, continuing within the soul of each of the participants . . . Out of this comes a kind of inner communion at the level of the Spirit so that, even when a difference of opinion cannot be bridged at the conceptual level, both parties instinctively look for a higher and deeper insight to which their opposing ways of expressing themselves are only partial approximations.*[15]

This interior dialogue was the key to the legacy left by Swami Abhishiktananda and his contribution to the future of Christianity's encounter and dialogue with the world's religions.

Summary

Much of what was said in the summary of the previous chapter could be repeated here. The world that Congar, von Balthasar, Rahner, Vatican II, Gustavo Gutierrez, and Abhishiktananda encountered had struggled to find its way amidst and after the wars of the 20th century. There were new means of communication—the phone, radio, television, and the internet—as society transitioned from one rooted in agriculture to one characterized by industrialization and ever new technologies, a burgeoning population, the end of colonialism and the ever-changing world of power politics. Yves Congar anticipated and called for a new ecumenism decades before Pope John the 23rd announced the convening of Vatican II. Named to the preparatory committee, Congar saw many of his hopes succeed in Vatican II. von Balthasar had moved beyond the neo-Scholasticism of his youth, and chartered some new

---

14. See Abhishiktananda, *Hindu-Christian Meeting Point*, 4-5.
15. See Abhishiktananda, *Saccidananda*, xi.

directions in Catholic thought prior to Vatican II. Karl Rahner had begun publishing his research already in the 1930s and came under some restrictions in the 1950s. When Pope John Paul XXIII announced the convening of Vatican II, Rahner was named to the preparatory committee. Many of the decrees of Vatican II have Rahner's fingerprints all over them.

Nostra Aetate or the *Declaration on the Relationship of the Church to Non-Christian Religions* is a ground-breaking teaching of the Catholic tradition. In calling for "dialogue and cooperation" with people of other faiths it opened a new chapter in the life of the Catholic Church.

Latin American liberation theology initiated by Gustavo Gutierrez was an important development following Vatican II, though the Vatican during the time of Pope John Paul II placed some restrictions on it. Even prior to the 2nd Vatican Council, Father Henri LeSaux had begun a profound dialogue with Hindu Ways. He assumed a Hindu name, Abhishiktanada (Bliss of the Anointed Lord) and began the dialogue with the great Eastern traditions of spirituality.

Review

1. What struck you as important in our brief encounter with the thought of Congar, von Baltharsar, or Rahner?
2. Vatican II and especially *Nostra Aetate*?
3. How would you characterize Liberation theology?
4. Who is Abhishiktananda? What contribution did he make to Christian thought?

Chapter 24

The Great Conversation Revisited
Beginning the Third Millennium

We now find ourselves in the opening decades of the third millennium of the Christian era. We have attempted here to recount something of the remarkable history of Christian thought that has unfolded over the past two millennia. It is a conversation that still has at its heart the mystery of Jesus as the Christ, the one who reveals the human face of God. For almost two thousand years now, men and women of faith, in varying circumstances and with varying intentions, have turned again and again to the apostolic witness of Scripture and to the traditions of thought, piety and spiritual practice in Christianity to wrestle with the perennial question of the meaning of it all. What it means was not given all at once in the beginning; it is a revelatory event whose meaning we are still probing and unpacking. The great conversation has been ongoing and inexhaustible because, from the beginning, Christians believed that somehow Jesus Christ led them into the mystery of God—that the Way that Jesus invited them to embrace had its center and heart in God.

In presenting the story of the great conversation among Christians, I have sought to guide the interested reader into some of the writings of those that have contributed to that conversation. My hope is that in this account you will have encountered some figures that you might return to in the future.

We have seen that the history of Christian thought is an ongoing conversation about the Christian faith: its assumptions and foundations, its content and dimensions, its significance and meaning. From its very beginnings in Galilee, Christian thinkers have reflected on the meaning of Jesus the Christ, his life, death and resurrection. Throughout two millennia, they have been convinced that in Christ God had drawn near to our suffering world. Thinkers as diverse as Justin Martyr, Irenaeus, Gregory of Nyssa, Augustine, Thomas Aquinas, Julian of Norwich, Martin Luther, Jonathan Edwards, Karl Barth, Martin Luther King, Jr., Bede Griffiths and countless others have contributed to this great conversation about the meaning of our life that comes from God and goes to God.

We have seen how over the centuries questions recur time after time and how certain emphases are lost for a while only to resurface at a later point. We see development and repetition. We see themes explored, only to be forgotten, probes abandoned and new departures undertaken. We never seem to reach any point when we can say that the great conversation that is the history of Christian thought has now come to an end, or to conclusions that cannot be re-visited. Throughout the ages Christian thinkers, trying to understand the revelation rooted in the events that are witnessed to in the Christian Scriptures, have turned, again-and-again, to the enigma of the one who asks, "And who do you say that I am?"

Looking back over that long history there are, in my view, three obvious failings in Christian thought. The first arises from its pervasive patriarchy, leading to the ambivalent attitude towards women that pervades Christian thinking. Mary Malone, my colleague for many years at St. Jerome's University in the University of Waterloo, has admirably chronicled that painful dimension of in her three-volume *Women in Christianity*. As Mary Malone remarked in noting that ambivalence:

> *Women have been included, called, graced, inspired and canonized by Christianity throughout the centuries. On the other hand . . . women have not always felt appreciated . . . and indeed have often felt excluded and oppressed by church leaders.*

She continued, "The 'good news' for women . . . is rooted in the gospel portrait of the relationships between Jesus and women."[1] There one sees that women were part of the early Jesus movement and were portrayed in a positive way. However, she noted, that quickly gave way to a "negative message of exclusion, trivialization and often quite astonishing hostility."[2] In the fourth century, Jerome, who translated the Bible into Latin, was supported in his work by women and he dedicated his commentary on Galatians to Marcella, a remarkable Roman Christian woman. He would later write:

---

1. Malone, *Women and Christianity*, 17.
2. Ibid., 1.

"woman is classed among the greatest of evils."[3] The eleventh-century saint Peter Damian excoriated women in this appalling way: "O charmers of the clergy, appetizing flesh of the devil, that castaway from Paradise, poison of minds, death of souls, companions of the very stuff of sin, the cause of our ruin" and so on.[4] Yet we also find Mary, *theotokos* or Mother of God, exalted and venerated from the early centuries on. Mary Malone has shown how the Catholic traditions of Christian thought failed to deal with the feminine and suppressed the voices of women, even though there have been remarkable voices of women in that history.

This ambivalence towards women has been a blot on Christian thought. However, beginning in the nineteenth century and especially at the end of the twentieth century, a powerful movement has arisen within Christianity that seeks to redress this longstanding failing of Christian thought. Raising the question of women in Christian thought will, I believe, prove to be one of our time's significant contributions to the continuing great conversation. Already the great conversation is challenged, enriched, and transformed by the very significant voices of women. Here I need only mention the name of a contemporary Christian thinker like Rosemary Radford Ruether or Elizabeth A. Johnson, or Elizabeth Schussler Fiorenza or Ursula King to point in that hopeful direction.[5]

Some mainline Protestant churches, such as the United Church of Canada, began to ordain women as ministers in the 1930s. The number of denominations with women priests (Anglican) and ministers (Lutheran, Reformed and others) grew significantly in the 1970s. The place of women is a major issue on the agenda as Christian thought enters the third millennium.

The second great failing of Christianity is its failure to deal with the reality of other faiths. The bitterest aspect of this failing is in relation to the tradition out of which Christianity emerged. As early Jewish Christianity moved into the gentile world, its attitude towards its Jewish parent underwent a troubling and destructive change. Already in some of the writings that became the New Testament, the Jewish traditions are seen as superseded by the Christian revelation. Even though the early Church rejected Marcion's view that rejected the Hebrew Bible, there emerged an antipathy towards Judaism that has skewed much Christian thought. After

---

3. Ibid., 138.
4. Ibid., 18.
5. See Ruether, *Faith and Fratricide* (1974), *Women and Redemption* (1998), or Johnson, *Quest for a Living God* (2002), or Elizabeth Schussler Fiorenza, *In Memory of Her: A Feminist Theological Reconstruction of Christian Origins* (1983) or Ursula King, *The Search for Spirituality: Our Global Quest for a Spiritual Life* (2008).

Christianity was made the religion of the Roman Empire, Christian thought tended to either ignore or denigrate other religious traditions.

This occurred again when Islam emerged in the 600s. We saw that some very early Christian thinkers, like Justin Martyr, saw Greek thought in a positive way, and others, like Augustine, worried about the "pious pagans," but generally Christian thinkers failed to acknowledge and address other traditions of faith and life. This occurred again when Islam emerged in the seventh century. Christianity's failure to acknowledge other traditions persisted through the Middle Ages and into modern times.

In recent times, however, there have been some important new developments in this area. As we saw, the Second Vatican Council opened up the possibility of dialogue with other faiths, and this has been a concern of the World Council of Churches, a community of Protestant and Orthodox churches, as well.

Father Bede Griffiths was one figure who charted some new directions in this area. Bede Griffiths was a Christian monk who spent much of his life in India, and in his writings, he wrestled with Christianity's relation to the other great traditions, especially those of the East. No less a figure than His Holiness the Dalai Lama has said of Bede Griffiths' work that:

> "His vision has guided him to open the hearts and minds of mankind to gain understanding and acceptance of all the major religions with respect and dignity, to gain a sense of peace and unity to further the cause and goodwill of all people."[6]

Starting in the last third of the twentieth century, Christians have undertaken significant dialogue with Buddhists, Muslims, Hindus, Jews, Sikhs, Confucians and people of other religious traditions. Here we see the beginnings of a new chapter in the story of Christian thinking as the Christian faith begins to explore its relations with people of other faiths.

The third issue is one that has emerged in recent times: the well-being of our environment, our planet. Rachel Carson's *Silent Spring* (1962), that documented the negative impact of pesticides on the environment and especially on birds, was the wake-up call for many. Her book gave rise to an environmental movement that quickly expanded to include the full range of impacts that human activity was having on the biosphere: the loss of species, the degradation of water and the pollution of the sea, diminishing forests, mountains of garbage and so on. Christians also responded to this new situation. At the World Council of Churches, "Caring for Creation" became a major focus in the 1970s. Catholic popes since Paul VI (1897–1978) have

---

6. See the back cover of Bede Griffiths, *Universal Wisdom*, for these words by HH the Dalai Lama.

spoken out on environmental issues. Pope John Paul II (1920–2005) proclaimed Francis of Assisi (1182–1226) the patron saint of ecologists in 1979.

Perhaps the most remarkable contemporary Christian thinker on these issues is Professor Thomas Berry (1914–2009), a priest, cultural historian and eco-theologian—"Earth scholar" was his preferred description. Thomas Berry taught at Fordham University in New York and in 1989 published his remarkable *Dream of the Earth*, a series of essays that mark out the contours on a new global earth consciousness, one that sees "the universe . . . as a single, glorious, celebratory event."[7] Influenced by Teilhard de Chardin, Berry went on to write *The Universe Story* with physicist Brian Swimme, arguing that the "universe is a communion of subjects, not a collection of objects." He summarized his efforts in *The Great Work: Our Way into the Future* as "a new story of the universe."[8]

At the beginning of the third millennium, Christian thinkers face new challenges; some of those challenges are unprecedented. First among challenges, facing humankind is the looming environmental crisis that we already see in global warming, the loss of topsoil, the devastation of the rainforests and other forest cover, the desertification of large areas, the collapse of fish stocks and the other signs of our disturbing impact upon this "good earth." This must be at the forefront of the new challenges facing Christian thought. Can we respond to this challenge? While some have questioned the continuing vitality of these long and varied traditions of the great conversation, the capacity of Christian thought repeatedly to renew and reform itself throughout the ages should give us an element of hope. As long as we hold to the light given to us in this great conversation, we are poised to continue that story into the future that is already coming our way.

A New Postscript

On March 13, 2013, as I was completing this account of the great conversation, the Catholic Church elected a new pope, Cardinal Jorge Mario Bergoglio, who chose the papal name Francis after St. Francis of Assisi. An Argentinian bishop and Jesuit, Pope Francis quickly brought a new tone to the papacy. On May 24, 2015, he issued an encyclical (letter) entitled *Laudato Si'* (Praise be to You, O Lord), which includes these words from St. Francis's Canticle of the Sun: "Praise be to you, my Lord, through our Sister, Mother Earth, who sustains and governs us." Subtitled "On Care for

---

7. See Berry, *Dream of the Earth*, 132.

8. See also Swimme and Berry, *From the Primordial Flaming Forth to the Ecozoic Age*, and Berry, *The Great Work*.

Our Common Home," the encyclical seeks to "address every person living on this planet" and "enter into dialogue with all people about our common home."[9]

After citing the contributions of previous Popes, Pope Frances turns to look at our common home. He is concerned that "we have come to see ourselves as her [Mother Earth's] master, entitled to plunder at will," rather than seeing, as did Francis of Assisi, "nature as a magnificent book in which God speaks to us and grants us a glimpse of his infinite beauty and goodness."[10] After these introductory remarks, the encyclical is divided into six chapters: (1) What is happening to our Common Home, (2) the Gospel of Creation, (3) The Human Roots of the Ecological Crisis, (4) Integral Ecology, (5) Lines of Approach and Action and (6) Ecological Education and Spirituality.

In Chapter 1, Pope Francis articulates the many dimensions of the challenges facing us. He begins with pollution of our water, land and seas, our throwaway culture, and our failure to recognize the climate as a common good. He points out that the threat of global warming is "mainly the result of human activity" and is a global problem. He also cites the loss of biodiversity, the decline in quality of life, global inequity and "the cry of the earth and the cry of the poor"—and more. Throughout he affirms the consensus of science concerning climate change.

In Chapter 2, Pope Francis turns to some Christian teachings that are relevant to caring for our earth. Five of those principles stand out. First, there is "the dignity of each and every human being." Second, human life is "grounded in three relationships: with God, our neighbour, and the earth itself. Third, "creation has a broader meaning than nature" and human beings are "subjects that can never be reduced to objects." Fourth, "all of us are linked by unseen bonds and together they form a kind of universal family, a sublime communion which fills us with a sacred, affectionate, and humble respect." Fifth, "the natural environment is a collective good, the patrimony of all humanity and the responsibility of everyone."[11]

In Chapter 3, he explores technology, acknowledging its creative gifts but warning of the limitations of the technological paradigm and its globalization. In Chapter 4, he calls for an "integral ecology" that links environmental, economic and social ecology, and urges attention to cultural ecology, preserving cultural diversity, and attending to the ecology of daily life and the principle of the common good.

---

9. See *Laudato Si: On Care for Our Common Home*, at https://laudatosi.com. In the encyclical, each paragraph is numbered. The footnotes indicate the paragraph where the quoted words are located.

10. Ibid. para. 2.

11. Ibid. para. 27, 32, 35, 39.

In Chapter 5 on Lines of Approach and Action, Pope Francis urges dialogue on the environment in the international community and on new national and local policies. He also proposes dialogue on "transparency in decision making," on politics and economics for human fulfillment, and between religion and science. He then concludes with Chapter 6 on Ecological Education and Spirituality, where he recommends simplicity rather than extreme consumerism in lifestyle, education for a covenant between humanity and the environment, ecological conversion, joy and peace, and civic and political love. He closes this chapter with attention to sacramental signs and celebrations, the Trinity and the relationship between creatures, Mary as queen of all creation, and the beauty of God. He then concludes with two prayers: one for the earth, the other a prayer in union with creation. They include the following words:

> Teach us to discover the worth of each thing
> to be filled with awe and contemplation
> to recognize that we are profoundly united
> with every creature
> as we journey toward your infinite light.
>
> and
> God of love
> show us our place in the world
> as channels of your love
> for all the creatures of this earth.[12]

This seems a fitting place to bring this exploration of the great conversation a close. The encyclical is an indication that Christian figures will continue to address the challenges that face humankind as we enter the age of our planetary society.

APPENDIX

Words from the Great Conversation of Christian Thought

Letters of Paul (c. 45-60)

Letter to the Romans

I appeal to you, brethren, to take note of those who create dissentions and difficulties in opposition to the doctrine, which you have been taught; avoid them. For such persons do not serve our Lord Christ, but their own appetites...I would have you wise as to what is good and guileless as to what is evil...Now to him who is able to strengthen you according to my gospel and the preaching of Jesus Christ, according to the revelation of the mystery which was kept secret for long ages but is now disclosed and through the prophetic writings is made known to all nations... (The Holy Bible, Revised Standard Version, New York: Thomas Nelson & Sons, 1953, Romans 16:17-18, 25-26)

Letter to the Corinthians

...we preach Christ crucified a stumbling-block to Jews and folly to Gentiles, but to those who are called, both Jews and Greeks, Christ the power of God and the wisdom of God. ((The Holy Bible, Revised Standard Version, New York: Thomas Nelson & Sons, 1953, I Corinthians 1:22-24)

Gospel of Mark (c. 60)

In those days, Jesus came from Nazareth of Galilee and was baptized by John in the Jordan...and a voice came from heaven. 'Thou are my beloved Son, with thee I am well pleased." (The Holy Bible, Revised Standard Version, New York: Thomas Nelson & Sons, 1953, Mark 1:9-11)

Gospel of Matthew (c. 70)

The book of the genealogy of Jesus Christ, the son of David, the son of Abraham. Abraham was the father of Isaac, and Isaac the father of Jacob...So all the generations from Abraham to David were fourteen generations, and from David to the deportation to Babylon fourteen generations, and from the deportation to Babylon to the Christ fourteen generations. (The Holy Bible, Revised Standard Version, New York: Thomas Nelson & Sons, 1953, Matthew 1:1, 2 & 17)

Gospel of John (c. 90)

In the beginning was the Word, and the Word was with God, and the Word was God. He was in the beginning with God; all things were made through him, and without him was not anything made that was made. In him was life, and the life was the light of men. The light shines in the darkness, and the darkness shall not over come it...And the Word became flesh and dwelt among us, full of grace and truth; we have beheld his glory, glory as of the only Son from the Father. (The Holy Bible, Revised Standard Version, New York: Thomas Nelson & Sons, 1953, John 1: 1-5, 14)

The Acts of the Apostles

So when they had come together, they asked him, "Lord, will you at this time restore the kingdom of Israel?" He said to them, 'It is not for you to know times or season which the father has fixed by his own authority. But you shall receive power when the Holy Spirit has come upon you; and you shall be my witnesses in Jerusalem and in all Judea and Samaria and to the end of the earth. (The Holy Bible, Revised Standard Version, New York: Thomas Nelson & Sons, 1953, Acts 1:6-8)

Gospel of Luke (c. 70)

And he came to Nazareth where he had been brought up; and he went to the synagogue, as his custom was, on the Sabbath day, And he stood up to read...the book of the prophet Isaiah...'The Spirit of the Lord is upon me, because he has anointed me to preach good news to the poor. He has sent me to proclaim release to the captives and recovering of sight to the blind, to set at liberty those who are oppressed, to proclaim the acceptable year of the Lord.' And he closed the book...And he began to say to them, 'Today this scripture has been fulfilled in your hearing.'... And they rose up and put him out of the city... (The Holy Bible, Revised Standard Version, New York: Thomas Nelson & Sons, 1953, Luke 4:16-21, 29)

Gospel of Thomas (c. 150-180)

"These are the secret words which Jesus the Living spoke and (which) Didymus Judas Thomas wrote. And He said: He who will find the interpretation of these words will not taste death." (112)

Jesus said: Let him who seeks not cease in his seeking until he finds; and when he finds, he will be troubled, and if he is troubled, he will marvel, and will be a king over the All. (114)

Jesus said: . . . the kingdom is within you and outside you. . . . When you know yourselves, then you will be known, and you will know that you are the sons of the living Father. (115)

His disciples said: Show us the place where you are. . . He said to them: He who has ears, let him hear! There is light within a light-man and it illuminates the whole world, if it does not illuminate it, it is darkness. (138)

Jesus said: If they say to you, (Who are) you? Say, We are his sons, and we are the elect of the living Father. (152). . . Jesus said: I am the light, which is over everything. I am the All; (from me) the All has gone forth and to me the All has returned. Split wood: I am there. Lift up the stone, and you will find me there. (167)

Source: Robert Grant & David N. Freedman, The Secret Sayings of Jesus (London: Fontana, 1969).

Didache, Or the Teaching of the Twelve Disciples (c. 130)

The Lord's Teaching. . .by the Twelve Apostles: There are two ways, one of life and one of death. . .

Now, this is the way of life: First, you must love God who made you, and second, your neighbor as yourself." And whatever you want people to refrain from doing to you, you must not do to them. (171)

. . .Do not turn your back on the needy, . . .share everything with your brother. . .hate hypocrisy. . .confess your sins. . .That is the way of life. (173)

. . .the way of death is this: First of all, it is wicked and. . .blasphemous: murders, adulteries, lusts, thefts. . .duplicity, deceit. . .jealously. . .boastfulness. Those who persecute good people, who hate truth, who love lies. . .have no pity for the poor. . . (174)

Now about baptism: this is how to baptize. Give public instruction . . .then baptize in running water "in the name of the Father . . .the Son . . .the Holy Spirit. If you do not have running water, baptize in some other. If not in cold, then in warm. If you have neither, . . .pour water on the head three times. . . Before baptism. . .the one who baptizes and the one being baptized must fast. . .(174)

Our Father in heaven, hallowed by your name. . .You should pray . . .three times a day. (174)

Welcome every apostle on arriving, as if he were the Lord. But he must not stay beyond one day. . . .If he stays three days, he is a false prophet. . .If he asks for money, he is a false prophet. (176) On every Lord's Day . . . come together and break bread and give thanks. . . (178)

Source: Cyril Richardson, ed., Early Christian Fathers, Vol. I (Philadelphia: Westminster Press, 1953), "The Teachings of the Twelve Apostles, Commonly Called the Didache," pp. 171-179).

Justin Martyr (c. 100-165)

Plea for a Fair Hearing: "To the Emperor Titus Aelius Hadrianus Antoninus Pius Augustus Caesar, and to Verissimus his son, the Philosopher, and to Lucius the Philosopher, son of Caesar by nature and of Augustus by adoption, a lover of culture, and to the Sacred Senate and the whole Roman people—on behalf of men of every nation who are unjustly hated and reviled, I, Justin, son of Pricus and grandson of Bacchius, of Flavia Neapolis in Syria Palestina, being myself one of them, have drawn up this plea and petition. . .

Reason requires that those who are truly pious and philosophers should honor and cherish the truth alone, scorning merely to follow the opinions of the ancients, if they are worthless. Nor does sound reason only require that one should not follow those who do or teach what is unjust; the lover of truth ought to choose in every way, even at the cost of his own life, to speak and do what is right, though death should take him away. So do you, since you are called pious and philosophers and guardians of justice and lovers of culture, at least give us a hearing—and it will appear if you are really such. (17-18)

What sound-minded man will not admit that we are not godless, since we worship the Fashioner of the universe, declaring him, as we have been taught, to have no need of blood and libations and incense, but praising him by the word of prayer and thanksgiving for all that he has given us? (19)

. . . [T]hat Jesus Christ alone was really begotten as Son of God, being his Word and First-begotten and Power, and becoming man by his will he taught us these things for the reconciliation and restoration of the human race. (19)

We have been taught that Christ is the First-begotten of God, and have previously testified that he is the Reason of which every race of man partakes. Those who lived in accordance with reason are Christians, even though they were called godless, such as, among the Greeks, Socrates and Heraclitus. . . But those who lived by Reason, and those who so live now, are Christians, fearless and unperturbed. For what cause a man was conceived of a virgin by the power of the Word according to the will of God, the Father and Master of all, and was named Jesus, and after being crucified and dying rose again... (21-22)

For why should we believe a crucified man that he is First-begotten of the Unbegotten God, and that he will pass judgement on the whole human race, unless we found testimonies proclaimed about him before he came. And was made man, and see that things have thus happened? (22)

Christian rites & practices: This food we call Eucharist, of which no one is allowed to partake except one who believes that the things we teach are true, and has received the washing for forgiveness of sins and for rebirth, and who lives as Christ handed down to us. (23)

"After these services...those who have more come to the aid of those who lack, and we are constantly together. Over all that we receive, we bless the Maker of all things through his Son Jesus Christ and through the Holy Spirit... On the day called Sunday there is a meeting in one place of those who live in cities or the country. There... the memoirs of the apostles or the writings of the prophets are read...the president in a discourse then urges us to the imitation of these noble things. Then we all stand together and offer prayers... Then bread, wine and water is brought and distributed to all there... and a collection taken. [Money is used, says JM,]... to take care of the orphans and widows and those who are in want on account of sickness or any other cause... and the strangers who are sojourners amongst us..." (24)

Source: Kerr, Hugh T. Readings In Christian Thought (Nashville: Abingdon, 1978), pp. 17-18, 19, 21, 22, 23, 24....

Perpetua (c. 181-203)

"While I was still with the police...my father out of love for me tried to dissuade me from my resolution. [But I replied...] "Father, I cannot be called anything else than what I am, a Christian."

...my father stayed away... We were baptized and the Spirit instructed me not to request anything from the baptismal waters except endurance of physical suffering. A few days later we were imprisoned. I was terrified because never before had I experienced such darkness. What a terrible day!

[Arrangements were made for the prisoners to spend some of their day in "better" areas of the prison.]... We all went about our own business. I nursed my child, who was already weak from hunger... I was granted the privilege of having my son remain with me in prison. Being, thus, relieved of my anxiety and concern for the infant, I immediately regained my strength. Suddenly the prison became my palace, and I loved being there..."

"One boy as we were eating we were suddenly rushed off for a hearing... When my turn came my father appeared with my boy...he begged: "Have pity on your son!" Hilarion, the governor, said, "Have pity on your father's grey head...offer sacrifice for the emperor's welfare." But I answered, "I will not." Hilarion asked, "Are you a Christian?" And I answered, "I am a Christian."... Then the sentence was passed. all of us were condemned to the beasts. (pp. 24-28)

Source: www.eyewitnesstohistory.com/martyr.htm

The Martyrdom of Saint Polycarp (c. 170)

We write you, brethren, the things concerning those who suffered martyrdom, especially the blessed Polycarp... For almost everything that led up to it happened in order that the Lord might show once again a martyrdom conformable to the gospel....to the end that we also might be imitators of him... Blessed and noble, indeed, are all the martyrdoms that have taken place according to God's will... (149)

The text tells of Polycarp's arrest and his appearance before the proconsul (a Roman official).

...the proconsul asked him if he were Polycarp. And when he confessed that he was, he tried to persuade him to deny [the faith] saying, "Have respect to your age... swear by the fortune of Caesar, change your mind...Curse Christ...Polycarp said, "Eighty-six years I have served him...How can I blaspheme my King who saved me?... I am a Christian." ... And when he said these things and many more besides he was inspired with courage and joy, and his face was full of grace... (LCC, I, 152-153)

They then bound him and built a fire to burn him.

So they did not nail him, but tied him. And with his hands put behind him and tied, like a noble ram...read for sacrifice...he looked up to heaven and said, "Lord God Almighty, Father of thy beloved and blessed Servant Jesus Christ...I bless thee, because thou has deemed me worthy of this day and hour, to take my part in the number of the martyrs..." And when he had concluded the Amen...the men attending to the fire lighted it.... (154-155)

Source: Cyril Richardson, ed., Early Christian Fathers, Vol. I (Philadelphia: Westminster Press, 1953), "The Martyrdom of Saint Polycarp, Bishop of Smyrna as Told in the Letter of the Church of Smyrna to the Church of Philomelium," pp. 149-158.

Irenaeus (c. 130-202)

Christ became what we are so that we could become as he is. (29)

Against Heresies: . . .John declared that there was one God Almighty, and one only-begotten Christ Jesus, through whom all things were made, and that he was the Word of God, that he was Monogenes [only-begotten], that he was the creator of all things, that he was the true light that giveth light to every man, that he was the creator of the world, that he came to his own, that he was made flesh. . . (30)

Regula Fidei: The Church, although scattered over the whole world even to its extremities, received from the Apostles and their disciples the faith in one God, the Father Almighty, Maker of heaven and earth, the seas and all that in them is. . .Christ Jesus, the Son of God, who became incarnate for our salvation, and in the holy ghost, who by the prophets proclaimed the dispensations, the advents, the virgin birth, the passion and resurrection from the dead, the bodily ascension of the well-beloved Christ Jesus our Lord into heaven, and his Parousia [second coming] from the heavens in the glory of the Father to gather up all things in Himself and to raise the flesh of all mankind to life. . .(31)

This Kerygma and this faith the Church, although scattered over the whole world, diligently observes, as if it occupied but one house, and believes as it had but one mind. . . (31)

The rule of truth we hold is, that there is one God Almighty, who made all things by His Word, and fashioned and formed that which has existence out of that which had none. (31)

For God needs nought of such things; but it is He who by His Word and Spirit makes, disposes, governs and gives being to all things, who created the universe, who is the God of Abraham, Isaac and Jacob. Above Him there is no other God, neither initial principle, nor power, nor *pleroma* [fullness]. He is the Father of our Lord Jesus Christ. (31)

The Plan & Purpose of God: It is well that we should begin from the first and principal heading—the Creator God, who made the heaven and earth and all that is therein; whom they blasphemously describe as the "fruit of a defect," and show that there is nothing above Him nor after Him, and that it was not by compulsion but of His own free will that He made all things, since He alone is God, alone is Lord, alone is Creator, alone is Father, alone is the container of all things and the cause of the existence of all things. (32)

. . .It is God in Himself, predestinating all things according to His inscrutable and ineffable plan, who made all things just as He willed. It is He who distributes to everything the harmony, order, and beginning of its creation, a spiritual and invisible order to the spiritual. . .an earthly to the earthly, giving to each its proper substance. He made all things that were made by His unwearied Word. (32)

Many and various are the things that are made. When you take them in detail they are mutually antagonistic and discordant. But, taken in connection with the whole creation, they are agreeable and harmonious. (32

...[I]t is not proper to say that the Supreme Deity is the slave of necessity... (32)

He only is God who made all things. He alone is omnipotent. He only is Father who made and created all things, visible and invisible, objects of sense and objects of understanding, things in Heaven and things in earth by the Word of His Power. (34)

He is Creator, Maker and Fashioner. He is the Moulder and Lord of all. And neither is there anything above or beside Him..... But there is only one God, the Creator. (34)

The Apostolic Tradition: Any one who wishes to discern the truth may see in every Church in the whole world the Apostolic tradition clear and manifest. (34)

...have their salvation not written on paper with ink, but by the Spirit on their hearts...and carefully keep the old tradition, believing in one God the Maker of heaven and earth and of all therein, by Christ Jesus the Son of God. (35)

Incarnation, Recapitulation, Redemption: [According to the Gnostics] neither the Word nor the Christ ever entered this world, that the Saviour never really became incarnate or suffered, but that he descended as a dove upon that Jesus who belonged to the dispensation, and then when he had proclaimed the unknown Father, he again ascended into the Pleroma. (36)

... [A]ccording to no school of the Gnostics did the word of God become incarnate. (36) ....Others hold that the Christ only suffered in a fictitious way... (36)

...Him who is truly God, not knowing that His Only-begotten Word, who is always present with the human race, united and blended with his own creatures according to the Father's pleasure, and being made flesh, that he is Jesus Christ our Lord, who both suffered for us and rose on our behalf, and will come again in the glory of the Father to raise all flesh, and to manifest salvation, and to show the rule of a just judgment to all under him. (36)

Man is in every respect the formation of God, and therefore he [Jesus Christ] recapitulates men into himself, the invisible becoming visible, the incomprehensible comprehensible, the one superior to suffering becoming subject to suffering, and the Word becoming man. (36)

... [T]he Word who was in the beginning with God, through whom all things were made and who was always present with the human race, even he in the last times according to the time appointed of the Father, was united with His creation, and became man subject to suffering, the argument of those who say, "If he was born then, he was not Christ before," is overcome. (37)

...It therefore behoved him who assayed to slay sin and redeem man, who was guilty of death, to become that very thing which he was, namely, man, who had indeed been drawn into bondage by sin and was held fast by death...(37)...[T]he Word became flesh. God recapitulating the ancient creation of man in Himself, in order to slay sin, to remove death's sting, and restore man to life.

It has been shown that the teaching of the Church is everywhere constant and abiding, and is supported by the testimony of the prophets, Apostles, and all the disciples... (37)

The teaching of the Apostles is the true gnosis [knowledge]. (38)

Source: Kerr, Hugh T. Readings In Christian Thought (Nashville: Abingdon, 1978), pp. 28-38.

Tertullian (c. 160-c. 220)

Why Heresies: For worldly wisdom culminates in philosophy with its rash interpretation of God's nature and purpose. It is philosophy that supplies the heresies with their equipment. . ... A plague on Aristotle, who taught them dialectic... (40) (On Jerusalem & Athens) I have no use for a Stoic or a Platonic or a dialectic Christianity. After Jesus Christ we have no need of speculation, after the Gospel no need of research. (40)

My first principle is this. Christ laid down one definite system of truth which the world must believe without qualifications, and which we must seek precisely in order to believe it when we find it. . ..

You must seek until you find, and when you find, you must believe. (41)

The Rule of Faith [apostolic tradition; creed]—to state here and now what we maintain. . .there is but one God, who is none other than the Creator of the world, who produced everything from nothing through his Word, sent forth before all things; that this Word is called his Son, and in the Name of God was seen in divers ways by patriarchs, was ever heard in the prophets and finally was brought down by the Spirit and Power of God the Father into the Virgin Mary, was made flesh in her womb, was born of her and lived as Jesus Christ; who thereafter proclaimed a new law and a new promise of the kingdom of heaven, worked miracles, was crucified, on the third day rose again, was caught up into heaven and sat down at the right hand of the Father; that he sent in his place the power of the Holy Spirit to guide believers; that he will come with glory to take the saints up into the fruition of the life eternal and the heavenly promises and to judge the wicked to everlasting fire, after the resurrection of both good and evil with the restoration of their flesh. (41)

Provided the essence of the Rule is not disturbed, you may seek and discuss as much as you like. (42) Our Lord Jesus Christ...taught...what he was laying down as man's duty. (42)

Their [the church's] common unity is proved by fellowship in communion, by the name of brother and the mutual pledge of hospitality-—rights which are governed by no other principle than the single tradition of a common creed. (42)

Source: Kerr, Hugh T. Readings In Christian Thought (Nashville: Abingdon, 1978), pp. 37-42.

Origen (c. 185-254)

The holy apostles, when preaching the faith of Christ, took certain doctrines...which they believed to be the necessary ones and delivered them in the plainest terms to all believers. . .. The grounds of their statements they left to be investigated by such as should merit the higher gifts of the Holy Spirit and in particular by such as should afterwards receive through the Holy Spirit himself the graces of language, wisdom, and knowledge. (44-45) ...the kind of doctrines which are believed in plain terms are the following: First, that God is one, who created and set in order all things and who, when nothing existed, caused the universe to be... Then again: Christ Jesus, he who came to earth, was begotten of the Father before every created thing...then again, that the Holy Spirit is united in honor and dignity with the Father and the Son... (44)

Scriptures: The right way...of approaching the scriptures and gathering their meaning, is the following... (46):

[T]he meaning of the sacred writings is impressed in a threefold way upon one's own soul, so that the simple man can be edified by what we may call the flesh of the scripture, this name being given to the obvious interpretation; while the man who has made some progress may be edified by its soul, as it were;...the man who is perfect...may be edified by the spiritual law. For just as man consists of body, soul, and spirit, so in the same way does the scripture, which has been prepared by God to be given for man's salvation." (46-47)

[T]here are certain passages of scripture which, as we shall show in what follows, have no bodily...sense at all...(47)

Now what man of intelligence will believe that the first and the second and the third day, and the evening and the morning existed without the sun and the moon and the stars?...And who is so silly as to believe that God, after the manner of a farmer, "planted a paradise eastward of Eden," and set in it a visible and palpable "tree of life,"...And when God is said to 'walk in the paradise in the cool of the day"...I do not think anyone will doubt that these are figurative expressions which indicate certain mysteries through a semblance of history and not through actual events. (47)

For our contention with regard to the whole of divine scripture is, that it all has a spiritual meaning, but not all a bodily [literal] meaning; for the bodily meaning is often proved to be an impossibility. Consequently the man who reads the divine books reverently, believing them to be divine writings, must exercise great care. (48)

Source: Kerr, Hugh T. Readings In Christian Thought (Nashville: Abingdon, 1978), pp. 43-50.

Augustine (354-430)

The Confessions: "Great art thou, O Lord, and greatly to be praised; great is thy power, and infinite is thy wisdom" (Ps. 145:3). And man desires to praise thee, for he is a part of thy creation; he bears his mortality about with him and carries the evidence of his sin and the proof that thou dost resist the proud. Still he desires to praise thee, this man who is only a small part of thy creation. Thou hast prompted him that he should delight to praise thee, for thou hast made us as for thyself and restless is our heart until it comes to rest in thee. (52)

I wish now to review in memory my past wickedness . . . not because I still love them, but that I may love thee, O my God. [When an adolescent] But what was it that delighted me save to love and to be loved?. . . ..the mists of passion steamed up out of the puddly concupiscence of the flesh, and the hot imagination of puberty, and they so obscured and overcast my heart that I was unable to distinguish pure affection from unholy desire. (54)...the world so often forgets thee, it's Creator and falls in love with thy creature instead of thee. (54) But, fool that I was I foamed in my wickedness as the sea... (54)

I stole away from Alypius, for it seemed to me that solitude was more appropriate for the business of weeping. . . . I was weeping in the most bitter contrition of my heart, when suddenly I heard the voice of a boy or a girl..."Pick it up, read it; pick it up, read it." [This is the famous *Tolle, lege; tolle, lege.*] ...I ceased weeping and began most earnestly to think whether it was usual for children in some kind of game to sing such a song... (57) I got to my feet, for I could not but think that this was a divine command to open the Bible and read the first passage I should light upon.... I snatched it up and in silence read thee paragraph on which my eyes first fell: "Not in rioting and drunkenness, not in chambering and wantonness, not in strife and envying, but put on the Lord Jesus Christ, and make no provision for the flesh to fulfil the lusts thereof" (Rom. 13:13). I wanted to read no further, nor did I need to. For instantly, as the sentence ended, there was infused in my heart something like the light of full certainty and all the gloom of doubt vanished away. (58)

Time & eternity: How, then, shall I respond to him who asks, "What was God doing before he made heaven & earth?" [Augustine says it is a silly question since before creation] "There was no "then" when there was no time.... There was no time, therefore, when thou hadst not made anything, because thou had not made time itself." (58) The distinguishing mark between time and eternity is that the former does not exist without some movement and change, while in the latter there is no change at all... the fact is that the world was made simultaneously with time... (65)

The City of God: [M]y first plan was to challenge the view of those who hold that the Christian religion is responsible for all the wars desolating this miserable world and, in particular, for the recent barbarian sack of the City of Rome. (60)

Foreknowledge & Free Will: The conclusion is that we are by no means under compulsion to abandon free choice in favor of divine foreknowledge, nor need we deny—God forbid—that God knows the future, as a condition for holding free choice. We accept both. As Christians and philosophers, we profess both—foreknowledge as a part of our faith; free choice, as a condition of responsible living." (61) The fact is that the human will does not achieve grace through freedom, but rather freedom through grace... (67)

Source Kerr, Hugh T. Readings In Christian Thought (Nashville: Abingdon, 1978), pp. 51-67.

Benedict of Nursia (480-547)

Prologue: Listen, my son, and with your heart hear the principles of your Master. Readily accept and faithfully follow the advice of a loving Father, so that through the labor of obedience you may return to Him from whom you have withdrawn because of the laziness of disobedience... (43)

...encompass ourselves with faith and the practice of good works, and guided by the Gospel, tread the path He has cleared for us. (44)

We are about to open *a school for God's service* in which we hope nothing harsh or oppressive will be directed... As our lives and faith progress, the heart expands and with the sweetness of love we move down the paths of God's commandments. Never departing from His guidance, remaining in the monastery until death, we patiently share in Christ's passion, so we may eventually enter into the Kingdom of God. (45)

An abbot should always remember what he is called (Abba = Father) and carry out his high calling in his everyday life. In a monastery he is Christ's representative... The abbot should always remember that he will be held accountable on Judgment Day for his teaching and the obedience of his charges... (47)

Chapter 4: the instruments of good works: 1. love the Lord God with all our heart, soul, and strength. 2. To love one's neighbor as oneself. 8. To respect all men. 14. To comfort the poor. 28. To speak the truth with heart and lips. 42. To attribute to God the good one sees in oneself. 70. To pray for one's enemies for the love of Christ. (52-54)

The vice of private ownership must be uprooted from the monastery. No one...shall give, receive or keep anything...nothing at all. (76)

Source: Anthony Meisel & M.L. del Mastro, translators, The Rule of St. Benedict (Garden City, NY: Image Books/Doubleday, 1975).

Dionysius (c. 5th or 6th century)

Divine Names: "...we must not dare to resort to words or conceptions concerning that hidden divinity which transcends being...the unknowing of what is beyond being is something above and beyond speech, mind or being itself, one should ascribe to it an understanding beyond being. Let us therefore look as far upward as the light of sacred scripture will allow, and, in our reverent awe of what is divine, let us be drawn together toward the divine splendor."...We must not dare to apply words or conceptions to this hidden or transcendent God...

And yet...the Good is not absolutely incommunicable to everything. By itself it...draws sacred minds upwards to its permitted contemplation, to participation, and to the state of becoming like it....they are raised firmly and unswervingly upward..."(49-50)

We cannot know God in his nature, since this is unknowable and is beyond the reach of mind or reason...We therefore approach that which is beyond all as far as our capacities allow us and we pass by way of the denial and the transcendence of all things and by way of the cause of all things. God is known in all things and as distinct from all things. . .through knowledge and through unknowing. . . On the other hand he cannot be understood, words cannot contain him, and no name can lay hold of him. . .This is the sort of language we must use about God. (108-109)

Mystical Theology: . . .*to strive upward as much as you can toward union with him who is beyond all being and knowledge. . . (135)*

Source: *Classics of Western Spirituality,* Pseudo-Dionysius, *The Complete Works* (New York: Paulist Press, 1987).

John of Damascus (c. 674-c.749)

Two natures in one person: "We do not say that man became God, but that God became man. For, while He was by nature perfect God, the same became by nature perfect man. He did not change His nature and neither did He just appear to become man. On the contrary, without confusion, alteration or division He became hypostatically united to the rationally and intellectually animated flesh which He had from the holy Virgin and which had its existence in him. . ... (68)

The natures were united to each other without change and without alteration. *(69)*

We have repeatedly said that *substance* is one thing and *person* another, and that *substance* means the common species including the persons that belong to the same species—as for example, God, man—while *person* indicates an individual as Father, Son, Holy Ghost, Peter, Paul. One must furthermore know that the terms *divinity* and *humanity* are indicative of the substances or natures. . . Since, then, in our Lord Jesus Christ we recognize two natures in one composite Person for both, when we are considering the natures, we call them divinity and humanity. . .

Worship of images: "Since not all know letters nor do all have leisure to read, the Fathers deemed it fit that these events (those of Scripture) should be depicted as a sort of memorial and terse reminder. It certainly happens. . .that we may see the image of His crucifixion and, being thus reminded of his saving Passion, fall down and adore. But it is not the material we adore, but that which is represented. . . the honor paid to the image redounds to the original. . ." (73)

Source: Kerr, Hugh T. Readings In Christian Thought (Nashville: Abingdon, 1978), pp. 68-73.

APPENDIX

TWO CREEDS

Apostles: I believe in God the Father Almighty, Maker of heaven & earth: And in Jesus Christ his only Son our Lord: Who was conceived by the Holy Ghost, Born of the Virgin Mary; suffered under Pontius Pilate, was crucified, dead and buried: He descended into hell: The third day he rose again from the dead: He ascended into heaven, And sitteth on the right hand of God the Father Almighty: From Thence he shall come to judge the quick and the dead. I believe in the Holy Ghost: The holy Catholic Church: The Communion of Saints: The forgiveness of sins: The Resurrection of the body: And the Life everlasting. Amen

Nicene: I believe in one God the Father Almighty, Maker of heaven and earth, And of all things visible and invisible: And in one Lord Jesus Christ, the only-begotten Son of God; Begotten of his Father before all words, God of Gods, Light of Light, Very God of very God; Begotten, not made; being of one substance with the Father: By whom all things were made: Who for us men and for our salvation came down from heaven. And was incarnate by the Holy Ghost of the Virgin Mary, and was made man: And was crucified also for us under Pontius Pilate; He suffered and was buried: And the third day he rose again according to the Scriptures: And ascended into heaven, And sitteth on the right hand of the Father. And he shall come again with glory to judge both the quick and the dead; Whose kingdom shall have no end. And I believe in the Holy Spirit, the Lord and Giver of Life, [Who proceedeth from the Father and the Son;] Who with the Father and the Son together is worshipped and glorified; Who spake by the Prophets: And I believe one Catholic and Apostolic Church: I acknowledge one Baptism for the remission of sings: And I look for the Resurrection of the dead: And the Life of the world to come. Amen

Source: Kerr, Hugh T. Readings In Christian Thought (Nashville: Abingdon, 1978), pp. 75-76

Anselm (1033-1109)

An Argument/Proof for the Existence of God: "I began to ask myself whether there might be found a single argument which would require no other for its proof than itself alone: and alone would suffice to demonstrate that God truly exists, and that there is a supreme good requiring nothing else, which all other things require for their existence and well-being (1)

I have written the following treatise, in the person of one who strives to lift his mind to the contemplation of God, and seeks to understand what he believes. . .(2)

The *prayer* that proceeds the argument: "Enter the inner chamber of thy mind; shut out all thoughts save that of God, and such as can aid thee in seeking him; close thy door and seek him. . . Speak now to God, saying, I seek thy face. . . I was created to see thee, and not yet have I done that for which I was made. . .Teach me to seek thee and reveal thyself to me. . . for I cannot seek thee, except thou teach me, nor find thee, except thou reveal thyself. . . Lord, I acknowledge and I thank thee that thou hast created me in this thine image, in order that I may be mindful of thee, may conceive of thee and love thee. . .I long to understand in some degree thy truth, which my heart believes and loves. For I do not seek to understand that I may believe, but I believe in order to understand. For this also I believe -- that unless I believed, I should not understand. (5-7)

Source: Anselm: Basic Writings, translated by S. W. Deane (LaSalle, Ill: Open Court, 1962).

The *argument:* Now we believe that thou art a being than which none greater can be thought. Or can it be that there is no such being, since "the fool hath said in his heart, 'There is no God'"? (84)

Thus, if that than which a greater cannot be thought can be thought of as not existing, this very thing than which a greater cannot be thought is *not* that than which a greater cannot be thought. But this is contradictory. So, then, there truly is a being than which a greater cannot be thought—so truly that it cannot even be thought of as not existing. (84) And, *thou* art this being, O Lord our God. (85)

Christ's Atonement for Man's Sin: Then remission of sins is necessary for a man, if he is to arrive at blessedness. (87)

Summary: The heart of the question was this; Why did God become man, to save man by his death, when it seems that he could have done this in some other way? You have answered this by showing, by many necessary reasons, how it would not have been right for the restoration of human nature to be left undone, and how it could not have been done unless man paid what was owing to God for sin. But the debt was so great that while man alone owed it, only God could pay it, so that the same person must be both man and God. Thus it was necessary for God to take manhood into the unity of his person, so that he who in his own nature ought to pay and could not, should be in a person who could. Then you showed that the man who also was God was to be taken from a virgin, and by the person of the Son of God, and how he could be taken from the sinful mass without sin. Moreover, you have proved most straightforwardly that the life of this Man was so sublime, so precious, that it can suffice to pay what is owing for the sins of the whole world, and infinitely more. (92).

Source: Kerr, Hugh T. Readings in Christian Thought (Nashville: Abingdon, 1978), pp. 84-94.

Abelard (1079-1142)

God's Love and Man's Redemption: It seems to us that we have been justified. . .in that his Son has taken upon himself our nature and persevered therein in teaching us by word and example even unto death—he has more fully bound us to himself by love; with the result that our hearts should be enkindled by such a gift of divine grace, and true charity should not now shrink from enduring anything for him. (95)

"Greater love than this no man hath, that a man lay down his life for his friends" (Jn. 15:13) (95)

[H]e came for the express purpose of spreading this true liberty of love amongst men. (95)

Source: Kerr, Hugh T. Readings In Christian Thought (Nashville: Abingdon, 1978), pp. 95-96

Bernard of Clairvaux (1090-1153)

The Three Kisses: A soul like mine. . .laden with sins. . .can make no smallest claim to such a grace.

Do not presume to lift yourself so high as to the Mouth of the Divine Bridegroom, but lie along with me before the Feet of the Lord. . .[I]f you would cease to be unhappy you must imitate this happy penitent, prostrate upon the ground, kissing His Feet and washing them with tears.

There is an intermediate stage—to kiss His Hand. . .So between Feet and Mouth you need this half-way house—his Hand, which first must cleanse you and then raise you up. How shall it raise you up? By giving you the grace of self-control, the fruits of penitence, which gifts will of themselves incite you to aspire to blessings greater still..

So this, then, is the way, the order we must follow. First we fall at the Lord's feet and bewail to Him Who made us the wrong things we have done. Next, we seek His Hand to lift us up and strengthen our weak knees, that we may stand upright. And, when we have won these two graces by many prayers and tears, we may at last, perhaps, dare to lift up our heads to that all-glorious Mouth, not only to behold it but to kiss. (97)

Source: Kerr, Hugh T. Readings In Christian Thought (Nashville: Abingdon, 1978), pp. 96-99

Francis of Assisi (1182-1226)

The Canticle of Brother Sun:

. . .

>Praised be thou, my Lord, with all Thy creatures,
>Especially for Sir Brother Sun.. . .
>Praised be Thou, my Lord, for Sister Moon and the stars. . .
>Praised be Thou, my Lord, for Brother Wind,
>Praised be Thou, my Lord, for Sister Water. . .
>Praised be Thou, my Lord, for Brother Fire. . .
>Praised be Thou, my Lord, for our Mother Earth
>Who sustains and rules us
>And brings forth divers fruits and coloured flowers and herbs. (102)

Source: Kerr, Hugh T. Readings In Christian Thought (Nashville: Abingdon, 1978), p. 102.

St. Bonaventure (1217-1274)

The Soul's Journey to God: (1) On the Stages of the Ascent into God...through His Vestiges in the Universe, (2). . .in His Vestiges in the Sense World, (3) . . .through His Image Stamped upon our Natural Powers, (4) . . .in his Image Reformed by the Gifts of Grace, (5) Through its Primary Name Which Is Being, (6). . .the Most Blessed Trinity in its Name Which is Good, & (7) Spiritual & Mystical Ecstasy . . ." (58)

In relation to our position in creation, the universe itself is a ladder by which we can ascend into God. . . (60) Just as no one comes to wisdom except through grace, justice and knowledge, so no one comes to contemplation except by penetrating meditation, a holy life and devout prayer. . . . We must ascend step by step. . . (63)

>We can contemplate God
>not only outside us and within us
>but also above us;
>outside us through his vestiges, within through his image
>and above through the light

>which shines upon our minds,
>
>which is the light of Eternal Truth
>
>since 'our mind itself is formed immediately by Truth itself.' (94)

In this passing over...all intellectual activities must be left behind and the height of our affection must be totally transferred and transformed into God. This, however, is mystical and most secret, which no one knows except him who receives it, and no one desires except him who in inflamed in his very marrow by the fire of the Holy Spirit whom Christ sent into the world. (115)

Source: Ewart Cousins, ed., Bonaventure: *The Soul's Journey into God, The Tree of Life*... (New York: Paulist Press, 1978).

Hildegard of Bingen (1098-1179)

From the *Book of Divine Works*: "... And I saw within the mystery of God...a wondrously beautiful image. It had a human form and its countenance was of such beauty and radiance that I could have more easily gazed at the sun than at that face...

I, the highest and fiery power, have kindled every spark of life...With wisdom I have rightly put the universe in order. I, the fiery life of divine essence, am aflame beyond the beauty of the meadows, I gleam in the waters, and I burn in the sun, moon, and stars... I awaken everything to life... The waters flow as if they were alive. The sun lives in its light, and the moon is enkindled, after its disappearance, once again by the light of the sun so that the moon is again revived... And thus I remain hidden in every kind of reality as a fiery power. Everything burns because of me in such a way as our breath constantly moves us, like the wind-tossed flame in a fire. All of this lives in its essence, and there is no death in it. For I am life. I am also Reason, which bears within itself the breath of the resounding Word, through which the whole of creation is made. I breathe life into everything so that nothing is mortal in respect to its species. For I am life. I am life, whole and entire... (8-11) I am life that remains ever the same, without beginning and without end. For this life is God... (11)

The Incarnation was the cause of sheer joy since God had bound God to Earth in such a way that human beings could behold God in human form... (79)

Source: Hildegard of Bingen, edited by Matthew Fox, Book of Divine Works (Santa Fe, NM: Bear & Company, 1987).

Thomas Aquinas (c. 1225-1274)

Reason and Revelation: There is a twofold mode of truth in what we profess about God. Some truths about God exceed all the ability of the human reason. Such is the truth that God is triune. But there are some truths which the natural reason also is able to reach. Such are that God exists, that He is one, and the like. (107)

Now, although the truth of the Christian faith...surpasses the capacity of the reason, nevertheless that truth that the human reason is naturally endowed to know cannot be opposed to the truth of the Christian faith. (109)

Whether God Exists?: The existence of God can be proved in five ways.

The first and more manifest way is the argument from motion. It is certain, and evident to our senses, that in the world some things are in motion. Now whatever is in motion is put in motion by another...Therefore it is necessary to arrive at a first mover, put in motion by no other; and this everyone understands to be God. (113-114)

The second way is from the nature of the efficient cause...Therefore it is necessary to admit a first efficient cause, to which everyone gives the name of God. (114)

The third way is taken from possibility and necessity...We find in nature things that are possible to be and not to be, since they are found to be generated, and to be corrupted, and consequently, they are possible to be and not to be. (114)

The fourth way is taken from the gradation to be found in all things. (114)

The fifth way is taken from the governance of the world...Therefore some intelligent being exists by whom all natural things are directed to their end; and this being we call God. (115)

The Effects of Sin: The good of nature that is diminished by sin, is the natural inclination to virtue, which is befitting to man from the very fact that he is a rational being; for it is due to this that he performs actions in accord with reason, which is to act virtuously. (115)

Consequently, its diminution may be understood in two ways: first, on the part of its root, secondly, on the part of its term. In the first way, it is not diminished by sin, because sin does not diminish nature....But it is diminished in the second way, in so far as an obstacle is placed against its attaining its term. (116)

[T]here is the wound of ignorance...there is the wound of malice...there is the wound of weakness...there is the wound of concupiscence.

Accordingly, these are the four wounds inflicted on the whole of human nature as a result of our first parents' sin. (116)

Humanity's restoration Through Christ: To restore man, who had been laid low by sin, to the heights of divine glory, the Word of the eternal Father, though containing all things within His immensity, willed to become small.

The reparation of human nature could not be effected by Adam or by any other purely human being.

Hence divine Wisdom judged it fitting that God should become man, so that thus one and the same person would be able both to restore man and to offer satisfaction.

There are also other reasons for the divine Incarnation.

Furthermore, the human race had need that God should become man to show forth the dignity of human nature... (120)

Lastly, the Incarnation puts the finishing touch to the whole vast work envisaged by God. For man, who was the last to be created, returns by a sort of circulatory movement to his first beginning, being united by the work of the Incarnation to the very principle of all things. (121)

Source: Kerr, Hugh T. Readings In Christian Thought (Nashville: Abingdon, 1978), pp. 106-121.

Julian of Norwich (1342-c.1423)

Showings/Revelations of Divine Love: ...it was in [God's] eternal purposes to create human nature...and so in our making, God almighty is our loving father...God all wisdom is our loving Mother... I saw and understood these three properties: the property of the fatherhood, the property of the motherhood, and the property of the lordship in one God. In our Father, we have our protection and our bliss...in the second person...we have our perfection...our restoration and our salvation, for he is our Mother...and in the Holy Spirit we have our reward and our gift... In the first we have our being, in the second we have our increasing, and in the third we have our fulfillment. (293-294)

...I saw...that the high might of the Trinity is our Father, the deep wisdom of the Trinity is our Mother, and the great love of the Trinity is our Lord...I saw that the second person...is our Mother...in our substantial creation, in whom we are founded and rooted, and he is our Mother of mercy...(294)

Thus, in our Father, God almighty, we have our being, and in our Mother of mercy we have our reforming and our restoring...and through the Holy Spirit...we are fulfilled. (294-295)

So Jesus Christ...is our true Mother.... As truly as God is our Father, so truly is God our Mother...(295) And so Jesus is our true Mother...all the lovely works and all the sweet loving offices of beloved motherhood are appropriated to the second person...(296-297)

This fair lovely word 'mother' is so sweet and so kind in itself that it cannot truly be said of anyone or to anyone except of him and to him who is the true Mother of life and of all things. (299)

Source: Julian of Norwich, Showings/Revelations of Divine Love, translated by Edmund Colledge & James Walsh (New York: Paulist Press. 1978).

Martin Luther (1483-1546)

Sin and Justification: ...Christ, our good Samaritan, brought the man who was half dead, his patient, to an inn and took care of him (Luke 10:30 ff.) and commenced to heal him.. ...He does not reckon him his sin, i.e., his sinful desires, for death, but in the meantime, i.e., holding up to him the hope that he will get well, he forbids him to do or not do anything that might impede his recovery and make his sin, i.e., his concupiscence, worse. Now can we say that he is perfectly righteous? No; but he is at the same time both a sinner and righteous, a sinner in fact but righteous by virtue of the reckoning and the certain promise of God that he will redeem him from sin in order, in the end, to make him perfectly whole and sound. (142)

So then, this life is a life of cure from sin; it is not a life of sinlessness, as if the cure were finished and health had been recovered. The church is an inn and an infirmary for the sick and for convalescents. Heaven, however, is the palace where the whole and the righteous live. (143)

Three Roman Walls: [A]ll Christians whatsoever really and truly belong to the religious class, and there is no difference among them except in so far as they do different work. . .. [W]e have one baptism, one gospel, one faith, and all are equally Christian. For baptism, gospel, and faith alone make men religious, and create a Christian people. (146)

Hence we deduce that there is, at bottom, really no difference between laymen, priests, princes, bishops, or, in Romanist terminology, between religious and secular, than that of office or occupation, and not that of Christian status. (146-147)

Freedom and Service: We conclude, therefore, that a Christian lives not in himself, but in Christ and in his neighbour. Otherwise he is not a Christian. He lives in Christ through faith, in his neighbour through love. By faith he is caught up beyond himself into God. By love he descends beneath himself into his neighbour. . .. (154)

Faith is a living, bold trust in God's grace, so certain of God's favor that is would risk death a thousand times trusting in it. Such confidence and knowledge of God's grace makes you happy, joyful and bold in your relationship to God and all creatures. . . .. Joyfully do well to everyone, serve everyone, suffer all kinds of things, love and praise the God who has shown you such grace.

Source: Kerr, Hugh T. Readings in Christian Thought (Nashville: Abingdon, 1978), pp. 142-157.

John Calvin (1509-1564)

The Bible and the Word of God: Any man then who would profit by the Scriptures, must hold first of all and firmly that the teaching of the law and the prophets came to us not by the will of man, but as dictated by the Holy Spirit.

. . .The author of the Scriptures is God.

. . .Scripture. . .contains the perfect rule of a good and happy life. . . .. God gave us Scripture for our good, and not to satisfy our curiosity. (163)

. . . [I]f we would know Christ, we must seek him in the Scriptures. (164)

How do we know God?: Experience teaches that the seed of religion has been divinely planted in all men. (164)

[A] sense of divinity is by nature engraven on human hearts. (165)

[B]ut with the aid of spectacles will begin to read distinctly; so Scripture, gathering up the otherwise confused knowledge of God in our minds, having dispersed our dullness, clearly shows us the true God. This, therefore, is a special gift, where God, to instruct the church, not merely uses mute teachers but also opens his own most hallowed lips. (166)

Sin and Total Depravity: Therefore all of us, who have descended from impure seed, are born infected with the contagion of sin. In fact, before we saw the light of this life we were soiled and spotted in God's sight. . . ..Hence, rotten branches came forth from a rotten root.

[L]et us define original sin. . .Original sin, therefore, seems to be a hereditary depravity and corruption of our nature, diffused into all parts of the soul, which first makes us liable to God's wrath, then also brings forth in us those works which Scripture calls "works of the flesh" (Gal. 5:19). (167)

. . .[T]he mind of man has been so completely estranged from God's righteousness that it conceives, desires, and undertakes, only that which is impious, perverted, foul, impure, and infamous. (168)

Christ: Redeemer and Savior: What the Mediator was to accomplish was no common thing. His task was so to restore us to God's grace as to make of the children of men, children of God. (168)

We see that our whole salvation and all its parts are comprehended in Christ. (169)

The Holy Spirit is the bond by which Christ effectually unites us to himself. . . .. (169)

Source: Kerr, Hugh T. Readings In Christian Thought (Nashville: Abingdon, 1978), pp. 161-172.

Richard Hooker (1554-1600)

Church and State as One: . . . [T]he care of religion should be the common concern of every state.

We see, therefore, that according to our view the Church is a society of men organized first of all as a public or civil government, and second. . .by the exercise of the Christian religion. (178-179)

. . .Church and state are two corporations. Here in England there is not a man who is a member of the Church of England who is not a member of the commonwealth; and there is a man who is a member of the commonwealth who is not a member of the Church of England. The relation of the Church and state is like the relation of the two sides and base of a triangle. (179)

The Church and the commonwealth, therefore, are a single corporation, which is called a commonwealth in relation to its secular law and government, and is called a church in relation to its submission to the spiritual law of Jesus Christ. (179)

Source: Kerr, Hugh T. Readings In Christian Thought (Nashville: Abingdon, 1978), pp. 178-179.

Menno Simons (1496-1561)

The Community of the Faithful: I tell you the truth in Christ, the rightly baptized disciples of Christ, note well, they who are baptized inwardly with Spirit and fire, and externally with water, according to the Word of the Lord, have no weapons except patience, hope, silence, and God's Word. (186)

They verily are not the true congregation of Christ who merely boast of His name. But they are the true congregation of Christ who are truly converted, who are born from above of God, who are of a regenerate mind by the operation of the Holy Spirit through the hearing of the divine Word, and have become the children of God, have entered into obedience to Him, and live unblamably in His holy commandments, and according to His holy will all their days, or from the moment of their call.

And since the worldly church is no such amiable, obedient bride but one who has left her lawful husband, Christ.... I seek to accomplish nothing by my writing and teaching (according to the talent God has pleased to give me) but to reclaim this adulterous bride, the erring church, from her adulterous actions, and return her to her first husband... (187)

Source: Kerr, Hugh T. Readings In Christian Thought (Nashville: Abingdon, 1978), pp. 185-186

Council of Trent (1545-1563)

Decree Concerning Canonical Scripture: ...the Holy Scriptures, our Lord Jesus Christ, promulgated first with His own mouth and then commanded it be preached by His Apostles to every creature as the source at once of all saving truth and rules of conduct...and of all the Latin editions of the sacred books now in circulation...declares that the Latin Vulgate Edition...is authentic... (180-181)

Justification & Works: Justification is not only a remission of sins but also the sanctification and renewal of the inward man through the voluntary reception of the grace and gifts whereby an unjust man becomes just and from being an enemy becomes a friend...Canon 1. If anyone says that man can be justified before God by his own works...let him be anathema...Canon 5. If anyone says that after the sin of Adam man's free will was lost and destroyed...let him be anathema...Canon 19. If anyone says that nothing besides faith is commanded in the Gospel... or that the Ten Commandments in no way pertain to Christians, let him be anathema...

Eucharist & Transubstantiation...the holy council teaches...that after consecration of bread and wine, our Lord Jesus Christ, true God and true man, is truly, really and substantially contained in the august sacrament of the Holy Eucharist under the appearance of those sensible things...

Source: Kerr, Hugh T. Readings In Christian Thought (Nashville: Abingdon, 1978), pp. 180-184.

St. Ignatius (1491-1556)

This expression "Spiritual Exercises" (SE) embraces every method of examination of conscience, of meditation, of contemplation, of vocal and mental prayer, and of other spiritual activity... For just as...walking and running are bodily exercises, so spiritual exercises are methods of preparing and disposing the soul to free itself of all inordinate attachments, and after accomplishing this, of seeking and discovering the Divine Will regarding the disposition of one's life, thus insuring the salvation of his soul. (37)

As is true in all of the following Spiritual Exercises, one uses the intellect for reasoning while the will is employed in giving expression to the affection...Four weeks are assigned to the following SE....: the first, which is the consideration and contemplation of sin; the second, the life of our Lord Jesus Christ up to and including Palm Sunday; the third, the passion of Christ our Lord; and the fourth, the Resurrection and Ascension... (38)

The purpose of these exercises is to help the exercitant to conquer himself and regulate his life so that he will not be influenced in his decisions by any inordinate attachment... Man is created to praise, reverence and serve God our Lord, and by this means to save his soul. All other things on the face of the earth are created for man to help him fulfill the end for which he is created...

Source: St. Ignatius, The Spiritual Exercises of St. Ignatius, translated by A. Mottola (Garden City, NY: Image Books/Doubleday, 1964).

Teresa of Avila (1515-1582)

Of the Interior Castle, "I was told...that the nuns of these convents of Our Lady of Carmel need someone to solve their difficulties concerning prayer, and as...women best understand each other's language and also in view of their love for me, anything I might say would be particularly useful to them. (24)

I began to think of the soul as...a castle made of a single diamond...in which there are many rooms, just as in Heaven there are many mansions. Now if we think carefully over this, sisters, the soul of the righteous man is nothing but a paradise, in which...God takes His delight. (28)...He created us in His image and likeness [and]...we do not understand ourselves or know who we are..."(29) Learn to understand yourselves and take pity on yourselves... (35)

You must not imagine these mansions as arranged in a row...but fix your attention on the centre...the room occupied by the King. (37)...It is very important that no soul that practices prayer, whether little or much, should be subjected to undue constraint or limitation. Since God has given it such dignity, it must be allowed to roam through these mansions... It must not be compelled to remain for a long time in one single room...unless it is the room of self-knowledge."(37)...self-knowledge is so important that, even if you are raised right up to heaven, I should like you never to relax your cultivation of it... As I see it, we shall never succeed in knowing ourselves unless we seek to know God. (38)

1st mansion is self-knowledge...the 7th is spiritual marriage with God. (66)

Source: Teresa of Avila, Interior Castle, translated by E. Allison Peers (New York: Image Books/Doubleday, 1961)

Philip Jacob Spener (1635-1705)

How much good it would do if good friends would come together on a Sunday and instead of getting out glasses, cards or dice would take up a book and read from it for the edification of all or would review something from sermons that were heard. If they would speak with one another about the divine mysteries, and the one who received most from God would try to instruct his weaker brethren...by virtue of their universal Christian priesthood...p. 13.

Our whole Chistian religion consists of the inner man or new man, whose soul is faith and whose expressions are the fruits of life, and all sermons should be aimed at this. p. 116

Source: Philip Jacob Spener, Pia Desideria (Philadelphia: Fortress Press, 1964).

John Wesley (1703-1791)

A Methodist: The distinguishing marks of a Methodist are not his opinions of any sort. His assenting to this or that scheme of religion, his embracing any particular set of notions, his espousing the judgment of one man or of another, are all quite wide of the point...We believe, indeed, that "all Scripture is given by the inspiration of God:" and herein we are distinguished from Jews, Turks, and Infidels. We believe the written word of God to be the only and sufficient rule both of Christian faith and practice... We believe Christ to be the eternal, supreme God... (195-196)

A Methodist is one who has "the love of God shed abroad in his heart by the Holy Ghost given unto him;" one who "loves the Lord his God with all his heart, and with all his soul, and with all his mind, and with all his strength." God is the joy of his heart, and the desire of his soul; which is constantly crying out, "Whom have I in heaven but thee? And there is none upon earth that I desire beside thee! My God and my all! Thou art the strength of my heart, and my portion forever!" (196)

Dost thou love and serve God? It is enough. I give thee the right hand of fellowship. (197)

"It is hard to find words in the language of men, to explain the deep things of God. Indeed, there are none that will adequately express what the Spirit of God works in his children." (191)

Perfection: Christian perfection. . .is only another term for holiness. They are two names for the same thing. Thus, everyone that is holy is, in the Scripture sense, perfect. (198)

In what sense, then, are Christians perfect? . . ...Every one that hath Christ in him, the hope of glory, "purifieth himself, even as He is pure" (I John 3:3). He is purified from pride; for Christ was lowly of heart. He is pure from self-will or desire; for Christ desired only to do the will of His Father, and to finish His work. And he is pure from anger, in the common sense of the word; for Christ was meek and gentle, patient and long-suffering. (199)

Source: Kerr, Hugh T. Readings In Christian Thought (Nashville: Abingdon, 1978), pp. 194-200.

Jonathan Edwards (1703-1758)

Religious Affections: The Author of the human nature has not only given affections to men, but has made them very much the spring of men's actions. As the affections do not only necessarily belong to the human nature, but are a very great part of it; so. . .holy affections do not only necessarily belong to true religion, but are a very great part of that. . ... [T]he affections are very much the spring of men's actions, this also shows, that true religion must consist very much in the affections.

Such is man's nature, that he is very inactive, any otherwise than he is influenced by some affection, either love or hatred, desire, hope, fear or some other. These affections we see to be the springs that set men agoing, in all the affairs of life, and engage them in all their pursuits: these are the things that put men forward, and carry them along. . . (203)

There are false affections, and there are true. A man's having much affection, don't prove that he has any true religion: but if he has no affection, it proves that he has no true religion. (204)

God has given to mankind affections, for the same purpose which he has given all the faculties and principles of the human soul for, viz. That they might be subservient to man's chief end, and the great business for which God has created him, that is the business of religion. (205)

Source: Kerr, Hugh T. Readings In Christian Thought (Nashville: Abingdon, 1978), pp. 201-208.

Friedrich Schleiermacher (1768-1834)

The Essence of Religion: I ask, therefore, that you turn from everything usually reckoned religion, and fix your regard on the inward emotions and dispositions... (219)

The Essence of Christianity: Christianity is a monotheistic faith, belonging to the teleological type of religion, and is essentially distinguished from other such faiths by the fact that in it everything is related to the redemption accomplished by Jesus of Nazareth.... (221)

The Redeemer: The Redeemer, then is like all men in virtue of the identity of human nature, but distinguished from them all by the constant potency of His God-consciousness... (223)

The Redeemer assumes believers into the power of His God-consciousness, and this is His redemptive activity... (225)

Source: Kerr, Hugh T. Readings In Christian Thought (Nashville: Abingdon, 1978), pp.218-227.

Walter Rauschenbusch (1861-1918)

Social Gospel: Individualistic Christianity has almost lost sight of the great idea of the kingdom of God, which was the inspiration and center of the thought of Jesus. Social Christianity would once more enable us to understand the purpose and thought of Jesus and take the veil from our eyes when we read the synoptic gospels. (267)

As we have seen, the industrial and commercial life of to-day is dominated by principles antagonistic to the fundamental principles of Christianity.... (267)

The conviction has always been embedded in the heart of the Church that "the world"—society as it is—is evil and some time is to make way for a true human society in which the spirit of Jesus Christ shall rule. (268)

The Kingdom of God

1. The Kingdom of God is divine in its origin, progress and consummation.

2. The Kingdom of God contains the teleology of the Christian religion.

3. Since God is in it, the Kingdom of God is always both present and future.

4. Even before Christ, men of God saw the Kingdom of God as the great end to which all divine leadings were pointing.

5. The Kingdom of God is humanity organized according to the will of God. (269)

6. Since the Kingdom is the supreme end of God, it must be the purpose for which the Church exists.
7. Since the Kingdom is the supreme end, all problems of personal salvation must be reconsidered from the point of view of the Kingdom.
8. The kingdom of God is not confined within the limits of the Church and its activities. It embraces the whole of human life. It is the Christian transfiguration of the social order. (270)

Source: Kerr, Hugh T. Readings In Christian Thought (Nashville: Abingdon, 1978), pp. 266-270.

Soren Kierkegaard (1813-1855)

On Being a Christian: How strange is the way of the world! Once it was at the risk of his life that a man dared to profess himself a Christian; now it is to make oneself suspect to venture to doubt that one is a Christian. Especially when this doubt does not mean that the individual launches a violent attack against Christianity with a view to abolishing it... (275)

Do you not perform your duties at the office like a conscientious civil servant; are you not a good citizen of a Christian nation, a Lutheran Christian state? So then of course you must be a Christian." (275)

...Suppose that Christianity is subjectivity, an inner transformation, an actualization of inwardness, and that only two kinds of people can know anything about it: those who with an infinite passionate interest in an eternal happiness base this their happiness upon their believing relationship to Christianity, and those who with an opposite passion, but in passion, reject it—the happy and the unhappy lovers. (276)

But if Christianity is essentially subjectivity, it is a mistake for the observer to be objective. (276)

The invisible Church is no historical phenomenon; it cannot be observed objected at all, since it exists only in the subjectivity of the individuals. (277)

But to treat Christianity in the same manner is simply to invite confusion. Since man is a synthesis of the temporal and the eternal, the happiness that the speculative philosopher may enjoy will be an illusion, in that he desires in time to be merely eternal. Herein lies the error of the speculative philosopher. Higher than this speculative happiness, therefore, is the infinite passionate interest in a personal eternal happiness. (278)

Christ as God Incognito... Christ willed to be incognito, just because He willed to be the sign of contradiction. (279)

It was Christ's free will and determination from all eternity to be incognito. (280)

He is God, but chooses to become the individual man. This, as we have seen, is the profoundest incognito, or the most impenetrable unrecognizableness that is possible; for the contradiction between being God and being an individual man is the greatest possible, the infinitely qualitative contradiction. (282)

Whether Christianity Exists: . . .[I]nasmuch as Christianity is spirit, the sobriety of spirit, the honesty of eternity, there is of course nothing which to its detective eye is so suspicious as are all fantastic entities: Christian states, Christian lands, a Christian people, and (how marvelous!) a Christian world. (284)

. . . [I]n comparison with the Christianity of the New Testament, it is playing Christianity. (285)

Source: Kerr, Hugh T. Readings In Christian Thought (Nashville: Abingdon, 1978), pp.275-286.

Karl Barth (1886-1968)

The Bible is the concrete medium by which the Church recalls God's revelation in the past, is called to expect revelation in the future, and is thereby challenged, empowered, and guided to proclaim. The Bible is, therefore, not itself and in itself God's past revelation. . .But the Bible speaking to us and heard by us as God's Word attests the past revelation. . ." (284)

Between God and man there stands the person of Jesus Christ, Himself God and Himself man, and is mediating between the two. In Him God reveals Himself to man. In him, man sees and knows God.(288) The attitude of God in which the faithfulness of the Creator and therefore the unchanging relationships of the human being created by Him are revealed and knowable, is quite simply His attitude and relation to the man Jesus: His election of this man; His become and remaining one with Him; His self-revelation, action and glorification in Him and through Him; His love addressed to Him and through Him to those who believe in Him and to the whole of creation. . .(295)

Source: Kerr, Hugh T. Readings In Christian Thought (Nashville: Abingdon, 1978), pp. 293-310.

Eugen Rosenstock-Huessy (1888-1973)

God becomes known to us in all the powers which triumph over death, and from earliest times men have called any such power divine... The climax in conquering death, and therefore in man's knowledge of God, was the crucifixion and resurrection of Christ. By him, at last, death was included as a positive factor within life and was thereby finally and completely overcome: death became the gateway to the future, to new life.... The living God thus revealed by Jesus must be forever distinguished from the merely conceptual God of philosophers... The Christian dogma is not an intellectual formula but a record and promise of life... The four Gospels give a model example of this rule that one truth must be expressed in different ways for different times of life, and that the whole truth is conveyed only on several such levels together...

...the third article of the Creed is the specifically Christian one: from now on the Holy Spirit makes man a partner in his own creation... In this light, the Church Fathers interpreted human history as a process of making Man like God. They called it "anthropurgy": as metallurgy refines metal from its ore, anthropurgy wins the true stuff of Man out of his coarse physical substance. Christ, in the centre of history, enabled us to participate consciously in this man-making process... (Christian Future pp. 98 ff.)

Source: Eugen Rosenstock-Huessy, The Christian Future or the Modern Mind Outrun (New York: Harper & Row, 1966).

Our passions give life to the world. Our collective passions constitute the history of mankind... A different type of man and woman is produced by stimulating or repressing different potential passions; and any special society is based on a peculiar selection in admitting or negating the innumerable desires of our hearts... The heart of man either falls in love with somebody or something, or it falls ill...And the great question for mankind is what is to be loved or hated next, whenever an old love or fear has lost its hold.... The creation of humankind, then, is the topic of this book...

It is sheer nonsense to put before us the choice between Evolution and Revolution... [they are} reciprocal ideas... Creation goes on as God's creation has always done. A thunderstorm of destruction clears the air; then follows the low rustle of growth and reconstruction... In history creation is going on all the time, and eternal recurrence of the created kinds is also going on all the time... Revolutions do not create man; they build nurseries, as we have said before, for his reproduction in a certain way and according to a certain type..." (Out of Revolution pp. 1-5, 466-467)

Source: Eugen Rosenstock-Huessy, Out of Revolution, *the Autobiography of Western Man* (Norwich, VT: Argo Books, 1969).

Paul Tillich (1886-1965)

Theology, as a function of the Christian church, must serve. . .two basic needs: the statement of the truth of the Christian message and the interpretation of this truth for every new generation. (338)

It is not an exaggeration to say that today man experiences his present situation in terms of disruption, conflict, self-destruction, meaninglessness, and despair in all realms of life. . . The question arising out of this experience is not . . .the question of a merciful God and the forgiveness of sins. . . It is the question of a reality in which the self-estrangement of our existence is overcome. . .of reconciliation and reunion, of creativity, meaning and hope. . . If the Christian message is understood as the message of "new being. . ." Source: Kerr, Hugh T. Readings In Christian Thought (Nashville: Abingdon, 1978) pp. 342-343.

Christ, Salvation & New Being: To experience the New Being in Jesus as the Christ means to experience the power in him which has conquered existential estrangement in himself and in everyone who participates in him. "Being," if used for God or divine manifestations, is the power of being, or, negatively expressed, the power of conquering non-being. The word "being" points to the fact that this power is not a matter of someone's good will but that it is a gift which precedes or determines the character of every act of the will. (125)

In an ecstatic experience the concrete picture of Jesus of Nazareth became indissolubly united with the reality of the New Being. He is present wherever the New Being is present. . . (157)

With respect to both the original meaning of salvation (from *salvus*, healed) and our present situation, it may be adequate to interpret salvation as "healing." It corresponds to the state of estrangement as the main characteristic of existence. In this sense, healing means reuniting that which is estranged, giving a center to what is split, overcoming the split between God and man, man and his world, man and himself. Out of this interpretation of salvation, the concept of the New Being has grown. . . where there is revelation there is salvation. . .Revelation is not information about divine things; it is the ecstatic manifestation of the Ground of Being in events, persons, and things. Such manifestations have shaking, transforming, and healing power. (166-167)

Source: Paul Tillich, Systematic Theology, *Vol. II, Existence & the Christ* (Chicago: University of Chicago Press, 1957).

Pierre Teilhard de Chardin (1881-1955)

Hymn to Matter: Blessed be you, harsh matter, barren soil, stubborn rock. . ./ Blessed be you, perilous matter, violent sea, untameable passion: you who unless we fetter you will devour us. /Blessed be you, mighty matter, irresistible march of evolution, reality ever new-born; you who, by constantly shattering our mental categories, force us to go ever further and further in our pursuit of the truth. /Blessed be you, universal matter, immeasurable time, boundless other, triple abyss of stars and atoms and generations: you who by overflowing and dissolving our narrow standards or measurement reveal to us the dimensions of God. ./Blessed be you impenetrable matter. . ./Blessed be you, mortal matter. . . /Without. . .your uprooting of us, we should remain all our lives inert, stagnant. . .ignorant both of ourselves and of God. /You who batter us and then dress our wounds. . ./you who shackle and liberate, the sap of our souls, the hand of God, the flesh of Christ: /It is you, matter, that I bless./I bless you, matter, and you I acclaim. . .as you reveal yourself to me today, *in your totality and your true nature.*/You I acclaim as the inexhaustible potentiality for existence and transformation. . ./I acclaim you as the universal power which brings together and unites, through which the multitudinous monads are bound together and in which they all converge on the way of the spirit./I acclaim you as the melodious fountain of water. . ./I acclaim you as the divine *milieu*, charged with creative power. . ./ This I now understand. Raise me up then, matter, to those heights. . .[until] it becomes possible. . .to embrace the universe. (68-70)

Source: Pierre Teilhard de Chardin, Hymn of the Universe (New York: Harper & Row, 1961).

Abhishiktananda (Henri LeSaux) (1910-1973)

On Dialogue: The time is. . .ripe for the Church—indeed, for all Churches together—to enter into official contact with these religions. . . it is even more important that the faithful followers of Christ and of the great world religions should try to understand each other in a profound spirit of humility, sincerity and charity. Each will be aware of the irresistible attraction of the unfathomable mystery of God in the depths of his own being, and will recognize that the religious beliefs and practices of his neighbour are the outward signs of an awareness of that Presence and of a desire to respond to it that is closely akin to his own. . . (4)

The Oriental world, however, whether Hindu, Buddhist, or Taoist seems to have reacted to that experience of the indwelling Mystery that lies at the root of all genuine religion quite differently from the cultural and religious world of the Mediterranean...

In India men have not felt the need to objectify, to project outside themselves, the mystery sensed in the depths of their own being and at the very heart of the universe...For him adoration can only be expressed in a wordless 'recollection' at the heart of Being, in the experience of sat-cit-ananda (being- consciousness- bliss). (p.5)

Hindus and Christians must learn to accept each other as they actually are, in their concrete historical situation. This is the essential prerequisite for any dialogue... (116-117).

Source: Abhishiktananda, Hindu-Christian Meeting Point: *Within the Cave of the Heart* (Delhi: ISPCK, 1969).

Bibliography

Abbott, Walter M., ed. *The Documents of Vatican II*. New York: Guild/America & Association, 1966.

Abhishiktananda. *Guru & Disciple: An Encounter with Sri Gnanananda, A Contemporary Spiritual Master*. Delhi: I.S.P.C.K. 1970.

———. *Hindu-Christian Meeting Point, Within the Cave of the Heart*. New Delhi: ISPCK, 1976.

———. *Saccidananda: A Christian Approach to Advaitic Experience*. Delhi: I.S.P.C.K. 1984.

———. *The Secret of Arunachala: A Christian Hermit on Shiva's Holy Mountain*. Delhi: I.S.P.C.K. rev.ed. 1997.

Anselm. *Basic Writings*. LaSalle, IL: Open Court, 1962.

Aquinas, Thomas. *The Summa Theologica*. Translated by L. Shapcote, revised by D. J. Sullivan. Chicago: Encyclopedia Britannica, 1952.

Augustine, *City of God*. Harmondsworth, England: Penguin Books, 1972.

Bamford, Christopher. *The Voice of the Eagle: The Heart of Celtic Christianity*. Great Barrington, MA: Lindisfarne, 2000.

Barth, Karl. *The Epistle to the Romans*. Oxford: Oxford University Press, 1968.

Beck, Lewis W. *Foundations of the Metaphysics of Morals & What is Enlightenment?* New York: Macmillan, 1959.

Benedict. *The Rule of St. Benedict*. Translated by A. C. Meisel & M. L. del Mastro. Garden City, NY: Image Books, 1972.

Berry, Thomas. *Dream of the Earth*. San Francisco: Sierra Club, 1988.

———. *The Great Work: Our Way into the Future*. New York: Bell Tower, 1999.

Boethius. *Consolation of Philosophy*. New York: Modern Library, 1943.

"Bonaventure: The Soul's Journey into God." *Classics of Western Spirituality*. Edited and translated by Ewart Cousins. New York: Paulist Press, 1978.

du Boulay, Shirley. *The Cave of the Heart: the Life of Swami Abhishiktananda*. Maryknoll, NY: Orbis, 2005.

Calvin. *Institutes of the Christian Religion*. Edited by John T. McNeill. 2 Vols. Philadelphia: Westminster, 1960.

Dillenberger, John. *Martin Luther: Selections from His Writings*. New York: Anchor Books, 1962.

Dionysius. *The Complete Works*. New York: Paulist, 1988.

Gardner, Clinton C. *Beyond Belief: Discovering Christianity's New Paradigm*. White River Junction, VT: White River, 2008.

Goen, C.C. ed. *The Great Awakening: The Works of Jonathan Edwards*. 4 Vols. New Haven: Yale University Press, 1972.
Grant, Robert, and David N. Freedman. *The Secret Sayings of Jesus, According to the Gospel of Thomas*. London: Fontana, 1963.
Griffiths, Bede. *Universal Wisdom: A Journey Through the Sacred Wisdom of the World*. London: Fount, 1994.
Gutiérrez, Gustavo. *A Theology of Liberation*. Maryknoll, New York: Orbis, 1987.
Hardy, E.R. *Christology of the Later Fathers*. Philadelphia: Westminster, 1954.
Henderson, J.L.H., ed. *John Strachan: Documents & Opinions*. Montreal: McGill-Queens, 1969.
Hildegard of Bingen. *Book of Divine Works*. Santa Fee, NM: Bear & Company, 1987.
Himlick, Raymond. *The Enchiridion of Erasmus*. Bloomington, IN: Indiana University Press, 1963.
Hooker, Richard. *Of the Laws of Ecclesiastical Polity*. New York: Everyman Library, 1963.
Julian of Norwich. *Showings. Classics of Western Spirituality*. New York: Paulist Press, 1978.
Kerr, Hugh, ed. *Readings in Christian Thought*. Nashville, TN: Abingdon, 1978.
Klaaren, Eugene. *Religious Origins of Modern Science, Belief in Creation in Seventeenth-Century Thought*. Grand Rapids: William B. Eerdmans, 1977.
Leclercq, Jean. *Love of Learning & the Desire for God*. New York: Mentor, 1961.
Malone, Mary T. *Women & Christianity: Vol. I. The First Thousand Years*. Ottawa: Novalis, 2000.
McDonald, Neil, and Alf Chaiton, eds. *Egerton Ryerson & His Times*. Toronto: Macmillan Canada, 1978.
Meyerdorff, John. *The Byzantine Legacy in the Orthodox Church*. Crestwood, NY: St. Vladimir's Seminary Press, 1982.
Morgan, George. *Speech & Society, The Christian Linguistic Social Philosophy of Eugen Rosenstock-Huessy*. Gainesville, FL: University of Florida Press, 1987.
Norris, Richard A. *The Christological Controversy*. Minneapolis, MN: Augsburg/Fortress, 1980.
O'Callaghan, J.F. *The Autobiography of St. Ignatius Loyola*. New York: Harper & Row, 1963.
Olin, John C. *The Catholic Reformation: Savonarola to Ignatius Loyola*. New York: Fordham University Press, 1992.
Origen. *On First Principles*. Translated by G. W. Butterworth. New York: Harper & Row, 1966.
Palmer, Martin. *The Jesus Sutras: Rediscovering the Lost Scrolls of Taoist Christianity*. New York: Ballantine/Random House, 2001.
Parish, Helen R. *Bartolome de las Casas: The Only Way*. New York: Paulist Press, 1992.
Pope John XXIII. *Journal of a Soul*. New York: McGraw-Hill, 1965.
Rahner, Karl. *The Foundations of Christian Faith: An Introduction to the Idea of Christianity*. New York: Crossroads, 1982.
Rauschenbusch, Walter. *A Theology for the Social Gospel*. Nashville, TN: Abingdon, 1964.
Richardson, Cyril, ed. *Early Christian Fathers*. Vol. I. Philadelphia: Westminster, 1953.
Rosenstock-Huessy, Eugene. *The Christian Future, Or the Modern Mind Outrun*. New York: Harper & Row, 1966.

———. *Out of Revolution: The Autobiography of Western Man*. Norwich, Vermont: Argo, 1969.
———. *Speech & Society*. Norwich, VT: Argo, 1970.
Ryerson, Egerton. *The Story of My Life*. Toronto: Methodist Book & Publishing House, 1881.
Simons, Menno. *The Complete Works of Menno Simons*. Edited by J.C. Wenger. Scottsdale, PA: Herald, 1986.
Smith, Huston. *The Soul of Christianity: Restoring the Great Tradition*. New York: Harper Collins, 2005.
Smith, John. E., ed. Jonathan Edwards: *Religious Affections*. New Haven: Yale University Press, 1959.
Stillman, Drake. *Discoveries & Opinions of Galileo*. New York: Doubleday/Anchor, 1957.
St. Augustine. *Confessions*. Translated by R.S. Pine-Coffin. New York: Penguin Books, 1961.
Swimme, Brian, and Thomas Berry. *From the Primordial Flaming Forth to the Ecozoic Age: A Celebration of the Unfolding Cosmos*. New York: Harper SanFrancisco, 1992.
The Spiritual Exercises of St. Ignatius. Translated by Anthony Mottola, et. al. New York: Image Books/Doubleday, 1964.
Tillich, Paul. *A History of Christian Thought*. New York: Touchstone/Simon & Schuster, 1968.
———. *Systematic Theology*. Vol. I. Chicago: University of Chicago Press, 1951.
Teilhard de Chardin. *Writings in a Time of War*. New York: Harper & Row, 1968.
———. *Science & Christ*. New York: Harper & Row, 1968.
———. *The Divine Milieu*. New York: Harper & Row, 1960.
———. *The Phenomenon of Man*. New York: Harper & Row, 1959.
Wendel, Francois. *Calvin: The Origin & Development of his Religious Thought*. London: Collins/Fontana, 1963.
Werner, Martin. *The Formation of Christian Dogma*. Boston: Beacon, 1957.
Wrights, Ronald. *Stolen Continents: The New World Through Indian Eyes*. Toronto: Penguin Canada, 1992.

www.ingramcontent.com/pod-product-compliance
Lightning Source LLC
Chambersburg PA
CBHW071145300426
44113CB00009B/1095